MW00669209

Introducing International Relations

This exciting new textbook provides an accessible and lively introduction to international relations for students encountering the subject for the first time.

Presenting complex ideas, concepts, and arguments in a straightforward and conversational way, the textbook explains international relations from a diplomatic perspective, emphasizing co-existence in the absence of agreement, and developing students' ability to make sense of the current conditions of international uncertainty.

Introducing students to the major theories and issues in international relations, each chapter:

- is written to a common structure, dividing each topic into sections with learning objectives within each section to provide points of focus for students and instructors
- includes extensive text box examples and short case studies for reflection and discussion
- provides key terms, key takeaways and simple exercises which require short responses
- offers a suggested list of further readings for those who wish to explore a topic further.

The first introductory textbook to take a diplomatic approach, this text is essential reading for all those looking to take their first steps into the study of international relations in an era of uncertainty.

Paul Sharp is Professor and Head of Political Science at the University of Minnesota Duluth where he teaches courses in International Relations, Foreign Policy, Diplomacy, and International Relations Theory.

"Introducing International Relations is a *tour de force*, fast-paced and entertaining survey of the major theories and issues of international politics. It is destined to become widely viewed as the best IR textbook on the market."

Marcus Holmes, *College of William and Mary, USA*

"In a clear and engaging fashion, Sharp presents the diplomatic framework of understanding international relations by mapping out the field in a fair-minded, nuanced, and straightforward manner. A splendid teaching tool!"

Zhang Qingmin, *Peking University, China*

"In a refreshing conversational style, Paul Sharp, the diplomatic scholar, has composed an unusual core textbook that bridges the gap between diplomacy and international relations for the undergraduate. Assuming the reader knows little, Sharp digs into essential concepts, offers definitions, contemporary examples in case studies and points to further reading. Clearly a teacher, as well as a scholar, Sharp's original approach should meet the pedagogical demands of professors and help lower division college students get a grip on the human and systemic forces at work in our increasingly messy world."

Donna Marie Oglesby, *former diplomat (U.S.F.S. ret.) and educator at Eckerd College, USA*

"Paul Sharp has the rare ability to make International Relations theory readable, relevant and relatable. This textbook is a must-have for scholars and students alike, whatever their geopolitical interest or paradigmatic inclination."

Yolanda Kemp Spies, *University of Johannesburg, South Africa*

"This highly accessible textbook superbly synthesizes and advances current debates about whether and how diplomacy matters in the construction of world politics. Viewing the International Relations field through a diplomatic lens, Paul Sharp yields fascinating, and often challenging, insights about both theory and practice. In an appealing personal tone, Sharp's book will set students thinking and debating robustly amongst themselves."

Geoffrey Wiseman, *Australian National University, Australia*

"An excellent foundation for new entrants to the study of international relations. It provides excellent surveys of the leading approaches to International Relations. It also steers readers' attention to key questions that will help spark their own analyses of the problems of the discipline and the world."

Adam Quinn, *University of Birmingham, UK*

Introducing International Relations

PAUL SHARP

Routledge
Taylor & Francis Group

LONDON AND NEW YORK

First published 2018
by Routledge
2 Park Square, Milton Park, Abingdon, Oxon OX14 4RN

and by Routledge
711 Third Avenue, New York, NY 10017

Routledge is an imprint of the Taylor & Francis Group, an informa business

© 2018 Paul Sharp

The right of Paul Sharp to be identified as author of this work has been asserted by him in accordance with sections 77 and 78 of the Copyright, Designs and Patents Act 1988.

All rights reserved. No part of this book may be reprinted or reproduced or utilised in any form or by any electronic, mechanical, or other means, now known or hereafter invented, including photocopying and recording, or in any information storage or retrieval system, without permission in writing from the publishers.

Trademark notice: Product or corporate names may be trademarks or registered trademarks, and are used only for identification and explanation without intent to infringe.

British Library Cataloguing in Publication Data
A catalogue record for this book is available from the British Library

Library of Congress Cataloging in Publication Data
A catalog record for this book has been requested

ISBN: 9781138297654 (hbk)
ISBN: 9781138297678 (pbk)
ISBN: 9781315099064 (ebk)

Typeset in ITC Stone Serif and ITC Franklin Gothic
by Servis Filmsetting Ltd, Stockport, Cheshire

Visit the e-resources at: www.routledge.com/9781138297678

In memory of Patrick James Sharp

Contents

Figures

Tables

Acknowledgements

This textbook was made possible by the work, help, ideas, and advice of many people over many years. In particular I would like to acknowledge: Geoffrey Wiseman, Jan Melissen, Costas Constantinou, Zhang Qingmin, Rebecca Adler Nissen, Raymond Cohen, Halvard Leira, Geoffrey Berridge, Pauline Kerr, Donna Lee, John Hemery, Shaun Riordan, Cornelia Navari, Stuart Murray, David Clinton, Marcus Holmes, Iver Neumann, and Andrew Cooper.

My thanks also go to Nicola Parkin and Lucy Frederick at Routledge for their help, advice, and patience.

1 Introduction
Why study international relations and other basic questions

Reasons for studying international relations

Learning objectives

1. List the reasons for studying international relations.
2. Discuss the strengths and weaknesses of instrumental reasons for studying international relations.
3. Discuss the strengths and weaknesses of studying international relations just because it's interesting.

Why take a course on **International Relations**?[1] Three types of reasons are generally offered: first, because the course is instrumentally useful; second, because the issues the subject examines are important; and, third, because the subject is interesting. Needing the credit from the course to complete program requirements, obtain a degree, and secure a better job are examples of instrumental reasons. What the course is about takes second place to what passing the course does for you. These reasons matter, but their value is limited. Your instructor has instrumental reasons for teaching the course. She or he probably has house payments to make and daycare bills to pay; but you'd be disappointed and worried if these were the only reasons—or even the most important ones—why your instructor is showing up to teach the class. More reasons are needed to explain why people study International Relations as opposed to other subjects.

Questions of war and peace, economic interdependence, and globalization are examples of important issues which provide the second set of reasons for studying the subject. International Relations is a relatively new college subject. It developed after World War I in the 1920s when Political Science Departments in the US and Britain started adding it to their research and teaching missions. As we shall see in Chapters 2 and 3, World War I (1914–1918) resulted from a chain reaction which followed a Bosnian Serb student's assassination of the heir to the Austro-Hungarian Empire. What followed was a disaster in which tens of millions died, four empires were destroyed, and revolutionary communism became an international force based in Russia. No one was quite sure how it had all occurred, and so governments, private foundations, and rich individuals put up money for research on the following questions. Why did the war happen? Why in general do wars happen? When are wars more and less likely to occur?

It was hoped that answers to these questions would help people understand how to avoid war and preserve peace in the future. Part of the answer, said experts at the time, was that governments should be elected by the people and that the people should be educated about the dangers of war and the best ways to avoid them. That is why you find International Relations courses in most colleges today, even if those courses look at other things besides war and peace. War and peace are still big reasons for studying international relations. World War II (1939–1945) and the Cold War (1948–1989) made sure of that. During the Cold War, people were very aware that if things went badly wrong, everywhere in the world was just some 20 minutes or less away from destruction by nuclear weapons carried by rockets. Smaller wars persist today. Some occur between big states and smaller states they are trying to keep in line, for example the two US-led wars against Iraq in 1990 and 2003. Others are fought between governments of states, on the one hand, and terrorists and guerrillas fighting on behalf of revolutions, religions, and rebellions on the other, for example, the present wars between the Iraqi and Syrian governments and the Islamic State in Iraq and Syria (ISIS), and the recent war between the Ukrainian government and pro-Russian rebels. However, attention in International Relations, especially among students, has shifted somewhat away from questions of war and peace to other issues, even though, as it turns out, most of us still live within about 20 minutes (the flight time of the rockets carrying the nuclear warheads) of destruction.

One of these other issues is the rising importance of economics and international economic relations. The citizens of most states in the world expect their standards of living and those of their children to improve over time. This requires economic growth, and economic growth requires relations with other places around the world. It is from these other places that people obtain the raw materials, financial capital (invested money), customers, and technology for the goods and services they produce. They sell their goods and services to people in other places around the world and, if they are wealthy, they look to invest in those places to make more money. As a result, economies around the world have become more interdependent. They need what the others have got. Economic prospects in one part of the world increasingly depend on what happens somewhere else in the world. (See Figure 1.1.)

Just think of the attention you pay to the prices on the signs outside gas stations as you drive to school or work, or to the news about jobs, for example in computer engineering or call service centers, disappearing abroad because wages are lower there, or coming back because worker productivity is better in developed states like the US. If what happens in the rest of the world increasingly affects your economic prospects, then it is also true that what happens in your own state influences what happens in the rest of the world, especially if you happen to live in a rich, developed state. Right now, for example, the livelihoods of many people in China depend upon the willingness and ability of Americans to keep buying the cheap goods China exports for sale in shops like Target and Walmart. To make matters more complicated, the ability of many Americans to keep buying these goods depends upon their access to credit, some of which comes from Chinese sources.

Figure 1.1 Changing fuel prices in Karachi, Pakistan, December 2016
(Source: Asianet-Pakistan/Alamy Stock Photo)

Economic interdependence provides the core of another important issue which the subject of International Relations examines—globalization. Globalization can mean several things. Most often, it refers to a set of economic and technological processes by which the states and peoples of the world are becoming ever more closely linked. For example, vast amounts of electronic money move from one part of the world to another at the push of a button or in a preprogrammed response of computers to certain signals from the money markets, and this money moves around on a scale which can make or break national governments and their attempts at economic management.

In addition to economic and technological processes, however, people associate the way news and information about the world travel quickly and cheaply nearly everywhere with globalization. As a consequence, national traditions of music, drama, literature, and art are transmitted everywhere but are, in turn, influenced by similar transmissions from other states, peoples, and cultures. Americans are learning about soccer or football as the rest of the world calls it. Europeans are learning about football or American football as they call it. Different sets of moral standards collide as people, or knowledge about them, travels around the world. People in the Middle East are shocked by commercials from the West in which women are immodestly dressed, while people in the West are shocked to learn that some Asian peoples regard it as proper to arrange marriages for girls of thirteen and fourteen. As well as describing a process of interactions, the term globalization can also involve an argument that the governments and peoples of the world have, and ought, to think about issues which concern human beings on a global scale, not simply on a state, national, regional, or local scale. We cannot reduce the consequences of pollution, for example, simply by focusing efforts inside particular states. We find it harder to ignore governments which abuse their citizens when we hear about it and sometimes actually see this abuse live on our television sets, laptops, and mobile devices.

How does globalization change things? How, for example, does the development of a type of English as a global language affect non-English-speaking cultures? How does the search for new energy supplies to fuel developing economies affect global political relations? How do the results of consuming this energy affect the global environment and weather systems on which we all depend? And where does thinking globally take us—towards a world government, towards greater Americanization, or towards Westernization, at the expense of other cultures and communities? Will these other cultures and the independent states which protected some of them disappear in the face of the pressures to think and act on a global scale? Or will these pressures stimulate resistance in which local cultures and competing visions of a global world push back, like the French farmer who crashed his tractor into a McDonalds? If China and India become the dominant economic powers of the second half of the 21st century, how might globalization change from the way it looks today—for example, less English on international airport signs and more Mandarin and Urdu? (See Figure 1.2.)

These are all good reasons for studying International Relations. They do not exist separately from one another, but if you focus on one of them, this affects the way you see the others. If war and peace seem most important to you, then the way states become economically interdependent on one another may worry you. What happens to the states of Europe, for example, if they become dependent on supplies of natural gas from Russia? If you are focused on economic interdependence, however, then war may appear a terrible waste of lives and wealth and it is becoming, and ought to become, increasingly obsolescent. Why should China and the United States, for example, see each other as military rivals when

Figure 1.2 Multilingual international airport signage at Orlando airport in the US
(Source: Llene MacDonald/Alamy Stock Photo)

they are economically interdependent? China needs American markets, money, and business know-how, and, until recently at least, America has depended in part on Chinese imports and loans. If your focus is on globalization, then "petty" political, cultural, and economic concerns with local and national issues may seem like frustrating and fading obstacles to the challenge of getting things done. Why, for example, should a global agreement on the environment be put at risk by a few states' desire to continue polluting? Why should progress on fighting the Auto Immune Deficiency Syndrome (AIDS) and its consequences be held up by the fact that safe sex practices are politically or culturally unpopular with some men in one or a few states?

Each of these issues is important, and knowing about them may be useful in instrumental terms. You may have plans to become a Foreign Service Officer, to serve in the armed forces, or to work with a corporation or missionary service which has operations overseas. They may also be useful if you spend your life in your own state working as a business executive with foreign companies which have operations there, or as a law enforcement officer or social worker with individuals who are visiting or have immigrated. However, even if you have no intention of living the sort of life in which the material and ideas covered in this course may be useful, there is a third type of reason for studying International Relations. The subject is interesting. Through its study we see the drama of what it means to be human playing out on the broadest possible stage, that of the whole world. It is a stage on which human beings with often very different interests and different ideas of what it means to be human keep bumping into each other and, somehow, must find ways of relating to each other. For some people, this is reason enough for studying International Relations. Things do not always have to be directly useful to be valuable. For others, people whose taxes and tuition fees pay for the courses, for example, interest may not be enough. For them, the subject of International Relations should be useful, if only in the sense of helping to produce better educated and informed citizens.

Key term

International Relations   The academic study of international relations

Key takeaway

■ International Relations can be studied for instrumental reasons, because it deals with important problems and issues, and because it is an interesting subject.

Exercise

1. Which of the reasons for studying International Relations best applies to you as you begin the course?

1.2 Defining and studying the subject of International Relations

Learning objectives

1. Describe how international relations used to be defined in narrow terms.
2. Examine how broad definitions of international relations differ from narrow terms.
3. List the text's three main sources of uncertainty in contemporary international relations.

What is meant by international relations, and what does the subject of International Relations study? These used to be easy questions to answer. Until recently, it was generally agreed that international relations were the relations of sovereign states like China, the United States, and Germany. Notice that even though the name of the activity and the subject which studies it is inter*national* relations, it is the relations of states, not nations, which provided the original point of focus. The words "nation" and "state" are often used to mean the same thing, but a nation is best thought of as a culture group with a shared sense of identity, while a state is best thought of as a legal, political arrangement. As we shall see, not all nations have a state to themselves—think of the Welsh and the

Kurds, for example, and many states are made up of more than one nation or ethnic group—think of the United Kingdom, Russia, and China, for example (although one national group tends to be in a majority).

Each state had a territory, a people, and a government. Sovereignty meant that each state recognized no authority above itself. The system of sovereign states was assumed to have emerged in 17th-century Europe where it had been confirmed by the Treaty of Westphalia which ended the Thirty Years War in 1648. This system was then spread to the rest of the world by the European empires. The relations of these sovereign states and their governments were conducted by diplomats in time of peace. These diplomats worked from their own foreign ministries and out of their embassies in the capital cities of other states. They were professionals who shared a similar set of assumptions about how the world worked and how to operate in it. Their job was to advance the interests of their own state, but usually in such a way that peace between states was maintained. This required great skills in communicating and negotiating to ensure that misunderstandings did not create tension or lead to unintended war. When the diplomats failed and war broke out, international relations were turned over to the armed forces, although not completely. States generally kept talking to each other—either secretly or through third party mediators—even as they killed each other's soldiers and citizens. The role of diplomats was so important that people, especially in the United States, often used diplomacy as a synonym for international relations. As we shall see in the next chapter, studying international relations in these narrow terms came to be known as "the **state-centric** approach," especially by people who were critical of it.[2]

There is still a system of sovereign states today, and it is still very important. However, critics of the state-centric approach objected to focusing only on states for two reasons. First, some said it was wrong to concentrate on states to the neglect of the people who lived in them. The activity of international relations ought not to be dominated by states and the subject of International Relations ought not to focus only on them. It was people who mattered. After all, they argued, states should only exist to serve people. Others pointed out that states weren't the only actors in international relations. There were other types of actors: international organizations like the United Nations; multi-national corporations like Microsoft and Toyota; organized religious groups like the Roman Catholic Church; humanitarian organizations like Oxfam; and even influential individuals like the billionaires George Soros and Bill and Melinda Gates. Second, critics said that even if states—or the big rich states at least—were the most important and most powerful actors in international relations, they weren't just interested in war and peace. They were also concerned with economics, the environment, and a host of other issues. Therefore, anyone who concentrated only on the activities of diplomats and soldiers who represented sovereign states on matters of war and peace would be missing what "the **modified state-centric** approach," as Brown called it, regarded as a big and growing part of the story.

Over the last forty years or so, things have changed so much, some argue, that we no longer clearly live in a world dominated by sovereign states. What we have, they argue, is a network of relations between different kinds of actors of the sort listed above. In addition, the governments of states themselves can fragment into different parts. In the US, for example, the President, Congress, and various government agencies can seem to be engaged in a tug of war over what American foreign policy should be. Even some of these government agencies have broken down into parts pursuing their own agendas. In addition, computers, the Internet and developments in cameras and filming have made information cheap and plentiful to nearly everyone. Groups quickly form around shared interests, and just as quickly fall apart again in a world in which the boundaries between what is foreign and what is domestic are breaking down. You can get involved in a Saudi Arabian blog discussion on women's rights just as easily as Saudis can join a blog discussion on gun control in the US. In this "**transnational**" approach, as Brown among others refers to it, states seem to have lost a great deal of their former importance, but to whom? Some argue that the information revolution has reached a point where everyone can become an international player if they so choose, pushing their own agendas, and exposing the actions of diplomats, soldiers, and politicians in a way that never used to happen. Others argue that the Internet has given actors like the mass media, the corporations, and the intelligence services new influence through the powers of reporting, marketing, and surveillance.

These broad, transnational approaches say that all human relations which cross international boundaries are international relations and should be studied because they are becoming more important. Tourism, international phone calls, and online purchases from a seller in another sovereign state all qualify as international relations, just as much as diplomatic and military relations between states. The state-centric approach suggests this may be so, but the relations of states over war and peace are still the most important relations. Beyond indicating these broad and narrow approaches to definitions of international relations and International Relations, however, this textbook leaves you on your own. For you, the challenge involves listening to what other people say is important, figuring out what their approaches can and cannot tell you, and then doing your best to reach your own conclusions about the approaches you find most useful.

If international relations themselves are difficult to define, how is the subject of International Relations best studied? Again, there are multiple answers to this question. They depend on what people are interested in and what people regard as important. In addition, however, you will see that approaches to the methods of studying International Relations rest on some rock bottom, though conflicting, assumptions that scholars have about two big-named, but straightforward and very useful, ideas: ontology and epistemology. Ontology concerns inquiry into the nature of existence and being. What sort of world and broader universe do we live in, and what sort of beings are we? For example, are we, like the universe around us, just temporary arrangements of chemicals and electro-magnetic impulses, or do the materials of the universe simply provide shells for more spiritual essences which have meaning, purpose, and direction? Epistemology concerns inquiry into the nature of knowledge. What does it mean to know things? How do we come to know things? What is the relationship between the things we know and what is really out there? Indeed, how much really is out there independent of us thinking and talking about it?

In International Relations, we can identify a very rough divide between two groups of people with different responses to these questions. One group, whom we can call "Builders," assumes we can observe the world of international relations as if we were outside and separate from it. Human beings are part of the natural universe, they say, and are therefore subject to the laws which govern it. The challenge is to discover these laws just in the way a chemist or physicist investigates the behavior of elements or energy. We may not be able to come up with a science of International Relations which can predict what will happen in various situations the "Builders" accept, but by using the methods of science, they argue, we can build a better knowledge through theories about what is happening and likely to happen.

The other group, whom we can call "Interpreters," rejects this divide between the observer and the outside world. What we see, they argue, is profoundly shaped, possibly constructed, by who we are and the meanings which we assign to the world. The United States, for example, the Interpreters say, does not exist in the same way as the mountain called Mount Rushmore exists. As we shall see in Chapter 4, the existence of the United States is a social fact which depends on a lot of people thinking and acting as if it does exist. The existence of the mountain called Mount Rushmore is a material or "brute" fact which is independent of whether people say it exists or not. However, the existence of the mountain *as* Mount Rushmore is a social fact, and then only for some people, not all people— for others it exists as Six Grandfathers. This is not a trivial matter, as the fall of the Soviet Union demonstrates. Even superpowers can stop existing when enough people stop believing that they do. For the Interpreters, it is of critical importance to know people's own understandings of the situations they are in because this will have a big influence on what they do and what happens as a result.

Beyond this disagreement about material and social facts, however, most students of International Relations agree that they are doing social science. As K. J. Holsti says, this means they are interested in what typically happens in international relations.[3] For example, they do not ask why World War I broke out in 1914, why Somalia was wracked by famine in the 1980s, or why Norway is so rich today. They are interested in what each of these cases can tell us about why and when, in general, wars, famines, and economic success occur, under what conditions they are more and less likely, and how the challenges they present may be successfully dealt with.

Some International Relations social scientists are interested in identifying patterns of cause and effect. They ask, for example, how the internal politics of a state cause it to be more or less likely to engage in violent behavior. Are, for example, democracies more peaceful than dictatorships? Others are interested in how people's understanding of their international circumstances affects their actions. They ask, for example, why Canadians do not worry about the United States as a military threat, while Iranians do. Still others are interested in normative or moral questions. When is going to war justified, for example, and when is it not, and how do the ways governments answer these sorts of questions affect the way they act?

While social sciences like political science, sociology, psychology, economics, and communications dominate the academic subject of International Relations, it is important to note international relations can be studied in different ways. Historians, philosophers, theologians, and scholars of literature have shown great interest in international relations. International Law is a distinguished branch of the study of law. And a growing number of academics teach the subject entirely through the way international relations are presented in popular culture through media like television, film, and news outlets.

A major theme of the text is uncertainty. We can identify at least three sources of this uncertainty. The first is a traditional one. The balance of power in the world appears to be shifting away from the United States and Europe and towards other states like China and, possibly, India and Brazil, as these states industrialize and experience fast economic growth. However, there are fierce arguments about the rate at which power is shifting and the possible consequences of this shift. The second source of uncertainty is all the changes associated with the revolution in the technologies of communication and the transfer of information and their knock-on effects on political, economic, and social relations. The balance of power may be shifting between states, but, as noted above, some people, for example, Imad Salamey, suggest that the Internet and the massive amounts of information it makes cheaply available to anyone with a connection has crippled the power of states.[4] Look, for example, at the role of social networks and of flash mobs in toppling the Egyptian regime of Hosni Mubarak in 2011. The third source of uncertainty is the claim that our way of life is putting the health of the planet at risk. Politics—whether the great power politics of the US and China, the trade politics of economic interdependence, or the social activist politics of protests and rebellion—will all be rendered irrelevant if the natural environment which sustains all life is irreparably damaged.

As you will see as you read this text, the subject of International Relations probably adds more to this uncertainty. It certainly doesn't resolve much of it. For some, this is a sign of the undeveloped state of the subject. We know that for centuries, the medical sciences probably harmed as many people as they helped before the balance shifted in a positive direction. Perhaps International Relations is in an early stage from which it will grow. Perhaps all the competing voices of the present will be replaced by a few strong principles on which everyone can agree about how to make the world a more prosperous, just, and secure place. For other people, however, the competing views and uncertainties in International Relations are a sign of its strength and a source of fascination. They reflect the diverse range of experiences and understandings involved in being human beings occupying different positions in different parts of the world. If this is so, then as the conclusions in Chapter 15 will suggest, perhaps the old view of international relations as diplomacy will undergo a revival. It will not be the diplomacy of ambassadors, embassies, consulates, and foreign ministries, however. It will be a diplomacy which increasingly involves each and every one of us exercising the skills of living with different people and peoples under conditions where uncertainty is the norm.

Key terms

modified state-centric Term for approaches to International Relations which assume states to be the most important actors but regard other forms of international relations—especially economic ones—to be as important as diplomacy and war

state-centric Term for approaches to International Relations which assume states to be the most important actors and diplomacy and war to be the most important types of international relations

transnational Term for approaches to International Relations which assume other actors as well as states to be important and regard all forms of international relations to be potentially as important as diplomacy and war

Key takeaways

- There is no single way of defining international relations or single best way of studying International Relations.
- The state-centric approach is based on a narrow definition focusing on states, diplomacy, and war. The modified state-centric approach is broader, focuses on states, but adds economic and other forms of relations to diplomacy and war. The transnational approach is broadest of all and includes all sorts of relation between all sorts of actors which cross the boundaries of states.
- International Relations can be studied by looking for explanations of what happens in terms of causation, developing understandings of what happens in terms of how the social world is constituted and contested, and by examining normative arguments about what is right and wrong in international relations and about how they ought to be conducted.

Exercises

1. In what ways is the absence of a single accepted definition of international relations a strength, and in what ways is it a weakness?
2. In what ways are social facts different from material facts, and how does it matter?

1.3 Outline of the book

Chapters 2, 3, and 4 of the text examine the history of the subject of International Relations, its major theoretical perspectives, and the debates between them. Chapters 5, 6, and 7 look at sovereign states and how they act in the world through foreign policy, diplomacy, and war. Chapter 8 discusses attempts to regulate the behavior of states and others through international law, international organization, and processes of global governance. Chapters 9 and 10 shift the focus from politics and war to international economics, particularly the production, exchange, and distribution of goods and services, and the ways these activities are financed. Chapter 11 considers how states integrate with each other and how associations of states and individual states themselves can fall apart and disintegrate. Chapter 12 shifts the focus again from international relations to global problems—environmental, resource-based, and demographic—which face us all, plus the efforts to manage them. Chapters 13 and 14 return us to politics, not the politics of states however, but the political economy of wealth, poverty, and human development, the explanations for why at the global level the "haves" are so few, the "have-nots" are so many, and the arguments about how to narrow the gap between them. Chapter 15 concludes the text with a review of the sources of uncertainty, the arguments for why they are likely to increase, and a call for more diplomacy.

Notes

1 Throughout the text "International Relations" in upper case will refer to the study of international relations. The lower case form ("international relations") will be used to refer to the activity itself. When President Obama visits Canada, he is doing international relations. When you are reading this text or going to the class, you are doing International Relations.
2 See Chris Brown and Kirsten Ainley, *Understanding International Relations* (4th edition), Basingstoke, 2009, for this division of the field into state-centric, modified state-centric, and transnational approaches. Each of the three broad approaches contains variations or subsets, so it is possible to speak about, for example, state-centric approaches.
3 Kal Holsti, *International Politics: A Framework for Analysis* (7th edition), Upper Saddle River, 1994.
4 Imad Salamey, *The Decline of Nation-States after the Arab Spring*, New York, 2017, 72–73.

2 International theory, Realism, and power politics

As noted in Chapter 1, international relations are complicated, and they are becoming more complicated with the rise and acceleration of developments associated with globalization. As a result, people use theories to help them simplify, understand, and explain what is going on. Theorizing can be no more than thinking deeply and abstractly about how the world works. Everybody theorizes about the things which puzzle them, for example, why are most men supposed to be interested in football, why are most women supposed to be interested in clothes, and why does a text alert seem more interesting than the conversation you are having with a real live person which it interrupts. However, students of international relations, as social scientists, attempt to construct clearer and more explicit theories. They do so because they believe that broad and recurring patterns can be identified in the way that people, states, and others interact with one another. Realism, sometimes called Political Realism, is one of the oldest and most important International Relations theories in this sense. The people who accept Realism's view of the world are called **Realists**. There are problems with Realists' assumptions, arguments, and claims, but it is impossible to understand the subject International Relations, and almost impossible to understand actual international relations themselves, without having a firm grasp of what Realists have to say.

2.1 **Power** and politics

Learning objectives

1. List the three elements of politics.
2. Describe the way Realists see power.
3. Describe three sorts of **interests** which states and their governments have.
4. Explain how the Realists see their approach as being "realistic."

Realists claim that international relations should be viewed as a political activity. Politics may be defined in several ways. Classical thinkers like Plato

(424 BCE–348 BCE) for example, understood politics in terms of ruling. Plato saw ruling both as an inquiry into what is generally good for human beings and as the activity of arranging our societies so that good can be achieved.[1] As he put it, "I conceived that the art of the ruler, considered as ruler, whether in a state or in private life, could only regard the good of his flock or subjects." Later thinkers, like Niccoló Machiavelli (1469–1527), for example, saw politics and government in terms of the power struggles which human beings get into because they have an interest in ruling over one another and avoiding being ruled.[2] According to Machiavelli, if you were in charge, then your task would consist "mainly in so keeping your subjects that they shall be neither able, nor disposed to injure you."

More recent thinkers often see politics in economic terms. Harold Lasswell (1902–1978), for example, stressed the way politics was a way of conducting and settling arguments about how the things which people value get distributed. He said "Politics is who gets what, when and how."[3]

People tend to agree now that all three elements—some idea of pursuing a general and higher good; struggles or competitions for power and control; and decisions about who gets what—are present in all political systems. The important question to ask, however, concerns their relative strength in any particular system. To what extent, for example, are the American political system, the Iranian political system, and the international political system, about seeking some higher conception of what is good for all human beings? To what extent is each system dominated by struggles for power and control among some or all, of their citizens? And to what extent is each system absorbed with deciding who gets how much of the things we value like money, freedom, or social status?

When Realists say that international relations should be viewed as a political activity, they are talking about politics in terms of the second conception, the competition for power to control or avoid being controlled. Thus, Hans Morgenthau, one of the earliest and most important Realists in modern IR said that international relations should be primarily be viewed as the struggle for power and peace between the governments of states seeking to satisfy their national interests.[4] There may be a lot of other things going on. Governments, international organizations, private corporations, social movements, and most professors of International Relations, certainly talk as if there is more going on. According to Realists, however, these people are all mistaken because they are looking at the froth and missing the coffee (or the beer) underneath. For Realists, this power struggle is all-important, because everything else—doing good, obtaining wealth, enjoying respect—depends on having power.

At the heart of the Realists' conception of international relations as a political activity then is **power**. But what is power? This is a difficult, but important, question to answer. As we shall see, it will keep resurfacing in this textbook and it keeps resurfacing in actual international relations in the discussions and arguments of governments, diplomats, soldiers, and ordinary people. The Realists see power in two ways. First, they treat it as an attribute or a thing, something which states possess in specific quantities: armed forces, wealth, resources, and territory, for example. In these terms, we can see that the United States has a lot of power and the south Asian state of Bangladesh has much less. We can soon see the limitations with this approach, however. Saying that the United States and

Bangladesh possess specific quantities of the attributes of power tells us very little on its own. Thus, Realists ask, "relative to what?" and "in what context?" When the United States gets into an argument with North Korea over nuclear weapons, for example, we can see that Washington has a lot more power than Pyongyang, the North Korean capital.

North Korea is known for impressive-looking and menacing-looking parades in which large numbers of soldiers march past the government and military equipment is shown off (see, for example, http://www.youtube.com/watch?v=dH-nGLrMdWqw&feature=relmfu, or just google You Tube North Korean Military parade).

The power of North Korea and the United States

The Democratic Republic of Korea (North Korea) is one of the last communist dictatorships in the world. It has a population of around 25 million but is reputed to have the fourth largest armed forces in the world with 1.21 million military personnel. It also possesses a small but growing number of nuclear warheads and missiles with which it may soon be able to hit targets in the United States. Viewed in isolation, North Korea's military effort looks impressive. However, much of its equipment is obsolescent and its military effort inflicts a huge burden on North Korea's economy and people. In comparison, the world's leading military power, the United States, with a population of 312 million, has 1.4 million people on active duty and over two million reservists. The US armed forces are far more modern, backed by several thousand nuclear warheads, can be moved around the world, and impose far less of a burden on the American economy. In relation to its own size, therefore, North Korea's military effort is huge. In relation to the most powerful states in the world, however, the results of this effort remain modest.

Source for figures, *CIA The World Fact Book*, Washington DC, 2012.

When the United States gets into an argument with the People's Republic of China over what to do about North Korea's nuclear weapons, however, the question of how much power Washington has relative to Beijing is less clear. China has a lot more of the attributes of power than has North Korea. Similarly, in an argument between Bangladesh and its neighbor India over illegal immigration, for example, we can see that its capital, Dacca, has less power than New Delhi, the Indian capital. However, it is much more difficult to say who has more power when Bangladesh gets into an argument with its other neighbor, Myanmar (Burma), over persecuted Muslim minorities and immigration because the two states are more closely matched in terms of the attributes of power. (See Table 2.1.)

One way out of this difficulty is to ask who got their way in a real conflict or to imagine who would likely get their way in a hypothetical conflict between

Table 2.1 Attributes of power for selected states in 2016

Name/Indicator	Population	GDP in USD (at purchasing power parity)	Average GDP per capita in USD	Military Spending as percentage of GDP
United States	323,995,528	18.56 trillion	57,300	3.29
China	1,373,541,278	21.14 trillion	14,600	1.9
India	1,266,883,598	8.721 trillion	6,700	2.47
Bangladesh	156,186,882	628.4 billion	3,900	1.44
Burma (Myanmar)	56,890,418	307.3 billion	6,000	4.08
North Korea	25,115,311	40 billion	1,700 (in 2015)	Not available

Source: Table compiled from data presented in the Central Intelligence Agency *World Fact Book 2017*, at https://www.cia.gov/library/publications/the-world-factbook/

Note: Estimates for North Korean defense spending as a proportion of GNP frequently exceed 20 percent. See, for example, *NationMaster* at http://www.nationmaster.com/country-info/stats/Military/Expenditures/Percent-of-GDP

two or more states. Thus, in addition to seeing power as an attribute, Realists say it must also be seen in terms of a relationship. Who generally gets their way, for example, when the United States and Canada disagree about how to handle cross-border environmental pollution, or when Japan tries to get China to recognize its sovereignty over islands which they both claim in the East China Sea? As we shall see, there are sometimes surprising answers from a Realist point of view to these sorts of questions. Determining how much power a state has, and how much it has relative to other states, is a bit like the sort of pre-season analysis which goes into predicting likely Super Bowl contenders or pre-game analysis to predict the outcome of particular matchups. It is difficult, Realists concede, but people and states are going to make such estimates of the power of other states because the answers affect their own actions. If this is so, then such estimates might as well be done as carefully as possible. Besides, Realists add, in international relations, just as in interpersonal relations and professional sports, it is not that hard to establish who in general has the power to get their way and who in general does not. And when it is too close to call, as between Bangladesh and Myanmar in the example above, then this too can be a useful discovery.

States need power, according to Realists, because they are interest-driven and operate in a political anarchy of sovereign states where no one is in charge and no one else is obligated to help them. Arnold Wolfers identified three types of national interests or goals. There are things which states would like to acquire or hold on to which he called possession goals (see Chapter 5 for further discussion of foreign policy goals).[5] These can be concrete like territory; resources; armed forces. They can also be abstract, however, like achieving a peaceful reputation among other states, or a position of leadership in an alliance like the North Atlantic Treaty Organization (NATO) or an international organization like the United Nations (UN). There are what Wolfers called milieu goals. This term refers to creating conditions in the world which make it easier to pursue a state's interests. According to Realists, for example, the United States government works to create a world of democratic states with free market economies because it believes the US will prosper in such a world. For the same reason, the government of the

Figure 2.1 President George W. Bush on Air Force One after the 9–11 terrorist attacks on New York and Washington DC in 2001

(Source: White House Photo/Alamy Stock Photo)

People's Republic of China tries to create a world of states with strong governments which control economies because they believe China will prosper in such a world.

In 2001, President George W. Bush expressed the idea of creating a world which suited American interest and values in the following terms.

> America has a window of opportunity to extend and secure our present peace by promoting a distinctly American internationalism. We will work with our allies and friends to be a force for good and a champion of freedom. We will work for free markets and free trade and freedom from oppression. Nations making progress toward freedom will find America is their friend.
>
> George W. Bush, First State of the Union speech, February 27, 2001

In addition to possession goals and milieu goals, there are goals for which states make sacrifices. Wolfers describes these as self-abnegation goals. States, for example, may provide others with development assistance (foreign aid), or they may reduce the size of their armed forces or pull them back from bases around the world. However, Realists maintain that real self-sacrifices of this sort are rare, and can usually be explained in terms of serving self-interests. They say that states give aid, for example, to create political allies and economic partners.

For Realists power is important to achieving the interests of states for two reasons. First, one state will rarely help another state secure its interests unless it is in the interests of the first state. Thus, the United States only looks after

Canadian security because it is in the United States' own interest to do so. Secondly, the interests of states often collide with one another and are sometimes mutually exclusive. Most Israelis, for example, believe that the existence of a fully independent Palestinian state is incompatible with the requirements of Israel's security. Some Palestinians, in contrast, believe that the continued existence of Israel is incompatible with their own aspirations for a fully independent Palestine, while most believe that in the absence of an independent Palestine, Israel should never be allowed to be secure. Even apparently benign interests in general aspirations like world peace and world order can cause tension and conflict according to Realists. This is because each state will always have its own conception of what world peace and world order should look like. In the Cold War, the United States imagined and worked for a world of democracies with free market economies in which it would be well-positioned to prosper and to lead. The Soviet Union could see only a subordinate place for itself in this picture and offered its own vision of world peace and world order—a communist one—which was just as unattractive to the United States.

Not only do the interests of states tend to collide with one another, however. According to Realists, states generally put their own interests before everybody else's. The international system is what Kenneth Waltz called a self-help system, in which the only way for a state to get its own way on big issues is to have the power to insist upon it and to block others.[6] Thus, since power is so important to states getting their way, acquiring power and keeping it become interests in themselves. There is a circular character to the relationship between interests and power for states, just as there is to the relationship between money and the economic goods it enables people to acquire. Most of us work to get money to buy the things we need to live and live well. Making money seems like just a means to an end. However, most of us also make big choices, for example about getting educated or about where to live, so we can get the jobs which provide us with money. Making money, therefore, can also be an end, a reason why we do things. So can getting power.

According to Realists, most states' interest in power is stronger than most individuals' interest in money because the consequences of being powerless in international relations are worse than the consequences of being broke in ordinary life. The state and its people can expect no help and may face physical destruction. The individual, in contrast, can look to his or her family, charitable organizations, and the state of which they are a citizen for assistance, and rarely faces destruction unless the state itself is failing catastrophically.

Key history for Realists 1: Greece 416–415 BCE

Realists see the struggle for power and interests as a permanent condition of international relations. To support this they point to the "Melian Dialogue," an account of an episode in the Peloponnesian War, 431–404 BCE, provided by Thucydides (460c–395c BCE) in his historical study of the same name. Athens and its allies were at war with Sparta, and the Athenians were trying to get one of Sparta's allies, the island of Melos, to surrender and pay tribute.

The Athenians tell the Melians that if they refuse, they will be destroyed. The Melians try several arguments during the negotiations. They say the Athenians should spare them because Melos has a powerful ally, Sparta, who will come to its rescue. The Athenians should also spare them because then the rest of the Greek world will be impressed with Athens' generosity and mercy. The Athenians reply that any rescue, if it comes at all, will come too late to help Melos and that, if the Athenians spare the island, everyone else will think the Athenians are weak and scared. The Melians, they continue, have no choice if they want to live. This may not be fair, but in this life "the strong do what they can, and the weak suffer what they must." The Melians decide to fight, are defeated, the surviving men executed, and the women and children taken into captivity. The historical accuracy of the story can be challenged, as can the Realist interpretation of it. For Realists, however, it captures the way the powerful not only can, but must, act ruthlessly, and how the weak can do little about it.

Realists focus on international relations as a political struggle for power between states which is driven by competing, and sometimes mutually exclusive, interests. In doing so, they claim that their theory is based on how the world actually is—the real world as they see it, and not the ideal world for which we all might wish. The terms Realist and Realism were adopted by theorists of international relations who tried to explain why World War I (1914–1918) was followed so closely by World War II (1939–45). It was so after only twenty-one years and after a huge effort had been expended on constructing a new international order under the League of Nations which was supposed to prevent such wars occurring ever again. These efforts failed, according to the Realists, because they were based on the assumption that peoples were generally peace-loving, but would be prepared to resist those who threatened the peace. This assumption the Realists characterized as "idealist," desirable in principle but unrealistic in the present and for the foreseeable future.

Key terms

interests   Things which people and states seek to obtain and hold on to. The most important national interests of states are security, independence, prosperity, and power.

power   A state's ability to influence other states to do what they want.

realists   Theorists who see international relations as dominated by a struggle for power and interests between states.

Key takeaways

- Realists see international relations as a political struggle for interests and power between states.

- Power is hard to define. It can be seen as attributes—things which states possess in smaller or greater amounts which make them stronger. It can be seen as relational—how much power a state has in relation to another state, for example, or how much power it has in one particular situation as opposed to another.

- Realists regard it as both possible and necessary to come up with rough measures of how much power a state possesses. States need power to secure their interests in the face of challenges from other states whose interests may conflict with theirs.

- Realists see themselves as theorizing about the world as it actually is and not from how they might like it to be—an approach which they regard as Idealist. They can be criticized, however, for merely asserting that their approach captures the most important aspects of the reality of international relations, rather than making their case for why we should agree with them.

Exercises

1. How do Realists see politics and why is international relations a political activity?
2. Why do states need power according to Realists?

2.2   What Realists see in international relations

Learning objectives

1. List the characteristics of a sovereign state.
2. Describe what states are doing according to Realists.
3. Describe what a system of **sovereign states** looks like according to Realists.
4. Explain the Realist view of how international relations change and yet remain the same.

Realists look at the world and see an international or global political order made up of states. These states are sometimes called nation-states in which the state is the political-legal component, while the nation is the cultural component with shared sense of history, identity, and language. As we shall see in Chapters 3 and 5, the idea emerged in 19th century Europe that the world was divided into nations and that each nation should evolve to the point where it should get its own state if it wanted it. Realists, and others, accept that the nation state, where it exists, has often been a successful combination, but many states are not nation-states in the sense of one nation, one state. Most states have a dominant nation and minority nations. Therefore, Realists focus on the state, accepting that the cultural component which helps keep its people together can take several forms besides national, for example, ideological or religious.

These states vary greatly in terms of size (compare Russia to Israel, for example), wealth (compare the Norway to Yemen, for example) and power (compare the United States to Somalia, for example). However, they each possess territory, people, and a government. In addition these states enjoy the status of being sovereign. **Sovereign states** act independently and no higher authority can tell them what they must to do. For American students particularly, therefore, it is important to note that the 50 states of the Union do not qualify as states in the way the term is used in international relations because they are not sovereign. The federal government has authority over them in key areas. While the idea of the sovereign territorial state was developed by political theorists for governments in Europe during the 14th and 15th centuries, Realists regard this development as a recognition, clarification, and, perhaps, perfection of our ideas about conditions which always exist when people live in groups which are separate from one another. Go back in time to ancient Egypt, where people did not talk in terms of states, sovereignty, and independence, for example, Realists say, and you will still see political entities which look and act like states.

The Amarna letters

The Amarna letters were discovered near the town of that name in Egypt in 1887. They are a set of clay tablets dating from the 14th century BCE and provide a record of correspondence between the Egyptian Pharaohs, their allies, and other ancient empires (see Figure 2.2). The form of the letters strikes us as strange. They contain requests for gifts and brides from Great Kings who regard one another as brothers, and requests for protection from smaller players coming under pressure. Nevertheless, Realists maintain, they reveal a game of power politics being played over three and a half thousand years ago between insecure and jealous political leaders which should be very familiar to us today. Players, tactics, and technologies may change, but the game remains the same—the struggle for power and interests, however these are defined at particular times and places.

The Realists maintain that the same is true if you look at the peoples of the Americas prior to their contact with the Europeans, the peoples of the Greco-Roman world, and those of the Chinese and Indian empires. Wherever one looks, according to Realists, once peoples reach a certain level of technical, economic, and political development, they organize themselves into state-like entities. According to Realists, they have always done so. They do so at present. It is reasonable to suppose that they will do so in the future. Over time, the fortunes of particular states have fluctuated. Some new ones have been created (most recently, South Sudan, for example, in 2011). Others have disappeared (the Soviet Union in 1991, for example). Some have grown more powerful, to the point of seeming to dominate the world (the United States after the fall of the Soviet Union, for example). Others have lost power and faded into relative obscurity

Figure 2.2 Cuneiform tablet dating from 14th century BCE, part of a record of diplomatic correspondence between the Egyptian Pharaoh and other kings about gifts, agreements, and alliances

(Source: www.BibleLandPictures.com/Alamy)

(Austria, for example). According to Realists, however, the state principle as a way of organizing human beings has persisted down the ages. It will likely persist into the future, as will the processes by which particular states are created and rise, decline, and fall.

There are other actors in international relations to be sure. Realists do not deny that transnational companies like the Coca Cola Corporation, organized religions like the Catholic Church, human rights organizations like Doctors Without Borders, and even individual human beings like George Clooney and the Gates (mentioned earlier), can be seen to be acting internationally. These other actors may even, on occasion, affect the fortunes of individual, smaller, weaker states. Nevertheless, according to Realists, these other actors operate within a framework set by states and cannot have an independent and decisive impact on the ways in which states conduct their relations with each other. The big multinational oil company British Petroleum, for example, may be able to make demands on a poor West African state which is seeking its help in discovering oil. It can bargain fairly effectively with a big state like Nigeria about how much it can charge for its services. However, when it finds itself in the gun sights of the United States for polluting the Gulf of Mexico, or Russia when the Kremlin wants it to reassign its stake in a Siberian oilfield to a more friendly company, then British Petroleum has to do as it is told.

These states, which Realists see as the most important actors in international relations, are constantly seeking to increase their power and hold on to the power they already have. Their governments, diplomats, and armed forces are nearly always seeking opportunities to increase their influence over other states, and give this objective priority over all others. On the rare occasions that states stray from this path, according to Realists, they will get into trouble like Britain and France when both these states failed to stand up to Nazi Germany in the 1930s. France was invaded and occupied, while Britain survived but had to wait for the more powerful Soviet Union and United States to enter the war to defeat Germany and its allies, Italy and Japan.

Key history for Realists 2: Europe in the 1930s and the policy of appeasement

In 1933, Adolf Hitler and the Nazis gained sufficient support in the German elections to form a government. Hitler promised that he would restore Germany's prosperity, military strength, and self-respect, as well as punish the Jews, communists, and others whom he and his supporters held responsible for Germany's collapse at the end of World War I in 1918. He wanted to recover territory in what had become Czechoslovakia and Poland which had been taken from Germany by the Treaty of Versailles, and to bring his native Austria into a union with Germany. At each step of the way, the British government under Neville Chamberlain and its French allies agreed to Hitler's demands in the hope that once he was satisfied, the peace of Europe would be secured. In 1938, at a conference in Munich (Figure 2.3), they told Czechoslovakia to give up part of its territory to Germany in order to avoid the European war which Hitler was threatening. When Hitler took over the rest of Czechoslovakia, demanded that the Free City of Danzig be returned to Germany and attacked Poland for objecting to this in 1939, Britain and France decided that Hitler would not stop making demands and they declared war on Germany.

The policy of making concessions to others is known as appeasement, but the word has become linked to this period in history, and to the idea that if you let bullies have what they want out of fear they will only come back for more. The history of the period has been much argued over with some historians noting the problems posed by Britain's and France's military weakness and the fact that most of Hitler's specific demands were understandable and some quite reasonable, even if they were made by someone whom events proved to be evil and unstable. Nevertheless, the mud has stuck, and "appeasement" and "appeaser" have become terms of abuse in political argument. American Realists, in particular, were worried that an American public tired of fighting would want to appease the Soviet

Union at the end of World War II. Note, however, that Realists do not object to appeasement in principle, just to appeasing those whose appetites are unlimited and to sacrificing key national interests in doing so.

(To view the famous "Peace for Our Time" speech by which the British Prime Minister Chamberlain announced his agreement with Hitler in 1938, follow this link: https://www.youtube.com/watch?v=hQ95ffnU4Sw. Chamberlain had secured his agreement with Hitler that morning before flying back to London and believed it had preserved what he called in Parliament later that day "Peace for Our Time." Just less than a year later, Britain and France declared war on Germany in response to the latter's invasion of Poland.)

All governments and politicians talk of the need for peace and cooperation to solve the sorts of global economic and environmental problems which face the human race. According to Realists, however, the actions of states reveal that they are always maneuvering for advantage over each other and will rarely, if ever, sacrifice national interests for the global good. Look, they say, at how the United States drags its feet over environmental agreements which it believes disproportionately burden developed states like itself. Look at how China and Russia drag their feet over implementing UN-sponsored economic sanctions on Syria and Iran because they have better relations and do more business than the United States does with either.

Figure 2.3 British Prime Minister Neville Chamberlain, French Prime Minister Edouard Daladier, German Chancellor Adolf Hitler, and Italian leader Benito Mussolini meeting at Munich in 1938

(Source: World History Archive/Alamy Stock Photo)

Realists, like Hans Morgenthau, often divide states into two sorts. There are those which do well out of the world as it is presently set up and want to keep the world that way, and there are those who do not do well and would like to change it. E.H. Carr, although he was not a Realist in the conventional sense, called the first type status quo states and the second type revisionist states. Today, according to Realists, the United States and Japan would be examples of status quo states which are broadly content with the way power is currently distributed in the world. China and Iran would be examples of revisionist states seeking a change in the way power is distributed and improvements in their respective power positions. Russia, because of its recent international decline, would be an example of a state which is not quite sure whether its interests are best served by being a status quo state or a revisionist state.

Some Realists, associated with **defensive realism**, like Stephen Walt, see most states most of the time as trying to hang on to the power and the resulting influence they already have.[7] Most states, like most people, prefer the quiet life most of the time. Even defensive states can still clash with one another, however, because most states, unlike most people, inhabit a dangerous environment—the anarchic international system—and, as a result, feel insecure. The steps they take to secure themselves can appear threatening to other states and lead to a chain-reaction of arming themselves and allying with others. What John Herz called "the **security dilemma**" can lead to tension and even warfare between states which had few substantive reasons for falling out with each other.[8] For other Realists, associated with **offensive realism**, like John Mearsheimer, the situation is even more tense than the one presented by Walt and Herz. They see all states relentlessly and actively engaged in seeking to increase their power and reduce the power of others. Success in power politics, for Offensive Realists, is like success in riding a bicycle. States have to keep moving forwards in terms of pursuing power, otherwise, like the cyclist who stops without putting their foot down, they will take a tumble.[9] Thus, for Offensive Realists, the American-led wars against Iraq and in Afghanistan, for example, should not be seen as attempts to protect the US and the rest of the world from terrorists and local expansionist powers. They should be seen as attempts to extend United States power and the influence which flows from it into the heart of the Middle East and Central Asia. This is not to say that Offensive Realists regarded either of these two wars as a good idea, however. Indeed, some Realists of all stripes have been quite critical of United States policy in both wars on the grounds that neither serve what Realists regard as key national interests of the United States.

According to Realists, states pursue their interests, and especially their interest in acquiring and holding onto power, above all else. These interests frequently conflict with the interests of other states. A famous Realist image of international relations involves a pool table with balls of unequal size and weight, each representing a state, colliding and bouncing off each other. These pool ball/states have no one else who puts their interests first. There is no system of rules and laws to which other states will subordinate their interests when these conflict. And there is no reliable system of enforcement for the rules and laws which actually exist. Every government knows that it can expect help from others or the rules to be enforced by others only when this suits the interests of other states. When it does not suit anyone else's interests to help, then like Hungary, when the Soviet Union intervened in it in 1956, like Iraq when the United States and its allies invaded it in 2003, and like the United States when Japan attacked it at Pearl Harbor, each state must ultimately rely on its own efforts. There is no 911 phone number for states to call when they get into trouble or, at least, there is no one at the other end who is obliged to come and help.

As a result, the world of states, as seen by Realists, is a tense and potentially violent place characterized by **power politics**. That is to say, states are constantly maneuvering to defend and advance their power and interests by all means, including force if necessary. In this regard, according to Realists, international relations are qualitatively different from the "normal" human relations which take place inside states. Relations inside states are governed by laws which most citizens accept because they believe obeying the laws is sensible and right, and because they feel like they belong to the community the laws are supposed to serve. The laws are also enforceable by a system of justice and policing which is regarded as legitimate by most citizens and deals with those who are not prepared to accept the laws. Relations outside states are not governed by laws which most states accept even when doing so hurts their interests. There is no system of enforcement which states recognize as legitimate in the way that most citizens regard the justice system and police force of their own state as legitimate. Realists are not the only theorists who make what R.B.J. Walker has called the inside-out distinction between people's relations inside states and relations between states themselves. However, they are foremost among those who argue that it is impossible for students to gain a proper understanding of international relations if they do not recognize the "inside-outside" distinction. More importantly, governments which fail to recognize this distinction will soon get into trouble in their foreign policies. Realists argue, for example, that the United States gets into trouble when it assumes that if other states are democracies, then their people will agree with Americans on the big questions. Whether democracies or not, other states have their own interests which can diverge from the interests of the United States. It will also get into trouble, Realists argue, when other states see it pronouncing on and interpreting rules of international conduct for everyone else. They will resent this as threatening their sovereign independence.

American foreign policy, public opinion and the "Arab Spring"

A fruit-seller set fire to himself in Tunisia in 2011 in protest and frustration at being denied a sales permit by an official in a disrespectful manner. His response tapped into decades of popular anger at political corruption and incompetence which resulted in protests, first in Tunisia, then Egypt and then other Arab states where people demanded that the old elites leave power and new leaders emerge who would be more responsive to the needs of the people. In America and much of the Western world, it was assumed that successful protests would lead to democracies being established and that democracies would produce governments with which it would be easier to have friendly relations. Realists are skeptical about this line of reasoning, not because they think that Arabs are incapable of running proper democracies, but because they believe that key national interests have a way of holding up no matter who is in charge. Arab states hostile to the US would remain hostile whether they were democracies or not. Arab states friendly to the US would remain friendly whether they were democracies or not. This being so, Realists argued, the important thing for American interests was that there should be governments in friendly Arab states who could keep their people under control, and governments in hostile Arab states which could keep their hostility under control. For example, many American Realists argued that Hosni Mubarak, the Egyptian leader, looked better able to align Egyptian interests with America's than any likely alternative produced by a popular revolt. Even the anti-American Libyan leader, Muammar Gaddafi, looked like a better bet if the alternative was going to be chaos. The same might have been said about President Assad in Syria at the start of the Syrian civil war. Add to this the tendency of Americans to see continued arguments with new Arab governments as evidence that their shift to democracy is either incomplete or bogus and needs more help, and Realists see a prescription for disaster. Arab peoples will be angry that Americans do not respect the political changes they have undertaken. Americans will be angry that these changes have not resulted in the sorts of policy changes in Arab states which Americans think they should make. Unless other states are making trouble for your state, Realists conclude, don't interfere in their domestic politics.

According to Realists, international relations have always been characterized by power politics ever since human communities began to organize around agriculture, became sedentary, and managed to create a surplus which would feed priests and soldiers (see Chapter 7 for a further discussion of soldiers). Looking back into both the distant and the recent past, Realists maintain that we can see a pattern of international relations which is similar in its essentials to the international relations of today. They also maintain that the citizens of ancient Egypt, the Greek city states, the Roman Empire, the Iroquois confederacy and the European ancien régime, would have little difficulty in making sense of contemporary international relations once technical developments like the telephone, the internet, and the atomic bomb had been explained to them. Just as Alfred Lord Whitehead maintained that all political philosophy "is but a footnote to Plato," Realists might maintain that all International Relations is but a footnote to Thucydides and his account of the wars of the Greek city states. Now, as in ancient Greece, states fight each other. All seek to become stronger, either by building up their own power or making alliances with other states. Some grow weaker. Some grow stronger. Sometimes, peace is maintained for a considerable time because no state feels strong enough to take another on. Sooner or later, however, power shifts in such a way that the revisionist states are tempted to go to war to change things, or the status quo states are tempted to go to war to stop them changing. Over time, therefore, Realists identify a repetitive rhythm to international relations characterized by what Paul Kennedy, among others, called "the rise and fall of the great powers."[10]

Realists find it difficult to imagine a future in which human beings escape this pattern. Why should we want to escape it? Most Realists, like most of the rest of us, do not like the tensions and violence associated with power politics. Since these arise from the interactions of sovereign and independent states, however, they can be avoided only by getting rid of states or creating a single world state. To get rid of states would put at risk the peaceful and orderly life which Realists see states providing for the people living inside them. Setting up a world state would get rid of relations between states, at least at the definitional level, because there would only be one state. Realists note, however, that very few citizens wish to see their own state give up its sovereignty to a world state. They suspect that a world state would, in practice, amount to the rule of one particular state and its people over the rest, or that it would be seen as such. As a result, a world state would soon be faced by rebellions and civil wars through which it would disintegrate into a world of multiple states and the old pattern of power politics would resume again.

This may seem to be a depressing conclusion for at least two reasons. First, as Morgenthau noted, the wars by which power and relations are adjusted have become ever more expensive and destructive, especially with the invention of nuclear weapons. Even though he is regarded as the grandfather of American Political Realism, Morgenthau was torn between his sense that the dynamics of power politics were inescapable in a world of sovereign states, and his knowledge that the widespread use of nuclear weapons in a world war could lead to the extinction of the human race. If human beings continue to engage in wars, the probability is that sooner or later they will engage in one where nuclear weapons are extensively used.[11] The second reason this conclusion may be depressing, for Americans at least, is because right now the United States is the most powerful state in the world. It probably will be so for some time to come, but nothing in history gives grounds for believing that the United States will always be the most powerful state in the world. Of course, what is depressing for Americans and those around the world who like the kind of international order provided by US power, may be good news to others who like it less, and believe that their state's time as the world's leader is coming. Realists as theorists have no opinion about these sorts of changes, any more than meteorologists have opinions about different sorts of weather systems. As citizens, however, Realists tend to identify with their own state's interests and the sorts of values which are upheld and advanced by their own state's power.

Key terms

defensive realism   A view associated with theorists who see a world of mainly insecure states acting to protect their power and secure their national interests from the threats posed by other states.

offensive realism   A view associated with theorists who see a world of mainly aggressive states acting to acquire more power and advance their national interests over the interests of other states.

power politics   A type of politics in which the primary objective is to increase your own power while reducing the power of others. Realists (among others) maintain that international relations are mainly about power politics.

security dilemma   A concept which illustrates the way in which defensive measures taken by one state can be seen as offensive measures by another state which reacts by taking its own defensive measures which are seen as offensive by the first state, thereby starting a chain reaction.

sovereign states   A state is a political-legal entity composed of territory, people, and a government. Sovereignty is a condition of constitutional independence in which no higher political or legal authority is recognized. A sovereign state recognizes no higher authority over it. The people of a state are often said to be sovereign but, for practical purposes, that sovereignty is claimed and exercised by the state's government.

Key takeaways

- Realists see sovereign states pursuing power and interests in an anarchic system which has existed ever since the emergence of independent political communities.

- Realists see the international system as a self-help system in which states are forced to pursue their power and interests or lose their independence and freedom to other states.

- Realists see two sorts of states: status quo states which are broadly content with the international system and their position in it, and revisionist states which would like to change the system or greatly improve their position in it.

- Realists see little prospect of the state system ending since this could only be by one state or a few establishing a world government which no one else would like.

Exercises

1. What are the key properties of a state?

2. According to Realists, why is the world produced by states a tense and potentially violent place?

3. According to Realists, why are states probably a permanent feature of international relations?

What Realists understand is happening in international relations

Learning objectives

1. Describe how Realists see human nature results in people living in states.
2. Explain how Realists see the states system forcing all people to live in states.

Why do we live in states? Many Realists do not regard this as a very important question. The reality, they say, is that we do. There are over 190 sovereign states in the world at present. There are a few stateless individuals who have lost their citizenship in one state without gaining it in another. There are many more people who live in territories whose status is unsettled or in dispute, like Palestine and Kosovo, for example. With the exception of a few scientists in Antarctica, however, everybody lives in a state. With no exceptions, everyone is supposed to belong to a state, although some states use withdrawing citizenship as a form of punishment. To Realists, the reasons why people live in states seem obvious. States protect us from outside invaders and law breakers inside the state. They provide public goods like schools and roads which private interests are unable to afford or unwilling to provide. And they may help advance shared values like ending poverty or improving the health of the population. We argue about how states should do this, how many resources they should devote to it, and how much each of us, as citizens, should be expected to contribute to the effort. This is politics. Everyone agrees that this is what states do, however, and nearly everyone—except anarchists and some libertarians, agrees that this is what states ought to be doing.

It is easy to understand, therefore, why Realists generally think it is much more important to examine the consequences of people living in states than to understand the reasons why they do so. Realists do not completely ignore the latter question, however. They answer it in two sorts of ways. The first, associated with **classical realism** assumes a particular conception of human nature which all of us are said to share. This can be expressed in moral terms. Though we try to be good, Reinhold Niebuhr argued, we easily fall into sin by putting our own interests above the wellbeing of others.[12] We do so because we are physically and emotionally vulnerable to being harmed. We can be shamed, impoverished, hurt, and killed.

It is this sense of vulnerability which makes us fearful and suspicious of one another and makes us selfish, and potentially violently selfish, creatures. This sense of human nature can also be expressed in more scientific terms, however. Realists are very interested in, for example, the work of psychologists which associates aggressive impulses with the experience of frustration, the work of socio-biologists which identifies an impulse within mammals to establish and defend their territory, and the work of geneticists who see this impulse as a survival mechanism which has been developed and refined through evolutionary selection.

It is important to note that the strongest among us feel just as vulnerable as the weakest for—as the 17th-century English political theorist Thomas Hobbes pointed out—even the strongest person must sleep eventually, and then the weakest person has their chance. Indeed the strong may feel more vulnerable because they have more to lose. Accordingly, we set up states in which to live, with laws and enforcers like the police to secure us, reduce our sense of vulnerability, and allow us all to spend peaceful nights without a great fear of being robbed or murdered in our sleep. This peace of mind comes at a price, however, for the peace the state provides at home is not matched by peace between states. We know already that states are sovereign and independent, and thus have no one to regulate their relations with each other. According to some Realists, like Morgenthau, however, since states are collections of people and amplify their feelings, it may be in the nature of states to feel more insecure and vulnerable than we would otherwise expect.

The fact that we all live in states may be traced back to our human nature, according to Classical Realists. However, all human nature arguments have a problem which Realists, especially those associated with **structural realism**, acknowledge. If we explain a trait or tendency as the product of human nature, then how do we account for variations? How do we account for people disagreeing with the claim that we are all power-seekers and people who try to act as if this was not so? Are all people and all states equally driven by their senses of insecurity and vulnerability to seeking power and selfishly putting their interests above those of everybody else? Structural Realists approach the problems of variation presented by human nature arguments in a different way. They argue that we all have to live in states and states have to act the way they do, because some of us live in states and some states act the way they do. If some of us live in states, those who choose not to or are unable to will be put at a great disadvantage in terms of their power and interests. Look at what happened to the rest of the world when the states of modern Europe embarked on their age of expansion. Those who hung on to their traditional forms of politics, like China, were humiliated and defeated. Only those who adapted, like Japan, and built their own modern states were able to resist effectively. Similarly, if some states aggressively pursue their interests and reduce their insecurities and vulnerabilities through the accumulation of power, then those that do not or cannot will be at a terrible disadvantage.

This is an argument which has often been put forward in the United States when its isolationist culture and political history have made its people reluctant to get involved in world affairs. You cannot keep out of power politics, the Realists say. Sooner or later you are drawn in, and all you control are the terms on which you get involved—taken by surprise at Pearl Harbor, or taking the initiative to prevent Iran acquiring weapons of mass destruction by any or all means necessary including threatening and going to war. Note, however, that the argument does not depend on a human nature which we all possess. Rather, it stresses the systemic consequences of some people living in states and some states acting the way they do. According to Structural Realists this creates an international system whose pressures to conform are almost impossible to resist. There are two possible outcomes from the resulting competition. One state may come to dominate the rest for a time. As we shall see in Chapter 6, however, more often, a balance of power is created by which two or more states keep each other in check. Either way, the logic of the system, according to Structural Realists, forces all people and all states to behave in pretty much the same way. Just look at how the United States and India (see the text box on p. 36) started life as states determined to keep out of international relations as much as possible, yet got drawn in and became skillful, power-political players.

Classical Realists build their arguments from a conception of human nature and an understanding of history to make a case for how states and their governments should act if they are wise. **Structural Realists** (sometimes called "Neo-Realists"), like Waltz, build their arguments from abstract views of the properties of systems of sovereign states. The pressures these systems exert, they argue, make all states behave in the same way in very general terms, whether their governments and people like it or not. A third much smaller group associated with classical neo-realism, argue that the different internal characteristics of states—their political institutions and economic priorities, for example—may result in different responses to the same sorts of pressures exerted on all states by the international system of which they are members.

Key terms

classical realists Theorists who take a Realist approach focusing on states, power and interests, but who base their arguments on claims about human nature supported by historical examples.

structural realists Theorists who take a Realist approach focusing on states, power and interests, but who base their arguments upon claims about properties of the international systems in which states are situated.

Key takeaways

- Realists are more interested in the consequences of us living in states, which they regard as important, and less interested in the reasons why we do so, which they regard as obvious.

- Classical Realists see states as resulting from and rooted in human nature. States provide people with security but reflect, and possibly amplify, people's feelings of insecurity and vulnerability at the international system level.

- Structural Realists are less interested in human nature. Rather they stress the systemic consequences of some people living in states and some states pursuing their interests through power. Once some people and states do this, there is great pressure on everybody else to do likewise if they are to survive and prosper.

Exercises

1. Why might Realists not be very interested in why we live in states?
2. What is human nature like according to Classical Realists?
3. How does the international system force us all to live in states, according to Neo-Realists?

| 2.4 | What Realists explain in international relations |

Learning objective

1. Describe the parts of international relations that Realists are best at explaining.

Physicists look for a **general theory** which will be able to explain the universe using a few propositions about the relationships between the basic matter and forces of which it is composed. If they develop one, then everything else will be explained in terms of propositions derived from this single universal theory, at least in principle. Realists sometimes used to sound like they had discovered this sort of theory of international relations. The basic matter of their theory is interest-driven states whose behavior is governed through the forces set in motion by their quest for power. Understand this, Realists seemed to say, and everything else—why wars occur; how peace is best maintained; how states become powerful; why they fail—falls into place. Now, almost no one believes that the Realists have a general theory from which explanations of all aspects of international relations can be derived. Nearly everyone, Realists included, doubts that such a general theory of international relations is possible. There is too much going on which lies outside any single theoretical frame of reference.

Perhaps we cannot tell you much about relations between the United States and Canada, Realists concede, and perhaps we cannot explain what the consequences of rising levels of international tourism might be, or suggest ways of dealing with global warming, natural resource depletion and global pandemics. What we can do, however, is tell you why some of the international problems which people worry about today are not important and why others, no matter how important they seem, are unlikely to get fixed any time soon. Why, for example, do international conferences on global warming accomplish so little when everyone agrees there is a problem, and the scientific experts have told us how the problem can be solved (see Chapter 12)?

The Realists' answer is that an international conference on global warming is just like any other international conference in that it is attended by power-seeking, insecure states which put their narrow national interests before all else. Miss this and you are missing the real story of what is going on. You will have unrealistic expectations about what is possible in international relations and, if you are a government, you may well lead your state into trouble in a world where others remain much more ruthlessly self-centered.

Key term

general theory   The idea in any field of study of a simple set of propositions which account for everything important, or from which all other propositions which account for everything important, can be derived. Historically it has been associated with the study of economics and physics.

Key takeaways

- Realists do not have a general theory of international relations which explains everything. However, they claim to have a theory which shows what is still important—the interactions of self-interested, powerful states—and how this still limits what is achievable on problems like global warming, pandemics, and natural resource depletion.

Exercises

1. Why do Realists not have a general theory of international relations?
2. Why are our attempts to solve problems like global warming unlikely to be successful according to Realists?

2.5   What Realists say people ought to do in international relations

Learning objectives

1. Describe the Realist view of the role of **ordinary people** in international relations.
2. Explain the Realist view of the role of governments in international relations.

Realists have little to say about what ordinary people ought to do in international relations. It is states and the governments which lead them that matter most because they have most of the power. Realists are usually not interested in answering questions about what governments ought to do, either, especially in a moral sense. Realists are more interested in explaining what people and governments actually will do. Ordinary people ought to study international relations up to a point so that they can understand how different they are from ordinary human relations at home. This is especially so in democracies where they have a say in choosing the government, so that they can understand their state's vital national interests and foreign policy. However, Realists expect that most ordinary people will never play an active part in international relations.

Realists have a great deal to say to governments about what they should do in a practical sense. This is well summed up by two of President Trump's advisers,

H.R. McMaster and Gary Cohn, who in 2017 said ". . . the world is not a 'global community' but an arena where nations, non-governmental actors and businesses engage and compete for advantage . . . Rather than deny this elemental nature of international affairs, we embrace it."[13]

There are a number of problems with this specific claim, but there is a bigger puzzle lying behind them. If Realists think they have a theory which explains what states actually do, then it is not clear why they need to advise governments or anyone else regarding what to do. It should just happen. Nevertheless, Realists suggest the following:

- A government should be aware of the core national interests of its state and distinguish these core national interests from less important ones.
- A government should make sure that its state and people are mentally, emotionally, and physically prepared to defend and advance these core national interests, by force if necessary.
- A government should not trust the governments of other states to do anything except what serves their own national interests, and should judge them not by what they say, but by what they do and have the ability to do.
- A government should be constantly seeking to maintain and preferably increase the power of its own state, while reducing the power of others.

Key term

ordinary people   People who are not leading figures in government and/or do not possess sufficient wealth and power to influence a state's foreign policy.

Key takeaways

- Realists have little to say about what ordinary people ought to do in international relations. They do not expect them to do much beyond obtaining a basic understanding of the factors which shape their own state's foreign policy.
- Realists say that governments ought to know their states' core national interests and be prepared to defend and advance them by force if necessary.

Exercises

1. According to Realists, why should ordinary people in a democracy understand their state's foreign policy?
2. According to Realists, what are core national interests, and what should governments be prepared to do in order to defend and advance these core national interests?

2.6	Strengths of Realism

Learning objectives

1. Describe how Realists simplify international relations.
2. Describe how what Realists have to say about international relations seems like **commonsense** to many people.
3. Explain why Realism supports a pessimistic outlook regarding what is possible in international relations.

If international relations are complicated and becoming more so, then Realists perform a great service by simplifying what is going on. According to them, all states at all times in all places are acquiring and using power to protect and advance their interests. To paraphrase the poet Keats, Realists are telling us "that is all you know on Earth, and all ye need to know." It does not matter what presidents and prime ministers say their states are doing. They all say they want peace, friendship among nations, and to solve the problems of the world, but they want to build up the power and serve the national interests of their own state more. According to Realists, this is not just the governments of states other than our own, or powerful states, or dictatorships with aggressive and fanatical ideologies. It is all states, democracies like the United States and Canada, small states like Luxembourg, and poor states like Bangladesh too.

Trust not what states say; watch what they do: the case of India

The modern republic of India became independent from Britain in 1947. An important feature of its struggle for independence was the use of passive resistance and non-violent techniques associated with the Mahatma, Mohandas Gandhi. Gandhi was assassinated in 1948, but India's newly independent government under Prime Minister Pandit Nehru committed the state to a foreign policy based on the five principles of Panch Shile, or peaceful coexistence, renouncing aggression or interference in the affairs of others. Indian leaders saw the two World Wars and the Cold War as the products of a European, imperialist way of thinking about international relations which the rest of the world could avoid. To this end, India was one of the founders of the Non-Aligned Movement, a group of states which shared this view. Over sixty years on, however, India is a nuclear-armed great power with large and modern conventional armed forces. It has fought at least five wars with its neighbors and now dominates its region. So much for principles, say Realists; these always lose out to the pursuit of power and interests. It was the bad behavior of our neighbors which forced us to act in this way, say the Indians. Perhaps, say the Realists, but this simply underlines our point. Even states with the best intentions have to build their power if they are to survive and prosper, a lesson which Indian governments seem to have taken to heart.

It does not matter if religious leaders, business people, human rights workers, or professors say that international relations ought to be about much more than power politics; time and again, the way real international relations play out confirms, according to the Realists, that they are not. Once understood, the Realist claim about the simplicity of international relations seems like commonsense. Politicians, diplomats, journalists, and academics start talking in Realist terms when relations between states turn sour, crises develop, and war threatens. The great surprises of international relations, for example, capitalist America teaming up with communist China against the communist Soviet Union in the 1970s or Moslem Iran talking to Jewish Israel about making life difficult for Moslem Iraq in the 1980s, become obvious.

Unusual bedfellows: the case of China and the United States

China and the United States have had a long (by American standards) and difficult relationship. In the 19th century, American traders and missionaries interfered in Chinese affairs, and Chinese laborers were brought to the United States to help build the transcontinental railroads for low pay and working in bad conditions. China and the United States were on the same side in World War II fighting the Japanese, but once the Japanese surrendered, a civil war resumed in China between the Nationalists and the Communists. The Americans backed the Nationalists, but the Communists won in 1949 and established the People's Republic of China. China and its communist ally, the Soviet Union, competed with the US during the Cold War, supporting communists and others in civil wars in Korea and Viet Nam against allies of the United States. Although the weaker of the two, China was often seen as the greater danger by Americans because its leader, Mao Zedong, sounded more fanatical than the Soviets did about pursuing communism's expansion even at the risk of nuclear war. In the early 1960s, however, China and the Soviet Union fell out with each other over nuclear weapons-sharing and leadership of the international communist movement. Even so, much of the world was surprised to learn in 1972 that President Nixon, a staunch anti-communist, was to visit China seeking better relations and cooperation against the Soviet Union, China's communist former ally. Realists would have told us not to be surprised at all, either by China and the Soviet Union falling out or by China and the US making up. National interests are more important than ideologies. Both China and America were worried by their own weakness at the end of the 1960s and worried about the growth of Soviet power. It was only "natural" that they were pulled together in order to counter-balance this threat to them both.

National interests, according to the Realists, trump all other considerations, and, as we have seen, the result can be unusual partnerships like the one between the capitalist US and communist China. As Churchill, a convinced anti-communist, said after Hitler's Germany attacked Stalin's Russia during World War II, "if Hitler invaded Hell, I would make at least a favorable reference to the Devil in the House of Commons." Churchill did more than that. He offered the Soviet Union British help in its struggle against the two states' common enemy, Nazi Germany. At one level, therefore, Realists invite us to expect the unexpected in international relations. There is very little that states won't do, including engaging in murder and mayhem, if it is believed to serve core national interests.

National interests, national values and the atomic bombing of Hiroshima and Nagasaki

In the summer of 1945, fearing the high losses of Allied troops in which an invasion of the Japanese home islands would result, President Truman decided to use weapons of mass destruction on two cities to convince the Japanese that continued resistance would be both futile and unimaginably costly. Truman said he never had any doubt that he had made the right decision, although dropping the atomic bombs resulted in the deaths of tens of thousands of Japanese civilians who were playing no direct part in the war. Whatever controversies the attack gave rise to in terms of conventional morality, Realists would tell us not to be surprised. Even "good," liberal, democratic, free market states will violate their core moral principles both at home and abroad, if vital national interests suggest that they should. The lives, liberty, and pursuit of happiness of individuals, especially foreign individuals, may have to take a back seat when the survival, or even just the power, of the state is in question.

To be sure, some states seem more prone to murder and mayhem than others. As noted earlier, Neo-Classical Realists argue that variation in the internal political arrangements of states produce variations in the way they pursue interests and power. The concerns of their electorates may result in liberal democracies, for example, acting with more restraint or with more difficulty than other states up to a point. However, it is not easy to predict when that point will be reached and they will abandon restraint. Nor are Realists agreed on whether acting with more restraint is more effective. During the Cold War, for example, some American Realists harbored a grudging admiration for the way the Soviet Union appeared to work cautiously and patiently, if ruthlessly, towards objectives strategically determined by its ruling Communist Party. Meanwhile it seemed as though United States foreign policy fluctuated in response to the arguments and scandals of politicians, the sensationalism of the media, and the emotional reactions of American citizens to both.

At another level, however, Realists ask us to lower our expectations about what can be achieved in international relations. For Realists, the process by which great powers rise and fall—the "same old melodrama"[14] as Martin Wight called it—is the most important game, setting the boundaries for everything else. Greater prospects for order and stability may be associated with certain distributions of power—although Realists argue among themselves about which ones are best. The world may even run better when governments understand and accept the realities of international relations as these are understood by Realists. As for world peace, sustainable development, and ending poverty and disease in the poorest parts of the world, however, don't hold your breath.

Key term

commonsense   Seeing things or making sense of them in a straightforward and simple way; as theorists are fond of pointing out, however, things are not always straightforward or simple. Commonsense might suggest, for example, that the world is flat or, at least, that it is not round.

Key takeaways

■ A big strength of Realism is that it simplifies international relations. Realists claim that underneath all its apparent complexities, there is a struggle for power going on between self-interested states.

■ Understand this and a great deal of what governments, corporations, religious groups, media, and many academics say is or ought to be important can be ignored.

■ The sort of immoral actions and relationships in which even democratic states engage on occasions will not be surprising, but expectations about progress in international relations should be low.

2.7   Weaknesses of Realism

Learning objectives

1. Describe the difficulties with the Realist claim that people and states are motivated mainly by interests and power.

2. List the problems with the Realist claim that states are the only important actors in international relations.

The claims that states are concerned only with interests and power, and that this is rooted in human nature, are strong ones. They seem to be supported by the way international relations are presented in history books or appear in the news. Just look at any international crisis or conflict which is being covered in the media today. We can easily see strong individuals and groups competing for interests and power who are prepared to cause great harm and suffering to each other and innocent bystanders in the process. However, ask yourself if you or the people you know are concerned only with interests and power. Some people seem more concerned with interests and power than others; Hitler, for example, more than Nelson Mandela. All people become more concerned with interests and power in specific situations, such as where they feel insecure or threatened. Think of Americans the day before and the day after Pearl Harbor and the day before and the day after 9–11. And it is easier to imagine other people as more concerned than ourselves with interests and power. Chinese and Iranian people, for example, see Americans as working hard to preserve the United States' dominant international position while they see their own states as simply looking for a fair shake from the rest of the world. On the whole, however, the answer to the question "Are all people, and thus all states, at all times concerned with interests and power?" is likely to be "No." The claim that they are concerned only with power and interests seems to be based on a very selective reading of history, and on the way the media emphasizes bad international news.

It is possible to see every action undertaken by individuals and states in terms of interests and power. As noted above, for example, it can be argued that people give to charity and states give foreign aid mainly to buy friends. However, this is a weakness, rather than a strength, of the Realist position. If we can say that Adolf Hitler, Donald Trump, and Nelson Mandela are or were all motivated by self-interest and the desire for power, for example, then we have succeeded only in making the question of what we mean by self-interest and power more complicated. Why do they drive one man to violence and killing on a massive scale, another to talking tough but wielding power in a limited way for narrow ends, and a third to trying to lead by setting a virtuous example of self-sacrifice? Realists can be quite open to this sort of critique. They point out, however, that sovereign, independent states and the international system produced by the relations of these states provide the sort of situations in which the interest and power dimensions of human nature come to the fore. This may be so, but it raises two questions. First, are states the only important actors in international relations? Second, do other sorts of actors—like international organizations, transnational corporations, civil society groups, and organized religions—have the same preoccupation as states with power and interests?

Key takeaways

- There are problems with the Realist claim that states are motivated simply by interests and power. The people who make up states are motivated by and interested in other things. Besides, it is not clear what it means to say that people or states are motivated only by interests and power. Both ideas are too broad and can cover nearly everything that people do.
- Even if states and the state system bring out these aspects of human nature, there are problems with the Realist claim that states are the only important actors in international relations.

Exercises

1. Are you and the people you know concerned only, or even primarily, with interests and power?
2. Are states like the United States, Canada, and China different from people like Americans, Canadians, and Chinese in this regard? If so, why?

2.8   The future of Realism in an era of uncertainty

Realists claim that all the most important actors in international relations are independent sovereign states. As we shall see in Chapter 3, it is certain that this is not the case. There are many other actors, some of which are more important than some states. What is uncertain is whether the rise of other actors is simply making the world more complicated or is making states less important and, if less important, at what rate this is happening.

Realists claim that human nature and the sort of system you get when states conduct relations with each other combine to make states concerned with interests and power, especially military power, to the exclusion of everything else. It is certain that some states remain very preoccupied with interests and power in these terms. It is certain that all states have some level of preoccupation with interests and power in these terms, but it is equally certain that they are also concerned about other things, for example: economic growth, climate change, and human rights. What is uncertain is whether state preoccupations are shifting from interests and power in military terms to other concerns or if these new concerns are simply being added to the list of things about which states worry. States may not be the only actors in international relations, and they may not always be competing with each other in the pursuit of their interests and power. However, states remain very important, and when competition between them veers towards conflict, then the Realists still help us understand the dynamics of those conflicts and what the states involved in them are trying to achieve and avoid. The Realists also alert us to the reasons why cooperation between states, even on issues of great importance, can be very difficult to achieve.

Recommended reading

Scott Burchill, Andrew Linklater, Richard Devetak, Jack Donnelly, Mathew Peterson, Christian Reus Smith, and Jacqui True, *Theories of International Relations* (4th edition), Basingstoke, 2009.

E.H. Carr, *The Twenty Years Crisis: 1919–1939: An Introduction to the Study of International Relations*, London, 1939.

Martin Gilbert, *The Roots of Appeasement*, New York, 1966.

Café Press website provides an insight into the popular and commercial significance of the appeasement issue in contemporary US politics, accessed at *http://shop.cafepress.com/appeasement*

"I would have fired BP chief by now, Obama says," Disaster in the Gulf, MSNBC.com, June 8, 2010 accessed at *http://www.msnbc.msn.com/id/37566848/ns/disaster_in_the_gulf/t/i-would-have-fired-bp-chief-now-obama-says/#.TyWU-4G4KSo*

"New Blow for BP in Russia as Office Raided," Reuters US, August 31, 2011 accessed at *http://www.reuters.com/article/2011/08/31/us-bp-russia-raid-idUSTRE77U1EP20110831*

"Nigeria's agony dwarfs the Gulf oil spill. The US and Europe ignore it," *The Guardian*, May 29, 2010, accessed at *http://www.guardian.co.uk/world/2010/may/30/oil-spills-nigeria-niger-delta-shell.*

Paul Kennedy, *The Rise and Fall of the Great Powers*, New York, 1987.

Notes

1 Plato, *The Republic* (Penguin Classics), Harmondsworth, 1967.
2 Niccoló Machiavelli, *Discourses on Livy* (Penguin Classics), Harmondsworth, 1984.
3 Harold D. Lasswell, *Politics: Who Gets What, When and How*, Cleveland, 1936.
4 Hans J. Morgenthau, *Politics among Nations: The Struggle for Power and Peace*, New York, 1948.
5 Arnold Wolfers, "The Goals of Foreign Policy" in Arnold Wolfers, *Discord and Collaboration: Essays on International Politics*, Baltimore, 1962.
6 Kenneth Waltz, *Theory of International Politics*, Reading, 1979.
7 Stephen M. Walt, *The Origins of Alliances*, Ithaca, 1987.
8 John H. Herz, "Idealist Internationalism and the Security Dilemma," *World Politics*, 2, 2, January 1950.
9 John J. Mearsheimer, *The Tragedy of Great Power Politics*, New York, 2001.
10 Paul Kennedy, *The Rise and Fall of the Great Powers*, New York, 1987.
11 Hans J. Morgenthau, "Death in the Nuclear Age," September 1961 in *Commentary* (no date) accessed at *http://www.commentarymagazine.com/article/death-in-the-nuclear-age/*
12 Reinhold Niebuhr, *Christian Realism and Political Problems*, New York, 1944.
13 H.R. McMaster and Gary Cohn, "America First Does Not Mean America Alone," *Washington Post*, May 30, 2017.
14 Martin Wight, "Why Is There No International Relations Theory?" in Herbert Butterfield and Martin Wight (eds), *Diplomatic Investigations*, Cambridge, 1966, p. 26.

3 Liberalism and building world orders

Preamble

As a theoretical approach to international relations, Realism has two great advantages. Whether people agree with it or not, it appears clear and straightforward. The problems start when we try to apply it to concrete situations. The approach examined in this chapter—Liberalism—also appears clear and straightforward. It shares some of the assumptions on which Realism is based—especially the assumption that there is a world out there which we can see operating separately from our looking at it, in much the same way as natural sciences observe the physical universe and biological world. Critics call both Realism and Liberalism examples of "Positivist" approaches in this regard ("Post-positivist" approaches will be examined in Chapter 4).[1] Liberalism also shares with Realism assumptions about human beings as interest-driven individuals. However, there are important differences between Liberal and Realist assumptions about the potential for cooperation between interest-driven human beings, and about the role of human reason in improving the way people live by making war less likely and economic prosperity more possible. In addition, there are different types of Liberalism. Some focus on politics, some focus on economics, some focus on law, and others on moral questions. There are also important differences between Liberals regarding power and about the extent to which human groups hold together as a result of self-interested calculations of their individual members as opposed to a feeling of belonging to a community which all the members share. Taken together, these different aspects of Liberalism have produced the dominant understanding of how the world works and how it ought to work, first in developed capitalist states of the West by the end of the 20th century, then in the rest of the developed world by the end of the Cold War in the 1980s, and in the developing world by the beginning of the 21st century. Liberalism has always had its critics. Indeed, until the last 100 years or so, the arguments associated with it regarding human beings and their circumstances were less widely accepted than the arguments associated with Realism, especially about human nature. However, much of the present international uncertainty arises from a growing sense in some parts of the world that Liberalism does not satisfactorily address all the problems which people currently regard as important and that it may be creating problems of its own.

3.1 Liberal assumptions about people and politics

Learning objectives

1. List four key assumptions of Liberals about people and politics
2. Explain why Liberal assumptions are important in understanding international relations

Liberal and Liberalism are terms used to identify a set of assumptions about human beings, how they want to live, and how we should arrange society to best allow them to pursue what they want. It is very important to be clear that "liberal" here does not mean the same as when it is used in North American political debate. In the US, the term is often used to identify people who support the transfer of wealth from the rich and the comfortably off to the public good and the less well off by "big government" through taxation and spending. Liberal, as it is used here, conveys a different set of ideas which are all related to the idea of freedom and especially individual freedom.

The first key assumption of Liberalism is that we live our lives, first and foremost, as individual human beings, not as members of a family, a village, a nation or the human race. It is as **individuals** that we are born, experience pain and pleasure, happiness and sadness, and success and failure, and eventually die. Whatever they may say—either out of sympathy or to get your vote—other people do not actually feel your pain. In the words of the old song, each one of us walks the lonesome valley of life by ourselves.

The second key assumption of Liberalism is a little bit more cheerful. Human beings are reasoning and generally reasonable individuals. By using their reason, each individual is capable of defining and pursuing their own interests. Human beings can work out what they want in terms of what they think is good and bad or right and wrong, and what makes them happy, and each one wants to be free to do so. Indeed, each one of us is better at working these things out for ourselves than having someone else work them out for us. By being reasonable, however, each individual realizes they live in a world of other individuals who want the same sorts of things, and knowing this does not get them all bent out of shape and insecure in the way the Realists suggest. Indeed, **reason** and **reasonableness** allow individuals to realize that they can usually satisfy their individual interests better by cooperating with each other.

The third key assumption of Liberalism is that individuals should respect each other's right to pursue their interests as each of them sees fit, and they should have a duty not to infringe on that right in the pursuit of their own interests. Liberals argue this mutual respect is best guaranteed by some basic rules: individuals should respect each other's right to life; individuals should respect each other's right to property which is exclusively theirs; and individuals should keep promises which they freely make to one another.[2]

The fourth key assumption is that the social, political, and economic arrangements which individuals establish collectively should be limited to safeguarding these rights, and to doing very little else. For example, like the rest of us, Liberals know that if we cooperate with each other, rather than trying to do everything on our own, we can sometimes all be better off. The decision to cooperate, however, should as much as possible be one freely made by individuals. It should not be imposed upon them by a government or other form of authority claiming it knows the interests of individuals better than they know them themselves. Governments should only do things which make it easier for reasoning individuals to cooperate with each other in pursuit of their interests without infringing on the rights of other individuals to do likewise.

Particularly if you are a citizen of a developed, Western state like the US, Germany, Canada, and the UK, you will notice two things about these assumptions. First, they may strike you as familiar, obvious, and even obviously true. They are sometimes called embedded norms and assumptions which are taken for granted.[3] Second, you will notice that, unlike Realist assumptions, they seem to belong to the orderly world within states, not the disorderly world between states. They are not telling you how to safeguard yourself in a world where anything goes and you are on your own. They are setting out why we do not have to settle for such a world and how, through the use of our reason and reasonableness, we can develop something better in terms of security, prosperity, and freedom.

In studying international relations, it is important to be familiar with these ideas for three reasons. First, whether one agrees with them or not, they make strong claims which have profoundly affected the way the modern world has developed. Second, they are ideas which are closely associated with the most powerful, secure, and wealthy states of the developed world. Third, as we shall see in Chapter 9 on international trade, finance, production, and development, Liberal principles remain at the heart of a formal international consensus about why globalization has emerged and how it should be managed.

Key terms

individual The most important actor according to Liberalism, with each individual human being living primarily as themselves and not as part of a group or as an aggregate of other things like chemicals and electrical impulses.

reason The ability human beings have to think about who they are, what they want and how to get it.

reasonableness The disposition human beings have to allow for and sympathize with other individuals being like them to the point of preferring collaboration and competition to conflict with them.

Key takeaways

- Liberalism says that in politics, economics, and society we should start with individuals for reasons of fact and morality.
- Liberalism says that human beings can apply reason and reasonableness to improve their situations.

- Liberalism says that human beings have rights and have a duty to respect the rights of others.
- Liberalism says that institutions like government should be limited to safeguarding these rights.

Exercises

1. Why do Liberals say we must start with individuals in politics, economics, and society?
2. How do Liberals use the terms Reason and Reasonableness differently?

3.2	What Liberals see in international relations

Learning objectives

1. Describe the kind of international relations Liberals see.
2. Explain what Liberals say people ought to do in international relations.

Inside states, we usually see Liberals making arguments for less government and few rules in the name of increasing efficiency and strengthening freedom. In the field of International Relations, however, a curious inversion occurs, and we first encounter Liberals arguing for more rules and laws to regulate international relations and for stronger government action to enforce them. The Realists have told us that we live in an international anarchy which is dangerous, permanent, unchanging, and probably inescapable in its essentials. The Liberals say this anarchy is challenged by the universally valid, good, wise, and probably irresistible aspirations of reasoning and reasonable individual human beings for a freer, more orderly and peaceful world. As we saw in the previous chapter, it was this view which Realists regarded as "idealist." Indeed, they named themselves as Realists in opposition to those they called Idealists.

Given their assumptions set out above about individuals as the most important actors, an obvious problem for Liberals is why the world of international relations seems to begin and end with sovereign states. One response early Liberals made to this puzzle was more or less to say that this was not their problem since they were mainly interested in what went on inside states.[4] In international relations, there was no single sovereign government making and upholding laws for everyone, and so talking about democracy, freedom, liberty, rights, and duties at the international level, outside the sovereign state was almost a waste of time. Indeed, early Liberal thinkers used to use international relations to make a point about how awful life would be without a sovereign state to safeguard people's liberties, while suggesting that the disorder between sovereign states was the inevitable price which had to be paid for order within sovereign states.

This changed, however, for two reasons. First, Liberals, for all their gloomy individualism at times, were products of the period of European history between the 17th and 18th centuries known as **the Enlightenment**. They believed in the possibility, if not the certainty, of **progress**. Liberals thought things could be better, ought to be better, and would get better if people listened to reason and acted upon it. People would listen because, for the most part, they are reasonable and smart. Thus, in 18th-century Europe, a very important extension of the Liberal argument emerged, namely the claim that if states improved (became more liberal), then the relations between them would also improve almost by default. The Prussian philosopher, Immanuel Kant (1724–1804), for example, reasoned that only states which were constitutional republics would be capable of achieving a lasting peace among themselves.[5]

Second, Liberals shared the general dismay at how costly wars were becoming in terms of blood and treasure thanks to the development of industrialization, nationalism, and democracy in the 19th century. For Liberals, the slaughters of the French Revolutionary and Napoleonic wars, the great revolutions of mid-century, and finally World War I were all proof of what a murderous racket the international system of sovereign states could be. According to many Liberals, the national interest, the balance of power, and sovereignty itself were merely rationalizations (they would have called them humbug) by which some individuals (kings, emperors, tyrants, dictators, and successful revolutionaries) were able to impose their own interests, values, and visions on other individuals (workers, peasants, middle-class property owners, and other "ordinary" people).[6]

As a result, **Liberal Internationalists**, as they became to be known, began to focus more directly on international relations and the challenge of improving them through political, legal, and economic reform. Liberal reforms like limiting the power of government through review and elections, establishing new laws for protecting and strengthening the rights of citizens, and boosting efficiency and competition through allowing the free market to operate had made the citizens of states like Britain, France, and the United States more secure and prosperous in the 19th century. By the start of the 20th century, Liberals were confident that the application of their principles in other states and at the international level would have similar positive consequences for everyone. The British author and lecturer, Norman Angell, for example, argued that modern, integrated economies had made warfare costly to the point of it being irrational, although not impossible. Nicholas Murray Butler, a US international law expert, called for the cultivation of "the international mind," by which selfish state sovereignty could be transcended by the rule of international law. Most famously of all, Woodrow Wilson, 28th President of the United States, played a leading role in creating the League of Nations (see Figure 3.1 and text box p. 50). All three men were recipients of the Nobel Peace Prize, created as one of a series of prizes by Alfred Nobel as awards to be paid for from the great wealth he had accrued through the invention of dynamite and selling armaments.

Today, Liberals see the international system as a work in progress, incomplete but moving forward from the days when the national interests of states as defined by their leaders automatically took priority over every other consideration. The work is incomplete because some states remain controlled by powerful

Figure 3.1 Woodrow Wilson (1856–1924), US President 1913–1921
(Source: Archive Pics/Alamy Stock Photo)

individuals who, out of a warped sense of self-interest and plain ignorance, resist and subvert reforms. It is moving forward, however, because more and more governments and people are accepting Liberal principles and acting internationally in accordance with them. As a result, Liberals argue, the number of wars in the international system is declining to the point where some Liberals (for example, Michael Doyle) have put forward what is called "the **Liberal Peace**" thesis. There is no record of democracies in modern times fighting each other, although they fight other sorts of states. This, the Liberals argue, is because the governments of democracies have little desire to fight each other and because their peoples won't let them.[7]

What then have Liberal principles said that smart governments and people ought to do in their international relations if they are interested in peace and prosperity? Following Kant, they suggest that the first step is to reform states themselves to make their governments accountable to their people. The key assumption on which this call for reform is based is that ordinary individuals are, on the whole, peace-loving since they and their families are the ones who get hurt in wars. Only unaccountable leaders and their supporters would dream of going to war in the modern era because they would be the only ones not to suffer. Kant stressed constitutions which would constrain governments and produce leaders and citizens with new attitudes to politics and power. Others stress the importance of democratic elections which could unseat warlike leaders, and states set up on the principle of **national self-determination** where the leaders would belong to the same culture group, usually a nation, as the followers.

The second step, Liberals say, is to get states to submit themselves to a system of rules governing their conduct and how they related to each other, especially over disputes. Hidemi Suganami, among others, has called the assumptions on which this step is based, the **domestic analogy**.[8] In this view, life inside states is generally peaceful and prosperous because there is a sovereign government which makes and upholds laws, and people who, collectively as the nation or individually as citizens, accept the government's right to make laws and the principle that its laws, even ones they disagree with, should be obeyed. Life is even nicer in liberal states which are based on the consent of the people and which safeguard their freedom. In contrast, life outside states or between them is generally more prone to violence because these factors are missing. There is no single sovereign in the international system and there is no sense of international citizenship or global nationhood. Therefore, Liberals argue, make international relations more like relations inside states and they will become more peaceful and prosperous. For some Liberals (for example, Nicholas Murray Butler), the domestic analogy originally suggested that a representative world government exercising limited, but strong, power should be established.[9] Others, whatever they thought of this idea in principle, recognized that something less ambitious would have to be attempted. As a consequence, when World War I came to an end in 1918 with the victory of the mainly democratic states under the leadership of Wilson's United States, the first great experiment in Liberal Internationalism was launched (see Figure 3.2).

Figure 3.2 A meeting of the League of Nations in Geneva, Switzerland in 1926
(Source: Sueddeutsche Zeitung Photo/Alamy Stock Photo)

The League of Nations as a Liberal Internationalist idea

The League of Nations was established at the end of World War I in 1920. It was very much a product of what became known as Liberal Internationalist thinking. The League had a Council divided between great powers who were permanent members and other states which were elected to it for limited terms. The Council examined issues of international conflict, made recommendations, and could take actions. The League also had an Assembly in which all the member states of the League had a seat and a vote, an international court (see Chapter 8 on international law), and a Covenant or set of rules. To become a member of the League, states did not have to be democracies, but new members especially were supposed to reflect the principle of national self-determination. Also, to be a member, states had to commit to referring their disputes to the League for recommendations, refraining from the use of force except in self-defense or when permitted by the League, and contributing to a system of collective security in which an attack on one member was seen as an attack on all of them.

The League reflected many international arrangements such as Councils and Congresses which had been attempted in the past. These provided a place for many states to discuss issues and consider taking action on them, although they were usually dominated by the strongest states who claimed special responsibilities. However, the League also looked like a "government in embryo." It had an executive (the Council), a legislature (the Assembly), a judiciary (the International Court), a constitution and rules (the Covenant), and enforcement procedures (a system of economic sanctions and collective security). It was not a democracy, however, nor was it sovereign. Member states retained their sovereignty and, if they were willing to pay the price, could ignore the League Council's directions.

As we have seen in Chapter 2, the failure of the League to prevent the aggressions of the dictators in the 1930s and the outbreak of World War II is taken as damning circumstantial evidence of the shortcomings of Liberal ("idealist or "utopian" as the Realists called it) thought on international relations. In their defense, Liberals note the early successes of the League in settling disputes. They point to the scale of the challenge posed by Nazi Germany, Fascist Italy, and militarist Japan to world order and the weakness of the British, French, and American response. Most importantly, they also point to the general agreement in 1945 after World War II, even after everything had gone so badly wrong for the League of Nations, that a second attempt at institutionalizing international relations should be made—the United Nations. The League of Nations may have failed, but the League idea remains powerful and influential today.

The League of Nations did not restrict its attention to questions of war and peace between states. It had agencies concerned with, for example, health standards, labor conditions, and the status of minorities around the world. These reflected the Liberal assumption that the need for institutions and rules did not apply only to the relations of states on questions of war and peace. They also had a role in improving the living conditions of people and the economic relations between them. Liberal thinkers today, therefore, not only support big institutions like the UN (see Chapter 8 on international organizations); they also support the creation of what **Liberal Institutionalists** like Robert Keohane and Joseph Nye called **international regimes**.[10] These are systems combining informal understandings and conventions with more formal rules and laws. They are set up by states and international organizations for regulating transactions in which they have a shared interest. These regimes are often very practical in nature. The Montreal Convention, for example, is an agreement about international air travel which is regulated by the representatives of states and others in the International Civil Aviation Organization. Groups like this have decided in the past that English should be the recommended international language of air traffic control, and which airline should compensate you for losing your bag if it goes missing on a trip using multiple airlines.

Liberals say developing these regimes is a good idea because they solve practical problems efficiently. However, they also see these regimes moving international relations away from the power political state-centrism of the Realists and towards the more regulated relations of what Keohane and Nye call **complex interdependence**. States join regimes regulating human rights, trade, investment and a host of other issues because the issues are complicated and the relations of states are increasingly interdependent. They cannot afford to be left out. Then, according to the argument, states increasingly come to value their membership of these regimes, so much so that they will accept decisions which hurt their immediate national interests. Look, for example, at how angry some American politicians get at the UN when its members criticize the US, even though the US is still the biggest contributor to UN finances. No US government, however, seriously contemplates leaving the UN because its membership is beneficial and because the US would find it hard to influence what happens in the UN if it left. In Liberal terms, the US values keeping its membership of the UN over some of the costs which its membership entails.

Keohane and Nye looked at a series of arguments between the US and Canada in the 1960s and 1970s. The US is roughly ten times larger than Canada in everything except territory and so Realist assumptions, they argued, would predict an easy US victory in each case. In fact, Canada won more than half of them. The issues were often more vital to Canada than the US. The US was often distracted by other issues. The US political system was more open to Canadian lobbying than the Canadian political system was open to US lobbying. And on some issues, the US confronted Canada in multilateral regimes where Canada had more support than the US from the other members. In short, there were a host of factors that made sure that the simple power distribution between the two did not shape the outcome of all their disputes.

Today, the attractiveness of some regimes is such that states will not only adjust their foreign policies to join them, they will also attempt to reform their own political arrangements. Thus, former communist states of Eastern Europe which want to join NATO and the European Union are given a list of changes they must make—civilian control of the armed forces, real party political competition, increased human rights protections, and free and fair economic competition, for example, before they are allowed to become members. There are grades to pass, levels of membership, and states can be kept in the "waiting room" for many years by failing to pass these tests to the satisfaction of the existing members. As we shall see in Chapters 9 and 10 on international trade and finance, Liberals maintain that states and peoples have to take the Liberal road in their politics and economics if they wish to be peaceful, prosperous and free. They also maintain that any steps they take in this direction—joining regimes, for example—will draw them into taking further steps. The train of history is moving in a liberal direction, most Liberals argue. However, this is not to say that vested interests in old ways of exercising power and controlling wealth, together with the fearfulness, ignorance, and stupidity which human beings display on occasions, will not delay the arrival of the train or even derail it completely.

Key terms

complex interdependence   A description of how states are linked by mutual need through complicated networks of relations at all levels of society, rather than just government-to-government, plus an argument that these links create more conditions of more complex interdependence over time.

domestic analogy   The argument that relations between states can be made more peaceful and prosperous by making them more like the relations inside states.

the Enlightenment   A period in Europe in the 17th and 18th centuries when intellectuals argued for the replacement of faith, belief, and tradition by reason, knowledge, and the scientific method to explain and understand the world.

international regimes   Informal conventions and formal rules by which groups, associations, councils, leagues of states, and others regulate an issue or policy area of common interest to them.

Liberal Institutionalists   Those who see and argue for an international system in which sovereign states are bound by their membership of international organizations like the United Nations and accept their rules.

Liberal Internationalists   A term used to describe those who argued for international institutions like the League of Nations which would restrict the use of force by states and encourage the settlement of disputes by international law.

Liberal Peace   An observation that liberal or democratic states have not gone to war with each other and a hypothesis that this is because their internal political arrangements inhibit their using war against one another.

national self-determination The principle that, unless it is impractical or causes great trouble, each nation should have its own sovereign state if it wants it.

progress The idea than the way human beings live can be improved over time to provide more of what they want and value.

Key takeaways

■ Liberalism suggests the possibility, if not the certainty, of progress and improvement in international relations through the creation and development of international institutions.

■ Liberalism says that international relations can be improved by making states more liberal and representative.

■ Liberalism suggests that liberal arrangements are especially suited to delivering peace and prosperity in the modern era of industry and technology, and that nearly all governments and people, with varying degrees of willingness, recognize this is so.

Exercises

1. What do Liberals say we must do to improve international relations?
2. In what ways, according to Liberals, do international regimes become more important in international relations over time?

3.3 Strengths and weaknesses of Liberalism

Learning objectives

1. List the ways in which Liberalism may offer a more complete picture of International Relations than the one offered by Realism.
2. Explain the difference between pluralist and solidarist understandings of Liberalism.
3. Describe how the failure of Collective Security shows some of the weaknesses of Liberalism.

Liberalism opens up three lines of inquiry which for Realism remain more-or-less closed. First, Liberals draw our attention to the ways in which international relations can change. Realists tend to maintain that as long as there are sovereign states or their equivalents, the anarchical relationships between them will be limited, tense, and colored by the ever-present threat of war. Liberals, in contrast, suggest that different sorts of states can produce different sorts of anarchies which can result in different sorts of international relations. Liberal states, for example, are less likely to go to war, at least with one another, and an international anarchy in which states have interdependent relations based on trade and investment offers more opportunities for competitive cooperation, and fewer for war. Today's international relations are not the same as those of one, two or three hundred years ago, nor are they likely to be the same as international relations in one, two or three hundred years' time.

Second, Liberals open up the question of what kind of states and international relations would we like to have, whether in terms of our self-interests or in terms of what we think is right. Realists have little to say about how international relations ought to be or how states ought, at least in a moral sense, to act. Their advice for states to be strong and governments to act in the national interest can be seen in moral terms. The government has an obligation to look after the state since the state provides security for its people. However, this is the same advice which Realists would give to governments and states which treated their own people or other states very badly. Liberals, in contrast, start with individuals, their rights and their duties. The first question they ask is "why do individuals need a state?" If they can be convinced that some sort of state is necessary (a few of them aren't convinced), then they ask what sort of a state ought it to be? How can it best safeguard its citizens and their rights, and how is it to avoid restricting their security and their rights unnecessarily?

The world is not full of liberal states, and not all liberal states behave themselves in Liberal terms all the time. Nevertheless, the rise of Liberalism as both a social theory and a political ideology has had a big effect on forcing all states to provide justifications for what they do. It is much harder for states today to refuse to justify their actions to the rest of the world simply because they are sovereign and can do what they like. It is also much harder, but not as hard, to justify their actions on grounds of national security. As we shall see in Chapter 8 on international law, organizations, and governance, liberal pressures seem to be changing the terms on which states can claim sovereignty and have it recognized by others. The doctrine of Responsibility to Protect (R2P), for example, says that a state's sovereignty is conditional on it not engaging in wide scale violations of the rights of its citizens. As Realists are quick to point out, however, the effectiveness of Liberalism flows in part from it being the dominant ideology of the most developed and powerful states in the world. And as other critics note, those Liberal principles often seem selectively applied. Why, for example, is Syria held to account for denying basic human rights when Saudi Arabia and China are not?

Thirdly, Liberalism brings economics and law more clearly into our picture of international relations. This is not to say that Realism is uninterested in economics and law. However it organizes economics, law, geography, demographics, and other societal factors around how they contribute to a state's power and security. Liberalism, in contrast, organizes these factors, as well as states themselves, around how they contribute to the security, prosperity, and opportunities for happiness of individual human beings. Thus, as we have noted in Chapter 2, Realists have a hard time accounting for the collapse of the Soviet Union. By all the criteria in which they are interested, it was a very powerful, and therefore secure, state. When it did collapse, Realists were far more interested in the consequences. They did not see the causes as their problem. Stuff happens! Liberals, in contrast, were not surprised by the Soviet Union's collapse. The bigger puzzle for them was how it had managed to last so long. In their view, communism was doing nearly everything wrong given what individuals are like and how a modern society has to be organized to best help individuals get what they want.

Just like Realism, however, Liberalism does not just provide a single set of ideas about international relations. Beyond some core assumptions, it breaks into different sub-approaches with their own points of emphasis about what is important and where the world ought to be going. The Liberal Internationalists, like Angell, Butler, and Wilson, who argued for reforms like the League of Nations, focused on questions of war and peace. The road to peace, they argued, lay through international political institutions which channeled the power of cooperative states and constrained the power of the rest. Legal Liberals, in contrast, are more interested in establishing judicial, rather than political, processes for the establishment and practice of a more effective system of international law, and especially human rights law. Liberal Institutionalists such as Keohane and Nye, like the Liberal Internationalists before them, are interested in setting up political and administrative institutions for regulating international relations. However, they are more interested in the economic and, more recently, environmental dimensions to international relations. This focus is also reflected in their methods which are often borrowed from the study of economics and emphasize the importance of ideas like rationality and efficiency in producing desired outcomes.

However, below these differences of focus, there is also a deeper division between what have been termed **solidarist** and **pluralist** approaches.[11] Both are premised on the needs and wants of individuals, rather than states or other forms of social collectivities. However, solidarists tend to assume that all individuals have very similar needs and wants, and that this is revealed when individuals are sufficiently knowledgeable and free to express what their needs and wants actually are. The things that people have in common are stronger than the things which divide them and this gives rise to a feeling of "solidarity" among people. President Roosevelt spoke in 1941 of the "Four Freedoms" of speech and of worship, and from want and fear which people "everywhere in the world ought to enjoy."[12] And as we shall see in Chapter 13 on North-South gaps and Chapter 14 on human development, Liberals have assumed that since political democracies and free markets best deliver these, then it follows that they too are **universal values** shared by all free people.

The pluralists agree that there are universal values and that Roosevelt's four freedoms may provide as good a starting point as any for thinking about them. However, they are much more cautious about bundling such values with other ideas, and much more interested in paying attention to what individuals actually say they need and want and the relative importance they attach to them. People and peoples have much in common, but they also have many different interests, beliefs and values which distinguish them from one another. Suppose, for example, individuals say they like living in a state with other individuals of the same nation and that they are prepared to pay a price in terms of a lower standard of living or less individual freedom to do so? Suppose they say they do not want to live in a state at all, or that their religion says that they should not do military service or wear certain kinds of clothes even though everyone else does? While starting from the same basic assumptions as solidarist Liberals, pluralist Liberals are much more open to accepting that they might have to settle for a much more complex, diverse, and in many respects, illiberal world. They are so because they believe that individual self-interest is not enough to hold societies together. Their members have to have a sense of community as well, and this sense comes from variations—we drink tea not coffee, we play football not soccer, we take Friday off not Saturday or Sunday—which may be inefficient but which give individuals a sense of belonging to something bigger than themselves.

As with Realism, a major weakness of Liberalism is its account of people who do not act in accordance with its assumptions and what to do about them. Why, for example, did the League of Nations' collective security system eventually fail? The idea was that if a state attacked a member of the League of Nations, then all the other members would come to its aid. This was supposed to deter potential aggressors. Who in their right mind would attack another state when every other state would come to its rescue? Yet collective security failed. Japan invaded Manchuria, Italy invaded Abyssinia (Ethiopia), and Germany dismantled Czechoslovakia in the 1930s. No one from the League of Nations seriously wanted to accept the costs and risks of using force against these aggressors in the name of collective security.

As we have seen, the Realists had an answer. Wars are costly and dangerous. States will usually only fight them for the most immediate and important of self-interests. The wellbeing of a fellow member of the League on the other side of the world failed to qualify as such an interest. Even the wellbeing of a next door neighbor failed to qualify if the aggressor also lived in the neighborhood. Poland had no wish to antagonize Germany by standing up for Czechoslovakia in 1938, any more than Yugoslavia had been prepared to antagonize Italy by supporting Albania's appeal to the League of Nations in 1939. Indeed, Poland took the opportunity of German pressure on Czechoslovakia to grab a piece of Czechoslovak territory for itself. All Liberal Internationalists could say was that states were wrong not to take a longer-term view of their self-interests, as the subsequent invasions of Poland and Yugoslavia by Nazi Germany demonstrated. Hopefully, states and the individuals in them would learn from these experiences.

If states did not learn, then maybe their incentives should be shaped to encourage them to behave more reasonably in the future. This is the prescription suggested by Liberal Institutionalists who focus on regime-building. Increase the costs of undesired behavior and increase the rewards for reasonable behavior. However, the targets of these sorts of attempts to shape their behavior do not always like them. Developing states, for example, do not always see the offer of carrots and the threat of sticks to get them to pursue policies which Liberals say are universally recognized as the best policies for realizing universal Liberal values as help. They often see it as an attempt to coerce and manipulate states into cooperating with an agenda that serves someone else's interests.

Key terms

pluralist An approach which emphasizes properties, interests, and values which some human groups have and which are different from those of other human groups or, less often, which differ within a particular human group.

solidarist An approach which emphasizes properties, interests, and values which all human beings have in common or, less often, the members of a group have in common.

universal values Values said to be shared by all human beings. Most people agree that there are such values. Most people can agree on what some of them are, but there are often differences between people on other values they assume to be universal, what they actually are, and how important they are relative to other values.

Key takeaways

- Liberalism improves upon Realism by introducing the concept of change to the study of international relations.
- Liberalism improves upon Realism by raising the question of how international relations ought to change.
- Liberalism improves upon Realism by drawing our attention to the importance of law, economics, and social processes in shaping and improving international relations.
- Liberalism fragments into pluralist and solidarist approaches to understanding and explaining international relations.
- Liberalism struggles to explain why individuals and states do not always follow its prescriptions, and encounters resistance to its solutions—educating people and shaping their incentives to conform with its prescriptions.

Exercises

1. Why did Liberal Internationalists say international relations had to change?
2. If one member state of the UN attacked another today, would it be a good idea for your own state to come to the aid of the victim in line with the doctrine of collective security?
3. What are the advantages and disadvantages for your own state of its being a member of international regimes?

3.4 The future of Liberalism in an era of uncertainty

Liberals and Realists look at the same world of international relations yet see themselves drawing very different conclusions about what that world is like, why it is the way it is, and how states and people should act within it. So which has the better of the argument? Which approach does the evidence best support? Until recently, it has been possible to argue that Liberalism was "winning." In the academic subject of International Relations, especially in the rich, developed world, more and more attention has been devoted to the Liberal approach and its agenda of problems, while Realism has been presented as "old school," useful for explaining some things, but missing a big part of the story. In the actual world of international relations, as noted above, governments have engaged in "Liberal talk" about the importance of fostering cooperation through the creation of institutions and organizations at both the international and the regional level. They have also stressed the importance of democracy, respecting human rights, and renouncing the use of force except in self-defense. More importantly, they have followed through on this talk by creating and expanding institutions, being prepared to act in defense of human rights both at home and abroad, and reducing the number of wars fought between them. Realists have had an explanation for this—it is human nature among professors, governments, and people alike to avoid facing the reality of that nature. Even Realists, however, have had to acknowledge that, until recently at least, the tide has been running hard against them.

The key phrase here, however, is "until recently." One of the great sources of the current international uncertainty is that Liberalism has lost some of its standing as the dominant view of what is going on in the world. The Realists have a ready, if overly simple, explanation for why this is so. Liberalism, they argue, is the ideology of the United States, the most powerful state in the world. The United States is undergoing a relative decline in its power and as it declines, so too does its ability to make its ideas and preferences stick through getting others to accept them. Prepare, the Realists say, for the return of normal, power politics as the US declines and China rises. However, there is much more going on. As we shall see in Chapters 9 and 10, the great financial crisis of 2008–9 has been widely seen as a demonstration of the shortcomings of Liberal principles when it comes to allowing banks and businesses to operate, and people to move around, with less and less regulation. As we shall also see in Chapters 12 and 13, Liberalism has been widely seen to be failing to address pressing problems of increasing economic inequality and environmental degradation. While it is highly unlikely that we are poised to return to the business as usual of power politics between the great powers as the Realists imagine, they are on to something in pointing to the relationship between power and ideas. It is to this relationship between power and ideas, and between the two of them and technology—especially the technologies of communication—that we turn in Chapter 4 on post-positivist theories of international relations.

Recommended reading and viewing

Norman Angell, *A Study of the Relation of Military Power to National Advantage*, New York, 1910.

Per Hamerlund, *Liberal Internationalism and the Decline of the State: The Thought of Richard Cobden, David Mitrany, and Kenichi Ohmae*, Basingstoke, 2005.

Robert O. Keohane, *After Hegemony: Cooperation and Discord in World Political Economy*, Princeton, 1984.

G. John Ikenberry, *Liberal Leviathan: The Origins, Crisis, and Transformation of the American World Order*, Princeton, 2012.

Notes

1 Steve Smith, Ken Booth, and Marysia Zalewski (eds.), *International Theory: Positivism and Beyond*, Cambridge, 1996.
2 Hedley Bull, *The Anarchical Society*, Basingstoke, 1977.
3 Sanjeev Khagram, James V. Riker, and Kathryn Sikkink, *Restructuring World Politics: Transnational Social Movements, Networks, and Norms*, Minneapolis, 2002.
4 Martin Wight, "Why is there no international relations theory?" in Herbert Butterfield and Martin Wight (eds.) *Diplomatic Investigations*, Cambridge, 1968.
5 Immanuel Kant, *Perpetual Peace: a Philosophical Sketch* (1795) at https://www.mtholyoke.edu/acad/intrel/kant/kant1.htm
6 See, for example, David Hume, "Of the Balance of Power," in *Essays Moral, Political, and Literary (Part II, Essay VII)* (1742) at http://www.econlib.org/library/LFBooks/Hume/hmMPL30.html and also Richard Cobden, "The Balance of Power," in *The Political Writings of Richard Cobden (Volume I, Part II)* (1835) at http://www.econlib.org/library/YPDBooks/Cobden/cbdPW6.html
7 Michael W. Doyle, *Liberal Peace: Selected Theories*, Oxford, 2012.
8 Hidemi Suganami, *The Domestic Analogy and World Order Proposals*, Cambridge, 2008.
9 Nicholas Murray Butler, *The Family of Nations*, New York, 1938.
10 Robert Keohane and Joseph Nye, *Power and Interdependence: World Politics in Transition*, Boston, 1977.
11 Barry Buzan, *From International Society to World Society: English School Theory and the Social Structure of Globalization*, Cambridge, 2004.
12 Franklin D. Roosevelt, 1941 State of the Union Address, "The Four Freedoms" (January 6, 1941), Voices of Democracy: US Oratory Project accessed at http://voicesofdemocracy.umd.edu/fdr-the-four-freedoms-speech-text/

4 Post-positivist theories of international relations

Preamble

This chapter examines three Post-positivist theories of international relations: the English School, Social Constructivism, and Feminism. There are also other Post-positivist approaches, for example: critical theory, some types of Marxism, and Post-colonial theory, which will not be covered here because they appear in later chapters. What do these examples of Post-positivist theorizing have in common? As noted in Chapter 1, they share the assumption that a complex relationship exists between the social world out there and how we see it. Indeed, some of these approaches suggest it is a mistake to think we can separate a world out there from our ideas about it. How we think, speak, and write about the social world not only shapes our view of it, Post-positivists argue. We also think, speak, and write that social world into existence. It exists nowhere else except in efforts to describe, explain, and understand it, and in the way people act upon the results of those efforts. We noted in Chapter 2 that international relations appear to be becoming more complicated and that theorizing is useful in that it attempts to simplify and capture the essentials of what is going on. Realism and Liberalism can both be seen as examples of such attempts. The theories that we are about to examine cannot. Initially at least, they make things seem more complicated. This is intentional, for one of the points which they want to make is that there can be a high price to pay for simplifying or over-simplifying what the world is about—the result can be that some people's view of the world is imposed on other people and peoples. Making sense of Post-positivist approaches is difficult, but it is wellworth the effort. It helps us understand, for example, how Realists and Liberals can claim to be looking at the same world, yet offer such contrasting views of it. Beyond agreeing on the value of this sort of payoff, however, Post-positivist approaches have their own big debates and disagreements, both between the approaches and within each approach. They leave us with more questions than answers about international relations. However, they also provide us with grounds for treating with caution those who claim to have all the answers.

| 4.1 | Post-positivist approaches to international relations |

Learning objectives

1. List four features that Post-positivist approaches generally share.
2. Explain how Post-positivists see the relationship between how social **identity** is formed and how identity shapes the way people see the social world.
3. Describe how ideas can become **privileged**.
4. Describe the idea of an **emancipatory** commitment.

Post-positivism is a very broad label covering many approaches to the study of human relations in general and international relations in particular. Nevertheless, we can identify four features which Post-positivist approaches have in common.

First, as noted earlier, they assume that the relationship between language and ideas, on the one hand, and the social world of human relations which they attempt to describe and understand, on the other, is not straightforward. People's ideas about the social world and the way they act on those ideas play a big part in actually creating or producing that social world. Think, for example, about a key element of international relations—the borders between states.

According to Post-positivists, the US-Mexican border (Figure 4.1) only exists insofar as a sufficient number of significant people say it does and act as if it does. Even if you painted a line (or tried to build a wall) the length of the border as it exists today, it would have no objective existence if Mexicans and Americans

Figure 4.1   The US–Mexican border from Tijuana, Mexico
(Source: Tom King/Alamy Stock Photo)

decided that it should no longer exist or simply forgot that it did. The same is true for all international borders. Now notice this is not to say that these borders do not exist and that you can just ignore them and walk across them if you feel like it. If sufficient people, and especially powerful people, say there is a border, then there are very real, physical consequences—checkpoints, walls, fences, and patrols are established and controls are imposed on who can and cannot cross such borders. However, we can see from history that borders change. Old borders can disappear, new borders can come into existence, and the significance of borders can change, even if they are still in place. The borders between Ireland and Northern Ireland, for example, used to be very important, are less important at the moment, but may become important again when Britain leaves the European Union. Sometimes, these changes can take place almost overnight. A wall was built across Berlin in 1961 in a matter of days, dividing the part belonging to the German Democratic Republic (East Germany) from the part which would eventually belong to the Federal German Republic (West Germany). Permitted crossings of this border were very restricted and unpermitted attempts to cross could result in death or severe punishments if people were caught rather than killed. Then, in 1989, almost in a matter of hours, the Berlin Wall, as it was known, ceased to exist as a barrier. Guards stopped controlling the checkpoints, individuals started breaking holes in the wall, and crowds surged through. The Berlin Wall was a formidable barrier, but once enough people—crowds and guards at the Wall itself plus political leaders who gave orders—decided it should no longer exist, then it disappeared. The Berlin Wall is a spectacular example, but as we shall see below, Post-positivists want us to be aware of the extent to which all social life is dependent on people believing things to be so. States, like other social groups, exist when there is a sufficient **intersubjective consensus** among people who believe and act as if they exist.

Secondly, while Post-positivists show how ideas produce and shape the social world, they also want to stress how people and the ideas they have are shaped by where they are in terms of both geographical space and the social hierarchy, when they are in terms of historical time, and who they are in terms of the various elements that make up people's personalities and identities. This sounds complicated, but what it amounts to is that different people, and different groups of people, can see the same world differently. Think of how most (although not all) people assume that their own state is right when it gets into a dispute with other states. At worst, we tend to think of our own state as making honest mistakes, whereas we are more willing to think that other states actually have wicked intentions. Other people think about their own states like this too. This process of seeing the same things differently is very common. Think about people's reactions to policing policies, especially when police officers use violence against members of racial minorities. Clearly identifiable groups, for example, young people of color, old white people, and police officers will be pretty sure they know what happened. They will have different degrees of sympathy and levels of trust regarding the people involved in the violence. And they will struggle to understand why others do not see what happened in their terms because it will strike them as obvious. Indeed, these differences will increase the lack of trust and re-enforce prejudices. Post-positivists emphasize that how we see things is framed by our experiences and our sense of who we are. They also suggest, however, that the "real" story of what actually happened, the facts of the matter, do not really exist separate from the stories that different people tell about what happened. One state invaded another. One person killed another. This is what happened, but we almost immediately want to know how it happened and why it happened, and then we become involved in interpretation—making sense of what happened in terms of who we are, our experiences, and our sense of how the world works.

The third assumption most Post-positivists make is that the process by which one particular view of the world becomes established is not simply one of scientific research or intellectual debate. It often involves processes in which some ideas and ways of seeing are privileged over others. Sometimes, the fact that people see the world differently poses no problems, and they go their separate ways, or co-exist without having to resolve their differences. Sometimes, however, it does matter. Think of the mutual lack of comprehension which resulted when the first Europeans came to North America and asked the native population questions like "which river branch is the real source of the Mississippi?" and "who owns this particular piece of land?" Such questions had about as much meaning to the Native Americans as their own inquiries about the totemic animal groups to which they belonged had to the Europeans. In the case of "real" source of the Mississippi, the lack of mutual comprehension did not matter much. Find out that the Europeans meant the longest branch of the river and show them that. In the case of asking questions of land ownership, in contrast, Europeans used the native people's lack of a concept of exclusive ownership to conclude "Well, if no one owns it, we'll call it ours," and they usually had the power to make their claim stick. Often then, establishing, or privileging someone's meaning over someone else's becomes a highly political matter of interest, power, and control where the strongest get to impose their meanings and understandings. Post-positivists do not always regard privileging as a political matter, however. Privileged ideas are not necessarily imposed. They may simply be taken for granted because they appear obvious and natural. When, for example, a course in International Relations begins with the state-centric approach described in Chapter 1, as opposed to starting with a transnational approach, it is privileging the idea of states, but doing so does not necessarily involve making a political move. Things become interesting, however, when what has seemed obvious and natural up to now or to most people becomes challenged by changing circumstances or different people.

The fourth and final assumption of Post-positivist approaches is that we study and think about the world and international relations not just to understand them, to paraphrase Karl Marx, but to improve them. What it means to try and "improve" things varies considerably both between and within Post-positivist approaches. Some argue for an explicit emancipatory commitment which people ought to have. They see human beings as desiring freedom, the amount of freedom they enjoy varying by place and time, and freedom being denied by conditions of ignorance and processes of oppression and exploitation. History, in these views, is about extending freedom, and we all ought to be playing a part in removing the barriers to it. For many Post-positivists (for example, James Der Derian, Costas Constantinou, and Runa Das), the task of those who study human relations in general and international relations in particular begins with discovering and critiquing the ways in which existing social relations, and particularly relations of power, get in the way of human freedom.[1] The struggle is waged on many plains from the battlefield and conference chambers to the workplace and classroom. Why is it, for example, that Feminism is always at the back of the bus in the theory chapters of text books, and Realism is always at the front? What sort of world does this reflect? What would have to change for the batting order to be reversed, and how are we going to accomplish that change? In this critical view, theory is never neutral. It is always, in Robert Cox's words "for someone and for some purpose" and the challenge for theorists is to **problematize** privileged ideas to show that they are not necessarily natural, normal, or the only way of looking at things.[2]

Other Post-positivists (for example, Paul Sharp and Halvard Leira), in contrast, employ much less ambitious understandings of what improving things involves.[3] Their main concern is with avoiding the disasters which they believe can result from treating things like states and national interests, and even social classes and genders, as if they are independently existing things with their own objective properties which exert an independent influence on the world. For example, one of the big themes to emerge from the study of the crisis in 1914 which led to World War I is of a loss of control by the governments involved. Time and again, statesmen said that they knew they were on the road to disaster, but that the logic of great power politics, national interests, and credibility dictated that they had no choice. We hear the same theme sometimes today when, for example, after a terrorist act, journalists and politicians say the US has to respond with force whether it likes it or not, or whether it thinks it will work or not. Similar arguments occur regarding the North Korean nuclear program. The demands of the moment seem compelling, but think of how odd the claim of governments in 1914 seems to us today that they had no choice but to send their young men to kill and die in their millions for God, King, and State. Even the claims of the Soviet and American governments that they had no choice but to accept the possible deaths of hundreds of millions in a nuclear exchange at the height of the Cold War may seem odd today. At a minimum, Post-positivists want to say to these governments, "yes, you do have a choice." Taking these terrible actions may even be the right one, but never think that some automatic, objective requirement of states is forcing you or other governments to play out these parts without choice.

The Neo-Neo Synthesis[4]

One contribution of Post-positivist approaches is well captured by Ole Waever's phrase above. When people begin studying international relations, they are often presented (as you have been here) with the great contest between Realism and Liberalism. Realism emphasizes sovereign states trapped in an anarchy of their own making and doomed to pursue power and interests in competition with their rivals. Liberalism emphasizes a more benign anarchy in which economics is increasingly important, cooperation is both possible and necessary, and states (plus others) build the institutions which will broaden and deepen this cooperation. The names change with the use of the "neo" prefix. The issues become more complex and the actors more sophisticated. However, the basic debates remain unchanged and polarized around the great differences between these two approaches. Which is it to be, students of International Relations are asked, and which do you think is right?

However, are these two approaches so different? As Waever notes, they both assume self-interested states to be the most important actors, the construction of a stable, prosperous world order to be the most important challenge, power to be the most important instrument for meeting this challenge, and the US to be the most important wielder of this power. This may be how the big issues look from along a Washington-London axis of governments, think-tanks, mass media, and universities. Beyond that axis, however, the neo-Realist/neo-Liberal divide and the issues which they argue over become foreshortened, less distinct, and very narrow-looking. The views from New Delhi, Beijing, and Brazil, for example, may be quite different. How do we foster economic development and how do we get our share (or more) of it? And the views of the peoples of the Naga Hills in India, the Salars of the Yellow River in China, and Yanomami of the Amazon rain forest in Brazil, are probably different again. They have little interest in how development is to be fostered, and no interest in whether Realism or Liberalism is right about how global order is best sustained. Realism and Liberalism would seem very similar to them, and have little to say about their big international relations' concern with preserving themselves, their children, and the immediate habitats on which their ways of life depend.

Key terms

emancipatory   Something which contributes to freeing people or making them more free.

identity   How an individual or group is defined, by themselves and/or others in terms of who they are, what their place is in society, how they should act and how they should be treated.

intersubjective consensus   the idea that social groupings like states have no objective existence, but exist only insofar as enough people subjectively believe they exist and act as if they exist.

privileged   For Post-positivists, anything, in this case an idea, accepted by or imposed on everyone without an extended process of rational inquiry to demonstrate its accuracy or value.

problematize   The process of challenging privileged ideas about the world by making them look less normal and natural.

Key takeaways

- Post-positivist theories share the assumption that relations between social reality and ideas about it are complex, and that the existence of social groups like states depends on the existence of an intersubjective consensus among their people.

■ Post-positivist theory suggests that many ideas about societies and international relations are taken for granted by people, imposed by leaders, or both, rather than produced by rational discussion.

■ Many Post-positivist theorists suggest that the study of human beings and international relations should be directed at ending oppression and emancipating people.

Exercises

1. In what ways do your lectures and group meetings in this class reflect an intersubjective consensus?
2. Give an example of a privileged idea in the study of international relations.

4.2 The English School

Learning objectives

1. Describe the English School's idea of an **international society**.
2. Explain the English School's '**traditions of international thought**' approach.

The English School, sometimes called the International Society School, nicely illustrates some of the puzzles and paradoxes in which Post-positivists are interested. To begin with, three of the four people usually associated with its beginnings were a Welshman, a South African, and an Australian. Only one was English, although they were all at British universities. In addition, all of them would have rejected that they were setting up a school or "ism" like Realism or Liberalism. They believed that researchers should follow the evidence where it took them, and that they should not join groups which risked insisting on a particular view of how the world works. It was scholars who came after them who started using the term "English School"—one scholar to argue that they were all on the wrong track, and another, who happens to be a Canadian, to argue the case for building a very distinctive approach to making sense of international relations.[5]

Members of the English School have two things to say of interest to us here. The first is about international relations. They agree with the Realists that international relations at present are mainly the relations of sovereign states occurring in an anarchy which results from their claims to sovereignty. However, they disagree with those Realists who said that this was how international relations had always been and were always likely to be. They agree with the Liberals that states could achieve high levels of cooperation under conditions of anarchy. As Hedley Bull argues, this anarchy can look like an international society with its own understandings and rules which shape and constrain the actions of states.

These understandings and rules are maintained by international institutions: great powers, diplomacy, the balance of power, international law, and war.[6] They disagree with the Liberals, however, that this international society is necessarily being driven by economic and technological logic in a direction which reduces the importance of states or that it ought to do so. In recent years, however, arguments have emerged within the English School regarding whether the international society of states is being displaced by a global society of states, international organizations, multinational corporations, humanitarian organizations, social movements, and individual human beings and, if so, whether or not this is a good thing.

The second interesting point that members of the English School have to make is about how international relations are studied and understood. In the subject International Relations, Realists and Liberals produce hypotheses about important questions in international relations; for example, do close economic relations make war between two states more or less likely? They then gather evidence to see if it supports their hypotheses or contradicts them. In contrast, English School theorists are interested in what sorts of questions people ask about international relations, how they answer them, and with what consequences. Realists and Liberals ask questions like "what are the properties of states?" English School theorists remind us that the sovereign state today is a result of people thinking and writing about problems in the past which they argued might be solved by creating and establishing sovereign states. Martin Wight argues that if we look at people thinking and talking about international relations from the past to the present, we can identify three main traditions of international thought in the sense of familiar sets of assumptions and habitual paths of argument derived from them. Think of standard openings in a game of chess or standard patterns of bidding in a game of bridge. Thus Wight presents Machiavellianism as focused on power and being like Realism, Lockeanism as focused on reason and being like Liberalism, and Kantianism as focused on revolution. Over time, Wight maintains, these three basic approaches keep resurfacing, and the arguments between them never get permanently resolved.

The traditions of international thought approach may seem a bit wishy-washy to people interested in getting hard and fast answers to the big problems presented by international relations. As noted above, however, if there are hard-and-fast answers, there is no general agreement on what they are. Can we imagine a time in the future when the Realists or the Liberals will finally win the argument about who is right and, if not, why is this so? Not only do the arguments between the camps seem to rumble on, but people like presidents, prime ministers, professors, and preachers seem to slide back and forth between the approaches, sounding like a Realist in one situation, a Liberal in another, and Revolutionary in still another. Different contexts help to produce different responses from the same person. Further, ideas and theories not only guide us. They also seem to be selected by us when we believe they will help us get what we want. When governments want to increase spending on armaments, for example, they will present a very Realist picture of the world in which their state operates. When they want to sign an agreement with another state, they will present a very Liberal picture of the world in which trust and cooperation are not only possible, they are necessary. So, if you've struggled to make up your mind about whether you are a Realist, a Liberal, or a Radical as you work your way through the course, if you find yourself changing your mind in response to what the international news of the day happens to be, don't worry. You are in really good company.

Key terms

international society   In the English School, the idea that a system of sovereign states may be held together by shared understandings, rules, and institutions which its member states value and accept.

traditions of international thought   In the English School, the idea that most thinking about international relations follows one of three main paths: Machiavellianism (focused on power), Lockeanism (focused on reason), and Kantianism (focused on revolution).

Key takeaways

- The English School suggests that sovereign states have developed an anarchical society which lacks an overarching government, but which has rules, understandings, and institutions which regulate it.
- The English School suggests that the international society today is the product of a history of thinking and arguing about international relations in terms of traditions of international thought.

Exercises

1. Is the state you live in restrained from doing what it would like to do by its support for the understandings, rules, and institutions of international society?
2. Do you find yourself shifting back and forth between seeing international relations in Realist and Liberal terms? If so, when are these shifts likely to take place?

4.3   Social Constructivism

Learning objectives

1. Explain the distinction Social Constructivists make between "**brute facts**" and "**social facts**."
2. Describe how Social Constructivists say the social world is constructed/produced.

Like the English School, Social Constructivism says we must look beyond international relations and the way it has traditionally been studied for insights into what is going on. Where the English School looks to history, philosophy, and legal thought, however, the Social Constructivists look to sociology and psychology. Again, we will focus on two points they make which are of interest to us here and which we encountered in Chapter 1. The first point is the distinction between what John Searle and Alexander Wendt have called "brute facts" and "social facts."[7] As we noted above, a sovereign state and a border are not facts in the same way a piece of land and a river are facts. Sovereign states are social facts which exist because some people claim them to be the case and enough people accept the claim. Think again of what happened to the Soviet Union once enough people no longer accepted the claim that it should exist, and its leaders no longer thought it was worth coercing them to keep them in line. It disappeared even though all the brute elements of its existence were still in place. Maintaining a social fact like a sovereign state takes a great deal of work. Think of the way symbols of the UN, for example the flags of all the member states flying outside the UN buildings in New York, encourage people to think in terms of ideas like the international community or the community of nations as if this was something real. State ceremonies like the US President's annual address to Congress to which all the members of the diplomatic community are invited, international conferences where leaders from other states fly in and are treated to a greeting with a red carpet, a band playing, and a guard of honor, or the opening ceremonies of an international sporting event like the World Cup or the Olympics, all are means by which the idea of our own state among a system of states is produced. In addition to high state ceremonies, we also have what Michael Billig called "banal nationalism." By this he meant the patterns of daily life by which the idea of living in a state are produced, for example: pledges of allegiances at the start of the school day; newspaper weather maps in which the territory (and weather) of neighboring states is left blank; and television news reports which focus almost exclusively on matters of national or local interest.[8] By practices ranging from the occasional, formal, and highly symbolic to the daily, informal, and banal, Social Constructivists say human beings symbolically produce, construct, and enact social facts like the states in which we live into existence and maintain them there. Brute facts like the land and the river need no such consensus among human beings in order to exist.

The second point is that relations between states are also socially constructed. Wendt invites us to revisit the Realist claim regarding sovereign states, anarchy, and the possibility of war. States have to look after themselves. They cannot trust anyone else to do this for them, and any state with the power to hurt them is a potential threat. As soldiers are fond of saying, we have to pay attention to the actual military capabilities of other states, not to what their leaders say they will or will not do with them. If this is the case, then why does the US worry about the possibility of Iran acquiring a few nuclear weapons in the future, when France has over two hundred nuclear warheads and could blow the US to kingdom come right now? The answer is obvious. Iran is a rival and potential enemy. France is a trusted ally. This, however, is the Social Constructivist's point. All anarchic relations are not the same and do not have to be treated the same. Some are between enemies like the US and Cuba until recently. Some are between friends like the US and Britain. Some are between states which are indifferent to each other like Nepal and Uruguay. Each relationship depends on an identity which is socially constructed by the ideas, arguments, and actions of the participants. Each relationship needs reproducing if it is to have consequences. Without them it may change and may even disappear.

Brute facts, social facts, and main battle tanks

Consider the two images (Figures 4.2 and 4.3) of an American tank and a Russian tank. As brute facts they are arrangements of metal, rubber, oil, and explosive materials which can move over rough territory and fire projectiles. As social facts they are called "tanks," at least in the English-speaking world, because this was a code name the British gave to them to conceal what they really were at an early stage of their development. It is a very odd name for them when compared to what the Germans call them, *Panzerkampfwagen* (roughly, armored war wagon/car). Further, as social facts, some people might find the image of one of these tanks ("our" tank) reassuring, while the image of the other one ("their" tank) looks threatening. Social Constructivists focus on what goes into the production of the identities and relations which provide the context for why we see one tank as threatening and the other tank as reassuring.

Figure 4.2 Brute and social fact 1, a US Abrams tank
(Source: Purestock/Alamy Stock Photo)

Figure 4.3 Brute and social fact 2, a Russian T.55 tank
(Source: Gyula Gyukli/Alamy Stock Photo)

Key terms

brute facts   Facts of nature like mountains, rivers, rocks, water, and gas which exist independent of human interpretation, recognition, and acceptance.

social facts   Notional facts like families, cities, and states and relations between them which depend on human interpretation, recognition, and collective acceptance for their full existence.

Key takeaways

- Social Constructivists suggest that the social world is continually being constructed, produced and enacted by human beings.
- Social Constructivists suggest that relations between states are also constructed and that this permits a wider range of possible relations than those suggested by Realists and Liberals.

Exercises

1. What sorts of things do you do which Social Constructivists would suggest help produce the idea of the state in which you live existing as a social fact?
2. How is the relationship between the state in which you live and its closest neighboring state constructed, produced, and enacted?

Feminism

Learning objectives

1. Explain what feminists mean by ideas about society and how we live being **gendered**.
2. Describe what feminists mean when they talk about the apparent absence of women from international relations.

Feminism is itself an umbrella term covering a number theoretical, practical, social, and political ways of seeing the world and suggesting how people should act in it. Here we will simply look at some aspects of feminist scholarship and what they tell us about international relations. Post-positivism suggests that the relationship between the social world and ideas about it is complex. Social Constructivism suggests that social reality results from the ongoing thought and action of human beings which constructs, produces, and enacts it. Feminist approaches have their own distinctive understanding of the social facts which make up the world of international relations. Men and women are different, may think differently, may see things differently, and prioritize different things, at least up to a point. There is considerable overlap between most men and most women on many things. Some women are more like most men on some matters, and some men are more like most women on some matters. Thus, for example, if you are a man, you are more likely to have accepted the socially constructed difference between the two tanks pictured above. This may go as far as seeing them as one of "our" tanks intended to protect "us" and one of "their" tanks posing a threat to "us." If you are a woman, you are more likely to have accepted the brute facts of the images and, perhaps, their brutish similarities as instruments designed for killing. Notice that we say, "more likely." We must be careful about gender stereotyping which suggests that all men see things one way and all women see things another. We must also be careful about assuming that men or women in one place or time see things in the same way as men or women in another place or time. Most men, for example, seem to value courage, but in some cultures that involves showing no emotions, whereas in others it means showing them. Most men value comradeship, but in some cultures that involves holding hands with one another whereas in others men holding hands is viewed as inappropriate. The occasional bearhug or handshake will suffice. Most women value the freedom to dress as they wish, but many will disagree over whether "modest" or "immodest" dress in terms of the extent to which a woman is covered or uncovered in public is an expression of that freedom.

Feminists, like other social theorists, are interested in gender identities in the sense of what a society says its men are supposed to be like and what its women are supposed to be like. They maintain that, at least in part, gender identities are socially constructed, produced, and enacted. We have all experienced this process of from early childhood and even before. Most of us were named and some of us had our bedrooms painted blue or pink before we were even born. Some of us have suffered as a result of socially constructed gender expectations not fitting who we feel we are, or from there only being two gender roles on offer. In addition, however, feminists make two points which are of interest here. First, not only is the social world constructed, and not only is there always a political battle over whose particular construction of the world will beat out the others, but the winner represents a gendered view of the world.[9] Some feminists borrow the term **patriarchy** from anthropology to describe this condition. By this they mean that ways of thinking usually associated with masculinity (for example, either-or rationality requiring clear definitions and solutions, hierarchical organization, and the permissibility and even desirability of using force on occasions) are privileged over ways of thinking associated with femininity (for example, both-and rationality which does not require forced definitions and solutions, horizontal or egalitarian organization, and the need to avoid direct and especially violent conflict in most circumstances). Those statesmen from the 1914 crisis (see p. 64) who said they felt trapped by circumstances and necessity were arguably trapped in masculine ways of thinking about power, threats, and credibility, according to feminists. Worse, they were willing collaborators in their own entrapment because the privileging of masculine ways of thinking gave them power. To preserve both, they were prepared to pay a huge sacrifice in the lives of millions of other human beings. And, as feminists point out, if you count up all the deaths that occur in wars, not just the battle deaths, the number of non-combatants killed—largely women, children, and old men—is often greater than the number of men as soldiers. Viewing war through masculine eyes, this fact is often obscured by the focus on military campaigns, grand strategy, and great war leaders. Indeed, as Carol Cohn has noted, military language not only uses euphemisms to obscure what it is talking about. It often uses euphemisms which present acts of violence in terms of sex acts.[10]

Making a difference: women, power, and visibility

International relations remain a man's game, at least at the level of states, governments, armed forces, and diplomatic services, although this is beginning to change. Relatively few women have reached the top leadership positions in states, and even fewer have reached the top in states which play major roles in international affairs. Women have been actively excluded from such positions. India and Israel had women prime ministers (over thirty and forty years ago respectively). Britain had a woman prime minister nearly a quarter of a century ago, and recently acquired a second one. Pakistan, Indonesia, Norway are among those who have also had women as chief executives. Germany currently has Chancellor Merkel and Bangladesh has Sheikh Hasina Wazed. The US, modern Russia, and modern China are still waiting (although in recent years women like Madeleine Albright, Hillary Clinton, Condoleezza Rice, and Susan Rice have occupied very senior positions in US foreign policy-making). In no state has the proportion of women leaders come close to matching the proportion of women in the population over any period of time. Women also remain underrepresented in the armed forces, and diplomatic services of states, as well as in the academic study of International Relations, although this too is beginning to change.

There are a number of ways of accounting for this underrepresentation. One is to say that international relations are about fighting, competition, and risk-taking where people need to be strong and ruthless. It is obvious that men are more physically and psychologically suited to meeting these demands. To this can be added the claims that women are not often interested in international relations and, therefore, this is not a problem. Another response is to say that it would make no difference if women were more involved in international relations. To succeed, they would have to adjust to the rules of the game, or they would soon be out of office.

The Israeli prime minister, Golda Meier, the British prime minister, Margaret Thatcher, and the American Secretary of State, Hillary Clinton, are sometimes cited as supporting evidence for this claim. Golda Meier led Israel through a costly and dangerous war when Israel was attacked in 1973. She made no concessions to Israel's enemies, bargained fiercely with Israel's allies for their support, and threatened catastrophe if that support was not forthcoming. Margaret Thatcher led Britain to a victorious war against Argentina to win back the Falkland Islands in 1982, taking terrible risks for something which much of the rest of the world did not think was worth fighting for (until she won). She was also one of the few political leaders who said that nuclear weapons were a good thing rather than a regrettable necessity. Hillary Clinton, during the 2008 presidential election campaign, said Iran would face "massive retaliation" from the US with nuclear weapons if it used a nuclear weapon against Israel. As Secretary of State in the first Obama administration, she was known for hawkish views regarding the possible use of American military power against Iran and in Syria, despite also being associated with so-called "soft" issues like economic development, involving women in foreign affairs, and developing the internet as a tool of digital diplomacy. Women in power, the argument runs, behave pretty much like men in power, because international relations leave them no choice.

Feminists, among others, maintain that these arguments are missing big parts of the story. First, they reject the claim that men (and women) need to be strong, tough, and ruthless because that's just the way international relations are. Why are international relations like that, they ask. Is it because they have historically been dominated by men, or at least masculine ways of seeing how the world works and how to act in it if you are going to succeed? If so, then it is not surprising that the relatively few women who have reached the top have been as "manly" or more "manly" than the top men in international relations. Either this is how ambitious women have to be if they want to succeed in the face of male hostility to their advancement, or these are the relatively few women who actually do take a "manly" approach to the world. And, feminists note, if we drop the "masculine" preoccupation with who's at the top of the hierarchy, women become visible to us working at other levels of society in international relations. Look at anecdotal accounts of Sacajawea's role in the Lewis and Clark expedition or the calming influence of (some) young women in Saturday night parking lots when (some) young men want to fight. Or examine more systematic research on the links between the status of women in societies and the likelihood of those societies using force to solve problems. There is mounting evidence, feminists note, that where women are present and powerful, there is less likelihood of violence and more likelihood of men behaving themselves, and that women have always been present in great numbers in those parts of international relations that masculine gendered perspectives have encouraged us to ignore.

Key terms

gendered   This term is used by feminists to suggest that ways of seeing the world, understanding how it works, and prioritizing what ought to happen in it are profoundly shaped by and associated with masculinity and femininity.

patriarchy   This term is used by some feminists to describe societies where priorities associated with masculinity are privileged and men are powerful.

Key takeaways

- Feminists suggest that most societies, including states, and the relations between them are socially constructed to reflect gendered priorities like hierarchy, and are maintained by methods associated with masculinity.
- Feminists suggest that women have been excluded from positions of power and privilege in international relations.
- Feminists suggest that women appear invisible in international relations partly because they are excluded but also because our view of what constitutes important international relations is itself gendered.

Exercises

1. In what ways have women been excluded from leading roles in international relations?
2. In what ways could it be said that the way this textbook is organized is gendered?

| 4.5 | Strengths and weaknesses of Post-positivist approaches |

Learning objectives

1. Describe the problem of difficulty in Post-positivist approaches.
2. Explain the value of critique in Post-positivist approaches.
3. Describe the problem of grounding in Post-positivist approaches.

One great weakness of Post-positivist approaches to making sense of international relations is that they can be difficult to understand. They involve reflecting at length on the fact that much social life is lived "as if" social facts like states and other human communities really are as they appear. Most of us, most of the time, tend to accept that states are real and that they shape who we are and the way we act. Post-positivists tell us that this is only part of the story. Social facts exist because people are constantly producing them through their thought and action. States are produced by the thought and action of people. They do not exist independently of that thought and action. This difficulty may seem like a problem for people, and especially for students preparing for a test. However, it is also Post-positivism's problem, and it is especially a problem for those who take the emancipatory dimension to social theory seriously. What is the point of knowing the truth if you cannot describe it quickly and explain it simply to the people you want to reach? The dangerous temptation for Post-positivists is that of producing ever more refined versions of what they have to say for the small group they believe actually "gets it."

The difficulty which many people experience with Post-positivist approaches, however, is not merely an intellectual one. It is also an emotional one. Post-positivist approaches contain within them an element of critique noted above which challenges people's understanding of the world, often in troubling ways. The critique occurs on two levels. The first is the immediate or political level. Feminism and other critical sociological approaches, for example, focus on the gap between the stories we tell ourselves of what the world is like and what they say the world is actually like in terms of patterns of injustice, exploitation, and domination. They also seek to expose the ways in which those whom they regard as powerful and privileged try to cover up the gaps between how the world is supposed to be and how it actually is. Such revelations often produce upset and anger, either at the wrongs revealed or at those who are making the revelations. The second level of critique is less apparent but possibly more disturbing. Even the low key apolitical accounts of traditions of international thought produced by English School theorists contain within them the possibility that there is no great empirical or moral Truth to be discovered about how people should live. There are only human beings thinking and acting on the basis of their thoughts, the thoughts and actions of others, and the thoughts and actions of people who have gone before them. Worse, we are not let off the hook of trying to think things through just because there are no big answers. The questions are still there presenting problems which require choices about how we are to act.

Difficult and disturbing though Post-positivist approaches can seem, however, they can also be valuable, useful, and even fun. In terms of value, many Post-positivists see themselves engaged in trying to make the world a better place and encouraging others to do likewise. Their work is often explicitly political or has obviously political implications. How far people agree with particular Post-positivist approaches in this regard is up to them to work out for themselves. Even when people disagree with particular arguments, however, it is good to have what seems obvious and natural challenged, for it encourages people to reflect on why they think about things the way they do. This is an important point because accounts and theories of international relations often present themselves as truth claims. They do not say, here is a way of looking at the world. They say, this is the way the world actually is, and they make calls to action based on those claims. Post-positivism is valuable in that it encourages skepticism about such claims. It is, for example, harder to get someone to kill and die for a social construct produced through the thought, action, and compliance of many people than it is to get someone to kill and die for King and State, the Fatherland, the Faith, or some general idea like Freedom or the Revolution.

In terms of usefulness, Post-positivist approaches can help people answer puzzles like the one noted above. Why do the big arguments about society in general, and international relations in particular, not get resolved? It is tempting to conclude, especially if you are directly involved in such an argument yourself, that it is because people, especially other people, are stupid, wicked, or both. This may sometimes be the case, but it is not always the case, and it is certainly a bad place from which to start when looking at what other people have to say, especially those who disagree with you. Instead of dying completely, major ideas and arguments about them seem to wax and wane. In the early 1990s, for example, Francis Fukuyama argued that Liberalism had triumphed with the end of the Cold War and that socialism was finished.[11] Many international relations theorists added that Liberalism had also triumphed over Realism to the point that some Realists came to regard themselves as a persecuted sect. We can understand why these things were said at the time, but no one would make Fukuyama's claim about Liberalism with the same confidence today. Socialism—albeit not the same socialism that was declared dead in the 1990s, is back on the intellectual and political agenda. Realism has survived, almost unchanged, and its agenda of problems worth worrying about: great power politics; the balance of power; and the limits to what international organizations can achieve, is attracting both intellectual and political attention again. Context, the Post-positivists remind us, provides our problems, it provides the language and concepts with which we are equipped to deal with those problems, and there are times when that language and its concepts become problems themselves. Think, for example, about the debate in Britain over leaving the European Union and the role of restoring Britain's sovereignty in the arguments. The people in favor of leaving defined sovereignty in terms of an independence which probably cannot be regained. The people who wished to stay defined sovereignty in terms of a concept of shared or pooled sovereignty which makes no sense. The idea of sovereignty hindered rather than helped people understand what was at stake.

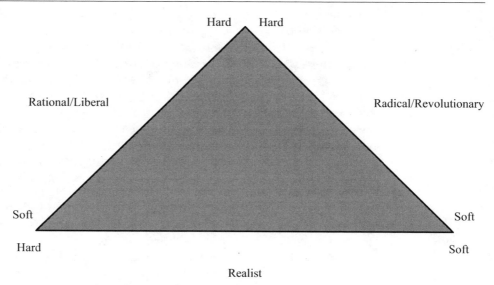

Figure 4.4 The triangle of traditions of international thought
(Source: by permission of Professor Richard Little)

In showing us how the same old problems in international relations and responses to them persist or mutate, but never completely disappear, Post-positivists alert us to the possibility that asking which response is right or true is probably a waste of time. It may be more useful to map out the field of International Relations by asking what each approach is interested in, what questions it finds important to answer, and how it goes about answering them. Richard Little attempted this by placing each of Wight's three traditions of international thought along a side of a triangle, calling each side of the triangle a general objective or worldview (Figure 4.4). He then named the triangle points as follows: "Hard/Hard, "Soft/Soft, and "Soft/Hard" to produce a continuum between them of methods for achieving the objectives or world views. This allowed Little to identify six approaches to international relations: soft Realists, soft Liberals, soft Radicals, hard Realists, hard Liberals, and hard Radicals.

Thus, for example, on the revolutionary side of the triangle, Lenin and Trotsky, the Bolshevik revolutionaries, would be towards the "hard" point as they were prepared to use force to achieve their objectives. Gandhi and Nelson Mandela, on the other hand, would be towards the soft point at the end of the revolutionary side. Gandhi preached non-violent protests to achieve revolutionary change in India. Mandela argued for peaceful reconciliation in South Africa (at least in his later years). Offensive Realists would be towards the hard point on the Realist side ready to use force to increase power, and Defensive Realists would be towards the soft point, cautious about using force. Franklin Roosevelt might be placed towards the hard point on the Liberal side and Jimmy Carter might be placed towards the soft point. This exercise is useful, even fun, yet there are clear limitations. Ronald Reagan might also qualify as a hard Liberal and Ron Paul, the American libertarian, might qualify as a soft one—yet Reagan and Roosevelt, and Carter and Paul seem unlikely pairs. Historians would argue over whether the Prussian/German chancellor Bismarck was a hard Realist with a master plan for forceful expansion, or a soft Realist reacting and improvising in response to political developments in Germany which he did not like and over which he had little control. On close examination, it becomes clear that boundaries between approaches are not firm. Thus, we can identify Kantians (radicals or revolutionaries) who, beyond their acceptance of the importance of working for social transformation, take a more-or-less Realist view of power and how it operates in the world. We can identify Realists who take a Liberal approach to the organization of international economic relations. And we can identify Liberals who use Realist arguments against becoming extensively engaged in international relations.

Mapping the way different approaches to international relations relate to each other, overlap, and sometimes merge is useful. Trying to place famous political figures on the map may be fun. It is important to know that social facts are different from brute facts, and that contexts and power play an important part in producing and maintaining social facts. Once this claim has been made, however, what is there left to say? Don't the critiques Post-positivists make of other theories apply to their own theories as well? Where do you stand to make claims about what the social world is like and what it ought to be like? Are we all just saying what we say because of who we are in terms of identity and where we are in terms of context? This is sometimes called the **grounding** problem in Post-positivist theory, and it is one which is not easily resolved.

There are at least three possible responses. The first response is to close this book and give up on trying to study social relations generally and international relations in particular. If we live in a "post-Truth" and "fake fact" world, why listen to what other people, especially those with whom we disagree, have to say at all? Why not just try to get on with our own lives? In response to this reaction, professors are fond of quoting the Greek philosopher Socrates (470/469–399 BCE), who is reputed to have said that the "unconsidered life is not worth living." This is, of course, not actually true. Good and useful lives can be lived without much reflection. As we noted in Chapter 2, however, most people seem to be curious about the world, and most people say they agree with the idea that they are better off knowing how things are than not knowing. Even fake facts are worth knowing about because they can have very real consequences when they are used to justify particular policies.

The second response to the grounding problem is to say that even in a world of social facts, it is still possible to see things like the exploitation of the rich by the poor, the domination by the powerful of the weak, and the exclusion of people from all the things people value on the basis of their race, nationality, class, gender, and age. These and other social practices strike us as morally wrong and we should embrace whatever it takes to identify, counter, and put an end to these practices. This embracing of, some say retreat into, a commitment to making the world a better place leads many scholars to move away from seeking an objective account of the world. Objectivity is an illusion, they argue, and neutrality between right and wrong is impossible. Indeed, attempting or pretending to be objective and neutral contribute to keeping things the way they are. This is an understandable response to the world—particularly the world of international relations with its dangers, injustices, and failures. However, it courts the risk of becoming a source of some of those problems itself because, while most people can agree that they are against things like exploitation, domination, and exclusion, they have big disagreements about what constitute examples of them, what their causes are, and what can be done about them. Think of the current angry and polarized politics of some developed states. The problem is not so much that no one knows what is wrong and what is to be done, but that everyone thinks they know what is wrong and what is to be done, and they disagree with each other.

The third response to the grounding problem, and the one which is followed by this textbook, is to acknowledge the critiques of the Post-positivists, particularly about Positivist theorists who claim to know things about social facts in the same way that we know things about brute facts. States, for example, do not have objective national interests which compel them to act in a particular way because states, properly speaking, do not have interests, even an interest in self-preservation. Only people have interests which they choose, or may be forced, to express in certain ways. Having acknowledged those critiques, however, we are still stuck in a world in which social facts like states are capable of having brute and brutish consequences. People acting in their name can disagree and go to war. They can agree and reach a climate treaty. And we are still stuck with doing our best to make sense of all this. Even the most committed people usually attempt to make the best sense they can out of situations, even if only to improve their chances of achieving what they want. Even those who try hardest to be objective and neutral, have biases in how they see the world and what they would like to happen in it. And everyone, at times, holds up their hands in despair at the complexity of the world and the difficulties involved in thinking about it. Most of us engage in all three responses and Post-positivists would tell us to be aware, but not surprised, that this is so.

Key term

grounding   The presentation of social facts as if they were brute facts conforming to properties and laws of the natural world.

Key takeaways

- Post-positivist theories challenge the assumption that social facts can be understood in the same terms as brute facts.
- Post-positivist theories share the same grounding problems that they identify in Positivist theories.
- Post-positivist theories alert us to difficulties in trying to make sense of international relations, but do not absolve us from trying our best to do so.

Exercises

1. How might knowing that the state of which you are a citizen is a constructed social fact influence your attitude to it?

2. What problems might the attempt to remain objective and neutral in making sense of international relations encounter?

3. What problems might the attempt to commit to exposing, critiquing, and righting wrongs in making sense of international relations encounter?

4.6 | The future of Post-positivism in an era of uncertainty

Post-positivism undermines our confidence in the sort of claims which Realists and Liberals make about international relations. Some Post-positivists attempt to substitute moral commitments for scientific truth in organizing their research and teaching, but all of them are struck by the way the big arguments never seem to get settled decisively. They weren't settled when the world was dominated by a few powers with a single, shared civilization. If they were not settled then, how likely are they to be settled now that different centers of power, influence, and ways of seeing things are re-emerging? Indeed, even the scientific model on which the Positivists attempt to base their own theories appears to be severely challenged by a quantum physics which calls into question what appeared to be commonsense about space, time, identity, laws of causation, and regularities of effects. We can see power politics in international relations, but it doesn't quite look like the competition between the great powers in which the Realists say we are more or less trapped. We can see the growth of economic collaboration through regimes and institutions, but it doesn't quite look like the rational and open economic order to which the Liberals said we are and ought to be headed. Perhaps it is better, the Post-positivists suggest, to worry less about which theoretical approach is right, and to focus more on how to live in an uncertain world of multiple orders and multiplying conceptions of what is going on in it. Perhaps so, but what does this involve? As we have seen, the particular arguments of Feminist, Social Constructivist, and English School theorists of international relations reviewed above encounter major problems of their own, some very similar to the criticisms they make of Realists and Liberals. And as we shall see in the following chapters, the world of states and other actors, socially constructed though they all may be, continues to pose problems and puzzles on its own terms which call for investigation and answers.

Recommended reading and viewing

James Der Derian and Michael Shapiro (eds.), *International and Intertextual Relations: Post Modern Readings of World Politics*, New York, 1998.

Barry Buzan and Richard Little, *International Systems in World History: Remaking the Study of International Relations*, Oxford, 2000.

Barry Buzan, *An Introduction to the English School of International Relations*, Cambridge, 2014.

Nicholas Onuf, *Making Sense: Making Worlds: Constructivism in Social Theory and International Relations*, Abingdon, 2013.

James Der Derian, "Critical Theories: Practices of Media," *You Tube* at http://www.youtube.com/watch?v=lzcx9a6lOC8

J. Ann Tickner, *Gender in International Relations: Feminist Perspectives on Achieving Global Security*, New York, 1992.

Valerie M. Hudson, Bonnie Ballif-Spanvill, Mary Caprioli, and Chad F. Emmett, *Sex and World Peace*, New York, 2012.

Notes

1 James Der Derian, *On Diplomacy*, Oxford, 1987, Costas Constantinou, *On the Way to Diplomacy*, Minneapolis, 1996, and Runa Das, *Re-Visiting Nuclear India*, New Delhi, 2015.
2 Robert Cox, "Social Forces, States and World Orders: Beyond International Relations Theory," *Millennium—Journal of International Studies*, 10, 1981, 126–155.
3 Paul Sharp, *Diplomatic Theory of International Relations*, Cambridge, 2009, and Halvard Leira, "A Conceptual History of Diplomacy," in Costas Constantinou, Pauline Kerr, Paul Sharp (eds.), *Sage Handbook of Diplomacy*, London, 2016.
4 Ole Waever, "The Rise and Fall of the Inter-Paradigm Debate," in Steve Smith, Ken Booth, and Marysia Zalewski (eds.), *International Theory: Positivism and Beyond*, Cambridge, 1996.
5 Roy E. Jones, "The English School: a Case for Closure," in *Review of International Studies*, 7, 1, 1981, 1–13, and Barry Buzan, *An Introduction to the English School*, Cambridge, 2014.
6 Hedley Bull, *The Anarchical Society*, London, 1977.
7 John Searle, *The Social Construction of Reality*, London, 1995, Alexander Wendt, *Social Theory of International Politics*, Cambridge, 1999.
8 Michael Billig, *Banal Nationalism*, London, 1995.
9 Jacqui True, "Feminism," in Scott Burchill, Andrew Linklater, Richard Devetak, Jack Donnelly, Terry Nardin, Mathew Peterson, Christian Reus-Smith, and Jacqui True, *Theories of International Relations* (4th edition), Basingstoke, 2009.
10 Carol Cohn, "Sex and Death in the Rational World of Defense Intellectuals," in *Signs: Journal of Women in Culture and Society*, 12, 4, 1987.
11 Francis Fukuyama, *The End of History and the Last Man*, New York, 1993.

5 Foreign policy

Preamble

Even the most Post-positivist of international theorists examined in the last chapter would agree that we appear to live in a world of sovereign states. Most of the rest of us tend to assume that we actually do. There are over 190 sovereign states which vary greatly in terms of their geographical and population sizes, their levels of economic development, their ethnic and cultural homogeneity, and their military strength. Some, like Iceland and the Maldive Islands, have populations no larger than that of a medium-sized North American city, just over 300,000 each. Two of them, China and India, have well over a billion people each, which taken together equals more than thirty-five percent of the world's entire population.

While sovereign states differ in many ways, they share the following. They are all based on territory. They all have people. They all have governments which possess a near monopoly on the means and use of legitimate violence. They are all recognized as sovereign, principally by each other. No one outside these states is legally or politically entitled to tell them what to do unless they give their consent to being told in advance. As we have seen, people argue about how important these states are when compared to other actors. After all, people live in other things too besides states; for example, families, neighborhoods, towns, cities, counties, nations, and non-sovereign states or provinces. People also argue about what is happening to states over time—are they becoming stronger or growing weaker and possibly disappearing—and should we be glad or worried if they are. What nearly everybody agrees on, however, is that when you are studying international relations, the relations between states are important, distinctive, and provide a good place to start. Relations between states are important because some states are the most powerful actors in the world, and because the majority of people see themselves as citizens of a particular state, believe that this is right, and feel that it is good. Relations between states are distinctive because, as relations between sovereigns who recognize no one in authority above them, they are potentially tense, dangerous, and violent. Relations between states provide an obvious place to start, because when we first think about international relations, it is hard to see what else there is to look at besides the relations of states.

Taking these conversations and interactions between states all together, we call them international relations. However, from within a particular state, our own state for example, we talk about them as **foreign policy**. By policy, people sometimes mean a position that they take on a particular issue, for example, when your college says it has a no smoking policy, or the United States government says it has a policy of not talking to terrorists. More often, however, people use the term to mean a goal or set of goals, together with the instruments or means by which they will try to achieve them; for example, the policy goal of getting people not to text while driving, the instruments of establishing fines for doing so, and running TV ads about the consequences of doing so.

We distinguish foreign policy from domestic policy. Domestic policy is conducted inside a state, or what is often called the domestic environment, by its government. As Chris Brown and Kirsten Ainley note, we often assume that after discussions and votes, the government pursues the policy it wants by passing laws which allow it a high degree of control over what happens.[1] Foreign policy, in contrast, is directed abroad towards other states in what we often call the external environment. Governments have a lower level of control in their external environments compared to their domestic environments. They cannot pass laws for the external environment which other states have to obey and so foreign policy is conducted by discussions about the right or smart thing to do, negotiations about trading favors, promises of rewards, threats of punishment, actual rewards or punishments, and sometimes the use of force.

The study of foreign policy examines the following:

- the **foreign policy goals** which states typically pursue;
- the way states make foreign policy decisions about which goals to pursue;
- the foreign policy instruments available to states for achieving the goals they chose.

There exists a tradition of doing **foreign policy analysis** in these terms. As we shall see, however, there also exists a rising tide of questions and doubts about how foreign policy is actually made, whether the differences between foreign policy and domestic policy are becoming increasingly blurred, and whether the idea of foreign policy as it is set out here has much future at all.

5.1 Foreign policy goals or objectives

Learning objectives

1. List the foreign policy goals states typically pursue.
2. Describe the terms in which states think about their security.
3. Explain why independence seems to be a foreign policy goal of declining importance for many states.
4. Explain why economic welfare appears to be a foreign policy goal of increasing importance for most states.

5. List ways in which states seek to increase their international prestige.

6. List some national values which states try to advance as goals of their foreign policies.

Every day we see foreign policy reported and discussed in the news. Usually, however, the focus is on a particular foreign policy of a particular state. What, for example, are the goals or objectives of US foreign policy towards the European Union (EU) on trade, investment, and human rights? What are the goals and objectives of Saudi Arabian foreign policy towards Iran on the future of Syria, control of the Persian Gulf, and the price at which oil and gas trade on international markets?

As students of International Relations and as social scientists, however, we ask if there are general foreign policy goals or objectives in which all states may be said to be interested. What sorts of things do they all typically want from other states in their external environments? It is fairly easy to come up with a general list in these terms. As K.J. Holsti has suggested, all states seem to be interested in maintaining **security**, exercising **independence**, fostering economic **welfare**, and acquiring **prestige**.[2] To these, we can add that all states seem to be interested in promoting their **values**, their ideas about right and wrong. These are very general goals, and they are not achieved only by foreign policy. They provide a useful way of analyzing particular foreign policies, however. Think of the United States' policy of supporting Israel, for example. We can ask how this policy, which involves providing military, economic, and humanitarian assistance, is supposed to serve the United States' security, independence, economic welfare, prestige, and values. We could ask exactly the same questions about China's policy of supporting North Korea and Iran's policy of supporting the Syrian government. So far so good; but as we shall see, what the governments of states mean by security, independence, economic welfare, prestige, and values can change hugely by time, place, and even immediate situations. Then the story of foreign policy goals becomes a bit more complicated.

An important, some scholars and many politicians say *the most* important, foreign policy goal is security. Feeling secure means feeling unthreatened. Security then is a psychological or emotional state experienced by individuals on behalf of themselves and those for whom they are responsible. What makes people feel secure and what they regard as threats to their security can vary considerably. Think about walking home across campus late at night after a long study session in the library. Depending on who you are: man; woman; white person; black person; young person; or old person, and depending on what kind of campus you are on: large; small; private; public; inner city; rural, you might feel quite insecure and take steps to counter this, or you might not even recognize your late night walk as a security situation at all.

States and their governments vary like this too. Luxembourg, a tiny state surrounded by more powerful neighbors, barely worries about being attacked, partly because the neighborhood is friendly and partly because it believes that nothing it could do, for example expanding its armed forces or acquiring nuclear weapons, would make it more secure. Russia, on the other hand, a large and powerful state, spends a great deal of time worrying about its security even though it is more powerful than all its neighbors, because its history suggests both that it is vulnerable to attacks and is capable of fighting them off if it makes the effort.

Americans, Russians, geography, and security

Historically Americans have felt safe. Their immediate neighbors (Native Americans, Mexicans, and Canadians) have been weaker than them in military terms. Two oceans lie between them and more serious rivals. Historically, Russians have felt insecure. They were originally weaker than their neighbors in military terms and no oceans, mountain ranges, or river systems provide effective natural barriers behind which Russians can shelter.

With relatively little military effort, Americans extended their control across North America because they could and they thought it was right. With a massive military effort, Russians extended their control into Europe and across Asia because they thought they had to if they were going to survive. Historians argue about how their different experiences have shaped American and Russian attitudes to security. Americans expect to feel secure, for example, but seem to have less tolerance of threat levels which other states would regard as normal, especially after shocks like Pearl Harbor and 9–11. Russians expect to feel insecure, but the measures they have taken to correct this—big armies, expansionist policies and a suspicious view of the world—arguably have made them more insecure by frightening their neighbors.

Historically, governments have seen the security of their states in largely military terms and worried about preventing threats to their territory, people, values, beliefs, and to the leaders themselves. By securing the state and themselves, governments have argued, they secure all these other things. The most obvious way in which states have tried to increase their security is by building up their own armed forces to deter other states from attacking them and to compel other states to do what they want. In addition, Holsti suggests they have attempted four basic foreign policy strategies to make themselves stronger and, thus, more secure: isolation, neutrality, expansion, and alignment.

Isolation involves a deliberate attempt to cut off, or keep to a minimum, all your contacts with other states. The basic assumption is that the fewer contacts others have with you, the fewer reasons they will have for getting into arguments with you. It is an unusual approach which depends on the government's ability to block foreigners and control its own people. Geography, for example, made it possible for the United States to isolate itself from European affairs during its first hundred years (although it did not isolate itself from other parts of the world). Just about every single development in the technologies of warfare, travel, and communication has made it increasingly difficult and unattractive to attempt to achieve security by a policy of isolation, however. Even states which can be seen trying to pursue a policy of isolation like Myanmar (Burma), until recently, and North Korea, find it difficult and seek at least some links with the outside world.

Isolation (*Sakoku*): the case of Japan

In 1543 a Portuguese ship made the first known European contact with the Japanese islands. It was followed by ships from other European powers bringing adventurers, traders, and missionaries who made the unstable politics of Japan worse with their soldiers' guns, their traders' goods and their missionaries' unsettling messages. After a while, the local authorities decided these contacts were too disruptive and might enable the Europeans to take over. They steadily reduced them until by the early 1700s only one ship—a Portuguese—was allowed a year, ordinary Japanese were forbidden contact with the Europeans, and those who held on to their new Christian faith were persecuted. The policy of *Sakoku* lasted until the mid-1800s when, by a combination of threats and promises, a US navy squadron under Commodore Perry persuaded the Japanese to open up their harbors and enter into diplomatic and trade agreements with the US and, subsequently, the European great power states.

Neutrality was originally a legal status that a state claimed in regard to a war between other states in which it did not want to participate. It involved rights like being able to trade peacefully with those involved in the war, and duties like not providing anything to them which would give them an advantage in the fighting. However, the concept was extended from the 19th century onwards to also mean a policy by which a state had full political, economic, and diplomatic relations with other states but which refused to participate in wars other than direct attacks on themselves and refused to join alliances in peacetime. The basic assumptions were that by joining wars, you made them worse and that by joining alliances, you made wars more likely. Switzerland and Sweden are examples of what became known as "permanent neutrality." Ireland is an example of a state whose neutrality can be seen as a protest policy, in this case resulting from what it saw as the continued occupation of Irish territory by its most likely ally, Britain. And Austria and Laos can be seen as examples of externally imposed neutrality resulting from agreements among rival great powers to leave them alone. The Non-Aligned Movement established by newly-independent states in the 1950s provides an example of a group of states cooperating to keep out of a particular conflict, in this case the Cold War.

Neutrality: the cases of Belgium and Switzerland

Governments can choose a policy in the way that people can choose a course of action, but this doesn't mean it is going to work. In 1914, Belgium had a policy of neutrality in the arguments between Germany and France.

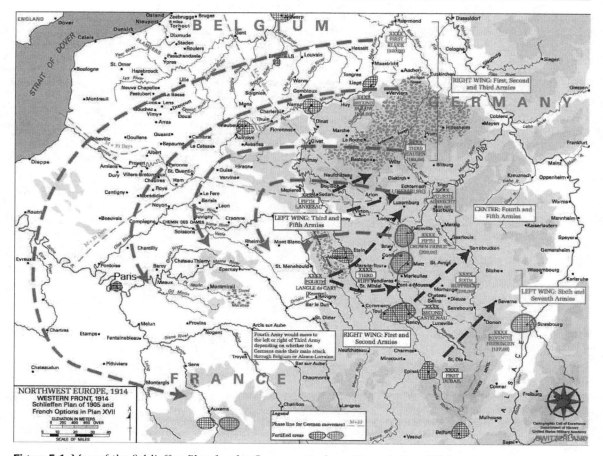

Figure 5.1 Map of the Schlieffen Plan for the German attack on France before 1914

(Source: http://en.wikipedia.org/wiki/File:Schlieffen_Plan.jpg Permission granted by the Department of History, United States Military Academy)

Note: This map shows how the German troops (light gray arrows) planned to move across Belgium and Luxembourg to get behind the French forces and strike at Paris.

It could not keep out of World War I, however, because Germany's war plans involved sending its troops across Belgian territory, thus violating its neutrality (see Figure 5.1). In the 1930s, Belgium, alarmed by the failure of the League of Nations to protect small states from big ones, shifted its policy from collective security to neutrality again. In 1940, the Germans invaded France again by passing through Belgian territory, albeit on a different line of attack (see Figure 5.2).

It is hard for a state to be neutral if it lies on the invasion routes of a more powerful state, unless its territory is difficult to cross and/or it maintains large armed forces. Switzerland has successfully maintained its neutrality since 1815 even though it lies on important communications routes from northern to southern Europe. These routes run through and under the Alps, and the Swiss have maintained strong armed forces. This combination has made others more wary of attacking them.

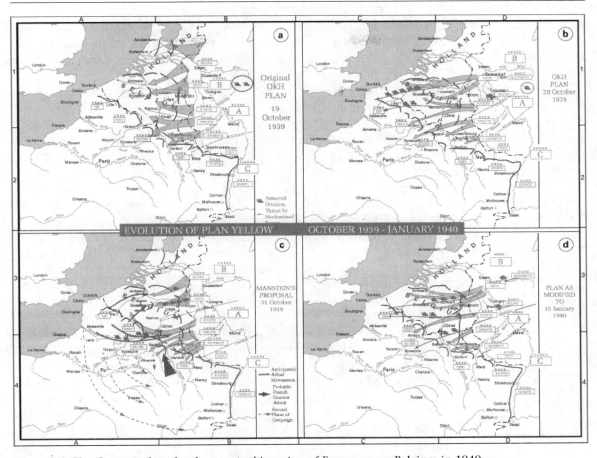

Figure 5.2 The German plans for the eventual invasion of France across Belgium in 1940

(Source: https://en.wikipedia.org/wiki/File:Evolution_of_Plan_Yellow.PNG Permission granted by the Department of History, United States Military Academy)

Neutrality has become a difficult policy for the same sorts of reasons which have made isolation hard to pursue, because of the moral issues raised by staying out of a war widely regarded as just (against the Nazis, for example), and because of the tendency of the great powers to ignore the neutrality of small states when it suited them in both the world wars of the 20th century.

Alignment involves a state reaching an agreement with one (bilateral) or more (multilateral) other states about how to deal with a common security threat. By combining their strength, the states in alliances make themselves stronger, but at the price of losing some of their freedom of action to their alliance partners. Originally, alliances were just promises recorded on documents, to take specific actions in specific circumstances, usually if one of the parties to the alliance was attacked. There are strong alliances like the bilateral ones between the old Soviet Union and its communist allies in Eastern Europe. These said if one state was attacked, the other would join the fight against the attacker. There are weak alliances like the multilateral agreement between the 28 members of the North

Atlantic Treaty Organization (NATO). Article Five of the North Atlantic Treaty says that the member states regard an attack on one of their number as an attack on all of them, but it commits them only to consult with each other about what to do. They are not committed on paper to fighting, although they probably would. Note that the use of "weak" and "strong" here refers to the degree of commitment the members make to each other, not the overall strength or power of the alliance.

NATO is interesting in that it shows the shift from the old sort of alliance—an agreement on a piece of paper—to so-called standing alliances with armed forces permanently in position and big military and civilian bureaucracies engaged in planning and practicing for how to deal with an attack. Before World War II, it was assumed that there would always be a period of time between a declaration of war and serious fighting while the armies got into position to attack. The use of airpower and mechanized forces during World War II suggested, however, that attacks could come almost instantaneously and at any moment. Alliances had to be permanently ready to fight, therefore, because there would be no time to prepare once the shooting started. NATO is also interesting for other reasons. First, it shows how some of the hottest political arguments take place, not between alliances, but inside them, especially when some members of an alliance are richer and more powerful than others. Politicians in the United States, most recently President Trump, frequently complain that America's allies are coming up short in terms of sharing the burden of providing troops and funding. Only three of NATO's members have managed to reach the alliance target of spending two percent of GNP on defense recently (see Table 5.1). Politicians in the other NATO members frequently complain that the United States expects their support but ignores their input into policy discussions.

It is important to note that people argue about the accuracy and significance of figures such as these. NATO shows how most states, even rich, developed states like Britain, France, and Germany, cannot afford to maintain large armed forces with state of the art military equipment on their own. As we shall see in Chapter 7, they increasingly have to pool their resources.

Secondly, NATO is interesting because it also shows how changing conceptions of security can change the role of alliances. Originally, NATO was

Table 5.1 Defense spending, select great power states 2015

Country	Billions of US Dollars	Global Percentage	GDP Percentage
US	596,010	35.5	3.3
China	210,493	12.5	1.9
Russia	66,419	4	4.9
United Kingdom	53,862	3.1	1.9
France	55,342	3.2	2.2
Germany	40,985	2.3	1.2
World Total	1,676,000	100	2.6

(*Source*: Spending totals and GDP percentages obtained from *Sipri Yearbook*, 2016 "Military Expenditure Database" at https://www.sipri.org/databases/milex)

created to deter an attack on Western Europe by the Soviet Union and its allies, and to fight off such an attack if deterrence failed. How to pursue this traditional task in an era of increasingly destructive nuclear weapons posed a problem it never quite solved, but fortunately never had to. NATO also had a mission to socialize its members into a successful, like-minded community of liberal states enjoying good relations with each other under the leadership of the United States. With the collapse of the Soviet Union, the deterrence and defense mission faded, at least in Europe, and the socialization mission, especially in regard to shrinking and democratizing the armed forces of former communist states in Eastern Europe, came to the fore. Now, NATO's socialization mission has been folded into the war against terrorists and Taliban in Afghanistan, far away from its original area of operations. Yet just to complicate matters, Russia's invasion of the Crimea and its intervention in other parts of the Ukraine in 2014 have got NATO planners thinking once again about how to protect its members—this time, Poland, Latvia, Lithuania, and Estonia.

We can identify two ways, therefore, in which security as a foreign policy goal is changing. First, security in the traditional sense of defending against other states has become too expensive for all but a few states to undertake on their own. At the moment, only the United States can develop and afford the very best weapons and forces across the board, and there are signs that even it is feeling the economic strain of doing so. Secondly, the way people think about security has broadened beyond the traditional military sense to ideas like human security, economic security, and environmental security (see Chapters 12 and 14). Viewed benignly, this process of securitization can be seen as getting foreign policy past worrying about the Russians, the Chinese, or the Americans as potential enemies, to thinking about how we should address the things which make human beings in any part of the world feel insecure. Less benignly, securitization can be seen as subordinating every sphere of human life to our own state's national security.

The foreign policy goal of independence was once assumed to be as, or more, important than security. In the formal sense of a state having the right to do what it wants, this is still the case. In the practical sense of being actually able to do what it wants by its own efforts, the picture is not quite so clear. Independence is a bit like wealth. Many peoples who don't have it crave it as the answer to their problems, while those who have it say it's not all it's cracked up to be. Independence, in the sense of not being under the orders of any higher authority and being free to make one's own decisions, has been the jealously guarded hallmark of sovereign states. Actions which impinged on the independence of a state, for example when the armed forces of another state entered its territory, airspace or waters, or when the ambassador of one state intervened in another by expressing a preference for a particular political candidate during an election, are still regarded as grave matters. The Turkish air force shot down a Russian military jet in 2015 after it had been in their airspace for 17 seconds, although the reasons why they did this remain complicated.

Pakistan and US drone strikes

The US, and increasingly other states, use pilotless aircraft known as drones. Their controllers can be hundreds or thousands of miles away. Drones can provide images of the territory they fly over and they can launch rockets to kill people and destroy property. The US uses drone strikes to attack Taliban and Al Qaeda leaders whose followers wage guerilla and terrorist campaigns in Afghanistan, Pakistan, Yemen, and elsewhere.

The Pakistan government is embarrassed by these attacks when they take place in its airspace without its agreement, especially when they kill innocent people. Pakistan asks the US to stop the drone strikes, saying they violate its sovereignty and independence, and make it look weak in the eyes of its own people. The US refuses, saying the drone strikes might not be necessary if the Pakistan government would fight the terrorists more effectively itself. The Pakistan government cannot stop the drone strikes and cannot fight the terrorists more effectively without great risk to itself. Its independence is doubly challenged, therefore, by the strikes and by its inability to stop them or make them unnecessary.

The processes by which most states today became independent involved the use or threat of at least some force, and on occasions a great deal of bloodshed. And many peoples who do not have an independent state of their own; for example, the Palestinians and the Kurds pursue independence policies for which they think it is worth fighting.

Jews, Palestinians, and a state of their own

The ideology of nationalism developed in 19th-century Europe. It said the world was divided into nations, and that each nation needed its own state so it could be independent and develop to its full potential. The Zionist Movement among the Jewish people took this message to heart. Centuries after most of the Jews had been dispersed from Palestine, the Zionists argued the Jews needed an independent state back in their old homeland if they were to escape persecution and manage their own destiny. This message became stronger after the slaughter of European Jews during the Holocaust in World War II, and the independent state of Israel was declared in Palestine after the war in 1948. As the plight of the Pakistanis suggests above, having an independent state of their own may not solve all a people's problems. Most Israelis would probably agree today, but the message remains a powerful one. Very few Israelis would want to give up their independence, and their Palestinian neighbors, watching Israel's success, have taken the lesson to heart. They have no chance, most Palestinians believe, of avoiding being pushed around and developing their full potential until they satisfy their goal to be independent in a state of their own.

Nevertheless, in developed states at least, independence does not seem to be as important a foreign policy goal as it was in the past. People have become more aware of the distinction between independence in the formal sense of their state having its own flag and postage stamps, and independence in the practical sense of their state, not only having the right to go its own way, but the ability to actually do so too.

Canadian independence

Canada is a sovereign state with its own independent constitution, system of law, money, and armed forces. Situated next to the US, however, a state which is over ten times its size in all respects except actual territory, some Canadians worry "Are we 'really' independent when our economy and defense are locked into a North American system dominated by the US?" The answer, of course, is yes. Canada is independent and this lets it decide important things—its health care policy, its firearms policy, its Cuban policy, and its banking policy, for example—in ways which California or New York cannot. However, there is virtually no important policy decision a Canadian government can make without carefully considering how it might affect US–Canada relations.

More importantly, and as we shall see in the next section, the other things which states want, most notably economic growth and prosperity, seem to involve them making sacrifices in terms of their political independence. This is not to say that independence is no longer an important goal of foreign policy. When states believe their sovereignty has been clearly violated, this will usually produce a strong response. Germany, for example, was angry when the US Congress passed legislation in 2017 which would make it possible to punish German companies for ignoring US sanctions on trade with Russia. We will trade with whom we want, Germans said. Similarly, Iran responded angrily when the UN told it that it was not allowed to process uranium in the way many other states do. Iranians claimed their state was being picked on unfairly.

One of the biggest challenges to independence as a foreign policy goal is the concern of every government with economic welfare. For most states in the world, the reason they have a foreign policy is to help advance the economic interests of the state and its citizens. Two hundred years ago, this would have seemed a strange thing to say in most states. Governments were supposed to be concerned with the security of their citizens, protecting them from law-breakers at home and foreign invasion. Economics—the processes by which wealth is created, exchanged, and distributed—was supposed to take care of itself. This was never completely the case. Individuals, companies and banks always lobbied their governments for help, for example, in protecting shipping, trading posts, and access to resources. Governments have always been interested in the economy as a source of resources and revenues through taxation, especially in times of war to build ships, create armies, and pay soldiers and sailors. Even when their foreign policies started to take on economic priorities in the 19th century, however, their status was subordinated to security concerns. The so-called "high politics" of war and diplomacy, was the concern of monarchs, nobles, and the most talented diplomats. The "low politics" of boosting exports and seeking foreign investment in the national economy was supposedly left to those of more modest talent and background.

Exporting washing machines for Britain

As late as the mid-20th century, the British (and others) saw Britain as a great power with global responsibilities, although its international position had declined since the heyday of the British Empire. Even so, people began to realize that its future living standards and power would depend on it competing successfully in the international economy. As a result, the British Foreign and Diplomatic Services were told they must devote more time to seeking markets for British exports and attracting foreign investment to the British economy to create jobs. At the time, stories surfaced of British ambassadors who had enjoyed the prestige and excitement of negotiating with world leaders on issues of world importance proclaiming that they had not joined the Service in order to help export washing machines for foreigners to buy! The stories are almost certainly apocryphal, even if they captured a mood. Today, however, few professional diplomats of any state would dare to say that helping boost exports was not a big and important part of their job.

In most states, this snobbery has almost disappeared. Governments proclaim improving their state's economic position in the world as their primary objective. They re-arrange and re-name their government departments concerned with foreign policy to reflect these shifting priorities, and an almost reverse snobbery of disavowing that they are still engaged in the old, dirty business of pursuing political and military advantage has crept in. There are three different but interlocking reasons for this change and the rise of economic concerns in foreign policy.

First, we can point to the rise of democratic and popular expectations since the political, social, and technological revolutions in America, France, and Britain respectively at the turn of the 18th and 19th centuries, and the 20th-century revolt against empires and colonialism. Since that time, governments have increasingly needed to secure the support of their citizens by claiming that they can help improve their economic circumstances. Even the religious theocracy in Iran and the communist dictatorship in North Korea claim to serve the economic needs of their citizens (although the latter more-or-less lies in this regard).

Second, over the same period, military competitiveness has increasingly come to depend on the wealth and technological innovation that only a developed economy can provide. The two great communist powers, the Soviet Union and China, embarked on their economic reforms in the second half of the 20th century partly to provide their peoples with better lives, but also because their leaders believed their states could not compete either economically or militarily unless these economic reforms were made.

Third, and over the same period again, it became increasingly clear to governments that if they wanted developed economies, their people needed access to the goods, services, capital, markets, workers, investment opportunities, technology, and knowledge to be found outside their own territory. Without this international economic dimension, even the biggest national economies would not grow as fast as the ones which had it, and the smaller national economies would not grow at all.

In short, if governments wanted to be loved by their own people and feared, or respected, by foreigners, they needed developed economies which could provide the necessary consumer goods and military power. If they wanted developed economies, however, they needed access and openness to the production, trade, and investment of the rest of the world. Priorities varied by states. As the costs of staying in the front rank of military power increased, more and more states have joined a majority which sees its foreign policy in primarily economic terms. Ask the diplomats of any state, powerful or not, how they spend their working days and they will likely say they spend them mostly looking for two things: export markets for their state's goods and services, and investments which will create jobs back home. How they and their governments do this, we will examine in more detail in Chapters 9 and 10.

Strong military power and high levels of wealth and standards of living contribute to the foreign policy goal of prestige or reputation. States, or more accurately their governments and people, value their reputations because we all tend to be both vain and moral beings. Most of us want to be admired for being successful, attractive and good, and we tend to think that a strong reputation in these regards will make it easier for us to get what we want. States value their reputations in the same way. Prestige, then, is an old term for an aspect of what today is often called soft power (see p. 118). States acquire prestige in different ways. The United States and the Soviet Union, for example, both impressed the world with their space programs which demonstrated their scientific achievements and, slightly more subtly, their military power. Canada enjoys a reputation for providing even-handed technical and logistical assistance to United Nations peacekeeping operations. Sweden and the Netherlands are thought of as being generous in terms of their overseas development programs. China and South Africa recently joined an exclusive club of states who are able to put on world sporting events by hosting the Olympic Games and Association Football's World Cup competition.

The best prestige comes as a byproduct of being successful. Sometimes states are admired for things to which they barely pay attention themselves. For example, foreigners often admire the sheer convenience of modern life in the US (which Americans often assume is standard until they go elsewhere), the efficiency of the Germans (a view which many Germans do not share of themselves), and the ease with which Chinese gather in their neighborhoods to play games, take exercise and chat (something they just go ahead and do without much organizing). As with people, so with states, however, the temptation exists to undertake certain policies in order to acquire a reputation. The Soviet Union, for example, developed big warships which could show the flag in all the oceans of the world at a time when its economy was in great trouble. Many other governments regarded these ships as an unnecessary luxury which the Soviet Union could ill-afford. Some people, like the current leader of the British Labour Party, Jeremy Corbyn, regard the British and French nuclear forces in the same way, as misguided and useless efforts to show that both states are still in the major leagues when it comes to military power. An argument against the US withdrawing from Viet Nam in the early 1970s (and from Afghanistan today) was that it looked like defeat, and this could hurt American prestige and US influence.

The best example of a policy where prestige and reputation seem to be drivers rather than byproducts is perhaps offered by North Korea's nuclear and conventional military programs. Hundreds of thousands of soldiers, thousands of armored vehicles, hundreds of short- and medium-range missiles, together with an unreliable nuclear weapons program, are all maintained, while the state has difficulty feeding its people and keeping them warm. There is no doubt that the North Koreans feel threatened, but their defense efforts are reminiscent of a young man who starves himself and lives on the street in order to own and maintain an old and unreliable Corvette. Even when the car runs well, everyone is mindful of the struggle and sacrifice which is being made to keep something which he cannot really afford.

The foreign policy goals of security, independence, economic welfare, and prestige which all states pursue may be thought of in terms of state or national interests. In addition, however, governments talk about promoting the values of their peoples as foreign policy goals of states. Here is a value that we support and live by, they say, and the world would be a better place if everyone lived by this value. Thus, human rights, free markets, sustainable development, and political democracy are said to be goals of nearly every state in the world at present. In the past, peace, order, socialism, Christianity, and many other values were all put forward as foreign policy goals of states.

As we have seen in Chapter 2, Realists advise us to be suspicious when governments talk of values because of their view of people and states as self-interested power-seekers. When governments talk values, Realists say, they are either reformulating interests in moral terms, or talking hypocritical humbug. Certainly, governments like it when they have a chance to present a policy as both an interest and a value, a bit like the commercials for health bars which say "tasty and good for you too." On occasions, however, governments seem to do things in their foreign policy simply because it seems to be the right thing to do. And Realists don't have a good answer to why governments talk in terms of values and morals if it is actually true that we are all nothing but self-interested power-seekers. If that were so, why would governments bother to talk in terms of values and doing good, and why would we bother to listen?

Freedom and democracy from 30,000 feet

In the 1990s the Yugoslavian state disintegrated into its national and ethnic components, and the republics which had made it up became independent through a series of civil wars and massacres—plus interventions by outside powers. The final chapter in this process involved Kosovo, a province of Serbia in which ethnic Albanians, also called Kosovars, were in the majority and ethnic Serbs were in the minority. The majority campaigned and some of them carried out acts of violence in order to gain independence from Serbia on grounds of national self-determination. The Serbian government attempted to crush the campaign with intimidation and violence.

When the UN could not agree to act, NATO launched a bombing campaign against Serb forces in Kosovo and militarily significant targets in the rest of Serbia. They argued that these bombing attacks from a safe height of 30,000 feet above the Serbs' anti-aircraft systems would prevent war crimes and a humanitarian catastrophe as people fled the state. The policy was successful and controversial because it involved killing some people to save others. It also appeared to be a great power response to small power defiance. The main motive of the policy, however, seems to have been to save lives and to defeat those who threatened them. Few other motives, other than the desire to be seen to be saving lives, explain NATO's policy for there was little of military or economic value in Kosovo or Serbia.

We can see then that states pursue a variety of foreign policy goals. Each foreign policy action they take, however, can be analyzed in terms of the way it may serve all or some of these goals. For example, President Obama's 2011 decision to support the rebels in Libya against the government could be seen in terms of serving security (weakening a supporter of terrorists), welfare (securing Libyan oil supplies), and values (protecting ordinary Libyans' human rights). How the policy was supposed to serve American independence and prestige, however, is perhaps less clear. Presumably these were not key foreign policy goals in this particular case. Remember also that satisfying foreign policy goals often involves trade-offs. President Obama's Libyan policy made gains in security and values (the destruction of an unpredictable leader who was violating human rights) at the expense of welfare and prestige goals (the fighting cost money and the US let others lead the military operations after the original attacks). Now, as it turns out, it is not particularly clear how anybody's security has been strengthened by the removal of the Libyan leader Gaddafi, since Libya has descended into a chaos which is producing refugees and helping terrorists.

Key terms

foreign policy The goals or position which a state sets for itself in its external environment and the instruments by which it tries to obtain those goals or maintain its position.

foreign policy analysis The study of foreign policy in International Relations, usually focused on foreign policy goals, foreign policy decision-making, and the foreign policy instruments by which foreign policy is implemented.

foreign policy goals What states typically want from their external environment.

independence   The ability to act as one chooses or the formal right to try to do so by being sovereign. As a foreign policy goal, states typically try to maintain their freedom of action and avoid violations of their formal sovereignty.

prestige   Reputation and usually a strong reputation for being good at things or possessing qualities which others value and admire. As a foreign policy goal, states typically seek to increase their prestige in the eyes of other states and peoples as a good in itself and on the assumption that other states and peoples are more likely to cooperate with states and people they admire.

security   The absence of a sense of threat. As a foreign policy goal, states typically seek to reduce the threat from their external environment

values   Beliefs about what is good and the right way in which to live to best achieve what is good. As a foreign policy goal, states typically try to promote some of their own values as being good for other states and peoples. States also promote their own values on the assumption that they will be more successful in an external environment in which other states and people share those values.

welfare   Material (economic), psychological, and possibly spiritual wellbeing. As a foreign policy goal, states typically seek to increase their economic prosperity and the economic prosperity of their citizens.

Key takeaways

- States pursue foreign policy in their external environments.
- The external environment is different from the internal or domestic environment of states. States do not control the external environment.
- States pursue a variety of foreign policy goals or objectives: security, independence, economic welfare, prestige, and values.
- Every foreign policy action can analyzed in terms of the extent to which it serves each of these goals.
- Foreign policy actions often involve trade-offs between different foreign policy goals.

Exercises

1. In what ways do states attempt to satisfy their foreign policy security goal?
2. What are states doing when they promote their values through their foreign policies? How would a Realist answer this question? How would a Liberal answer this question?

5.2 Foreign policy decision-making

Learning objectives

1. Describe the assumptions of the rational actor model of decision-making.
2. Explain how psychological factors influence foreign policy decision-making.
3. Explain how organizational factors influence foreign policy decision-making.
4. List some of the major institutional participants in foreign policy decision-making.

We have a general answer to the first big question in foreign policy analysis concerning the goals which states typically pursue. The second big question in foreign policy analysis concerns how governments decide which goals to pursue and how to pursue them. In many respects, the study of **foreign policy decision-making** is just a subset of the study of how people—either as individuals or in groups—make decisions. The main question is why a person chose one particular course of action and not another or others. It may help, therefore, to think about you, your family, or your college, making decisions about security, independence, economic welfare, prestige, and values in the course of a day. When, how, and why do you make such decisions? What factors affect how you do this? Indeed, to what extent do you actually make explicit decisions, as opposed to drifting along in a current which seems to play a bigger part in shaping what you do than any decisions you actually make yourself?

Foreign policy analysis offers a number of ways of answering these sorts of questions for states. Sometimes it takes a leaf out of the pages of the diplomatic historians' playbook and tries to reconstruct all the circumstances of a clear, high profile, and an important foreign policy decision or set of decisions. There are libraries of books devoted to examining the decision of each of the great powers to go to war in 1914. As a result, we have learned a lot about the decisions which were made in the run up to that war, but not as much about why decisions led to war in this crisis but not in previous crises. Nor does our knowledge of the decisions leading up to war in 1914 necessarily tell us much about what sorts of decisions might be made if a big crisis between the US and China or Russia, for example, broke out tomorrow.

Foreign policy analysis has also looked to the economists and psychologists for insights about foreign policy decisions. These offer a number of models of how decisions are made. Note that a model is a small-scale simplification, like the aircraft kits that children (and some adults) build. You can't have a life-sized working model, for it would be the real thing. Social scientists who use decision-making models acknowledge that they do not capture the whole reality of what is going on in decision-making. Instead, they suggest these models either highlight the essential part of what is going on or they exaggerate a particular aspect of what is going on so we can see it more clearly.

Rational actor models of people's behavior begin by assuming that people have clear sets of preferences about what they want, and that they decide among options available to them the best one in terms of it giving them what they want. Notice the word **rational** is used in a narrow sense here. It says nothing about the reasonableness or morality of people's preferences. Ayatollahs, dictators, presidents, and prime ministers can all be rational so long as they believe that what they choose to do will deliver what they want. Prospect theory models, in contrast, focus not on people's goals so much as what they think the short-term consequences of different risky choices will be.[3] As noted on p. 96, for example, US governments kept fighting the Viet Nam war not because they thought they could win in the middle to long term, but because they could see very big costs occurring in the short term if they pulled out. Both approaches, however, share the idea of human beings calculating outcomes before acting.

Several objections can be made to assumptions about rationality. The first objection to the rational actor model is that people and governments sometimes have preferences and assumptions which are so strong that in a process referred to as cognitive dissonance they ignore evidence which challenges both. Joseph Stalin, the Soviet leader in World War II, thought he understood the German leader Hitler and believed he would not attack the Soviet Union before a certain date. Stalin's foreign policy goal was to build up Soviet strength so that when he was ready, he could strike the first blow against the Nazis if he wanted. His diplomats, spies, and foreign governments told him his assumptions about Hitler were wrong. The Germans were going to attack first, but this did not fit with Stalin's plans. As the German forces built up on the frontier and even after the attack began with bombing and shelling, Stalin could not accept that he had been wrong, and he initially hesitated over giving the order to shoot back even as the Germans attacked. Stalin seems to have had a complete nervous breakdown once he accepted he was wrong and took several weeks to recover. President George W. Bush said he firmly believed in 2003 that Iraq under Saddam Hussein possessed weapons of mass destruction (WMD) and was supporting international terrorist groups. UN arms control inspectors, foreign diplomats, and most friendly governments maintained this was not the case. Even America's own intelligence agencies were doubtful. Bush and his advisors, however, decided to proceed with the attack on Iraq. They maintained their belief that Saddam had WMD. They dealt with the objections by saying that even if he possibly didn't have WMD, the slightest chance that he might have them after all justified the attack. President Bush and his advisors were surprised when no WMD were found. Some of his advisors even maintained they must have been smuggled out of Iraq just in time to Syria.

A second objection to the rational actor model is that people and governments do not always have clear sets of preferences, and they cannot clearly see the options available. Psychologists note, for example, that how our perceptions of the world and what we want from it are made up is a complex and selective process.[4] In times of stress, like international crises for example, the need to "do something" becomes more urgent. People's sense of their options narrows, and they don't examine all of them. Instead, in a process Herbert Simon called **satisficing**, they examine them one after another until a "good enough" option comes up.[5] This is particularly the case when groups have to make decisions. Group think, as Irving Janis called it, concentrates on building up consensus and casting out objectors, rather than on reaching the best decision in the way the rational actor model suggests they should.[6] Recent work in clinical psychology also suggests that there is a great deal of brain activity of which we are barely aware going on when we engage in interactions with other people, creating, for example, empathy and trust, on some occasions, and their precise opposite on others.[7]

Graham Allison and the Cuban Missile Crisis

In 1962, the Soviet Union attempted to place nuclear-tipped intermediate-range missiles on the island of Cuba, its ally, to threaten the United States. The Soviet leader, Khrushchev's decision to do this was a classic case of "satisficing." He wanted to show the Cubans that the Soviet Union was a good ally. He wanted to keep his generals happy. They were complaining that the Soviet Union was falling behind the US in long-range missiles because of Khrushchev's spending on the domestic economy, and he needed a quick fix to the problem that the Soviet Union's long-range missiles were unreliable and few in number. Therefore cheaper, more reliable intermediate-range missiles which the Soviet Union already had, placed on Cuba seemed the answer to several prayers.

However, Khrushchev had not paid sufficient attention to how the US under President Kennedy would respond to this move. Kennedy said the Soviet Union had to remove the missiles or the Americans would do it for them, a step that would have involved war, and possibly a nuclear war. The United States Navy blockaded Cuba to prevent more supplies arriving and, after a few days of very tense negotiations, the Soviet Union agreed to withdraw the missiles in return for a series of, what the Americans maintained were, minor concessions.

Allison's study of the decisions made by both sides during the crisis is a classic. What makes it even more interesting is the fact that President Kennedy and his advisors had paid attention to what the experts had said about decision-making. They tried to set up a decision process that would be as rational as possible. Even so, Allison demonstrated that the rational actor aspects of the process were continually modified by the effects of bureaucratic politics and organizational processes.

At times, for example, the army, navy, and air force bureaucracies seemed more interested in competing with each other for influence than seeking the best policy. They all wanted the leading role in whatever was decided upon. And on occasions, options were ruled out or not even considered because of the standard operating procedures by which organizations responded to requests. The decision to rule out airstrikes because of high civilian casualties, for example, was heavily influenced by estimates based on European population densities rather than Cuban ones because that was the information the Air Force had available and provided when asked.

Allison's study confused generations of undergraduates by suggesting that the **bureaucratic politics** model with its turf wars and **organizational process** model with its standard operating procedures provided lenses or models which competed with the rational actor model to explain how policy is produced. They don't compete; they alert us to the factors which may modify the ability of people to behave like rational actors. In 2003, for example, the US policy planning group responsible for figuring out how to govern Iraq after it was occupied was divided between a majority who thought the occupation would not present great problems and a minority that thought the problems would be so big that it might not be a good idea to invade. People from the Defense Department took the majority view. People from the State Department took the minority view. The majority won because the Defense Department was more powerful. Eventually the State Department people stopped getting invitations to the meetings because, as studies of groupthink suggest, it is hard for a group to reach decisions when some of its members don't share the basic assumptions. Also, it should be remembered that Allison's models are more useful in some settings—the United States with its divided powers and responsibilities for example—than in others, and on some issues—old-fashioned, clear-cut great power crises, for example—than others. Nevertheless, Allison's impact on how we think about foreign policy decisions is profound.

Rational actor theorists, and those who follow them in foreign policy analysis, are aware of these difficulties. They try to allow for them in their case studies. More importantly, perhaps, they ask how are we to study decisions if we do not assume that people are at least trying to be rational in terms of having preferences about ends and choosing means that they believe will achieve them. If most people and the governments of states are not even attempting to behave as rational actors, then there is little point in studying them and they will not listen to what we have to tell them. Better to assume that governments are trying to be rational. Just remember two things. Rationality can be used in the service of all sorts of foreign policy goals—both good and bad—and the difficulties of the environment in which foreign policy is made make many foreign policy decisions look irrational from the outside.

The presidents, prime ministers, secretaries of state, and government agencies involved in foreign policy decision-making operate in an environment with many political and societal influences. Governments have to consider their own legislatures and the legislative committees, especially those which have responsibilities for following foreign policy, defense policy, and economic policy. The influence of these differs by state. In presidential systems like the US, they can be more important, especially when the president is not of the same political party as the majority party in the legislature. In parliamentary systems, the legislative influence is usually less, and in dictatorships it is often confined to a rubber stamping role.

In society at large too, there are a wide variety of groups and individuals which seek to influence foreign policy, sometimes in general, but usually on particular issues. Companies with a large market in a foreign state will work for good relations with it. General Motors, for example, has big operations in China and wants the US to have good relations with China. Toyota has big operations in the US and will want Japan to have good relations with the US. Companies which depend on exports will look to keep trade as open as possible, as will companies which depend on imports. Companies whose markets and suppliers are mainly at home, in contrast, will look for protection from imports, especially if they are having a tough time competing. For example, US companies which use lots of steel want good steel at a good price no matter where it is made, but US companies which produce steel do not like cheap steel imports from abroad which they argue are being "dumped" at a loss to their producer. All of these companies and their foreign partners attempt to influence the government's foreign policy by lobbying key decision-makers and legislators.

So, too, do a host of other issue-driven groups and individuals who care about, for example, human rights or working conditions everywhere or in a particular foreign state, environmental concerns across the globe, or good relations with the people of a state which is in poor relations with their own. Many Americans, for example, tried to keep contacts with Cuban, Russian, and Iranian citizens at times when their states' government-to-government relations were bad. The expansion of information and the breakdown of the barrier between foreign and domestic policy and issues have both contributed greatly to the increasing number of attempts by companies, groups, and individuals to influence the foreign policies of their states. Their levels of success vary by state, type of actor, and issue, however, and academics argue about the amount of importance with which they should be treated.

Key terms

bureaucratic politics A view of how decisions are made which emphasizes the competition between different sub-units in a bureaucracy for power and influence over their collaboration to come up with an agreed course of action to achieve the goals of the whole organization.

foreign policy decision-making The way the government of a state decides which foreign policy goals to pursue.

organizational process A view of how decisions are made which emphasizes the role of standard operating procedures designed to reduce complexity and to produce an efficient, uniform response in multiple decision situations over individual rational responses which emphasize the factors specific to each decision situation.

rational Choices where the course of action chosen can be reasonably supposed to achieve the goal desired, even if it fails to actually do so in practice.

rational actor model A view of how decisions are made which emphasizes the way individuals and organizations match decisions about what to do with reasonable expectations about how their choices will achieve their goals.

satisficing Choosing the first course of action which looks like it will achieve a goal rather than examining all options and then choosing the best, and choosing a course of action which offers the best chance of achieving several goals at once, even if it is not the best course of action for achieving each of the goals individually.

Key takeaways

- The study of how governments make foreign policy decisions is a subset of the study of how people make decisions. It can be approached in a number of ways.
- Diplomatic historians study a foreign policy decision or set of related decisions in great detail and try to tell a story or construct a narrative of how that decision was reached.
- Foreign policy analysts start with the rational actor model. This assumes that decision-makers, whether individuals or collective actors, have clear sets of preferences or goals and choose the course of action which they believe is most likely to deliver them.
- Nearly everyone accepts that in real life choices are affected by the imperfections of the people making them and the conditions in which they are working.
- People and governments tend to ignore what they don't want to see, resulting in cognitive dissonance. Making big choices makes people tense and they seek to resolve the tension by satisficing, accepting the first "good-enough" solution to come along rather than waiting for the best.
- Graham Allison's study of the Cuban Missile Crisis shows how, even when decision-makers try their best to be rational, factors such as bureaucratic politics and the processes by which large organizations deal with problems play a part in producing the decisions which are made.

Exercises

1. How do people choose their future husbands, wives, or partners? Do they act like rational actors, risk prospect minimizers, or satisficers?
2. Under what circumstances are governments more likely to act like rational actors in making their foreign policy decisions, and when are they more likely to act like satisficers?
3. Ask your professor if there are bureaucratic politics in his or her department and college. How did bureaucratic politics influence the outcome of the Cuban Missile Crisis?
4. Have you experienced organizational processes affecting the way you get your university funding or your access to courses at registration time? How did organizational processes affect the outcome of the Cuban Missile Crisis?

5.3   Foreign policy instruments

Learning objectives

1. List the **foreign policy instruments** states use to pursue their foreign policy goals.
2. Describe how states talk to one another through their people.
3. Describe how states talk to one another through their diplomacy.
5. Explain how states bargain with one another.
5. List the economic instruments states use in foreign policy.
6. Describe how states use violence, force, and war as instruments of foreign policy.

Once governments have chosen or decided on their foreign policy goals, they have to think about which foreign policy instruments to use to achieve them or get them implemented. If we look at this abstractly, we can say that governments enter into **negotiations** with other governments where they bargain with each other about what they want. We imagine their conversations to take the following form.

State A: "I will reward you with this, if you do what I want. I will punish you with this, if you refuse."

State B: "I will do what you want, if you reward me with that, but I want more. If you refuse to give me more, I will not do what you want, and if you try to punish me, I will punish you even more."

In this abstract view the basic foreign policy options are as follows:

- to talk
- to make requests with promises of rewards
- to make demands with threats of punishment
- to actually provide rewards
- to actually carry out punishments.

It sounds a bit like Mafia dons or drug gang leaders arguing over turf and, sometimes—Russia's negotiations with Ukraine, US negotiations with North Korea, and the European Union's negotiations with Greece, for example—the simple conversation above pretty much captures what is going on. Realists think it pretty much captures what is going on all the time. Of course, they say, governments don't actually talk to each other like this. They are far more polite, but they talk in a code and they all know the game. When President Obama and Secretaries of State Clinton and Kerry said to Iran in regard to halting its nuclear weapons program that "all options remain on the table," for example, they were not communicating a wide open state of mind about what to do. They were telling the Iranian government the US was prepared to use force, and the Iranian government knew that this is what they were saying. Whether it believed them, of course, is another, and crucially important, matter.

Diplomatic language: choosing words carefully

Diplomacy deals with tense and potentially dangerous issues. It has developed an ultra-polite form of communication between the representatives (ambassadors and other diplomats) of states designed to avoid giving unintended offense. In the past, a king's apparently casual comment to an ambassador that he regretted that the relations of their two states were not as good as they might be would be read as a threat of war by those who understood the diplomatic code.

In 1870, the German Chancellor Bismarck exploited this code by editing a telegram he had received from his own king about the conduct of the French ambassador. The telegram was then made public. The edits were designed to provoke the French emperor by showing a lack of respect for his ambassador and, by angering the emperor, contributed to the war that Bismarck wanted. As late as 1991, the Iraqi Foreign Minister rejected a note from the American Secretary of State, claiming it was written in language which was "unacceptable." The note almost certainly contained a threat to use nuclear weapons on Iraq if it used weapons of mass destruction in the looming war between the two states.

In 1990, the Iraqi dictator, Saddam Hussein, asked the US Ambassador to Iraq for America's views on Iraq's dispute with Kuwait. Ambassador April Glaspie said the US took no position on disputes between Arab states. She meant the US took no position on who was right or who was wrong in disputes between Arab states. She did not mean the US took no position on how Arab states solved their problems, as Iraq found out. Saddam may have taken her response as a green light from the US. He invaded Kuwait and the United States organized a major coalition to throw him out again in 1991.

In 2017, Nikki Haley, the US Permanent Representative to the UN, told journalists that getting rid of the Syrian dictator, Bashir Assad, was no longer a priority in US policy. A few days later, the Syrian government used chemical weapons against a rebel-held town full of civilians. Critics of the US government suggested that her remarks may have encouraged the Syrians to take this risk. It is unlikely, but it shows the importance of words. Shortly after, the US government made its views clear by launching cruise missile strikes on the airfield from which the attack had been launched.

There is a big problem with this idea of foreign policy as being mainly about the communication of promises, threats, rewards, and punishments, however. If you ask anyone who has been involved in foreign policy as a politician, diplomat, or even as a soldier, they will say that most of the time, it's just not like that. Most of the time, foreign policy is much more like your relations with other people. We can get a clearer sense of what they mean by employing a more concrete list of foreign policy instruments: propaganda and public diplomacy; diplomacy;

economic rewards; economic sanctions or punishments; espionage; force as punishment; force to destroy.

Propaganda and public diplomacy involve governments of states trying to influence each other by talking directly to all or some of the people of the state they are trying to influence. They do this through media broadcasts, embassy and foreign ministry web sites, speaking tours, educational programs and, increasingly, participation in social media networks like Twitter and Facebook. These attempts to influence governments by reaching out to their people can be official. See, for example, the US embassy Beijing web site at http://beijing.usembassy-china.org.cn/

They can appear to be independent, but be closely controlled by the government. See, for example, the front page of the Tehran Times at http://www.tehrantimes.com

They can be independent, but still be in sync with the state's foreign policy. See, for example, the British Council Website at http://www.britishcouncil.org/

All of the examples above focus mainly on getting the word out to the audience, but these sites can also incorporate interactive elements. See, for example, the Canadian department of foreign affairs' (currently called Global Affairs Canada) "Stay Connected" page at http://www.international.gc.ca/department-ministere/social-media_medias-sociaux.aspx?lang=eng

Describing these activities as propaganda has fallen out of fashion because the term has sinister connotations with the idea of damaging states by confusing their people through lies and distortions which weaken their support for their own government. Public diplomacy is the term more commonly used now, and the significance of public diplomacy has greatly increased with the plentiful and cheap information made available by the revolution in information technology. There are still two sides to public diplomacy, however. One focuses on strategic communication, is concerned with control and manipulation, and has been greatly enhanced by the application of modern advertising and marketing techniques from the private sector. The other is concerned with the possibilities for direct dialogue between governments and people, and possibly even direct dialogue through social networking between the peoples of the world, to build relationships without specific foreign policy objectives in mind. Both approaches are used by governments and others in pursuit of a wide variety of objectives, ranging from promoting exports and attracting investments to changing people's attitudes in a profound way. After the attacks of 9–11, for example, American governments have invested heavily in radio, television, and on-line efforts to change the images of the United States in the Middle East, especially among young people of the "Arab Street."

It remains far more common, however, for governments to talk to one another through their official representatives using diplomacy as an instrument of foreign policy. They do so through a network based on resident embassies and ambassadors established originally in Europe from the 15th century onwards, by meeting at international organizations like the UN and regional organizations like the European Union (EU) and the Association of South East Asian Nations (ASEAN) and, increasingly, by government leaders talking directly with each other at summit meetings. Thus, diplomacy can be conducted in the following contexts:

- bilaterally, between two states, as when diplomats in the Mexican embassy in Washington talk to the State Department about legislation affecting Mexican citizens who live in the US
- multilaterally, between three or more states, as when the 28 members of NATO meet in Brussels to discuss the alliance's policy on maintaining forces in Afghanistan
- polylaterally,[8] between states and other sorts of actors like transnational corporations or banks as when American and Mexican diplomats meet with representatives of BP and other oil companies to talk about their operations in the Gulf of Mexico
- universally, in multilateral settings where just about every state in the world is a member, like the UN General Assembly, and meets to discuss a global issue like the challenge of reducing carbon emissions.

In each of these settings governments can talk to each other through their diplomats in a number of ways:

- formally (as at the signing of the climate agreement in Paris in 2015, for example), or informally (as at the meetings between American presidents and their guests in sweaters and jeans at Camp David, the president's place to get away from it all, for example)
- officially (as when an ambassador of Syria was called in by the British Foreign Minister to receive a formal complaint about his government's violations of human rights, for example), and unofficially (as when Iranian and Israeli diplomats speak to one another at the UN even though their states officially have no diplomatic relations with each other, for example)
- directly (as in face-to-face meetings between the American ambassador and the Russian foreign minister or president over US missile defense policy in Eastern Europe, for example), and indirectly (as when the US and North Korea used the Swedish embassy in Pyongyang and contacts at the UN to help set up the release of the American student, Otto Warmbier, in 2017, for example)
- publicly (as when the American Secretary of State makes a speech about another state), and privately, as when she or he talks to that state's ambassador at the State Department about how they want the foreign government's ambassador to understand the speech.

The important point to note, however, is that most of the time states engage in what the French statesman Cardinal Richelieu called "continuous relations." They talk to each other, whether or not they have something specific in mind. And when they do have something specific in mind, they don't begin by bargaining, promising, and threatening. They appeal to moral principles which they both claim to support. A French diplomat might note to someone at the US State Department, for example, that both the United States and France are committed to the principle of free trade and no national biases in purchasing orders. She might then ask how the American government reconciled a particular act, for example the purchase of aircraft by an American airline from Boeing rather than

Airbus when (in her government's view) the Airbus was the better plane, with American support for free trade. Most governments, like most people, do not like making threats and do not like being threatened. Most governments, like most people, do not like using favors or bribes or being the target of favors and bribes. Most foreign policy, therefore, most of the time, involves the governments of states simply talking to each other and to other actors through diplomacy and diplomats. However, when a government badly wants something and simply talking is not working, then other instruments of policy come into play.

A series of economic instruments are available, especially to wealthy, developed states whose citizens are heavily engaged in international trade, finance, and production. These economic instruments of foreign policy can be divided into the promise of rewards and actual rewards, the threat of punishments and actual punishments. As we shall see in Chapters 9 and 10, international economic relations are becoming increasingly important as states engage in them to develop their power, wealth, and the wellbeing of their peoples. States use the measures discussed below to achieve economic advantage. Here, however, the discussion is focused on how economic instruments of policy are used to gain foreign policy goals.

Economic foreign policy rewards are mostly of two sorts. First, governments can give things to other governments and their peoples or promise to do so, or they can provide them on favorable terms. Second, governments can let their own people accept the things which the governments and peoples of other states are offering them. The governments of states can give the following:

- money as a gift, as a loan with a below-market interest rate, or goods and services as a gift or at below-market prices
- technical assistance, for example helping to build a dam, and technical know-how, for example on how to raise particular crops, organize a banking sector, or train students to be civil engineers
- goods, services, and know-how which they would not normally transfer to other states, for example, military aircraft, intelligence, and training which the recipient would normally have to do without or produce itself.

The governments of states can let others have the following:

- open or, when compared to others, advantageous access to their own markets for the other's goods, finance, or labor
- open or, when compared to others, advantageous access to owning property like land, buildings, and companies.

Economic punishments or sanctions are also mainly of two sorts (for a more extensive discussion of economic sanctions see Chapter 9). Governments can deny and withdraw, or threaten to deny and withdraw, benefits of the sorts in the lists above which they have previously given. They can also undertake new measures designed to hurt the economy of another state and the economic prospects of its people or its government. They can hurt the economy of another state by:

- placing taxes (import duties) on goods and services from that state
- placing quotas (top limits) on the number of units of goods imported from that state
- imposing administrative (for example, safety) restrictions which delay the entry of goods from that state
- generally prohibiting their own producers from trading with or investing in that state
- selectively embargoing (prohibiting) the export of certain goods to that state
- restricting or forbidding their own banks and companies from investing in that state.

These are some of the actions available as economic instruments of foreign policy to hurt or punish a state, its economy, or its people. It is important to keep the following in mind:

- these measures are often undertaken in conjunction with other states doing the same thing;
- these measures are rarely taken in isolation from other measures also designed to put pressure on a target state;
- the effectiveness of these measures depends upon the sensitivity (do the measures have immediate consequences for the target?) and vulnerability (can the target ignore the measures or find alternatives?) of the target state;
- all sorts of states can be sensitive to economic measures, but smaller states with less diversified economics are more vulnerable to them;
- the question of who sanctions hurt in the target state—governments and elites or the poor and vulnerable—is a big moral and political question;
- it is sometimes very difficult to tell whether economic measures are taken to support foreign policy objectives or for other reasons, for example, the use of technical measures and safety standards which prevented the import of Russian cars into the US when every other major Western state permitted their import.

Economic foreign policy and the fate of Iraq

Economic sanctions imposed by the UN after the first American-led war on Iraq in 1991 weakened Iraq's economy, its armed forces, and its people's support for Saddam Hussein, the Iraqi dictator. His regime collapsed quickly when attacked again in 2003. However, we do not know how big a contribution those sanctions made. We do know they did not work quickly. We do know that some people made a lot of money from smuggling to get around the sanctions. And we suspect one of the reasons the US and Britain went to war for a second time was that they feared the sanctions regime around Iraq was beginning to collapse.

Supporters of economic sanctions say:

- they are better than going to war because people are not killed and property is not damaged;
- they favor the richer side in any conflict;
- they can be targeted to hurt elites rather than the poor and the weak;
- they can be used when a government needs to show other governments or its own people that it is doing something.

Opponents of sanctions say:

- they kill indirectly, but just as surely, the weak and the poor who are deprived of the necessities of life;
- they make the population of the target state more dependent on its government for the necessities of life, thereby strengthening the government's control;
- they always provide someone with economic, political, or moral incentives to try and get round the sanctions which are hard to block.

The UN, the US, and the European Union attempted to deploy at least five rounds of economic sanctions against Iran in order to get it to stop refining uranium into fuel which could be used for both nuclear power plants and nuclear weapons. Most people agree that these sanctions played a part in securing the nuclear agreement of 2015 by which Iran agreed to slow down some of its programs and abandon others, in return for sanctions being relaxed. The US government under Donald Trump argues that the agreement did not accomplish enough and talks about maintaining, restoring, and developing new economic sanctions on Iran.

Information is of critical importance to foreign policy decision-making. Diplomats spend much of the time trying to find out what is going on, but other states often seek to conceal their foreign policy goals and their plans for achieving them. Accordingly, states use espionage to obtain secret intelligence about one another. They spy on each other, each other's companies and firms, each other's citizens and each other's military, diplomatic and, indeed, espionage services. The extent of these activities has been partially revealed and widely publicized recently by WikiLeaks and its allies. The public "dumping" of large amounts of electronic communications traffic by Chelsea (previously Bradley) Manning and Edward Snowden shows how developments in information technology have increased this sort of activity (it also provides a useful example of how individuals can become significant international actors). Enemies, rivals, and friends all spy on each other. They do so because they value information and especially information that others wish to keep secret. They want to know what others know and believe, and what they are planning to do. They also want to know how others are spying on them. They spy on each other in several different ways:

- with secret agents—sometimes James Bond hero-types who take great risks to steal secrets—but more often very low-key people working under the cover of regular jobs, especially out of the state's own embassy in a targeted state

- with recruited citizens of the target state who have access to information and will obtain it for money, to avoid blackmail, or for ideological reasons
- by monitoring, listening into, and analyzing radio telecommunications and hacking into digital communications within the target state and between it and others from communication centers at home, satellites, and specially equipped aircraft
- by obtaining satellite imagery of military bases, research facilities, and other places to which access is restricted.

It is important to keep the following in mind when thinking about espionage:

- the lines between diplomacy and espionage are often blurred: is an aircraft flying up and down the coast of another state, but outside its airspace, monitoring radio traffic, espionage? Is cultivating a government official who has a weakness for single malt whisky, which loosens his tongue, espionage?
- the lines between acceptable espionage and unacceptable espionage are blurred: all states tolerate being spied on up to a point as a price they pay for being able to spy on others, but there are limits to what they will put up with and sometimes other factors like political sensitivity and embarrassment will result in their trying to shut down each other's espionage operations;
- the lines between success and failure in espionage are blurred; it is very hard to know how well an espionage service is performing and very hard to demonstrate when something goes wrong that it was a failure of intelligence.

Pearl Harbor, 9–11 and intelligence

The US has undergone two major and spectacular surprise attacks in its history. However, Americans seem to have been more shocked than other victims of surprise attacks. They have not focused on the wickedness of those who attacked them as much as on trying to find out what went wrong and how the attack could have been avoided. One answer, put forward by conspiracy theorists, is to say their own government wanted the attacks to occur. Thus, Japan's attack on Pearl Harbor was allowed by the Roosevelt administration, and the 9–11 attacks may have even been carried out by the Bush administration to anger the American public into being ready to fight. These are discredited explanations. They are not true.

Another explanation, however, focuses on the failure of intelligence agencies. Some of the devastating consequences of Pearl Harbor might have been avoided, for example, if Japanese communications had been decoded more quickly and the information sent to people with the authority to make big decisions at the base. According to the official 9–11 inquiry, the whole attack might have been prevented had various intelligence agencies—notably the FBI and the CIA—been more willing to share information which when pooled would have given a far clearer picture of the developing threat (follow this link http://www.gpo.gov/fdsys/search/page details.action?granuleId=&packageId=GPO-911REPORT&fromBrowse=true for the 9–11 Commission Report).

It is difficult to evaluate such claims. More importantly, it is difficult to say whether the adoption of measures suggested to avoid such failures in the future will make a difference. The point about surprises is that they are surprises which, by definition, it is impossible to anticipate, and intelligence agencies remain reluctant to share information for both bad and good professional reasons. When a plot is discovered and foiled, then it no longer is a surprise. However, politicians, soldiers, and diplomats are not put in positions of responsibility to be philosophical and skeptical about problem-solving. That is the job of the academics. Public servants have to try, or at least be seen to be trying, to address these problems.

The lines between espionage and warfare can be blurred with espionage shading over into sabotage. Cracking someone else's codes to gather information can lead to disrupting and misleading their information systems. And, of course, digital electronic systems do not merely share and store information between people. Increasingly, they share and store information between themselves, while complex machinery like aircraft, cars, and military equipment are actually made to run by digital electronic information transfers. Disrupting such systems through computer hacking is referred to as cyber warfare, to which states allocate increasing amounts of money, personnel, and research. It is rumored, for example, that the code-crackers of a foreign power (Iran says the US or Israel) infiltrated and inserted a virus into the computer programs which regulate Iran's efforts to refine uranium to higher levels of purity. Similarly, it is strongly rumored that both China and Russia have engaged in cyber-attacks on the computer networks of other states, not only to discover secrets, but also to disrupt the operations of networks which maintain websites, online financial services, and power generation systems. A major and ongoing controversy of the 2016 election in the United States concerned the alleged role of hackers based in Russia accessing and publicizing information from the Democratic Party's computer records, and similar accusations have been made about hacking in the election of other states, notably the French presidential election in 2017.

Violence, force, and war, as the Realists and other state-centric approaches remind us, remain options when states cannot agree with one another yet believe they must get their own way. In the rest of this section, we will look briefly at how states try to use violence, force, and war as instruments of foreign policy. In Chapters 6 and 7, we will look in more detail at relations of conflict and competition, different types of wars, how they are fought, who fights them, how they are controlled, and how they are ended.

Most societies regard war as a dangerous pathology or sickness, or at least a sign that something, usually diplomacy, has gone wrong. Indeed, as we noted in Chapter 1, the academic subject of International Relations has its origins in studying, explaining, and solving the "problem" of war. Today, almost everybody says that war is a bad thing which people should not use except in self-defense and, possibly, to prevent the mass violation of human rights. By some measures, war, and certainly war between states, has been in decline for some years, although this is not the impression we get from the news headlines. The fact remains, however, that states use violence (the physical destruction of life and property), force (violence used purposefully), and war (force used by states for political purposes), as instruments of their foreign policy.

Historically, states have used war to satisfy a wide range of foreign policy objectives:

- the defense of their governments, people, territory, and honor
- the acquisition of new territories, resources, and glory
- the destruction of other states and the enslavement of their peoples
- the creation of other states and the liberation of their peoples
- the development of their own people as loyal, proud, and obedient citizens
- the spreading of beliefs, ideas, values, and ideologies around the world.

States have used war as an instrument of foreign policy in three basic ways: to punish resistance; to destroy the ability to resist; and to fight off attempt by others to do both. During the Viet Nam War, for example, the United States was unable to prevent North Viet Nam from committing troops and supplies to the war in South Viet Nam at an acceptable cost to itself. It therefore bombed North Viet Nam, in effect saying "we cannot stop you intervening, but we can make you pay a price in pain and destruction for continuing to do so which we hope you will decide is not worth it." For much of the war, North Viet Nam and its allies fought a war of punishment extracting a cost from the South Vietnamese for resisting and the Americans for staying in South Viet Nam. Once the Americans chose to leave, however, they fought a war of destruction, crushing South Viet Nam's capacity to resist. In World War II, in contrast, the United States, the Soviet Union, Great Britain, and their allies invaded Germany, conquered nearly all its territory and physically destroyed most of its armies. Germany did not choose to surrender; it had to because it no longer had the ability to resist. In Afghanistan, the United States and its allies have been fighting both wars of punishment and destruction. Aggressive patrols and drone strikes are designed to hurt the Taliban fighters who resist them and to destroy the leadership of Al Qaeda and its allies on the Afghanistan-Pakistan border. The Taliban, in contrast, cannot destroy the United States and its allies. Instead, it is trying to inflict pain on them in the hope that this will help them choose to leave Afghanistan.

Though it may be viewed as an instrument of foreign policy, war has generally been seen as different from other instruments because of the death and destruction it causes, the fear it arouses, and the risks it involves. Even those who view it as an instrument of foreign policy, however, pay attention to what it can deliver and at what price. There are two sorts of arguments: the moral or ahistorical approaches which say that no good obtained by war has ever justified the price in terms of lives destroyed and ruined; and the historical approaches which examine how the cost-benefit analysis of war changes over time and by place. Those who take ahistorical approaches claim that wars have never achieved anything lasting, that whatever they achieve comes at a terrible price and produces the resentment, misery, and brutalization which will lead to more wars. Look at the Israelis, for example. They have fought at least five very successful wars against their neighbors since 1948. Are they any more secure today than they were back then and, given the resentment created among their Arab neighbors by their successes, what are the trends for Israeli security in the future?

Those who take more historical approaches sound more skeptical and practical. In a world where some are prepared to use force, this seems to require everybody being prepared to use force. Israelis may be no more secure today than they were in 1948, but had they not been prepared to fight, there might be no Israelis left today to argue the issue. Nevertheless, those who take the historical approach note three trends over time:

- what Robert Osgood and Robert Tucker called "the expansion of force" by which states have exploited material technologies—like high explosives, the internal combustion engine, and nuclear energy—and social technologies—like national and democratic ideologies, to greatly expand the destructive power that states can mobilize[9]

- the currently declining value of the things a war can get you, most notably territory and people which were the traditional prizes of war, but which now often appear to drain the resources of those who succeed in capturing them

- the rising moral sense that war, except in a narrow set of circumstances, is unjustifiable for all the reasons provided by the ahistorical approach above.

The lessons from fighting in 19th-century Europe seemed to be that states should develop their armed forces into precise, controllable instruments of limited war for political objectives.

Prussia's wars of unification and Israel's wars of survival and consolidation

In 1864, Prussia, allied with Austria, fought a war against Denmark to drive it out of two border territories. The fighting lasted about six months with the Danes defeated. In 1866 the Prussians fought a war to destroy Austrian influence in what were then the independent states of south Germany. The war lasted seven weeks with the Austrians defeated. In 1870–1, Prussia fought a war against France to remove it as an obstacle to German unification. It lasted ten months (although the decisive fighting took place in the first two months). The French emperor and Paris were captured. A new French republic was established and a new German empire declared by the Prussians in Versailles. In June 1967, Israel, terrified that the Arab armies on its borders were about to invade, launched a pre-emptive series of attacks with its air and ground forces. The war lasted six days with the forces of Egypt, Syria, and Jordan (plus "volunteers" from other Arab states) defeated, and east Jerusalem, the Golan Heights, Gaza, and the Sinai desert as far as the Suez Canal captured.

The suffering and losses of those killed, wounded or displaced were terrible. In these "smart wars," nevertheless, clear objectives were gained over a limited period of time in victories which, in the short to medium term at least, were decisive. Most people, most of the time, do not want wars, but if there must be wars, politicians, soldiers, and diplomats say, let us plan, prepare, and practice for wars such as these. As the subsequent fate of Germany in the 20th century and Israel's continued insecurity both suggest, however, "smart wars" are difficult to carry out and, even when successful, rarely achieve all they were designed to deliver.

The lessons from fighting in 20th-century Europe seemed to be that wars would escalate out of control into total war which threatened the survival of states and, with the advent of nuclear weapons, the survival of the human species. War had become too dangerous, too destructive, and too expensive to be viewed as an instrument of foreign policy. The lessons so far from fighting in the 21st century seem to be that governments continue to try to limit and control war to make it a useful instrument of foreign policy, that they have succeeded in lowering the risks of blowing us all to kingdom come in a nuclear holocaust, but that they have lost some control of warfare to guerillas and terrorists, and that the cost-benefit analysis has become no clearer. War as an instrument of foreign policy can be effective at preventing things happening or denying what the other side wants, but it seems to be much less effective at making things happen or getting you what you want.

Key terms

bargaining   Processes by which the representatives of states and others seek to shape each other's behavior by offering and providing rewards and by threatening and carrying out punishments.

foreign policy instruments   The different types of actions which states undertake to achieve their foreign policy objectives, typically: propaganda/public diplomacy, diplomacy, economic rewards, economic sanctions, and war.

negotiations   Discussions between the representatives of states about shared problems, matters of common interest, and issues over which they disagree.

Key takeaways

- States use foreign policy instruments to obtain foreign policy goals.
- Mostly they just talk to each other, directly or through their diplomats, about what they want or what they think is right.

- Sometimes they bargain with each other using promises of rewards, actual rewards or threats of punishment or actual punishment.
- The key foreign policy instruments are: propaganda or public diplomacy, diplomacy, economic rewards and punishments (sanctions), and war.
- States may use these instruments singly or in combinations.

Exercises

1. The governments of states mostly just talk to one another about what they want. When are states more likely to bargain with one another, promising rewards, and making threats?
2. Why are the governments of states so careful about the diplomatic language they use in talking to one another?
3. How has the cost-benefit analysis of war as an instrument of foreign policy changed over the last 200 years?

5.4 The future of foreign policy in an era of uncertainty

The actions which states take to conduct relations with other states to secure their interests in their external environment are known as foreign policy. Foreign policy analysis examines the goals which states typically pursue, the ways in which governments make foreign policy decisions about which goals to pursue, and the foreign policy instruments available to them. The idea of foreign policy suggests that states can be viewed as coherent actors behaving rationally and strategically in the way they relate goals or ends with means or instruments. Sometimes the image of a chessboard and pieces carefully marshaled by players is offered in books about international relations to suggest what a clever, calculating, and cautious game foreign policy-making can be.[10]

However, a great deal of evidence casts doubt on this image. We have seen how a variety of different factors complicate the process of foreign policy making. Key decision makers do not always have the information available to make good choices. Foreign policy bureaucracies have their own interests in policy processes which can go beyond simply serving the national interest. Big organizations develop standard operating procedures for dealing with complexity and the flood of demands which are placed on them every day. As a result, when we look closely at states, they appear to dis-aggregate from one big actor into lots of different actors. When we look closely at international relations, they appear as networks between different types of actors who increasingly operate in a dis-intermediated way. That is to say, these actors do not seem to need governments, foreign ministries, and diplomats to mediate between them. They just talk directly to each other. Another consequence of looking at foreign policy and international relations closely, therefore, is that the distinction between the state's external environment and its internal or domestic environment breaks down. Most governments say they are concerned with promoting environmentally sustainable economic growth, for example, and this is neither a foreign policy issue nor a domestic one. It is both. US governments pursue foreign policies of strong support for Israel and, until recently, opposition to relaxing sanctions on Cuba. In both cases, domestic political considerations are very important. US governments argue that both policies serve American national interests, but their desire to retain the support of pro-Israel voters who are often, but not always, Jewish and Cuban-émigré voters respectively plays a part in shaping these foreign policies.

Finally, some International Relations theorists have borrowed from other fields of inquiry the insight that most power, most of the time, is not exercised in a bargaining game of carrots and sticks. They have advanced the idea of soft power, and many policy-makers, especially in the US, have adopted this idea. Soft power is an idea associated with Joseph Nye (see Chapter 3), an academic who has also worked for several US governments. Nye argues that we should regard the foreign policy use of carrots and sticks in negotiations as discussed above as forms of hard power. Hard power is used to manipulate the cost-benefit analysis of the target to get them to do what you want, but it does not set out to shape what they think of you. Soft power or the power of attraction, in contrast, works because the target finds you attractive and internalizes your values. Nye argues that soft power is becoming more important and that, when it works, it is more effective and lasting than hard power. He also argues this is good news for the United States. Its hard power assets like wealth and armed forces may be relatively declining. However, its soft power assets like its effectiveness at technical innovation, its strong education system, the movies and rock music of its popular culture, and its democracy and freedoms are becoming more attractive to the rest of the world. The US, he argues, is still "bound to lead" because no one else is as attractive in soft power terms or strong in hard power terms.

Critics raise several objections. The core idea of power through attractiveness is important, they say, but not new. Marxists have stressed the importance of ideology and conservatives have stressed the importance of culture and legitimacy in providing the social structures which shape how people act. We are not constantly faced with a barrage of sticks and carrots to get us to conform, yet most of us do conform most of the time. In fact we dislike overt attempts to manipulate us in this way. The "power of attraction" may be very effective, other critics add, but creating it and using it for specific foreign policy purposes is much more difficult. Lots of people around the world say they love American movies but do not like the US. Does watching American movies make them more susceptible to seeing things in terms the US government would like and doing what the US would want? Over time, the idea of soft power has gone mainstream and lost its distinctiveness. Even Nye struggles to maintain his original distinction between soft and hard power and slips at times into using the popular misreading that soft power is offering positive incentives while hard power involves the use of sanctions and force. Most recently, he has helped the Obama administration develop the idea of "smart power," which involves getting the combination of soft and hard power right. It is hard to disagree with this, but equally hard to say that it tells us very much. Perhaps what is most interesting is why the term "soft power" has become so attractive to governments and those close to the foreign policy process. They find it useful. Liberals and Post-positivists would say this is because it reflects the new forms of power made possible by the information revolution. Realists would say it reflects a simpler process. As British military and financial power declined, they note, the British became more interested in the idea of "British influence" through the English language, the BBC, Shakespeare, and Britain's wise and urbane diplomats. Now, they suggest, the US is engaged in a similar sort of mirror-gazing about its alleged attractions which is understandable but unlikely to be effective.

Most Realists and most historians argue there is very little which is new in all these claims about how foreign policy is changing. Foreign policy, they argue, has always looked like a messy business when examined under the microscope. The great foreign policy-makers are the ones able to exert control over all these complexities, ignore the clutter, and keep their minds focused on what is really important. Others, in contrast, especially Liberal Institutionalists, suggest that all the big trends in international relations point to states becoming further disaggregated in the future. Look at what is happening, they say, to France, Germany, and Britain in the European Union (see Chapter 11). Their governments have less and less control over the relations which cross their national boundaries, even between parts of their own governments. Post-positivists suggest the picture is not so clear. On the one hand, they note there has not always been a clear distinction made between foreign and domestic at every time and every place in the world. The term "foreign policy" came into use in 19th-century Europe. It may be time, they say, that it fall out of use again. On the other hand, when shocks to the system occur, for example, the terrorist attacks in Paris, Brussels, London, Manchester, Nice, and Barcelona between 2015 and 2017, these same states reassert control of their borders, mobilize their peoples for war and send French, British, and German armed forces—not European or UN ones—to the Middle East. Context seems to be everything in terms of shaping how states will conduct their foreign policies and how we see them acting.

Recommended reading

Graham Allison and Philip Zelikow, *Essence of Decision: Explaining the Cuban Missile Crisis* (2nd edition), New York, 1999.

Albert O. Hirschman, *National Power and the Structure of Foreign Trade*, Berkeley, 1945.

Christopher Hill, *The Changing Politics of Foreign Policy*, Basingstoke, 2003.

Steven W. Hook, *American Foreign Policy: The Paradox of World Power* (3rd edition), Washington, 2011.

Fred C. Iklé, *How Nations Negotiate*, New York, 1964.

Geoffrey Allen Pigman, *Contemporary Diplomacy*, Cambridge, 2010.

Paul Sharp and Geoffrey Wiseman (eds.), *American Diplomacy*, Boston, 2012.

Notes

1 Chris Brown with Kirsten Ainley, *Understanding International Relations* (4th edition), Basingstoke, 2009.
2 K.J. Holsti, *International Politics: A Framework for Analysis* (7th edition), New York, 1994.
3 Daniel Kahneman and Amos Tversky, "Prospect Theory: An Analysis of Decision under Risk," *Econometrica*, 47(2), pp. 263–291, March 1979.
4 Robert Jervis, *Perception and Misperception in International Politics*, Princeton, 1976.
5 Herbert Simon, *Models of Bounded Rationality*, Boston, 1982.
6 Irving L. Janis, *Victims of Groupthink*, Boston, 1972.
7 Marcus Holmes, "The Force of Face-to-Face Diplomacy: Mirror Neurons and the Problem of Intentions," *International Organization* 67(4), pp. 829–861, 2013.
8 Geoffrey Wiseman, "Polylateralism: New Modes of Global Dialogue," *Diplomatic Studies Programme Discussion Paper*, Leicester: Diplomatic Studies Programme, 59, November 1999.
9 Robert E. Osgood and Robert W. Tucker, *Force Order and Justice*, Baltimore, 1967, p. 41.
10 For example, Zbigniew Brzezinski, *The Grand Chessboard: American Primacy and its Geo-strategic Imperatives*, New York, 1997.

6 International conflict and competition

Preamble

The previous chapter ended with a discussion of the use of force and war as instruments of foreign policy. The next two chapters examine conflict and competition in more general terms. This chapter looks at different types of conflict and competition. Chapter 7 looks at how states and others conduct conflicts and wage wars. Conflict and competition are widely assumed to lie at the heart of international relations. Most people agree that they are generally bad things. Conflict in the form of **war** destroys lives, property, and habitat, and it does so just so some people can get what they want from others. Competition, it is widely assumed, can easily lead to conflict. The big arguments then are over whether it is possible to get rid of conflict and competition and how to live with them in the meantime.

Conflict and competition are both terms with multiple uses and meanings, however. We speak of politicians having conflicts of interests when they pass legislation affecting companies in which they hold shares. We speak of feeling conflicted, when we can't make up our mind whether the reasons we like someone outweigh the reasons for steering clear of them. Similarly, we speak of competition in terms of sports and business. We often say that competition is good for people. It may be good for the actual competitors because they try harder and work better when the possibility of beating or being beaten by others is put in front of them. It may be good for the rest of us—look at how competition from Japanese cars improved the reliability and design of American cars, for example, in the 1980s. If you have been in the Service, you will be familiar with the claim that even military conflict and competition can be good for us, developing the virtues of discipline, comradeship, and self-sacrifice. If you've been in combat, you will probably have strong views on how this is both true and not true at the same time.

It is important, therefore, to be clear what we are talking about here. By **international conflict**, we refer to situations in which one or more sets of peoples are threatening or using violence to get what they want from other peoples. By **international competition**, we refer to situations where for one or more peoples to gain what they want, other peoples have to lose what they want. This is sometimes called a zero-sum game. In this chapter, we will examine different types of international conflict and competition; possible explanations for why they exist; possible cures which might get rid of them; and possible ways in which we might live with international conflict and competition without making them worse, while we are trying to produce cures which may or may not work.

6.1   Types of international conflict and competition

Learning objectives

1. Describe how types of international conflict and international competition vary.
2. Explain why international conflict and competition may be on the decline.
3. Describe how international conflict and competition looked in the past and how they look today.
4. List the reasons people give for competition which can lead to international conflict.

There are different types of international conflict and international competition. They differ primarily in two ways:

- the size, scale, and duration of the conflict;
- what people say the competition associated with the conflict is about.

If we look at international conflicts in the past, we can see that they vary in size, scale, and duration. Anthropologists tell us that simple human communities tend to fight in small groups for short periods of time without causing huge destruction of life, property, or habitat. The popular military historian, John Keegan, provides an image of young, male Pacific (no pun intended) islanders lining up opposite each other, making faces, trading insults, throwing rocks, and swiping at each other until someone actually gets hurt, then packing up and going home.[1] The conflict has a stylized dimension to it, similar to most confrontations between the hooligan supporters of rival soccer teams in Europe in the 1970s or the New York gang rumbles of the 1950s (at least as these were presented in the musical *West Side Story*). The reasons for the limited nature of the conflict seem obvious and linked to the social and material capacities of these simple societies. These societies had few people. Their weapons technologies were not very destructive, and they could not afford to take much time out from hunter-gathering and simple farming. However, we have examples of such simple societies engaging in drawn out warfare—almost as a way of life—and examples of them waging such wars to the point of exterminating the other side. We might also note that soccer hooliganism and gang warfare generally remain limited in their violence despite the availability of far more destructive technologies like cars and guns. The relationship between the size, scale, and duration of a conflict and the social and material capacities of its participants is not always simple. Other factors sometimes play a part.

Is international conflict on the rise or the decline? At least three stories can be told about the rise of war—the use of force by legitimate authorities for political objectives—and its possible decline. The first story stresses the increase in destructive power that has taken place through the course of history, Osgood and Tucker's **expansion of force** referred to in Chapter 5. Human beings begin by punching each other and throwing rocks. Over time, we organize ourselves into ever bigger groups—tribes, kingdoms, empires, and states—and we equip ourselves with more and more effective weapons—bows and arrows, firearms, high explosives, bombers, missiles and, finally, nuclear, chemical, and biological weapons of mass destruction. Finally, we reach the age of **total war** where everybody is mobilized to fight or support the fight and, thus, everybody from soldiers to babies can be targets. The flight times of ballistic missiles armed with nuclear warheads (20 minutes or so from the US to Russia, ten minutes or so from Russia to Europe as noted in Chapter 1, and 30–40 minutes from North Korea to different parts of the US) represents just how close we are to national, state, and possibly species extinction. This story leads to quite pessimistic conclusions, especially once we realize that every weapons system developed by human beings has been used at some point or other.

(For a video clip of a series of nuclear tests from the Cold War merged together with a deliberately numbing rock track added see http://www.metacafe.com/watch/1579263/nuclear_bomb_clips/)

The second story is more optimistic. It notes that nuclear weapons have not been used since the first two atom bombs were dropped on Japan. While the first story emphasizes how wars have grown from local arguments to global affairs which might destroy us all, the second story notes a long running attempt to control or even outlaw wars, and the decline in the number of interstate wars which have taken place since the end of the Cold War between the US and the Soviet Union in the 1990s. As we saw in Chapter 5, there have always been people who thought that wars were wrong and never worth fighting. When wars became more costly, after World War I especially, other people, including governments, started listening to them.

It may not seem like war is declining if you live in or have been to Iraq, Afghanistan, Syria, South Sudan, and other war-torn places, but wars between states are becoming fewer in number, smaller in scale and less destructive (even if some of those fought still manage to last a very long time). The US and Russia, who still possess the world's largest nuclear forces, are both formally committed to getting rid of nuclear weapons completely. Perhaps then, as John Mueller has suggested, war and international conflict are on the way out, just like slavery, smoking, and driving under the influence of alcohol.[2] Perhaps, as the Bible suggests, swords will be beaten into plowshares and spears into pruning hooks (Figure 6.1), or at least, guns and bombs might give way to tasers and tear gas.

A third story of the fate of war is far less sure that we are moving in any long-term direction—whether towards violent catastrophe or lasting peace. Anthropology suggests that there are times and places where war has barely existed, and times and places where it has been waged in the most destructive ways available. History suggests similar variations. The international conflicts of the ancient world sometimes resulted in wars of annihilation, Rome's war

Figure 6.1 Yevgeny Vuchetich's "Let Us Beat Swords Into Plowshares": sculpture at the UN in New York City

(Source: Independent Picture Service/Alamy Stock Photo)

against Carthage in the 3rd and 2nd centuries BCE, for example, where peace was proportionate to the ability of one empire to dominate the rest. In the late medieval and early modern periods in Europe, in contrast, war became limited to the point that mercenary armies in Italy would "fight" battles of maneuver in which no one was killed. This period of **limited war** was followed by the devastating wars of religion in the 17th century which again were succeeded by a period in which monarchical states used relatively small professional armies for limited purposes. Then the French Revolution ushered in a period of mass mobilization by states to fight highly destructive wars. The French were told they no longer fought for their king, but for their nation and thus, in a sense, for themselves. The final defeat of France in 1815 ushered in a "long peace." International conflict in Europe was muted and brief until 1914 and World War I. There followed what Jeremy Black has called "the age of total war"[3] in the first half of the 20th century and then the apparent decline of war, at least in the "zones of peace" of the developed world. A pattern of successive expansions and contractions of warfare suggests itself from this summary. So too does a pattern where wars and conflicts inside states increase as wars and conflicts between states decline. However, this third story would urge caution about identifying any pattern over the long haul.

So what does international conflict look like, at least for the time being?

First, there are no wars currently between developed states.

- The last was between Argentina and Britain over the Falkland Islands (1982). Between some developed states which have fought each other many times in the past—France and Germany, for example, war currently seems unthinkable. Yet Russia and Ukraine have come very close to fighting a war against each other after Russia invaded the Crimea and offered support to pro-Russians in eastern Ukraine in 2014.

- This is not to say that some developed states do not think about war with one another. US, Russian, and Chinese military planners (if we regard China as developed) no doubt consider the possibility of their states becoming directly engaged in international conflict with each other. China, Japan, and other developed states in East Asia have declared that a real risk of war between them currently exists.

Second, developed states are currently engaged in violent international conflict but such wars tend to be against smaller, less developed states and groups within them.

- The US-led interventions in Kosovo (1999), Afghanistan (2001), and Iraq (1990 and 2003) are obvious examples of this sort of war.

- Kosovo involved airpower only and no casualties on the US-led NATO side. The wars against Iraq and in Afghanistan involved tens of thousands of soldiers, hundreds of aircraft and scores of warships, and many casualties on both sides.

- The Russian intervention in Georgia in 2008 was a similar sort of war to these, although it was on a much smaller scale and of shorter duration.

- The invasion of Georgia and the bombardment of Kosovo and Serbia had relatively quick, clean finishes.

- The operations in Afghanistan and Iraq began with quick victories over the governments of the weaker states and their regular armed forces, but then became long, drawn out struggles to preserve the new political orders against terrorist attacks and guerilla insurgencies.

- The air operations in support of rebellions against the Gaddafi regime in Libya (2011) helped end his rule and his life, but have produced an outcome which remains unclear.

Third, developing states fight each other.

- India and Pakistan (1999), Ethiopia and Eritrea (1999 and 2000), Sudan and South Sudan (2012), and North Korea and South Korea (2010), for example, have clashed over disputed territory on their shared borders.

- Iraq and Iran fought a murderous, lengthy war border war (1980–88) which ended in stalemate, and Iraq attacked and occupied Kuwait (1990) leading to the American-led and UN-sponsored intervention which drove the Iraqis out.

- Tense naval confrontations between China (if we regard China as developing), the Philippines, Viet Nam, and Malaysia around islands in the South China Sea have so far not involved extensive direct violence.

Fourth, and more common, are wars between states and armed groups and wars between armed groups.

- Israel, for example, fights armed groups operating from within the territory of Lebanon, in the West Bank between Israel and Jordan, and in the strip of territory around Gaza.

- The US and its allies have fought several different armed groups in Iraq, some of which also fight each other and some of which were won over to the US side. It also fights a large armed group in Afghanistan—the Taliban—which has allies in Pakistan.

- Britain, France, and the US have all fought armed groups in African states, as have African states operating in support of the African Union.

- Several states, including the US and China, conduct patrols against armed groups—pirates—in the Arabian Gulf and the Indian Ocean.

- States also conduct wars against armed groups on their own territories. For example, India has conducted wars against some Kashmiris and the Naxalite movement. Sri Lanka concluded a war in 2009 against members of its Tamil minority in its northern territory. Russia maintains a strong military presence in its southern territories in the Caucasus, although the situation there is temporarily calm.

- Democratic Congo (Zaire), Uganda, Rwanda, and Burundi fight a complex and confusing set of encounters against some of their own armed people and the armed groups of their neighbors in the African Great Lakes region, while these groups also fight each other.

■ Russia and the United States plus other American allies are currently involved in supporting various factions in the Syrian civil war and the war in Iraq against the Islamic State in Iraq and Syria (ISIS), some of these factions being opposed to one another. Currently (2017) ISIS looks like being defeated as a force capable of holding territory, but the outcome of the Syrian civil war remains unclear. Russia is also engaged in supporting armed groups on Ukrainian territory against the Ukraine government.

If we think of levels of violence as a spectrum between exchanges with nuclear weapons at the high end and rifles, spears, and rocks at the low end, most of these irregular wars are waged towards the low end of the spectrum. Wars between states and armed groups such as national, ethnic, or terrorist movements are often called **asymmetrical war** because one side—the state—has far more power and wealth than the other.

The impressions international conflicts and competition give today are as follows.

■ They seem untidy. Gone for now are the days when the same sorts of armies fought each other in offensive and counter-offensive operations which could be captured by dramatic red and blue arrows streaking across campaign maps.

■ The front lines which used to separate two sides seem to have been replaced by far more fluid deployments and movements. Different sides occupy the same territory at different times, and there are often more than two sides.

■ They seem indecisive. This is partly a result of media reporting which suggests that any conflict which is not resolved in a short space of time is dragging on. However, many of these conflicts stretch on for years without finishing. They may flare up in a spectacular operation—grabbing a hotel and taking hostages or killing a terrorist leader in a raid for example, and then they die down or go quiet for a while before starting up again.

■ They seem unusually cruel. A soldier hurts as much as anybody else when hit by a bullet, but civilians, and especially women, children, and old people, seem to be the unintended victims, and often the intended targets, of military operations. And sometimes it is hard to tell who are the combatants and who are not. Is the terrorist bomb-maker or the civilian controller of drone attacks, for example, a combatant or a non-combatant?

We must be very careful with such impressions, however. Older people in particular have a sense of what normal and "proper" wars should look like which is heavily based on their understanding of what John Keegan called "the Western Way in War."[4] In this conception, states fight each other in clear teams of alliances for clear objectives in wars which have a clear beginning and a clear end, in which most of the participants try to avoid hurting civilians unnecessarily, and where what it means to win and lose are clear. The European wars of the 19th century are viewed as models of this kind of international conflict, as are the two world wars, the first four Arab-Israeli wars, the first three India-Pakistan wars and the Korean War in the 20th century. The wars in Algeria and Viet Nam, plus the Soviet intervention in Afghanistan point the way to the sorts of nasty, messy drawn out conflicts which appear to have become the norm. As good military historians remind us, however, and as participants in those "proper" wars would no doubt tell us, they were by no means as tidy and decisive as we like to remember them. Most of us learn about wars today from an almost real time, twenty-four-hour news cycle which spares us the pain and destruction, but shows us the suffering, fear, and chaos, and encourages us to talk about it to an extent which is unprecedented. Perhaps with the passage of time these messy wars will come to look as purposeful and decisive as the world wars. Perhaps with the passage of time, we may move back to actually fighting such wars. At present, however, that does not seem likely. To understand why, we need to look at what people say the competition which leads to their conflicts is about.

Iraq's first war against the US and its allies, 1990–91

In August, 1990, as the Cold War was ending, Iraq invaded Kuwait. The Iraqi leader, Saddam Hussein, complained that the Kuwaitis were demanding repayment of debts which Iraq had incurred fighting Iran on behalf of all the Arab states, that Kuwait had been stealing oil from Iraq's part of a shared oil field, and that the Kuwaiti leaders had disrespected Iraq. Critics might have objected that launching another war so soon after an eight-year war of attrition which Iraq had started with Ayatollah Khomeini's Iran was not wise. They would have also suggested that Saddam had better be sure that none of Kuwait's friends would be so upset as to come to its rescue. But anyone from Thucydides down to Henry Kissinger would have recognized the game Saddam was playing. He was taking a chance, but he felt pressed to act because of Iraq's economic difficulties. Besides, the prize was a big one: Kuwait's oil fields and all the respect which destroying an arrogant monarch and American ally would bring him in the Arab world.

The attack was reasonably well executed and the Kuwaitis were crushed in hours. Saddam first installed Kuwaiti stooges as the new government and then annexed Kuwait to Iraq on the grounds they had been one territory under the old Ottoman Empire. He then halted to see if his gamble would work. It didn't. The US, under the administration of George H. Bush, might have decided to do nothing or even boost Iraq as its new policeman in the Gulf. After all the US had offered indirect military support to Saddam during his war against Iran. Saddam certainly hoped it would, but there is no evidence Bush seriously considered this option. Saddam's track record of aggression, cruelty, and paranoia suggested he would be a highly unreliable policeman at best.

With UN approval, Bush built a large coalition of Western, Asian, and Arab states (some like Syria which had been quite hostile to the US). After a massive air bombardment lasting weeks, these forces launched a big ground invasion across Iraqi territory in February, 1991 to get in behind the Iraqi troops defending the Kuwaiti frontier and to destroy the Iraq reserves waiting in the rear (see Chapter 7).

Most of the ground fighting was over in three days. After trying to destroy the Kuwaiti oilfields, the Iraqis retreated and, after a short and very destructive pursuit, the Americans and their allies halted. Neither the UN nor many of the allies wanted to see Baghdad captured or Saddam overthrown, and there is little evidence that Bush wanted to go further into Iraq and risk more casualties in what up to that point had been a war with few casualties for the Americans and their allies.

A ceasefire was negotiated which became a peace agreement placing lots of restrictions on the size, type, and permitted operations of Iraq's surviving armed forces. The campaign had a few blemishes. Captured allied pilots and Special Forces were roughed up by the Iraqis, for example, and they also placed civilian hostages around some of their key government and military buildings for a time. Allied aircraft hit targets full of Iraqi civilians on several occasions, and the Americans encouraged a revolt among Shia Iraqis which they were not prepared to support and which was bloodily crushed. The suffering and killing which occurred during the war were as painful, distressing, and wasteful as they always are. However, the war had a clear beginning and clear objectives for both sides. Once their claims had been tested by force of arms, the fighting stopped, the war came to an end, and Iraq—with Saddam still the leader—was offered a tough, but not impossible, road back to international respectability. (See Figure 6.2.)

Figure 6.2 Iraqi Generals surrendering to US and Saudi Generals at the end of Iraq's first war against the US and its allies, March 1991

(Source: Contributor: DOD Photo/Alamy Stock Photo)

Iraq's second war against the US and its allies, 2003

Iraq's second war against the US and its allies was a very different sort of international conflict. There was no obvious immediate cause. The terms on which the first war had ended left Iraq greatly weakened in military terms and placed its trade under UN sanctions. After the 9–11 attacks, however, the US, under George W. Bush's administration, decided that it would either have to be completely satisfied that Saddam had no program for developing weapons of mass destruction or it would go to war to destroy his government.

UN inspectors suggested that no evidence of active programs could be found. Intelligence agencies, including America's own, said they could find no definitive concrete evidence of such programs, but that they could not be sure there were none at all. The Bush administration said there was no margin for error with weapons of mass destruction. If you were wrong, whole cities might be destroyed. It suggested that the Iraqis might collaborate with international terrorist movements and did nothing to correct the mistaken impression among many Americans that Saddam was somehow involved with Al Qaeda and the 9–11 attacks.

As it built the case for war in the face of a skeptical audience, especially abroad, the Bush administration added the poor human rights record of Saddam's government to the arguments for acting. It suggested that overthrowing him would allow the Iraqi people to build a democracy which would be a beacon of freedom and hope for the rest of the Arab world.

The Iraqi leaders didn't want a war, but they did not help their case much. They tried to trick arms inspectors. They boasted about the way the system of UN sanctions was falling apart (the possible collapse of sanctions may have influenced the Americans into deciding on war) and they couldn't make up their mind whether "fessing up" to no weapons of mass destruction or pretending that they just might have some which they would use was the best way of preventing an attack (there is some speculation that Saddam might have believed he had some weapons because his advisors were too scared to tell him he hadn't).

Even so, only Britain among the major power states bought into the American argument, and when even its government had a few doubts, the Bush administration gave the impression it was quite prepared to undertake the attack with no allies at all. The operation went ahead and was hugely successful, partly because the Iraqi armed forces were so weak after years of sanctions, but also because of the wealth and effort the US had devoted to creating the best armed and best prepared military in the world. Baghdad was captured. Saddam fled and was later captured and executed.

However, things quickly began to go wrong. The invasion, as many critics has pointed out, was the easy part. What came next was much harder. There were no weapons of mass destruction, and instead of Iraqis setting up their own democracy, the divisions in their society which the old order had repressed came to the surface. A Sunni minority had ruled the state, and now the Shia majority and another minority, the Iraqi Kurds, said it was their turn. Sunnis, Shia, and Kurds began using force against each other. Cells of the Al Qaeda terrorist group established themselves in the state and, together with some of Saddam's supporters, started launching attacks on American and allied troops plus Iraqi civilians. At times, Iraq looked like it was about to fall apart. Over the best part of a decade, and at a high price in blood and treasure, the Americans and their allies stabilized a situation in which Shia parties with no great love of the US came to dominate Iraqi politics through processes which mixed democracy with coercion and corruption. When they pulled out in 2012, the Americans left a situation which was far from clear as was the balance sheet from their decision to intervene in the first place. At present, it looks like a small, but growing, number of American forces will be in Iraq for some time to help the government fight ISIS which established itself on Iraqi and Syrian territory in 2013–14.

Both Groucho Marx and Bugs Bunny are well known for having said "Of course, you know this means war" (Groucho Marx, *Night at the Opera* (1935) and *Long-Haired Hare* (1948). To see a video clip follow the link https://www.youtube.com/watch?v=BjIZwv5aENQ). What, however, are the reasons people actually give for either being willing to fight or having no choice but to go to war?

The historical record suggests that people may fight over practically anything. The result of an international soccer match, the severing of a sea captain's ear, the insulting language in telegrams, the desire to force opium on unwilling consumers, and objections to being taxed without having the vote have all been cited as reasons why peoples went to war. If we look at what they say more systematically we can see that, under certain conditions, states and others will fight for all the foreign policy goals listed in Chapter 5. They will fight, or be prepared to fight, for reasons of: security, independence, economic welfare, prestige, and values. This list is useful for it reminds us that governments usually give multiple reasons for fighting the same war. As we have seen, the US administration of George W. Bush said it was fighting Iraq to get rid of its weapons of mass destruction, to get rid of Saddam Hussein and his supporters, to secure the world's oil supplies, to secure America's influence and reputation in the Persian Gulf, to end the abuse of human rights in Iraq, and to create democracy in Iraq and possibly the whole of the Middle East.

What sorts of reasons have governments given for being prepared to fight and for actually fighting recently? **Self-defense** is the most obvious one. The governments of all the states in the world today say they are prepared to use force in self-defense. This is one of the few reasons "allowed" in the Charter of the UN, and it seems reasonable to nearly everyone. Only a few people are prepared to follow the strict and demanding code of pacifism when they are physically attacked, arguing that nothing, including their own life, is worth fighting and killing for. And even pacifists struggle with the idea that they have no moral obligation to defend the helpless, for example if they could stop a baby being killed by using force themselves.

Self-defense, however, turns out to be a very broad idea in practice. It is difficult to draw a sharp boundary between defensive and offensive measures. Is American support of the European members of NATO or Russian support for states like Syria or Venezuela defensive? Are naval patrols to keep sea lanes open around the world self-defense? Does self-defense always let the other fellow get the first hit, or can you defend yourself in a **pre-emptive war** by hitting the other fellow before he hits you, or **preventive war** by hitting him before he's even ready to hit you? As we have seen in Chapter 5, in 1967 Israel argued it was too small a state to allow the Arab states the first blow. A pre-emptive war was needed, its government said because the first blow might very well be the last. The United States made a similar argument regarding Iraq in 2003 and does so today in justifying the importance of restricting Iran's nuclear energy program. If Iran gets nuclear weapons it may use them with devastating consequences. Better, some argue, to knock them out before the problem develops. As we shall see in Chapter 7, however, there are problems with this. What if the other side looks at us in the same way as we look at them? The Iranians have argued that it is they who are threatened by the US and Israel, and not the other way round. Think of those tense moments in old cowboy movies where everybody's hands are poised just above their guns, their eyes are locked on each other, and the sweat is beginning to run. Is he going to shoot first? Does he think I'm going to shoot first? Self-defense is a popular and understandable reason. As the Canadian General Burns once said, however, it seems to be that defensive weapons are those I have pointed at the other fellow. Offensive weapons are those he has pointed at me.

Most states say they are prepared to fight to hold on to their own territory. No one was surprised when Kuwait tried to defend itself in the first Iraq war, and nearly everyone expected the Iraqis to fight harder once the fighting moved on to their own territory than they did in Kuwait. Most states say they are prepared to fight to defend their way of life, whether they define this in religious, economic, or political terms or a combination of all three. Most Iranians, most Israelis, and many Americans emphasize the religious character of their states as being critical to its identity and worth fighting for. Most North Americans, Western Europeans, Indians, and Japanese, would emphasize political democracy and freedom of expression as being critical to their identities and worth fighting for.

Increasingly, most states also say they are prepared to fight to defend the international or global order and the rules and the laws which hold it together. This used to be the preserve of the great powers, but now smaller states too will send members of their armed forces across the world to protect everyone from terrorists and pirates. Increasingly, states also say they are prepared to use force to uphold human rights, and to prevent other states from violating the human rights of their own citizens or to punish them for having already done so. American and European military operations in the Balkans, Somalia, Iraq, and Afghanistan have been justified completely or partly in terms of the principles of **humanitarian intervention** and "Responsibility to Protect" (R2P). This suggests that where a state violates the human rights of its citizens on a large scale, it forfeits some or all of its rights to be left alone under the doctrine of sovereignty.

Most states are prepared to use force against terrorists—non-state actors using illegitimate violence for political ends—and the states which support them. There are arguments about whether terrorists should be seen as military-strategic problems—that is people against whom you wage war—or as criminal-legal problems to be dealt with by police work. There are also problems with the idea of terrorists and terrorism captured by the overly-simple jibe that one person's terrorist is another person's patriot or mujahideen. Naming people terrorists seems straightforward when they smash planes into skyscrapers or kidnap and kill hostages. We can see the problem, however, when states we do not like or trust, for example Syria, start calling their armed opponents terrorists. Can people fighting brutal dictatorships be terrorists? Were the American colonists who intimidated, beat up, and tarred and feathered agents of the British Crown who were lawfully trying to collect excise duties terrorists or patriots? This suggests, of course, a dark side to the reasons why states fight. Some states and armed groups are prepared to fight to ethnically cleanse or kill people of other states, races, tribal groups or religions which they say are wicked, corrupting, or threatening. Westerners are used to thinking of the dynamics of international and transnational relations in African states like Rwanda and the Democratic Congo in these terms. Many Africans, Arabs, and some Asians are used to thinking of the use of violence on their people by Western states in similar terms.

What sorts of reasons have governments stopped giving for being prepared to fight and for actually fighting? This is harder to answer because much of the international conflict we see today seems, at least in part, to take place for reasons which are no longer regarded as acceptable. Most states are still prepared to fight for their own territory. However no one now says they are prepared to fight to gain new territory and the people and resources in it, the way, for example, Hitler invaded the Soviet Union in the mid-20th century to obtain more living space for the German people, the European great powers moved into African territories in the late 19th century to acquire colonies, and the United States expanded across the North American continent in the 19th century to reach what some Americans regarded as its "natural" or "God-ordained" boundaries. The problem with this apparent shift, however, is that some states and peoples are prepared to fight for territories which they maintain were taken from them and which rightly belong to them. Russia used force to recover the Crimea, for example, saying that it was historically Russian, the majority of its inhabitants are Russian, and it only became Ukrainian back in the days of the Soviet Union when real power was exercised from Moscow anyway. Some Palestinians and some Israelis are prepared to fight for territories in the West Bank for these reasons. Iran has made it clear that it will fight for territories on its border with Iraq and islands in the Straits of Hormuz which it regards as belonging to it. We have already considered the tense maneuvers between China, Malaysia, Viet Nam, and the Philippines over islands in the South China Sea. There are similar tensions between China and Japan over what they respectively call the Diaoyu and Senkaku Islands just off the coast of Taiwan. Indeed, as the technical ability to exploit undersea mineral resources has increased, this has made formerly remote islands and coastal territories more valuable.

Most states would no longer claim national honor or glory as acceptable reasons for going to war the way, for example, Mussolini's fascist Italy went to war in the 1930s in Abyssinia (Ethiopia) and Albania, and in Greece in the 1940s to prove to the world, and itself, that it was a virile nation and great power. The terrible destructiveness and costs of modern warfare, plus popular awareness of these through the mass media have been particularly hard on the claim that war is in any way glorious. Nevertheless, it is quite common for governments in conflicts to insist that backing down would not only be wrong and costly, but would also damage their honor, reputation, and sense of worth. Iran, for example, says it would rather fight than be intimidated into accepting the shame of abandoning its nuclear energy program. Honor and self-respect are involved in the reasons why neither Britain nor Argentina could make concessions in their dispute over the Falkland Islands (see text box below) in 1982, and many Americans worry about what it means for their state's reputation if most of their forces have left Iraq and will leave Afghanistan with the original missions not completed.

Some states seem to have foresworn the use of force, not in terms of reasons, but in terms of the identity of those with whom they may be in conflict. As noted earlier, it is currently hard to imagine the states of Western Europe getting into armed conflict with one another or with the US or Canada. This is so partly because they do not have the sorts of disputes with each other which could lead to war. Also, the armed forces of most Western European states have become so small and so specialized that they would find it very difficult to fight each other on a large scale until they had mobilized their societies. It is also the case, however, that it does not occur to them to use force against each other, a quite remarkable development after centuries of their being willing to do so and the last major European war ending just over 70 years ago.

Key terms

asymmetrical war   Wars between different sorts of actors—like states and terrorists—with different amounts and types of destructive power.

expansion of force   The increase in destructive power made possible by improvements in material and social technologies.

humanitarian intervention   The idea that force can be used against governments engaged in large scale human rights violations.

international competition   Situations in which for one actor to get what it wants, another actor must lose what it wants.

international conflict   Situations in which one or more actors are threatening or using force.

limited war   War conducted by limited means, in limited space, for limited objectives.

pre-emptive war   The idea that war can be used against an attack which is just about to occur.

preventive war   The idea that war can be used against a potential threat before it has become direct.

self-defense   The idea that force should only be used to fight off an attack.

total war   A war where there are no intentional limits on objectives fought for, means employed, and targets attacked.

war   The use of force by legitimate actors for political purposes.

Key takeaways

- International conflict refers to situations in which one or more sets of peoples are threatening or using violence to get what they want from other peoples.
- International competition refers to situations where for one or more peoples to gain what they want, other peoples have to lose what they want.
- International conflicts vary by size, intensity, and duration.
- People give many reasons for using force but the reasons which people agree are appropriate change by place and over time.
- At present most people agree that self-defense is the only good reason for using force, but the meaning of self-defense is easily stretched.
- At present more and more people are beginning to agree that preventing a government violating human rights on a broad scale is also an acceptable reason for others to use force.
- Governments give different reasons to different audiences for the same use of force.

Exercises

1. What sorts of reasons did Saddam Hussein give for invading Kuwait in 1990?
2. What sorts of reasons did George W. Bush give for attacking Iraq in 2003?
3. What is the self-defense rationale for using force, and what are the problems with it?

6.2   Explaining and understanding international conflict and competition

Learning objectives

1. List Rapoport's three **general explanations** for international conflict and competition.

2. Describe Waltz' three levels-of-analysis explanations for international conflict and competition.

3. Explain what a reflexive understanding of international conflict is.

The long-running dispute over the Falklands-Malvinas illustrates the difficulties involved in asking states and their governments why they engage in international competition and conflict.

The Falkland Islands-Islas Malvinas (1982) and the changing value of territory in international conflict

The Falkland Islands in the South Atlantic are a British colony claimed by Argentina. In international law, both states have plausible claims to them in terms of who was there first, who chased whom out, who has been in continuous occupation, and what the people who live there want. They are thousands of miles from Britain and hundreds of miles away from Argentina. The two states have argued over them since the early 19th century, but the arguments remained low key for many years. Britain was strong, Argentina was weak, the two states enjoyed good relations in other respects, and the windswept, cold islands were not very valuable. Fishermen, whalers, and other ships in difficulty used them. They became more important as a place to store coal for resupply as ships shifted from sail to steam power, and a British company attempted to make money bringing people in to raise sheep. When ships shifted to oil and developed longer ranges, the islands became less important to the British, but they remained of great symbolic significance to both Britain and Argentina and negotiations to work out a peaceful settlement of their future in the 1970s were unsuccessful (see the discussion of prestige in Chapter 5).

In 1982, the Argentine military government, under great economic pressure at home, invaded the islands successfully, but they were recaptured by the British a couple of months later in a costly, but short, war. The British were heartened by their success which came at a tough economic time for them too, and they put a stronger garrison on the islands. The Argentines were shamed by their failure and put the Malvinas issue on the back burner. Let the British spend a fortune on defending a couple of thousand islanders, penguins, sheep, and seaweed. Perhaps they would get tired of it and come to their senses someday.

More recently, however, rumors of oil under the seabed which have always circulated have been firmed up by oil company explorations. By international law, whoever controls the islands has exclusive economic rights to the seas around them and the resources below them to a range of 250 miles. Britain granted rights to oil companies to explore. Argentina protested, and by 2012, with both states facing economic difficulties, the dispute began to warm up again.

Argentina says it will only use peaceful means to recover the islands, but that the British refuse even to talk about sovereignty over them. Britain says it will talk about anything except handing over the islands. The armed forces of both states are weaker than in 1982, but the domestic politics of both states gives their governments little room to maneuver in terms of making concessions. If commercially viable oil or gas fields are discovered, the islands will have become valuable again and not just have symbolic significance. The pressure on Argentina to do something and on Britain not to give an inch will increase.

As the Realists remind us, we often see big gaps between what governments and others say and what they do, and even between what they say at one point and what they say at another. In the Falklands/Malvinas case above, for example, both Argentina and Britain are committed to the principle of not using force to settle disputes, but they are both prepared to fight for the islands—the Argentines in the name of the principle of national liberation, the British in the name of the principle of national self-determination, and both in the name of the principle of national self-defense. High principles are mixed with economic calculations for both sides. They are also mixed with the pressures of domestic politics. When the islands look less valuable and when domestic politics in both states are calm, the dispute simmers down. When the islands look more valuable—as in the days of coaling stations for ships and now with the prospect of oil and gas deposits to exploit—the temperature of the dispute rises, especially if both governments are faced with difficulties at home. Even if they don't want to fight, other factors make it hard for either side to offer concessions.

It is these gaps between what governments say about international conflict—it is a bad thing—and their willingness to engage in it nevertheless, which lead some academics and other experts away from asking governments and people why they fight. Sooner or later, people will give every reason under the sun for fighting if they think it will help their case. Instead, these academics ask different sorts of questions. How are the causes of international conflict and competition to be explained and understood? Anatol Rapoport grouped answers to these questions into three types of general explanations of international conflict and competition.

- Political or Clausewitzian (after Karl von Clausewitz) explanations accept the reasons given by people for fighting wars. They fight them because they think they can get or keep what they want by fighting.

- Cataclysmic explanations see wars as disasters or punishments which happen to humanity from time to time and which are visited on them by uncaring forces of nature or caring, but judgmental, angry, and vengeful gods. Whatever reasons people may have for fighting wars are soon swept away by the terrible destruction and suffering in which war invariably results.

- Eschatological explanations see wars as part of a meaningful history, usually as the last great battle before something very different, and usually very good, occurs. Religions often offer a conception of a final battle between good and evil like the Armageddon of Christians. So too do secular movements, however. H.G. Wells spoke of the war that will end war and this was borrowed by Woodrow Wilson in making his case for why America should enter World War I, and Karl Marx sometimes wrote in terms of a final great struggle between bourgeois and proletarians which would result in the establishment of classless, communist society.

Rapoport's framework is useful for getting us to think about explanations for war, but it has its limitations. Consider, for example, the US-led invasion of Iraq in 2003. To the American strategists and military planners it was a political war to get rid of a regime which was a threat to America's allies in the region and potentially a threat to the US if Saddam Hussein actually acquired weapons of mass destruction. To many of its supporters, it was the first blow in a final war to bring peace, progress, and democracy to the whole of the Middle East. To some Iraqi peasant farmers in its way, however, the invasion must have seemed like just one more disaster rolling over them for reasons beyond their control and understanding. In other words, the same war can be seen in each of Rapoport's terms.

Levels of analysis explanations have been used by political scientists like Kenneth Waltz, and other social scientists to offer more specific explanations for why and when wars occur.[5] Waltz said we can look for explanations of war at the following levels.

- The individual level—human nature can be seen either in natural-scientific terms or in religious-moral terms. Some biologists have argued that we may fight when someone threatens our physical space because, like many other animals, we are inherently territorial. Other biologists have suggested that our wars are so destructive because of our physical weakness. Lions, tigers, bears, and many other animals have the physical capacity to do huge damage to each other quite easily and have evolved behaviors for conflict avoidance. Look at how most domestic dogs offer signals of submission (rolling over and baring their necks for example) when confronted by a stronger dog and look at how the stronger dog usually accepts those signals.

  Human beings, in contrast, have been unable to do much harm very easily to each other for most of their existence, and lack the inhibitions of other animals, a dangerous situation once they started applying their intelligence to making better and better weapons. Some psychologists have argued that when we experience frustration, we quickly also experience aggressive impulses which can lead to violent acts (pounding the table on hearing bad news, or pounding the bearer of the news, for example). The religious-moral explanations for war we have already come across in our discussion of Realism in Chapter 2. We fight, they suggest, because we are frightened sinners (or at least some of us are) who would sooner hurt other people than risk being hurt by them.

- The state level—others blame the state or some types of state for war. The state can be seen as a hierarchical and exclusivist social structure designed for disciplining its citizens into being willing to fight against other people. Nazi Germany, Soviet Russia, and communist China are often presented in these terms in the West. Marxists, anarchists, and some socialists, in contrast, present western states as instruments of the wars that capitalists need to maintain their positions of dominance and exploitation in the world economy.

- The system level—finally, others, Waltz among them, say we do better to look to the whole international system to explain why wars occur. The anarchical international system forces states to wage war to advance and defend their interests. Where an imbalance of power between two or more states is believed to exist, the stronger state will take advantage and threaten force to get what it wants, leaving the weaker state with the choice of giving in, playing for time until it builds up its strength, or going to war.

Levels of analysis explanations applied to blaming Germany for World War II

The levels of analysis approach has a similar problem to Rapoport's framework. The same war can be explained in all the terms offered. However, it is still a useful framework for getting us to think about what might be important in explaining a particular war, and wars in general. Think about World War II. Here we will focus on Germany, but the same sort of analysis could be applied to Britain, France, Italy, Japan, the Soviet Union and the United States.

If we look at the individual level our attention is drawn to Adolf Hitler's role in appealing to the violent impulses of Germans, or German men, or some German men. What would have happened if Hitler had enjoyed a better relationship with his father, had been accepted to art school in Vienna, or had been close enough to the British gas shells which twice wounded him in World War I to have been killed off completely?

If we look at the state level, however, we ask why did anybody listen to this odd, former corporal with his crazy stories about racial pride, Jewish corruption and the need to guarantee German survival through wars of territorial conquest and extermination? Why did those who controlled the German state find his message useful? Why had the state produced citizens who would be receptive to what he had to say?

The answer, some argue, is to be found at the system level. Since it had come into existence in 1871, Germany had upset the European balance of power by being too big and too successful in terms of economic productivity and scientific innovation. It made its neighbors—France, Britain, and Russia—feel insecure and so they ganged up on it. This made Germany feel insecure and so it tried all the harder to be better and stronger than the rest. Only by cutting Germany back down to size, for example by dividing it in two as the victorious allies did at the end of World War II in 1945, or by letting Germany become the dominant power—as some say is happening now—could the peace and stability of the European system be restored.

Waltz's levels of analysis alert us to the sorts of factors which may be important in explaining the causes of both war in general and particular wars. We can then look at particular wars and ask two sorts of questions.

- What was the relative importance of individual level, state level, and system level factors in explaining why that war occurred? For example, was the second US-led war against Iraq in 2003 mainly the product of Saddam's or George W. Bush's individual priorities, the respective economic and political needs of their two states, or the dynamics of the political, economic, and oil production systems of the Middle East?

- What sorts of factors make war more or less likely at any given moment or particular situation in international relations? How important is the distribution of power and changes in that distribution? How important is the kind of political or economic system in place in the states in question? How important are particular leaders and their personalities to making war more or less likely?

Theorists seeking to explain the causes of international conflict and international competition that can lead to war advise us to mistrust the reasons people give for fighting. Instead, we should look for the real or underlying reasons—a war justified on humanitarian grounds, for example, may be really being fought for economic reasons. Or we should look for objective causes of conflict which are independent of people's reasons for fighting and of which they might not be aware. Think of people giving evidence in court for why they became involved in a drunken brawl. Whatever they say, we all know that being drunk probably had a lot to do with it. When you crowd rats into a restricted space, beyond a certain ratio of rats to space, they start fighting. Perhaps similar sorts of things might be said about people.

Explanations are nearly always complex, however, and it is hard to separate out causes to identify which one was most important. To make things worse, and as the **reflexive understandings** of Post-positivists we examined in Chapter 4 remind us, there is no clear separation between people's reasons for doing what they do and explanations offered by others for why they do what they do. If Hitler's wrong and wicked beliefs about Jews led him to seizing power and going to war, then they are part of the explanation of why World War II happened even though the beliefs were wrong and wicked. If we identify that states with democratic politics and free market economies do not go to war against each other—the Liberal Peace theory—then this observation becomes part of people's subsequent thinking about going to war. Liberal states, for example, may seek to define those states they want to fight as undemocratic. Think, for example, of how the US and other Western states draw a clear line between Iran and Pakistan in these terms even though the distinction is by no means as clear as they would like it to be. Think about how contemporary wars are justified primarily in terms of humanitarian or anti-terrorist reasons. To what extent is this so because humanitarian and anti-terrorist reasons for fighting are currently regarded as acceptable? Treat "objective" and "independent" explanations more like the reasons that people give for fighting, the reflexive approach suggests. Both function as beliefs in the minds of people. The challenge then is to examine how both independent explanations and reasons operate in the minds of people to allow them to compete to the point of violent conflict. What makes it alright to hit someone in this situation and not in another which is objectively similar? How do different people answer this question in different circumstances, and how do the answers differ by time and place? And, of course, if we regard violent conflict as a bad and dangerous thing, can we come to recognize the circumstances in which it is more likely and create the circumstances in which it is less likely by influencing how people think about these questions?

Key terms

general explanations   Explanations which identify the causes of all international conflict rather than particular conflict, and the sources of all international competition rather than particular competitions.

level of analysis explanations   Explanations which stress properties of individuals, or states, or the international system as a whole as the main cause of international conflict and source of international competition.

reflexive understandings   Understandings which treat people's beliefs about why international conflict in general occurs and their beliefs about the sources of international competition in general as influences on the likelihood of particular international conflicts and competitions occurring.

Key takeaways

- There are rarely single or simple causes of international conflict and competition. The causes are usually multiple and complex.
- The reasons people who fight give for fighting do not necessarily explain why a conflict exists.
- Explanations for international conflict, independent of the reasons given by those involved in the conflict may provide a fuller, but not complete, account of why a particular conflict and conflicts in general exist.
- Understanding international conflict and competition involves looking at reasons people give for being involved in fights, other reasons which they may hide, and causes of which they may not be aware.

Exercises

1. Do cataclysmic and eschatological explanations of international conflict and competition help us understand the "War on Terror"?
2. How far does blaming Hitler get us in explaining World War II?
3. What are the problems with relying on the reasons given by those involved for explaining international conflict and competition?

Cures for international conflict and competition

Learning objectives

1. List the reasons why international conflict and international competition can be viewed as pathologies in need of cures.

2. Describe how people might learn to end or reduce international conflict and competition.

3. Explain the difficulties which may face any attempt to put an end to international conflict and competition.

Nearly everybody agrees that international conflict and competition are bad things. The reasons for this are linked to what look like very basic human values which are necessary if we are to live together in societies. All societies, Hedley Bull maintains, have some sort of **basic primary social rules** like the ones we considered in Chapter 3 about protecting lives, safeguarding property, and keeping promises to each other without which they could not function.[6] These basic primary social rules can be modified by secondary social rules. The basic primary social rules of a society may say "thou shalt not kill" and "promises must be kept," for example, but the secondary rules may say, except in self-defense or except when the promise is coerced. Societies have different answers to the questions when is it alright to take lives and when is it alright to break promises, and their ideas about property differ too. In Sweden, for example, it is much easier to obtain an abortion and much harder to accumulate property and use it as you wish than in the US. Of course, in addition to these basic primary rules being necessary for maintaining societies, some people, like Mohandas Gandhi, the leader of the Indian independence movement, would argue it is just plain wrong to hurt others with violence, deprive them of what is rightfully theirs, or cheat them.

Nearly everybody agrees that international relations are a type of human relations where the secondary rules about when it is alright to hit other people, take their stuff and break promises to them are particularly strong. Historically, most people have assumed that any international society between states or world society between peoples is not as strong as the societies we find inside states, and that we can manage without strong international societies or world societies. Historically, most people have also assumed that they were not obliged and had no need to treat foreigners as well as they treated their own kind.

As we have seen in Chapters 4 and 5, some people always objected to making these distinctions between "Inside" and "Outside" and between "Ourselves" and "Others" as morally wrong. Some people always objected to the use of force even in self-defense. Consider Christ's injunction to the apostle Peter that he should not attempt to resist those who'd come to arrest him. Other people have come to the conclusion that modern weaponry is so destructive that war has become obsolescent as a way of getting things done. War might have been useful in the past, but it is not **obsolete** because there are still wars.

Is war obsolescent? Admiral Rickover's view

President Carter and Admiral Rickover, who developed nuclear submarines which could launch nuclear weapons, were interviewed by Dianne Sawyer in 1984. Carter said of Rickover, "One of the most remarkable things he ever told me was when we were together on the submarine and he said that he wished that a nuclear explosive had never been evolved. And then he said, 'I wish that nuclear power had never been discovered.' And I said, 'Admiral, this is your life.' He said, 'I would forego all the accomplishments of my life, and I would be willing to forego all the advantages of nuclear power to propel ships, for medical research and for every other purpose of generating electric power, if we could have avoided the evolution of atomic explosives." (The interview can be seen at this link: http://www.people.vcu.edu/~rsleeth/Rickover.html.)

If this is so, surely we ought to be getting rid of war before we blow up, irradiate or poison the whole planet by using weapons of mass destruction? But how?

One approach is to see if we can research and learn a cure to international conflict and competition. As we saw in Chapter 1, a main reason for establishing the academic study of International Relations after World War I was to find out why wars had occurred in the past, how to stop them, and how to avoid them in the future. It was hoped that through **peace research** we would find answers, and through **peace education** we would change the way citizens and governments thought about warfare and they would learn how to avoid it.

In a sense, the class you are taking right now is a product of these assumptions. Your professor almost certainly hopes that by taking this course you will learn not just why wars happen, but why they are tragic, wasteful, and dangerous, and that you would be very reluctant to vote for a politician who said otherwise. Peace research has done valuable work on issues like working out the real costs and destructiveness of war, and trying to establish correlations between, for example, the likelihood of violence occurring and basic economic and social conditions. It has done much to undermine older arguments about the necessity of war and some of the benefits said to flow from it. It has also identified the processes by which states prepare for war by spending on arms and who benefits from these processes. Peace education has done much to disseminate these findings and to advocate non-violent techniques for resolving disputes. Yet there are still wars. Some people have not got peace education's message about the destructiveness of war. Some people, like Adolf Hitler and other fascists, disagree with it or don't care about it. They are prepared to use force to get what they want. As a consequence, even most thoughtful, sensitive, and well-informed people who get the message of peace education are still prepared to go to war on occasions, even though they are well aware of its terrible consequences. Nearly everyone, it seems, values some things more than preserving peace.

Knowledge alone, therefore, has not provided a cure for war, at least not so far. Like medical researchers, however, peace researchers say that they spend less time thinking about a cure for all war, and more time thinking about how to influence the conditions in which international conflict and competition occur. We have no cure as yet for many illnesses such as cancer, Alzheimer's, and AIDS. Through research, however, we can discover how to reduce the odds of developing some of them, reduce some of their worst effects, and make life with them more manageable. People who study International Relations sometimes talk the same way. The challenge is not to find a cure for international conflict and competition; it is to manage them.

Key terms

basic primary social rules   The idea that there are certain primary rules which must be present for any society to exist and function. They are usually said to be about force, property, and promises, and can be greatly modified by secondary rules in particular cases.

obsolete   The idea that something no longer serves its function and therefore no longer exists or is no longer used. In contrast, obsolescent refers to something which no longer serves its function as well as alternatives might but is still used. Penny farthing bicycles and slavery as a legitimate institution could be said to be obsolete. Volkswagen Beetles and war could be said to be obsolescent.

peace education   Teaching the results of peace research to all citizens and training them in ways which will make it less likely that they use force themselves or support its use by others.

peace research   Systematic and multidisciplinary inquiry into the causes and conditions of war and peace, how wars are to be avoided, shortened and made less costly, and how peace is to be encouraged, strengthened, and made permanent.

Key takeaways

- Nearly everyone agrees that using force and violence against other people is nearly always bad and there are nearly always rules against it.
- Some people say that without rules against using force and violence against other people, societies could not function.
- Some people say that hurting other people is simply morally wrong.
- Nearly everyone agrees that force and violence can be used sometimes, like in self-defense.
- Nearly everyone agrees that force and violence are more likely in international relations than in domestic relations.
- As war has become more destructive, International Relations scholars have looked for cures for international conflict and competition and ways of managing them, through research and education.

Exercises

1. Why do we have basic primary social rules against using force and violence?
2. Why do we have secondary rules about when we can override the primary rules about force and violence?
3. Is war obsolete or obsolescent, or neither?
4. Are international conflict and competition curable?

6.4   Managing international conflict and competition

Learning objectives

1. Describe how international conflict and competition might be managed by balancing power.
2. Describe how international conflict and competition may be managed by a single powerful state.
3. Explain how international conflict and competition could be managed by re-organizing international relations.

A successful cure for all international conflict and competition has not been developed yet, and there may never be one. How then are international conflict and competition to be managed in the meantime? One answer is through maintaining a **balance of power**. The theory of the balance of power states that in any system of sovereign states which value their independence, if one of them becomes stronger than the rest, the others will try to balance its strength. The other states will try to balance the stronger state by building up their own strength and/or make alliances with each other. With any luck, the strong state will back off and reduce its strength. If it doesn't, however, the others will have to be prepared to fight it to put it back in its place. Very often, one of the winning members of the balance of power alliance will do better than the rest from the fight and emerge stronger. Then the mechanism shifts direction with the new strong state's allies joining sides with the state they have just defeated to put the new strong state back in its place. Between two states or two alliances, the balance of power would work like a simple pair of scales. Between several states, the balance of power would look more like the sort of mobile placed over an infant's crib or cot.

Modern European diplomatic history seems to confirm this pattern. First Spain emerged in the 16th century and was beaten by a balancing alliance led by France. France got stronger than the rest and was beaten by a balancing alliance led by the British and the Dutch. Then Britain became too strong and was defeated by an alliance of European states (plus the Americans), which let France back to the top by the start of the 19th century. France was defeated by a coalition led by Prussia (the core of the future German state), and then Germany came to the fore to be defeated in the two world wars. The middle of the 20th century was marked by a great contest between the US and the Soviet Union. The Soviet Union collapsed under the strain, leaving the US as the last superpower. If the balance of power theory is right, the United States will soon be confronted by a hostile alliance of states seeking to put it back in its place.

The theory of the balance of power seems simple and attractive. However, it has a number of problems.

- People use the term—balance of power—to mean different things. Sometimes, for example, they mean the distribution of power. Governments especially talk about achieving favorable balances of power which—if you think about it—are not really balances of power, but imbalances of power in their state's favor.

- What does it mean to say that a balance of power exists between two or more states? Do they have the same amount of power as each other and, if so, how do you tell, or does there just have to be a very rough balance so that no one is strong enough to be tempted to take advantage of anyone else? Is there, for example, a balance of power between the US and the rest of the world?

- Is it an **automatic balance of power** which operates no matter what governments think of the theory, or is it a **contrived balance of power** where states have to know and accept the assumptions of the theory for it to work? Remember from Chapter 2 how the US and China, even though they were scared to death of each other, started cooperating against the Soviet Union when they began to see it as a common rival or enemy. Also consider, however, how political thinkers in the US have disliked and reject the balance of power as a European-inspired racket. If a big state like the US does not believe in the theory of the balance of power, can a real balance of power operate?

- Does the historical record actually back the claim that states are interested in operating a balance of power to maintain their independence? In 1871, when France was going down to defeat at the hands of the Prussian—soon to be the German—empire, the theory would have suggested Britain coming to France's rescue to balance Prussia-Germany. The British, who supposedly liked the theory of the balance of power, refused to hitch their wagon to the failing French and stayed neutral.

- If the theory of the balance of power needs states to be willing to fight wars to preserve the balance of power, then is it really a way of managing international conflict and competition? It is often argued that the two world wars were fought because Germany had become too strong, but do we want to think of these two wars which killed millions as ways of managing international conflict and competition, as opposed to catastrophes which needed better management themselves?

The theory of the balance of power seems reasonable. We can see it operating very clearly on some occasions, usually when states or their governments see things in balance of power terms. Very often they do not, however, and sometimes when they talk in balance of power terms it is not clear that they are being honest. Why, after all, did the Soviet Union need balancing by the US, plus all its allies in the developed world plus China in the 1970s? This would seem like an imbalance.

And why is no one seriously trying to balance the US at the moment, even though it spends nearly as much as the rest of the world together on its armed forces and weapons? Indeed, given China's rise and the relative decline of the US, who needs balancing in the world today—China or the US? The theory of the balance of power is not very helpful when it comes to answering these sorts of questions.

One response to these difficulties, suggested by Stephen Walt, is to talk about a "balance of threat" rather than a balance of power.[7] The Soviet Union, in this view, might not have been as powerful as the states balancing it, but it posed the threat, not them. The United States today is not balanced, despite its strength, because it does not pose a threat to others. This argument foreshadows the sort of claims made by Wendt that we examined in Chapter 4, but it is not clear that the metaphor of balances and balancing works well with intentions and perceptions of them. Another approach gets rid of the idea of balances completely. **Hegemonic stability theory** says that balance of power theory is not very helpful because it's wrong. There is no automatic balance of power going on and states are not always wise if they try to contrive one. Balancing is way too difficult a game to play in a complicated world of imperfect information. States actually get more worried about each other when they are close to equal in power and a transition from one state being the most powerful to another being the most powerful looks likely.[8] Germany in 1914, for example, was the strongest European power, but its planners had calculated that within a few years its rivals—especially Russia—would catch up. It was the fear of being caught and overtaken that made it so aggressive during the first twenty years of the 20th century. It has been argued that the US exhibited this kind of aggressiveness in the 1960s as the Soviet Union appeared to catch up with it, and is starting to exhibit it again as China continues to rise.

Besides, critics of the theory of the balance of power argue, states are not interested in balances. They are interested in being secure. Most states do this by trying to keep out of trouble or lining up—**bandwagoning**—with the strong, if they cannot be strong themselves. A very few, big, powerful states try to make themselves secure by being a **hegemon**, the strongest state of all, leading the rest and making the rules for them. Hegemonic stability theory suggests that once you have a hegemon which is much stronger than everybody else, then no one will bother to try to balance it—a situation which is very good for the hegemon and very good for anyone else who is interested in minimizing international conflict and competition.

Not surprisingly, it is people in the hegemonic power and its closest allies who tend to be most sympathetic to this line of argument. US foreign and defense policy statements, although they do not use the "h" word, make it very clear that the US intends to be the most powerful and leading state in the world for as long as it can, because this is good for the US and for everyone else. China, Russia, and Europe do not need big military forces in this view, just enough for their local needs. Anything more would make everybody tense for no good reason since the US is already maintaining peace and an international order which suits everybody.

Equally unsurprisingly, it is people in states which have the potential to be hegemons themselves who are the least impressed with this argument. The

Russians and the Chinese, for example, argue that the US exercises world leadership for itself, rather than for everybody, and that all the great powers should act in **concert** with each other to provide collective global leadership. Since the US will not listen, they argue, they have to build up their own military power to get Washington's attention to their views, but they explicitly reject the idea of becoming hegemons themselves. The US is unimpressed with this argument. Russia and China both want to be hegemons, it suggests, and they would not be as effective or as good at it as the US. Rather than risk the dangerous rivalries that might emerge if they built up their power, the US says, they should accept a US global leadership which lets them have their say. If they won't listen to this argument, then the US should try to stay so far ahead of them in military terms that they become disheartened and stop trying to catch up with the US.

Balance of power theorists and hegemonic stability theorists both think in terms of great power states, or one great power state, managing international conflict and competition. Others focus on re-organizing international relations themselves. To these people, arguments about whether international conflict and international competition are best reduced by the balance of power between great powers, a concert of cooperating great powers, or a single great power hegemon who leads and makes rules for the rest often sound self-serving. This is especially so when they are made by the statesmen, politicians, and, sometimes, academics of the great power states in question. Under all this talk, critics and skeptics say, each of these big states is mainly out for itself, trying to be number one and, if it cannot manage that, stopping anyone else from being number one. It can be no other way so long as we live in the political anarchy which is the only sort of international system which sovereign states are capable of generating if left to themselves. As we saw in Chapter 2, each state has to look after itself in this sort of self-help system because no one else will, and this will invariably lead to collisions between them. If people really want to reduce international conflict and competition, therefore, critics say we have to change the basic rules of the game. We saw how the Liberal Internationalists attempted this after World War I with the League of Nations and collective security in Chapters 2 and 3. We will examine the collective security, peacekeeping, and peace-building approaches to the management of international conflict and competition undertaken by the UN and its members today in Chapter 8.

Key terms

automatic balance of power   A Positivist version of the balance of power theory that says the balancing process operates as a "natural" law or structural property of systems of states whether or not the governments of the participating states are aware of it.

balance of power   A theory that when one state becomes stronger than the other states and poses a threat to their independence, they will balance it by building up their own strength and/or making alliances with each other.

bandwagoning   A theory which says that under most conditions states are more likely to align with a powerful state than to try to balance it.

concert   An idea which suggests that two or more major powers can cooperate with each other to perform the role of a hegemon in an international system.

contrived balance of power   A Post-positivist version of the balance of power theory that says that the governments of states have to be aware of its principles—especially regarding restraining other states and self-restraint—and wise enough apply them for the theory to work.

hegemon   A state so powerful that it not only leads the rest but makes and upholds the rules by which they conduct their relations with each other.

hegemonic stability theory   A theory which says that an international system is more stable when there is a state strong enough to be the hegemon than when there is not, and that the order of the system will reflect the hegemon's interests, preferences, and values.

Key takeaways

- There may be no final cure for international conflict and international competition but people have attempted to manage them in ways which make them less likely, less costly and less damaging.

- The theory of the balance of power says that when one state becomes stronger than the rest, the others seek to balance it by building up their own strength and/or building alliances with others. It is one of the oldest approaches to managing international conflict and competition, but there are arguments over how the term is used and whether states actually try to balance.

- Hegemonic stability theory says that great power states do not try to balance. They try to boss and it is best if one of them is so powerful that it can manage by leading and making the rules without anyone trying to challenge it. This may be true, but the theory can be criticized as a rationalization of what the strongest state at any given moment wants. Other great power states are less impressed with the argument.

- Other approaches suggest that international conflict and competition can be managed by reorganizing international relations. The League of Nations with its domestication of international relations with rules backed by a collective security system to punish the rule-breakers is one example of such a re-organization. So too is the UN, although this adds peacekeeping, peace-building and concert approaches to managing international conflict and cooperation mainly through a concert of several powerful states.

Exercises

1. In what two ways is the balance of power supposed to work?
2. What problems are there with the theory of the balance of power?
3. In what way is hegemonic stability theory supposed to work?
4. What problems are there with hegemonic stability theory?

6.5	The future of international conflict and competition in an era of uncertainty

What might future international conflict and competition look like? They will both remain important. Competition risks conflict and conflict can kill, hurt and damage people, destroy property, and waste resources. The increasing destructiveness of warfare means that conflict and competition can put the entire planet and life on it at risk. The track record of using force and violence is generally regarded as poor except when they are used in response to others using force and violence first. Everyone says they are against the sort of international conflict and competition which leads to war, but nearly everyone believes there are some things for which it is worth fighting, killing, and dying.

People give all sorts of reasons for fighting. States have all sorts of motives for fighting—security, independence, economic welfare, and prestige—some of which they hide behind official reasons, some of which they are not really aware of themselves. Researchers are very interested in these motives on the assumption that if we can figure out when people are more likely to fight, then we can work for conditions which make it less likely they fight. The academic study of International Relations was established with the explicit idea of finding the cause of war and then finding a cure for it.

However, the "big ideas" about how to cure international conflict and competition continue to disappoint. They have not delivered in the big way their original authors hoped they might. The same can be said up to a point for human beings' "big ideas" about how to manage international conflict. Some point to a patchy record of military interventions, especially in recent years, and speak of progress. The former republics of Yugoslavia plus Kosovo, together with Liberia, Sierra Leone, Côte d'Ivoire, and Rwanda in Africa, can all be presented as places which are no longer the troublemakers they used to be for both themselves and their neighbors thanks to management by a mix of international organizations and great power states. In contrast, Afghanistan, Iraq, Syria, Libya, Sudan/South Sudan, can all be presented as places where managing conflict has not yet worked, may never work, and may have made things worse. They can also be presented as places, along with the Crimea, Ukraine, and Yemen, where the great powers and others intervened with force not to manage conflict so much as to get their own way. One of the reasons for these interventions has been the steady increase in the ability of non-state actors—guerilla forces and terrorists, for example—to gain access to violent means. The next chapter examines how states and others actually use force. As we shall see, states spend a great deal of time and effort fighting non-state actors with limited success. As we shall also see, however, one of the key elements of uncertainty in contemporary international relations is that states seem to be giving more thought and committing more resources to the reviving possibility that they may have to fight each other.

Recommended reading

Robert Ardrey, *The Territorial Imperative: A Personal Inquiry into the Origins of Property and Nations*, New York, 1966.

Helen Caldicott, *Missile Envy: The Arms Race and Nuclear War*, New York, 1985.

Robert Gilpin, *War and Change in World Politics*, Cambridge, 1981.

Ian M. Harris and Mary Lee Morrison, *Peace Education* (3rd edition), Jefferson, NC, 2012.

Michael Howard, *The Causes of War and Other Essays* (2nd edition), Cambridge, Mass., 1983.

Paul Kennedy, *The Rise and Fall of Great Powers*, New York, 1987.

T.V. Paul, James Wirtz, and Michel Fortmann (eds.), *Balance of Power: Theory and Practice in the 21st Century*, Stanford, 2004.

Stephen M. Walt, *The Origins of Alliances*, Ithaca, 1990.

Charles Webel and Johan Galtung (eds.), *Handbook of Peace and Conflict Studies*, London, 2007.

Notes

1 John Keegan, *A History of Warfare*, London, 1994.
2 John Mueller, *The Remnants of War*, Ithaca, 2004.
3 Jeremy Black, *The Age of Total War: 1860–1945*, Santa Barbara, 2006.
4 John Keegan, *A History of Warfare*, London, 1993, p. 391
5 Kenneth Waltz, *Man, the State and War*, New York, 1959.
6 Hedley Bull, *The Anarchical Society*, Basingstoke, 1977.
7 Stephen M. Walt, "Alliance Formation and the Balance of World Power," *International Security*, 9, 4, 3–43, 1985.
8 A.F.K Organski and Jacek Kugler, *The War Ledger*, Chicago, 1981.

7 Military power and war

Preamble

The previous two chapters examined force as an instrument of foreign policy and the types of causes of international conflict and competition. This chapter examines the way states and others actually use **force** and **violence** in the form of military power and **war**. War can seem exciting and glorious. However, most people, especially those who have been in wars, say that there is not much glory and there is a great deal of fear. Some wars may be necessary, but all of them cause pain, suffering, and waste. War poses complex practical problems which are fascinating to study. So too, however, did the Nazi request to German engineers in World War II to come up with the best way to kill millions of people efficiently. They came up with gas chambers as a practical solution. The old gospel song "Down by the Riverside" has as its chorus "I ain't gonna study war no more" (follow the link to see the song being sung at an anti-war march in Los Angeles in 2007: http://www.youtube.com/watch?v=vsBOh2Vp71U). "Study" is used in the sense of dwelling on something bad in an unhealthy way, but in studying war the way we do below, it is worth keeping in mind this caution.

The basic ideas about how to wage war are simple.[1] Armed forces try to defend the territory where their people live and attack their enemy's armed forces to beat them, capture territory, or both. In addition, navies and air forces seek "command of the commons" (the sea and air space used by everyone), to use those commons and to deny their use to enemies.[2] The strong in terms of power and numbers try to be "fastest with the mostest" to the critical spot on the battlefield. The weak try to avoid a showdown, escape destruction, and make nuisances of themselves. The weak also hope for a "David and Goliath" moment when technology or circumstance gives them a temporary advantage, as in the Bible when David brought down the heavily armed Goliath with a stone from his slingshot. The strong try to avoid such moments or to neutralize them, and to make their advantage in strength count.

As the Prussian staff officer and "philosopher of war," Karl von Clausewitz, noted however, actually executing the simplest task successfully is difficult because of the frictions and fog of war. Moving large numbers of people and supplies poses organizational problems. Soldiers can get tired and scared. Orders may not be received or understood. Equipment may break, supplies fail to show up, and information may be incomplete or wrong, especially about the opponent's strength, resolve, and intentions. In addition, social and technological changes produce old problems in new forms. Just who the combatants and non-combatants are has become harder to determine with the rise of guerrilla warfare and terrorism, and a new dimension to warfare has developed with the rise of cyberspace and attacks against the information networks on which complex military and civilian systems increasingly depend. Military planners and armed forces try to see through the fog of war and to reduce its frictions. They often fail and are forced to adjust and improvise once the fighting starts.

Even the simplest things are difficult: Operation Desert Sabre, February 1991

In the ground phase of the military operation to liberate Kuwait from Iraqi occupation, the American commander, General Norman Schwarzkopf Jr., faced an apparently simple problem. In front of his forces were large numbers of poorly equipped Iraqi troops who had been under air bombardment for weeks. They were, nevertheless, well dug in and many of them had combat experience. On the Iraqis' left flank was the sea, on their right flank, the open desert. Schwarzkopf had four options: a weak amphibious attack by sea; a direct, and possibly costly, frontal assault against the Iraqi positions; a move around the Iraqi right flank with his mobile, modern armored forces into the open desert; or combinations of all three. Schwarzkopf went for a combination, but with his main effort driving around the Iraqi right flank and on into Kuwait (Figure 7.1). This was no chess puzzle. The concept behind Schwarzkopf's plan was very simple, and he had all sorts of advantages over his opponent in the quality and quantity of his forces which made it possible for them to carry it out.

However, even this simple plan was difficult to execute and depended on hugely complex problems being solved. The superiority of Schwarzkopf's forces and their equipment did not just happen. It was the product of years of training and investment made possible by political decisions. Moving this great mass of people, plus keeping them supplied and fueled needed preparation and then improvisation as the attack began to develop. And the plan involved risks and courage. What if the chains of command and supply broke down and the armored forces were left stuck deep in hostile territory? What if the other side fought hard, and its best troops counter-attacked? In the end, most of the Iraqis did not fight hard because of the battering they had taken from the air. Schwarzkopf's troops advanced on all fronts, and the fighting was soon over. It looked simple and easy. Compared to some fights, it was easy. Even so, the execution of Schwarzkopf's plan was made possible by solving very difficult operational problems, minimizing risks and being willing to take those risks which remained. To achieve this sort of success also involves large and long-standing commitments on the part of a state and its people in terms of their wealth, time, and lives.

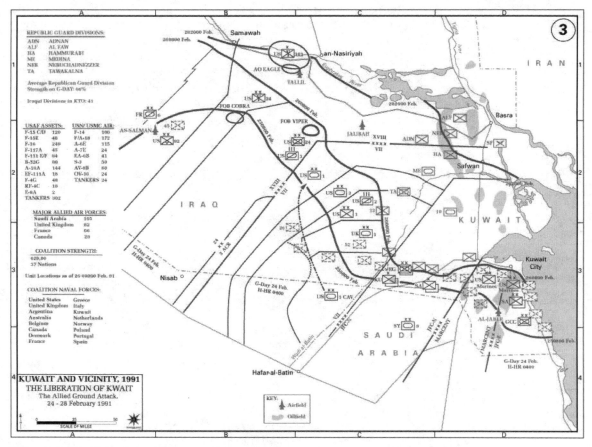

Figure 7.1 The liberation of Kuwait, 1991

(Source: http://www.usma.edu/history/SiteAssets/SitePages/First%20Gulf%20War/GulfWarFirst03.gif Permission granted by the Department of History, United States Military Academy)

Note: Allied forces in dark gray, Iraqi forces in light gray.

7.1 Land power

Learning objectives

1. List the key elements of contemporary **land power**.
2. Describe what land power is used for by states.
4. Describe **symmetrical warfare**.
5. Explain **asymmetrical warfare** and the problems it poses for the armies of states.

The longest established form of fighting takes place on land. Most human groups have developed some form of land power and engaged in fighting as a result of their willingness to use force to get what they want. There are variations, however, in terms of the resources they commit to fighting, how hard they fight, and their reasons for fighting. As noted in Chapter 6, some human groups have been content to have their young men line up to make faces and rude remarks, and lob things at the young men of the opposing group. Once someone got hurt, they might call it a day and go back home to their daily lives. Others have devoted far more effort to organizing themselves and fought with far more violence. Indeed, some peoples have developed warfare and the rewards it could bring in terms of captured land, goods, and slaves as a big part of their way of life. For physical and material reasons, the actual fighting was usually done by men and boys, although no one was exempt from supporting the "war effort" by growing food, tending the wounded, and encouraging their young men to fight. And no one—young, old, male, female—was exempt from the suffering, especially in defeat.

The idea of the state and many actual states have their origins in war. Food surpluses freed up some people to be leaders, priests, and warriors. This division of labor made it possible to have an army—an organized body of men and, increasingly today, women—trained to fight on land in defense of the state and against those its leaders say are the enemies of the state and its people. Different societies produce different types of armies. The early modern states of 15th-century Europe, for example, had economies sustained by agriculture. Their armies were restricted in size by how many people they could afford to take out of planting, growing, tending, and harvesting and for how long. A small social class of landowners produced knights and other military experts who mobilized and led their local peasants in usually short, local fights for limited objectives.

States, like those in northern Italy in the 15th and 16th centuries, which made their living from financial services and trade, rather than farming, tended to be smaller, richer, and composed of urban citizens even less willing to fight than their rural counterparts. Accordingly, these states often maintained small forces of highly trained professional soldiers—mercenaries—who were not often interested in getting themselves killed in the service of their paymasters. Exceptions to the general pressure to keep fighting limited did exist, however. Sometimes, during the Crusades, for example, a Big Idea like reconquering the Holy Land could capture the imagination of large numbers of people. And sometimes, empires in which one people ruled over others—like the Austrian or Ottoman empires—could maintain large armies and make war and conquest into a profitable business. By the 18th century, however, European states like France, Spain, Britain, Prussia, and Russia maintained relatively small professional armies of poorly paid, brutally disciplined, young men to be used in limited wars abroad and to preserve order at home. Life was tough for the soldiers, but they were fed, clothed, and, if they lived, might look forward to a retirement with a modest pension and a very modest amount of social status.

The great revolutions of the late 18th and early 19th centuries upset this formula. As we saw in Chapters 5 and 6, the social revolution in France claimed to transfer "ownership" of states from their kings to their citizens. Citizens could be mobilized in large numbers in the name of liberty, equality, fraternity, and patriotism to fight for their own state. The old professional armies of Austria, Russia, and Prussia were defeated by the citizen armies of France, until they responded in kind with their own mass armies motivated by similar ideas. And on both sides, as the losses mounted, citizen soldiers were increasingly replaced by conscripts, drafted in whether they liked it or not. The Industrial Revolution hugely expanded the destructive firepower of these armies. By the end of the 19th century each of the great European military power states (except Britain) possessed big armies maintained by the draft and supported by a system of reserves made up of former soldiers who could be called back into the service.

The effects of these revolutions were complex, however. Big armies of relatively highly motivated citizens were possible, but these citizens had their own ideas about why they fought, how they should fight, and when they should stop. Thus the outcome of World War I was decided partly by military victory, but partly by the citizens of some states no longer wanting to fight. By the start of World War II in 1939, European states either had to follow the very brutal approach to military and social discipline followed by the Soviet Union and the Japanese Empire, or they had to be very aware of the limits in terms of losses and sacrifices which they could impose on their own troops. Technology expanded the destructive power of land warfare with the continued development of machine guns, heavy artillery, tanks and other armored fighting vehicles. Unless a state could stay at the technical cutting edge in terms of the performance of its military equipment, it simply could not compete with those states which did. Yet weapons technology became increasingly expensive and complex and, as it did, this raised questions about the kind of soldiers needed to operate it.

The defeat of the Confederacy in the American civil war and the Boers by the British in South Africa suggested that the old martial virtues of warfare—horsemanship, marksmanship, field craft, and toughness—were losing out to the ability to mass produce and equip large armies. Instead, soldiers had to be highly educated—by historical standards—and well trained if they were going to operate military equipment effectively. As the Arab states showed in the second half of the 20th century, it was no good being able to afford the very latest military equipment if the soldiers—simple young men from the countryside—lacked the education which would make them trainable for handling sophisticated weapons.

Welsh longbows, Brown Bess muskets, and Kalashnikov rifles: complexities of weapons technologies and training

The Welsh longbow used by archers in medieval times was more accurate, had more hitting power and a higher rate of fire than several generations of firearms which followed. Young men had to train to the bow from boyhood, however, to develop the skills and right muscles. Musket men simply needed to be disciplined into loading and firing without running away under fire. The AK 47 (Kalashnikov) assault rifle was developed in the

Soviet Union at the end of World War II. Today, there are more accurate assault rifles with greater hitting power and a higher rate of fire, but none are as cheap and simple to manufacture and maintain as the AK 47. It is still widely used by armies, guerrillas, and terrorists. The best weapon is not always the best choice.

Today, a state's army will reflect the state's size, wealth, and level of economic development. It will also reflect its history, culture, and the neighborhood it occupies in terms of potential friends and enemies. Underlying all these factors is the steadily rising price of maintaining armies and their equipment. As a consequence, the armies of most states are quite small by wartime standards and lightly equipped. They consist of infantry—usually professional soldiers rather than drafted conscripts—who do their fighting on their feet, although trucks and armored fighting vehicles will be used to move some of them. There may also be some engineers for bridge and road building, some signalers for communications, and some small canon or mortars for providing light artillery support. The symbolic significance of these armies may be more important than their actual potential for combat. They are proof that their state is independent and sovereign. They are more likely to be used in helping with national disasters like earthquakes and floods, and on peacekeeping operations for the UN (see Chapter 8) and other international bodies than in wars with other states.

Even some quite large and wealthy states like Canada and the former European great powers—France, Germany, and Britain, for example—have relatively small, if up-to-date, volunteer armies. They use volunteers because the drafted citizens of developed states tend not to make effective soldiers except in times of national crisis when the survival of the state is in question. They keep their forces relatively small because equipping and paying their soldiers is very expensive. It is assumed that they are unlikely to be fighting other developed states and that, if they do, they will not fight alone but in alliances with others. It is also assumed that these small professional forces will form the experienced core of an expanded force should a state-to-state war occur and last long enough for a bigger force to be developed.

Other states, especially developing states whose relations with their neighbors are uneasy, try to maintain as large and as diverse armies as they can afford. They keep large armed force partly because it is usually easier to draft soldiers in developing states and they can be paid very little. They also maintain large armed forces because they feel threatened by neighbors outside the state and by opponents inside it. Many of the Arab states of the Middle East—Syria, Iraq, and Egypt—for example, have large armies in proportion to their respective size and wealth with infantry, motorized or mechanized infantry, artillery and missile or rocket units, and, above all, armor. As the television broadcasts of national day and May Day parades in some states show, the tanks of these armored formations, with their caterpillar tracks, traversing turrets, and long menacing gun barrels are impressive symbols of state power when they rumble by (see the last ten minutes of video clip of a 2017 North Korean military parade at the following link: https://www.youtube.com/watch?v=ZQxW_ipxEEo).

They have also been important during the ground wars in which these states have been involved. Fast moving, heavily armored tank formations are the most useful type of troops for surrounding and destroying enemy forces and quickly capturing territory for the infantry to hold. Yet these armored formations are often less impressive than they look or than they used to be. When they come up against the latest tanks of a first rate military power—like the United States or Russia—as they did in Iraq, they cannot compete. Their armor is not strong enough to resist the advanced shells of the American and other NATO tanks. Their shells cannot penetrate the advanced armor of the American and NATO tanks which also move quicker, fire faster and more accurately, and have much better information about where their opponents are and what they are doing.

A small, but growing, number of states are able to afford to buy or develop the very latest weapons. A smaller, but again, growing number—Russia, China, Japan, the European Union states perhaps if they act together, possibly India and Brazil, and the US—are able to deploy soldiers equipped with the latest weapons in great numbers. Only one, the US, has first rate capabilities in all the elements of land warfare: armor, mobile infantry, mobile artillery and missiles, combat and regular engineers, anti-aircraft and missile defenses, and special forces like paratroops and marines capable of undertaking aggressive assaults ranging in size from full-scale amphibious landings to precise hostage rescuing and assassination missions. Plus, only the US has the ships and aircraft to move its forces to nearly anywhere in the world.

The US worries about the challenge of staying ahead of the rest, and the rest worry about the challenge of trying to catch up in a world of spiraling defense costs and economic difficulties. Everybody also worries about what kind of armies they need. On the one hand, today's armies still assume that their primary mission is fighting each other—what the US military has termed symmetrical warfare. Russia and China are expanding their capabilities for fighting wars against other states, while the US and its allies continue to invest in the latest weapons for fighting such wars. On the other hand, the number of state-on-state wars has been in decline since 1945, especially for the military great power states. There have been no symmetrical wars between them since then. As we shall see below, states have been increasingly involved in irregular or asymmetrical warfare against usually small groups of lightly armed guerrillas and terrorists. The result is uncertainty and considerable debate in all the great powers about the extent to which they need different types of armed forces and the extent to which a one-size-fits-all army can accomplish very different sorts of missions.

What kind of war? Obama, Biden, and McChrystal

If there were rules about which wars to fight, Rule Two would be "never invade Afghanistan" (Rule One would be "never invade Russia"). Greek, Persian, Mongol, British, and Russian armies have all had a miserable time in Afghanistan trying to subdue, civilize, or shape the destiny of its peoples. Invaders (those who weren't killed) have left before they got what they wanted, and the US-led operation, following the 9–11 attacks in 2001, seems to be no exception. It began well. With US air support, the Afghan enemies of the Taliban government which had sheltered Al Qaeda, soon occupied the capital, Kabul. The Taliban fled, but they did not give up. Weeks turned into months. Months turned into years. More and more soldiers from the US and its NATO allies came to help the Afghan government, but control of large parts of the state kept slipping away. When President Barack Obama was first elected in 2008, he faced a difficult question. Should the US cut its losses or should it double down to see if it could rescue victory from the jaws of what was at best a stalemate? Over the next two years, the debate was fierce. Vice-President Biden suggested relying on missile strikes from the air and aggressive patrolling by Special Forces to target the Taliban leadership. Regular soldiers would be pulled back from remote areas to protect the towns, and this would allow the US and its allies to start bringing soldiers home. The US military commander, General McChrystal, maintained that if the US was still serious about winning, then drones, missiles, and Special Forces were no substitute for having lots more soldiers to clear and hold territory in which a new life for Afghans could be built from the bottom up.

The arguments were fierce, and McChrystal was fired after disrespectful remarks by his staff about Biden got into the press. Obama did increase the number of US troops, although he made it clear this was for a limited period of time to give the Afghan government's forces a last chance to improve. He worried that under Biden's plan the situation would get worse, but that the costs of McChrystal's plan were prohibitive—how many soldiers, for how long, and how would you know the plan was working? Obama's compromise between the two options possibly stopped a complete collapse. The US and its allies were still committed to leaving and almost no one was optimistic about what would happen to Afghanistan after their troops were gone. As a result, reduced numbers of American and allied troops remain in Afghanistan primarily in an advisory role, although their numbers may be expanded following advice to President Trump by his commanders.

Key terms

asymmetrical warfare War or armed conflict between different sorts of actors, usually heavily armed states on one side and lightly armed guerrillas and/or terrorists on the other with different types of armed forces and military power.

force The purposeful use of violence.

land power Armed forces designed to control, capture, and/or hold territory and other assets primarily by fighting on land.

symmetrical warfare War between similar actors, usually states, with similar types of armed forces and military power.

violence Acts of destruction which can have material, social, and psychological consequences.

war The use of organized collective force by a state or state-like actor for political purposes.

Key takeaways

- Armies provide the basic form of land power for states.
- States have armies mainly to hold and capture territory along with the people and resources in them.
- Today, nearly all states have armies, but only a few great military power states have large armies with up-to-date equipment, and only the US has the means to send large numbers of soldiers to nearly any part of the world.
- Most armies are organized, trained, and equipped to fight other armies in *symmetrical* wars.
- Most wars today are *asymmetrical* with one side consisting of a state or states.
- States find it difficult to engage in *asymmetrical warfare* for military, political, and economic reasons.

Exercises

1. Why do most developed states today maintain only relatively small armies?
2. Why is the US so effective at *symmetrical warfare*?
3. Why have the US and other great military powers struggled with *asymmetrical warfare*?

7.2 Sea power

Learning objectives

1. List the reasons why a state might want to have **sea power**.
2. Explain how sea power differs from land power.
3. Describe the factors which shape the type of sea power a state may try to develop.

Some states develop their sea power for the same reasons that some states develop their land power. They want to control the seas around them. They may also want to control the seas around other states. In addition, however, they may want to control or keep open for shipping the seas and oceans across which their people and goods need to travel. As with land power, this involves actions ranging from simple patrolling—policing the seas helping those in distress and protecting seafarers from piracy, to fighting big battles against the warships of other states, bombarding their territory and towns before landing soldiers, and sinking the merchant (trading) ships of other states.

Fighting at sea must have developed later than fighting on land for obvious physical and technical reasons. As soon as people learned how to travel on water, they learned to fight on it as well. John Keegan notes for most of human history fighting at sea took place by coasts in support of fighting on land.[3] It looked very much like fighting on land with the decks of ships providing the wooden "ground" on which soldiers fought in battles to capture each other's ships. As on land, fighting at sea was modified by the development of bows and arrows, catapults, and, eventually, firearms and cannon. It was also modified by technological developments which permitted ships specifically designed for fighting rather than carrying goods and people. From this point on, it was possible for cities, empires, and other types of states to maintain collections of fighting ships which we would call fleets, all the fleets of purpose-built warships of a state being its navy.

Originally, even purpose-built warships stayed close to home and were used primarily for **coastal defense**. Further developments in ship design, propulsion systems, and armaments allowed sea power gradually to spread from coastal areas to the blue water of the oceans far from land. China had the first **blue water navy** in the early 15th century, but scrapped it for economic and cultural reasons. By the late 18th century, the great European military power states had fleets of different types of sailing ships. Some of them were large, armed with heavy cannon to take their place in the line of battle, fighting the ships-of-the-line or battleships of other fleets. They fired at each other's masts and hulls, but their crews also boarded each other's decks to fight "land" battles as sailors had done for centuries. Smaller vessels of essentially the same design—known as frigates or cruisers—patrolled the shipping lanes of the oceans to protect their own merchant ships, and to attack those of other states. Still smaller ships—sloops, brigs, and corvettes—were used for a multitude of duties: escorting, exploring, surveying, and trying to catch smugglers.

There are two big differences between sea power and land power.

- Ships can sink and be sunk. The biggest and strongest ships can be vulnerable to the smallest and weakest in a way which is rarely the case with soldiers and armies.

- The oceans cannot be occupied like land, so there are two basic ways of using sea power. A stronger navy can try to gain what the American Admiral Mahan called **command of the sea**, blockading or defeating enemy fleets, chasing enemy merchant ships from the oceans, and patrolling the important sea lanes so friendly goods and armies move freely.[4] A weaker navy can pursue what the French called *guerre de course* avoiding pitched battles with the enemy fleet and using hit-and-run raids to disrupt the enemy's merchant shipping.

Ships shifted from sail to coal and then to oil to propel them between the 19th and the 20th centuries. Battleships became heavily armored, and their cannon were replaced by guns with ranges eventually over fifteen miles. In World War I, the biggest navies planned to gain command of the sea with their battleships by sinking the enemy fleet and blockading trade. They also developed small fast boats like destroyers, plus torpedoes, mines, and submarines to sink battleships and to wage a *guerre de course*.

The Battle of Jutland: "losing the war in an afternoon"

This battle was fought between the British Royal Navy's Grand Fleet and the German High Seas Fleet in 1916 during World War I. Both sides' strategies were shaped by the vulnerability of their own ships. Both sides dreaded losing them because construction expenses and construction time meant the ships could not be easily replaced. Both sides planned to catch a portion of the other side's fleet rather than fighting the whole lot at once. As a result, during four years of war, the two fleets only met once in a general battle which took place off the coast of Denmark. To start with, both sides thought they had run into a smaller portion of the other side's fleet. When they realized that it was the whole British fleet, the Germans, who were outnumbered, tried to retreat. The British went after the German fleet, but their caution and the chaos caused by smoke and eventually nightfall enabled the Germans to escape. The Germans sank more ships and killed more men, but their own ships were badly smashed up. The British, despite their losses, were ready for action again within a couple of days. Both sides claimed victory but their fleets never clashed on this scale again.

For some, Jutland is an illustration of the waste of warfare. Fortunes were poured into building these fleets, but they spent most of the war sitting in their harbors or patrolling. For others, Jutland demonstrates the tragic necessities being prepared to go to war imposes on people. Keeping their fleets in being, "doing nothing" prevented the other side gaining a great advantage. If either side had lacked a navy or its fleet had been sunk, this would have spelt disaster, especially for the British. Churchill said of the British admiral, Jellicoe, after the battle, "he is the only man who could have lost the war in an afternoon." This was an exaggeration, but it showed how precious and vulnerable great navies were (see a video clip of the Battle of Jutland at this link: https://www.youtube.com/watch?v=nCGOE6UiAWo).

Several factors shape how a state's navy is equipped today. The two basic logics of sea power remain the same. States with strong navies still want command of the sea, and states with weak navies still want to disrupt their enemy's trade. Ships can still sink and naval warfare always holds out the prospect of large, expensive warships being mined, torpedoed, rocketed or rammed by small, cheap ones. However, the way sea power is used was transformed by five developments in the 20th century.

- Flight and the development of aircraft carriers which allowed fleets to project destructive power over hundreds of miles instead of tens of miles, and made battleships vulnerable to air attack.

- Radar detection and guidance which allowed fleets to see one another's operations at greater distances, at night and in fog, and improved the accuracy of weapons.

- Nuclear propulsion which, from the 1950s onwards, radically improved the ability of ships equipped with nuclear reactors to stay at sea and, in the case of submarines, to operate underwater at speed and for long periods.

- Nuclear weapons as mines, depth charges, and warheads which expanded the firepower of warships so equipped. As we shall see below, nuclear warheads on submarine-launched ballistic missiles gave some navies a new and important role in the nuclear age.

- Rockets which threatened to make big warships obsolescent for a time because of their accuracy, speed, range, and relative cheapness.

- Cruise missiles (more like pilotless aircraft than ballistic rockets) which provided warships and submarines with a new role in delivering bombardments and highly accurate strikes over long ranges and inland.

The economic and technical demands of having a large, modern navy are challenging. A blue water navy now needs to be built around large aircraft carriers which can launch deep strikes. Yet only one state, the US, can presently afford such ships in any number because of their direct costs, the costs of the aircraft capable of operating from them, and the costs of providing warships to protect them from enemy aircraft, submarines, and warships. The Russians retain one medium-sized carrier, having sold several others after the collapse of the Soviet Union. The British are slowly building a two aircraft carrier force with one recently completed. However, economic difficulties dictate that they can only afford helicopters for one and none of the original aircraft planned for either at the moment. The British and French have talked about sharing France's one small carrier. A few other states have one or two small and obsolescent types. Only China is attempting to challenge the US monopoly. It has one modernized Soviet-era aircraft carrier acquired from Ukraine, and is building two or three more. It faces the same problem as the British in regard to acquiring suitable aircraft to fly off them. China is also attempting to compensate for its "aircraft carrier deficit" by building reefs up into artificial islands on which to position aircraft and troops in waters which it claims. Russia used its aircraft carrier for operations over Syria in 2017, but the other major naval powers focus on making contributions to alliance efforts, submarines for *guerre de course* and—in the case of Russia, China, Britain, and France—nuclear weapons operations. The navies of the rest are for coastal defense and patrols against pirates, smugglers, human traffickers.

War games in the Persian Gulf

The Persian Gulf lies between the oil-rich Arab states of the Arabian Peninsula and the oil-rich Islamic Republic of Iran. It is just over twenty miles wide at the Straits of Hormuz where it exits into the Arabian Sea.

Through these straits some twenty percent of the world's oil supplies flow, principally to Europe and Japan, but also and increasingly to China. During the 1980s both Iran and Iraq attacked each other's shipping in the Gulf and neutral tankers carrying each other's oil. The US and its allies sent warships to the Gulf to escort and defend shipping.

Iran has continued to threaten shipping and to "close" the Straits of Hormuz in support of its policies in the region, and as retaliation against anyone thinking of attacking it. In the recent past, it just had to threaten this to set shipping insurance rates and oil prices climbing. There were crises in 2008 and 2011–12 as the warships of both sides maneuvered to intimidate one another. The balance of forces is interesting. The Iranian navy has a few small surface warships and submarines. In addition, it has fast attack boats with anti-ship missiles and hundreds of power boats equipped with machine guns and rocket-propelled grenades. Most importantly, it also has a growing number of shore-based anti-ship missiles. In contrast, the US generally has a carrier battle group (an aircraft carrier escorted by anti-aircraft, anti-submarine and anti-ship cruisers, destroyers and frigates) in the Gulf. It can also pull two or more carrier battle groups into the area when relations become tense.

In a war, the Iranian warships would be quickly destroyed, and the US is confident that it could prevent missiles from hitting its ships or doing much damage. US warships and aircraft could also launch damaging, punishing cruise missile strikes and bombing raids against Iran in response to any attack on shipping. There is less certainty, however, about the US warships' ability to protect tankers from swarming attacks by Iranian power boats or about the consequences of Iran's growing force of anti-ship missiles. Weak navies have had successes with torpedoes, rockets, and mines against big warships in the past, but they have been one off spectaculars which have not affected the final outcome of the fighting. If a few tankers get hit, however, shippers will pull their tankers out. And what if the Iranians got lucky with a big hit on a carrier? An American admiral could not "lose the war in an afternoon" like Jellicoe at Jutland, but such a loss would force the US to consider getting into a much bigger war than planned, or backing off, humiliated.

Key terms

blue water navy   A navy capable of operating far from home in the deep oceans and in seas close to hostile states.

coastal defense   A naval policy which is directed at controlling only the sea spaces next to the shores of a state.

command of the sea   The ability to control the oceans and seas for a state's military and commercial purposes and to deny that ability to other states.

sea power   Naval armed forces designed to control oceans and seas and to deny them to others primarily by fighting other navies, protecting friendly merchant ships, and disrupting the trade of others.

Key takeaways

- Sea power can be used for command of the sea with a blue water navy and for protecting local waters with a coastal defense navy.
- Sea power can be used for a *guerre de course* against merchant shipping.
- Ships can sink, and big, expensive ships are always potentially vulnerable to attacks by small, cheap ships.
- Aircraft carriers have replaced battleships as the main ships for gaining control of the sea and bombarding enemy territory.
- Nuclear submarines with nuclear missiles have given sea power a new role.
- Ships and navies are very expensive and keeping them up-to-date requires great scientific and technical knowledge. Currently, only the US maintains a blue water navy equipped with many large aircraft carriers and the necessary escorting warships.

Exercises

1. How do the problems of maintaining and using sea power differ from those of land power?
2. Why did aircraft carriers replace battleships as the main fighting ships?
3. Why is the US the only state to maintain a large blue water navy currently?

7.3	Air power

Learning objectives

1. List the key elements of **air power**.
2. Describe what air power is used for by states.
3. Explain what factors shape how a state's air force is equipped.

Air power involves the use of aircraft by states to locate, observe, and attack the armed forces (including aircraft), people, economy, and government of another state. It is also used to prevent enemy aircraft carrying out similar missions. Air power threatens the viability of the territorial state in much the same way as gunpowder and cannon challenged the feudal state based around castles and walls. The first military missions were flown by heavier-than-air craft during the Italian-Turkish War of 1911. Air combat emerged early in World War I when the crews of opposing aircraft threw rocks and fired pistols at each other. Today, some states have supersonic jet aircraft equipped with missiles, intercontinental bombers able to attack targets on the other side of the world with great precision, and stealth aircraft which are almost impossible for conventional radar systems to detect. These developments have taken place in less than 100 years.

Initially, the use of air power was restricted to scouting and observation missions. When aircraft engines and airframes became strong enough to carry heavy loads over greater distances, and when basic problems like trying to get a machine gun to fire forward through the air screw (propeller) were solved, new missions quickly developed. The great military powers developed squadrons of aircraft known as air forces, although they were initially organized as sub-units of their armies and navies. By the end of World War I in 1918, bombers were being used to attack enemy troops and cities, while faster, lighter fighters were being used to attack bombers and one another. To begin with, the significance of air power was sometimes over-estimated and sometimes ignored.

Over-estimating and under-estimating the effects of air power

In the 1930s, bomber aircraft became faster, flew longer distances and with heavier bomb loads. Some people assumed they had made organized warfare impossible because, in the words of a former British prime minister, "the bomber would always get through."[5] Bombers could fly over land and sea defenses to attack cities, people, and governments directly. It was thought states would collapse as their citizens were reduced to panic and chaos by death raining down from the skies. World War II proved this prediction wrong. Anti-aircraft guns and fighter aircraft got better at identifying bombers and shooting them down. The bombers often struggled to hit their targets. Most importantly, even when cities were devastated by bigger and bigger bombing raids, their populations rarely panicked, production was quickly restored, and the cities quickly rebuilt after the war.

In contrast, many military men assumed that air power had changed nothing. Even after an American air force officer had an old battleship sunk by bombing, some admirals said the test would not be replicated in real combat. It took the sinking of two big British warships off the coast of Malaya (now Malaysia) in 1941 by Japanese aircraft to convince most admirals that airpower was a game changer. Generals were prepared to send their armies to war without protection from air attacks at the start of World War II. Polish, Dutch, Belgian, French, and British soldiers were pushed aside by German blitzkrieg (lightning war) attacks in which airstrikes played a major part in terrifying and destroying the defenders. By the end of the war, however, armies moved mainly at night if they could not be protected from air attacks.

To see the effects of airstrikes on Iraqi forces retreating from Kuwait in 1991 on the so-called "Highway of Death," follow this link: https://www.youtube.com/watch?v=hhmXleZXAr0.

People argue over the morality of the attack and the number of people actually killed.

Once it was realized that air power did not change everything, discussion of how to use it took on a familiar pattern. The primary purpose of an air force, experts agreed, was to achieve **command of the air** by denying that airspace to enemy aircraft. Once an air force controlled the skies, then it could conduct its other missions: reconnaissance (scouting), tactical bombing (of troops), and **strategic bombing** (of cities, economic targets and communications) unimpeded, and its own armies and navies could operate free from attack. Achieving command of the air involves a constant effort by a state in both peacetime and wartime to develop and produce aircraft which are faster, more maneuverable, better seeing, and equipped with more accurate weapons than those of potential enemies.

Technical improvements seem more important in air power than in power on the land and sea. The stronger air force quickly drives the weaker from the sky. However, the development of cheap, accurate rockets has opened up the possibility of a role for weaker air forces. At the beginning of the "Yom Kippur" War in 1973, Egyptian soldiers with simple, hand-held surface-to-air missiles were able to shoot down Israeli jets costing millions of dollars. The "War of the Cities," in which Iran and Iraq fired rockets at each other's capitals in the 1980s, and Iraq's Scud missile attacks on Israel and Saudi Arabia during the first US-led war against Iraq in 1991 showed how difficult it was to stop even old-fashioned, primitive rockets. In the 2006 Lebanon War, Israel could do little about the nearly 4000 rockets fired at it from over the border. While relatively cheap to maintain and difficult to stop, however, no rocket bombardment to date has come anywhere near producing the levels of destruction of which aircraft are capable.

Modern air forces present similar problems to modern armies and navies for states, but in a more severe form. A balanced air force today would have combat aircraft for establishing command of the air, strategic and tactical bombers for attacking a range of targets with precise, radar-guided so-called "smart bombs," communications aircraft equipped with radar and computerized information systems for obtaining and sending information about targets and threats and disrupting the enemy's information, and air tankers capable of fueling planes in mid-air to extend their ranges and allow them to stay airborne longer. Supporting these "teeth" of the air force would be a long "tail" of transport aircraft, helicopters, and vehicles, technicians, intelligence officers, plus bases and the people to construct and defend these bases where necessary. And this air force would need to be able to keep ahead of its rivals in terms of numbers, technical innovations and the training of its personnel.

Winning wars by air power alone?

When air power first emerged, supporters said it might be all a state needed in the future. Build a fast, large bomber force and attack first was the advice of the Italian general Douhet in the 1920s. Traditionalists objected that air power alone could never win a war. "Boots on the ground," i.e. infantry, would always be needed to seize and hold territory. This was never strictly true. Some "wars" in the past had been won by naval bombardment alone. In 1999, NATO launched an air war against Serbia to get Serbian troops out of Kosovo. They succeeded without losing a pilot (although a big army was getting ready to move in if the Serbs didn't leave). It might be argued that air power was decisive in weakening the Iraqi army in 1991 and that the ground war was just a giant mopping up operation (but the soldiers who did the fighting would have something to say about that).

Another contender for air power alone would be an air attack by the US and Israel (or either acting alone) against Iran's nuclear facilities to destroy its chances of getting nuclear weapons (although the likelihood of such an attack has been reduced by the 2015 nuclear arms agreement between Iran and the permanent members of the UN Security Council plus Germany and the European Union). "Smart bombs," cruise missiles and bombs designed for penetrating underground facilities and those built into mountains would be needed. If the attacks worked, there would be no need for a ground invasion. The same would be true for an attack on North Korea's nuclear weapons facilities and missile bases. No one is sure if air power only can actually do the job, however. It gets considered because neither the US nor anyone else has been interested in absorbing the costs and the risks of a ground invasion up to now.

The US maintains this full range of air power capabilities. Arguments over how many of the next generation F 22 and F 35 fighters should be deployed suggest, however, even the US is feeling the strain. Russia remains close to the US only in certain types of aircraft. China is beginning to develop a powerful air force but the quality of the aircraft and equipment remains uneven. India is further behind. Some EU states have shared the research, design, and production of tactical bombers and some are working on a joint fighter. For the Europeans, the tradeoff is between keeping an independent aviation industry going by making expensive aircraft, or buying US aircraft off the shelf which are less expensive, as good, and sometimes better.

Falling behind enemies is bad, but falling behind friends presents problems too. During NATO's bombing campaign over Serbia/Kosovo in 1999, the US found it difficult to work with the air forces of its allies. Some allied planes could not make use of the satellite-based systems of allocating targets and directing attacks, and could not operate effectively without putting themselves at risk of being shot down. Most medium-sized and small military power states maintain only small and obsolescent air forces. Some have considered whether it is worth having an air force separate from their armies and navies at all. States seem to think they can do without a separate air force more than they can do without a separate army or navy (although Canada merged all three, and China's air force, navy, and rocket force are formally organized as branches of the People's Liberation Army). Other states keep a few planes and helicopters mainly for border surveillance, rescue missions, and as a way of subsidizing the training of pilots for their civil aviation.

Key terms

air power Air forces designed to control air and sea spaces and to deny their use to other states primarily by fighting other air forces, and to destroy the armed forces, economies, and populations of other states.

command of the air A situation in which the air power of one state or side in a conflict has destroyed the air power of its enemy or has such superiority that the enemy air force is unable, or refuses, to fly.

strategic bombing Bombing attacks (usually on cities) designed to destroy the general capacity—both material and psychological—of an enemy state to make war, contrasted with tactical bombing which usually attacks enemy armed forces in the context of a particular military operation.

Key takeaways

- Air power has only developed over the last 100 years or so. It is relatively new.
- Air power has made land and sea forces more vulnerable than they used to be. It has also weakened the ability of states to protect their populations.
- Air power is used for command of the air, for strategic bombing of enemy cities, economies and populations, and for tactical bombing of enemy forces.
- Air power is technically demanding and expensive. Only a few states are able to maintain large, up-to-date air forces.
- Weaker air forces seem less useful than weaker armies and navies, although cheap ballistic rockets provide weak states with an air power option.

Exercises

1. How does air power threaten the defenses of the territorial state?
2. What are the missions fulfilled by a modern air force?
3. Why is the US the only state at the moment with a large, state-of-the-art air force capable of performing all these missions?

7.4   Weapons of mass destruction (WMD)

Learning objectives

1. List the chief characteristics of **weapons of mass destruction**.
2. Describe the key elements of the nuclear revolution in warfare.
3. Explain how **nuclear deterrence** and **Mutual Assured Destruction (MAD)** are supposed to work.

4. Describe the strengths and weaknesses of **chemical and biological weapons** of mass destruction.

5. Describe the factors which influence whether a state attempts to acquire weapons of mass destruction.

6. Describe the two types of nuclear proliferation.

Weapons of mass destruction (WMD) kill people indiscriminately and horribly as their primary purpose or as a side-effect of being used for other reasons. Most WMD kill in large numbers and may cause widespread damage to property and the environment. Most **nuclear weapons** fit this description, although some smaller ones are no more destructive than the most powerful conventional (non-nuclear) weapons. Most chemical and biological weapons fit this description. However, even when used in small amounts—to wipe out villages, to hinder the attacks of opposing armies, or to terrify the passengers on subway systems, for example—they are still, perhaps misleadingly, called weapons of mass destruction.

Nuclear weapons have been in existence for just over 70 years. The first ones—atom bombs—were used by the Americans on the Japanese cities of Hiroshima and Nagasaki in 1945 (Figure 7.2). None have been used since, only tested.

Figure 7.2 Atomic bomb explosion over Hiroshima, Japan, 1945
(Source: MARKA/Alamy Stock Photo)

Atom bombs are based on the energy released when atoms are split (fission). The Hiroshima and Nagasaki bombs had yields of about 12–15 and 20–22 kilotons respectively. A kiloton is the equivalent of 1,000 tons of TNT (or conventional explosive). Together, they immediately killed over 100,000 people by blast and heat. That figure doubled shortly after, and tens of thousands succumbed to the effects of radiation sickness in the following months and years. Hydrogen bombs or thermonuclear weapons, first tested in 1952, are based on the energy released when atoms are smashed together (fusion) to increase the size of a fission reaction. Their destructive power is sometimes measured in megatons (millions of tons of TNT equivalent). One large thermo-nuclear weapon deployed by the US had a yield of up to 25 megatons, over a thousand times more destructive (in principle) than the Nagasaki atomic bomb. Larger thermo-nuclear weapons were developed, especially by the Soviet Union. Some megaton weapons still exist today, but the trend is towards more accurate, "smaller" (although almost eight times more powerful than the Hiroshima bomb) warheads.

Many people believed when the atom bombs were dropped on Hiroshima and Nagasaki that this spelt the end of war. In a single moment, single bombers, each with a single bomb, caused destruction it would have taken several hundred bombers several days to achieve with thousands of conventional bombs. How could a state defend against this sort of attack? The Japanese quickly surrendered. However, it soon became clear that military planners regarded atom bombs as just big bombs to be used in what some called "broken backed warfare" between states crippled by atom bomb attacks but still fighting to defend and win territory. So several states that were able to do so developed atomic warheads for bombs, missiles, cannon shells, depth charges, and mines, and then prepared for the next war.

As Lawrence Freeman argues, the real nuclear revolution came later than 1945 and developed around the following:[6]

- The Soviet Union getting atom bombs of its own from 1949 which created the problem of **retaliation**.

- The development of powerful thermo-nuclear warheads in the mid-1950s which made it possible that human beings might destroy themselves and all other life on the planet.

- The development of long-range intercontinental ballistic missiles (rockets) in the late 1950s which were fired toward space and then brought back down on the target by gravity. These could carry thermo-nuclear warheads to almost any part of the planet's surface in twenty to thirty minutes.

Then people asked again, what possible use might such destructive, unstoppable weapons have, and what dangers did they pose for humanity? Albert Wholstetter suggested that the Soviet Union and the US had created "a delicate balance of terror" between their nuclear forces which was unstable.[7] Like two gunslingers in a Hollywood western, they did not want to launch an attack because they might be killed. If they let the other side launch first, though, they'd be killed for certain. The pressure on both sides would be to strike first. Slowly the US and the Soviet Union, followed by other nuclear weapons states—Britain (1952), France

(1960), and China (1964)—began to work towards the conclusion that the only sane use for nuclear weapons was to deter attacks by others. If you use them on me, I will use them on you. They were too destructive for anything else. This conclusion, however, created a new set of questions about nuclear deterrence.

What sorts of attacks could be deterred, nuclear attacks only, or other sorts of attacks? If the Soviet Union attacked with conventional (non-nuclear) forces in Europe, for example, could the US retaliate by using nuclear weapons and, if so, in Europe or against the Soviet Union itself? What was the best way to deter attacks? Some argued that it was to make your own nuclear forces survivable. The US "strategic nuclear triad," for example, involved some hydrogen bombs carried by jet bombers, some warheads on rockets in hardened "silos"—tubes sunk into the ground—so they could survive anything but a direct hit, and other warheads on rockets in nuclear submarines so they could not be located. Anyone thinking of a sneak attack or first strike on the US, therefore, knew that they could never get away with it. They would be faced with assured destruction by a US second strike. Thus, if they were rational, they would not attack in the first place.

If both sides concentrated on survivable forces, then there would be a situation of mutual assured destruction (MAD), and the dangers of the delicate balance of terror might be avoided. Imagine if our two Hollywood gunslingers were equipped with guns that fired slow-acting sedative darts, so the second shooter could shoot back before they went down. The pressure, according to the argument, would be off both of them and a situation of stable deterrence would emerge.

Suppose deterrence failed, however, and an attack was launched anyhow. How should a state try to protect its people from nuclear attack? Should it build shelters or antiballistic missiles that could destroy incoming rockets? MAD suggested no. States shouldn't do anything which made the other side less sure about its second strike, because this would tempt it to hit first. MAD became the semi-official position of the US and its allies, but the answers it provided were never fully satisfactory. The Soviet Union rejected MAD. It simply said, we won't use nuclear weapons first, but if anyone else uses them, we will launch everything we have, so don't even go there. The way the US developed rockets which carried many highly accurate warheads on each rocket suggested it was still looking for ways to hit the Soviet rocket force first before it was launched. So did its threat to use nuclear weapons in Europe at some point in response to a conventional, non-nuclear Soviet attack—a policy referred to by NATO as extended deterrence. Extended deterrence left the Germans unhappy with the prospect of their state becoming a nuclear battlefield, and wasn't believed by the British and French who acquired their own nuclear weapons. The French, especially, argued that no US president would expose an American city to nuclear attack by using nuclear weapons to try to stop the Soviet Union invading Western Europe.

The critics of MAD listed a set of problems with it:

- Governments were not rational enough to make it work. Their military bureaucracies and defense industries would continue to develop weapons systems on the basis of their technical feasibility and fear of the other side getting them first, rather than in a way which would be consistent with MAD, no matter what official policy was.

- The US and Soviet governments simply could not develop the levels of mutual trust needed to operate MAD. Even with the best will in the world (which neither of them had), both would be tempted into cheating by the fear of the other side cheating first.

- If deterrence under MAD failed, then one side, both sides, and possibly the world, would face a catastrophe because nothing had been done to try and protect people from the consequences of a nuclear exchange.

The recommendations of some of the MAD critics were just as worrying, however. Despite the nuclear revolution, Colin Gray argued, the old way of deterring someone remained the best way. The US, he argued, had to convince the Soviet Union's leaders that in any nuclear exchange, their state would come off worse and the Soviet leaders themselves be killed.[8] The US had to be prepared to win a nuclear war with accurate warheads of "modest" size, and measures taken to limit the damage to itself and its population. The problem with this was that millions of people on both sides would still be killed, and the planet's eco-system might be fatally damaged by the great clouds of smoke and ash created by just a few bombs blocking out the light from the sun. By the 1990s, the US had adopted the Strategic Defense Initiative (or "Star Wars"), to develop lasers and rockets to destroy incoming ballistic missiles. President Reagan said their eventual purpose would be to make all nuclear-tipped missiles obsolete, and he would share the system with the Soviets. Critics and supporters agreed that in the short term, they might make possible a first strike by the US, assuming that they could be made to work effectively.

Much of the public attention to arguments over nuclear weapons disappeared with the end of the Cold War. The Russians and Americans have made large reductions in their nuclear forces which are ready for action, even if they retain many more nuclear warheads than the media and the public assume. The official US position is to get rid of all nuclear weapons. Today, the US and its allies seem to worry more about small nuclear weapons from weak states than big exchanges with Russia and China. It is against these weak states that ballistic missile defenses continue to be developed. Nevertheless, and as noted in Chapter 1, most of us still live between ten and thirty minutes away from nuclear annihilation and experts still wrestle with the bizarre problems generated by nuclear weapons.

Global Zero

In 2009, President Obama announced that US policy was working for a world without nuclear weapons. In doing so, he echoed an aspiration of President Ronald Reagan. He added, however, that the US would be the last state to get rid of them. Earlier, the British Prime Minister, Margaret Thatcher, had dismissed the idea. Even if all nuclear weapons were scrapped, the knowledge of how to make them would still exist. In a crisis, states would race to rebuild their nuclear forces. The winner of that race, she added, would be the state which had cheated all along and kept some bombs. Thatcher saw getting to zero as impractical, unrealistic, and undesirable. Nuclear weapons stopped the Cold War becoming World War III in her view. However, her critics note the statistical probabilities of nuclear weapons being used again and say those who are prepared to accept this risk and its catastrophic consequences are the unrealistic ones. The US and Russia continue to reduce the number of nuclear warheads they possess, but they also continue to modernize the warheads and rockets which they still have. The Russians are probably developing an intermediate-range rocket in a category banned by international treaty, and other nuclear weapons states have done very little or nothing to reduce the size of their much smaller arsenals.

(To see US President Obama's speech in Europe in 2009 saying the US is seeking a world without nuclear weapons, follow the link: http://www.youtube.com/watch?v=9tKNihT2UxQ.)

(To see US President Ronald Reagan's best quotes on nuclear weapons, follow the link: http://www.thereaganvision.org/quotes/?doing_wp_cron=1347047005.727842092514038085 9375.)

(To see British Prime Minister Margaret Thatcher talking with Soviet leader Mikhail Gorbachev about nuclear weapons in 1987, follow the link: http://www.youtube.com/watch?v=tTelFoU3v8E.)

Chemical and biological weapons can be as destructive as some nuclear weapons, are easier to develop, and can be easier to use. Many of them are less effective in terms of killing people, and all of them are less effective in terms of destroying property or military equipment. All of them attack basic functions of the body such as the way people breathe or the operations of their central nervous systems. Some infect people with diseases. Others, like tear gas, simply incapacitate people and make it difficult for them to function.

Chemical and biological weapons have long histories. Catapulting animal carcasses into besieged cities, poisoning water holes, and giving infected materials such as blankets to people to make them sick could all be regarded as types of biological warfare. In World War I, the Germans, British, and French all used poison gas against each other's soldiers, as did the Iraqis in their war against Iran and on their own people. Chemical weapons have been used in Syria, almost certainly by government forces and possibly by their opponents. The use of radiation as the product of a nuclear blast which makes people sick is a form of chemical warfare. Until recently, the military great power states, as well as others, kept stocks of both kinds of WMD, offering the argument that this deterred their use by others. Some states retain them as a sort of "poor man's nuclear weapon." They can be dropped as bombs, fired from canon or on rockets, and some of them can be delivered by individuals releasing, for example, biological agents into the water supply of a city, or mailing letters.

It is a puzzle why chemical and biological weapons have been hardly used at all by terrorists and not much more by states after World War I. Poison gas is hard to control. It depends on which way the wind blows. Perhaps biological agents are more difficult to use than we have imagined. As noted above, chemical weapons have been used on a small scale in Syria since 2013, killing civilians. The political consequences of images of suffering and dead civilians for the Syrian government were so bad that it was nearly attacked by the US and its allies in 2013. Only the promise to the UN that it was destroying all its chemical weapons persuaded them to suspend the attack. When the Syrian government almost certainly used chemical weapons again in 2017, the US launched cruise missiles against the airbase from which it said the attack had been launched.

Why do some states have weapons of mass destruction? They are very expensive to develop, difficult to use except as a deterrent, and their existence places all of humanity in terrible danger. Most states don't bother with nuclear weapons precisely for these reasons. We can point to three basic motives for states acquiring WMD:

■ Fear is the great driver, especially fear of the consequences of being without such weapons when other states have them. The US and the Soviet Union thought a war between the two was likely in the 1950s and assumed that the other side would use nuclear weapons if there was no chance of retaliation. London and Paris hoped that by being able to destroy Moscow and Leningrad, they would convince the Soviet Union that Britain and France weren't worth attacking in the first place. This "life insurance" approach has also been adopted by Israel, North Korea, Pakistan, and possibly in the future it will be adopted by Iran. Anyone who makes problems for the military great powers today sees that nuclear-armed North Korea has not been attacked, whereas non-nuclear Iraq and Libya (which actually gave up its small WMD programs) have been attacked and their former leaders are both dead.

■ Freedom, or a sense of it, comes with the possession of WMD. US military operations in the Persian Gulf and Russian military operations in the Caucasus are undertaken under a nuclear umbrella. This is not to say the Americans and the Russians plan to use nuclear weapons, but they are there in the background, nevertheless. No one has used nuclear weapons since Hiroshima and Nagasaki, but the US and Russia have both threatened their use in international crises. Israel worries about Iran acquiring nuclear weapons because it might use them on Israel. The US and its other allies worry that Iran simply possessing them will encourage it to take more risks, while inhibiting the freedom of action of the US and Israel in countering Iran.

■ Prestige comes with the development, possession, and display of weapons of mass destruction by a state. Cheering crowds in both states greeted the successful weapons tests of India and Pakistan, for example. Prestige may also explain why states find it hard to give up the weapons they've acquired, even when they aren't sure they want them anymore. South Africa may have managed this after a revolution, but could Britain give them up while France still had them?

Nuclear proliferation means the spread of nuclear weapons. Horizontal proliferation means more states getting them. Vertical proliferation means more nuclear weapons of more types coming into existence. Today there are nine states out of over 130 states which actually have nuclear weapons (see Table 7.1). Should

Table 7.1 The spread of nuclear weapons

State	Date of First Test	Size and Status of Force
United States	1945	6,800 warheads of which 1411 are deployed
Russia	1949 (as Soviet Union)	7000 warheads of which 1765 are deployed
Britain	1952	215
France	1960	300
China	1964	270
India	1974 for a nuclear device and 1998 for a nuclear weapon	130
Israel	1979 (possibly)	80
Pakistan	1998	140
North Korea	2006	10

Note: Russian and US warheads are divided between those which are waiting to be scrapped, those which are stored but could be reactivated, and those which are ready to be deployed at short notice. There are different estimates of the numbers of warheads states possess, especially Israel and North Korea.

Source: The figures for warhead numbers used in this table are taken from "2017 Estimated Global Nuclear Warhead Inventories" provided by the Arms Control Association at https://www.armscontrol.org/factsheets/Nuclearweaponswhohaswhat

we be dismayed at the spread of nuclear weapons or surprised at how slowly the number has grown?

Most states agree nuclear proliferation is undesirable on the assumption that more weapons mean a greater risk of war. However, Kenneth Waltz disagrees. He argues that when states acquire nuclear weapons, they sober up, quit taking chances, and become more cautious. There have been huge diplomatic efforts to reduce the numbers of weapons of mass destruction (and other weapons) through nuclear **disarmament** treaties and to reduce the dangers posed by them through arms control and confidence-building measures treaties (see Table 7.2). Disarmament involves reducing the number of weapons. Arms control involves agreeing to the number of weapons—whether this involves reducing, increasing or keeping them the same. Confidence building involves better communications about what each side is up to avoid surprises and misunderstandings. The "hot line" link set up between the White House and the Kremlin after the Cuban Missile Crisis is an example of a confidence-building measure.

Negotiating these agreements is difficult for three reasons:

- States worry about losing advantages to others as a result of agreements. India used to argue, for example, that states with nuclear weapons were more concerned about *horizontal proliferation* that *vertical proliferation*, because these states wanted to stop others getting the weapons while keeping their own. Recently, Russia has argued that the US was keen to have a treaty banning the testing of all nuclear weapons because the Americans were better than the Russians at running virtual "tests" through computer simulations.

- The subject matter is difficult. In reducing forces, what to count and how to count it are big issues. Weaker military powers may want to cut proportionally (let's both get rid of ten percent of our rockets, for example), stronger powers may want to cut arithmetically (let's both get rid of ten of our rockets), and

Table 7.2 Some important disarmament, arms control, and confidence-building treaties

Name and Date of Treaty	Type of Treaty	Description
"Hotline" Agreement 1963	Confidence Building	Established direct teleprinter (later telephone) contact between US and Soviet leaders after the Cuban Missile Conflict
Test Ban Treaties 1963, 1996	Arms Control	Stopped nuclear weapons testing in the atmosphere, space, at sea, and underground (1996)
Non-Proliferation Treaties 1968/95	Arms Control	Non-nuclear states gain access to peaceful nuclear technologies in return for not acquiring nuclear weapons and allowing inspections. Nuclear weapon states promise to reduce the size of their forces
Strategic Arms Limitation Treaties 1972/79	Arms Control	Capped the number of US and Soviet rockets to be deployed and restricted the number of ballistic defense missile systems
Biological Weapons Convention 1972	Arms Control	States promised not to develop, produce, or stockpile chemical weapons and to destroy the ones they already had
Ottawa Treaty (Land Mines) 1997	Disarmament	States promised not to use, stockpile, produce, or transfer anti-personnel mines and to destroy the ones they had
Strategic Arms Reduction Treaties, 1991/93 and 2010	Disarmament	Russia and the US committed to reducing the number of nuclear warheads and delivery systems they had to agreed levels
Chemical Weapons Conventions 1997	Disarmament	States promised not to develop, produce, stockpile, or use chemical weapons and to destroy those they had

Note: Initially, only states which signed these agreements were bound by them.

states with better missile defenses might prefer lower numbers of missiles all round.

■ The subject matter has become increasingly complex. At a modern arms control conference, the diplomats are joined by teams of physicists, mathematicians, and engineers who try to reach agreement on the character and capabilities of different weapon systems.

Key terms

chemical and biological weapons Weapons which expose people to dangerous chemicals or infectious and harmful biological agents causing sickness, disease, and death.

disarmament A process by which one or more states agree to reduce the number of weapons they possess, possibly to the point of zero. Disarmament is a form of arms control, a process by which states attempt to manage the quantity and quality of their forces to reduce the unwanted threat they pose to each other. Under arms control, weapons levels can rise as well as fall.

Mutual Assured Destruction (MAD) A state which can use nuclear weapons without fearing retaliation has a "first strike" capability. A state which can retaliate with nuclear weapons after absorbing a nuclear attack from another state has "second strike capability." Where two states have "second strike" capabilities the situation is described as one of Mutual Assured Destruction (MAD). The assumption, often challenged, is that two states in a condition of MAD are unlikely to attack each other.

nuclear deterrence   A situation in which one state refrains from attacking another state with nuclear weapons because it fears nuclear retaliation. The argument is often made that nuclear weapons are so destructive that the only reason for a state to have them is to deter another state from using nuclear weapons against it.

nuclear proliferation   The spread of nuclear weapons to more states (horizontal proliferation) and the general increase in numbers of nuclear weapons (vertical proliferation) by new states or states already possessing nuclear weapons acquiring more.

nuclear weapons   Weapons which cause huge explosions and release dangerous levels of radiation by exploiting the energy released when atoms are split (fission producing atomic bombs), or smashed together (fusion plus fission producing hydrogen bombs, also known as thermo-nuclear weapons).

retaliation   The act of striking back after being attacked. The nuclear revolution is regarded as having only completely occurred once more than one state had developed nuclear weapons. This created the problem of nuclear retaliation.

weapons of mass destruction   Nuclear, biological, and chemical weapons capable of killing people, destroying physical structures, damaging natural features and harming the environment on a very large scale.

Key takeaways

- Weapons of mass destruction (WMD) kill people indiscriminately and usually in large numbers as their primary purpose or as a side effect of being used for other purposes.

- They take the form of nuclear, chemical, and biological weapons, usually explosive devices which can be put on rockets, dropped from planes, fired from guns, buried in the ground or (although this has not happened yet) hidden in property.

- Two atom bombs were dropped on cities killing tens of thousands of people in 1945. Chemical and biological weapons have been used more often, but on a smaller scale.

- The nuclear revolution emerged when a second state acquired nuclear weapons—creating the problem of retaliation, destructive thermo-nuclear weapons were successfully tested, and long range intercontinental ballistic missiles were developed.

- The destructiveness of most WMD makes them difficult for states to use other than to deter their use by other states. There are big arguments about whether nuclear deterrence is best achieved through MAD or being prepared to win a nuclear war.

■ The arguments over nuclear weapons have declined since the end of the Cold War. There are now far fewer nuclear weapons since Russia and the United States have reduced their forces through disarmament and arms control agreements. They worry more about smaller states acquiring nuclear or chemical and biological WMD.

Exercises

1. What are the key characteristics of weapons of mass destruction (WMD)?
2. Why do some states acquire WMD?
3. Why is it hard for states to use WMD?
4. Why is it hard for states to get rid of WMD?

7.5 Terrorists, guerrillas, pirates, and criminals

Learning objectives

1. Describe terrorism.
2. Describe guerrilla warfare.
3. Explain why terrorism attracts attention, but may not be a big national security threat.
4. Explain how pirates and criminals might pose national security threats.

Most of the military effort of states prepares their armed forces to fight the armed forces of other states in symmetrical warfare. However, most of the fighting at present takes place between the armed forces of states on one side and families, clans, tribes, ethnic groups, religious radicals, social revolutionaries, and criminal gangs on the other. This is not new. Ever since there have been states, there have been people who wanted to fight them but were not strong enough, rich enough, or popular enough to create armed forces which could go directly up against them. Instead, they hide or move to remote places, and launch tip and run attacks on states and their supporters to hurt them, rob them, frighten them, and make them look weak.

There is a sense today though that states are finding it harder to cope. During the attack widely known as 9–11, the US—the richest, most powerful state in the world—was unable to stop nineteen young men from highjacking four planes, smashing three of them into buildings, and killing more people than were killed in the Japanese attack on Pearl Harbor. All the great military power states currently devote a major effort to fighting what is at the most a few thousand, lightly armed, often poorly trained, but fanatical terrorists and guerrillas. Have we reached one of those "David and Goliath" moments in history then when the powerful but clumsy may be brought down by the weak but committed? Probably not, but the use of terror by **terrorists**, **guerrillas**, and others is receiving more attention than it did in the past.

Terror is an emotional condition in people caused by the prospect of losing something very dear to them—their life or the lives of their loved ones, for example—in the near future. It works through causing pain, the prospect or memory of pain, and showing others in pain or being killed. People use terror for different reasons: for power; for wealth; for pleasure; to bring what they believe to be truth and freedom to the world; to fight enemies; and to catch criminals (including terrorists). When people talk about terrorists and terrorism, however, they usually have something more specific in mind.

- Terrorists are said to be people who use terror in an indiscriminate way—setting off car bombs in a crowded market place, for example, to kill some people and to frighten many more.

- Terrorism is said to be a strategy by which terrorists use this kind of violence to advance their interests and their beliefs by weakening their opponents.

Different types of people use terror and some—notably states—use violence in ways which have terrifying effects. This is how it is easy to come to the conclusion that one person's terrorist is another person's freedom fighter. The British used to call the Irish Republican Army (IRA) terrorists because they shot people and let off bombs. Irish nationalists used to call the British army terrorists because they smashed up homes when searching for weapons, beat up people and shot IRA men and women. Therefore, people usually add the following about terrorists and terrorism:

- Terrorists are generally not regarded as legitimate users of violence. When the US invaded Iraq, for example, or Russia invaded Georgia, some other states disagreed with the policies, some said the use of force was inappropriate in these cases, but no state denied the general right of the US and Russia to use force.

- Terrorists, like other private citizens, are not seen as having such a right unless they are seen to be fighting an illegitimate source of authority. If the Syrian government uses violence against its people, then they can use violence back. However, can they plant bombs indiscriminately, in a pro-government TV station, for example, without being called terrorists?

- Terrorists use indiscriminate violence primarily to create terror, whereas states try to use violence for specific objectives and often, but not always, try to minimize the terrifying consequences of its use. When **Al Qaeda** attacked New York and Washington, for example, or bombed the Shi'a pilgrimages in Iraq, it was trying to kill and frighten as many people as it could. When a US drone launches a missile against a compound in northern Pakistan, its purpose is to kill terrorist leaders and not others. Indeed, drone and other strikes operate under strict rules about only firing when there is a clear shot, although many Pakistanis and Afghans who have seen the effects of these missiles find this hard to believe.

Neither of these qualifiers is entirely satisfactory. People use violence for the same motives, whether they are acting on behalf of states or not. They offer up the same sort of reasons to justify their use of violence and to condemn its use by others. We can simply accept what our side says on this and discount the other side. Or, we can take on the difficult job of examining the claims made by all sides and testing them against the evidence. How does the Taliban use violence in Afghanistan? How do the US and its allies use it there?

Guerrillas and guerrilla warfare present similar problems since terror is a major weapon of guerrillas and those who fight them. The term means "small war" and was given to the Spaniards who fought Napoleon in the 19th century after he had defeated the regular Spanish army. Today, guerrilla wars are being fought in Central and South America, Africa, the Middle East, India, Afghanistan, the Philippines, Burma (Myanmar), Central Asia, and along some of the southern borders of Russia. They usually begin as risings by people in the countryside against their government. Other governments often get involved in helping the guerrillas, however, and their wars can spill across borders.

In Africa, for example, the Democratic Republic of the Congo is facing a rebellion in its eastern territories and some of the Congolese rebels have based themselves across the border in Rwanda. Meanwhile, the Rwandans are also facing a rebellion, and some of the Rwandan rebels have set themselves up across the border in the Congo. Sometimes there is a four-way fight with each side's rebels helping the other's government. Sometimes they help each other against the local government and its UN supporters. Sometimes their leaders simply help themselves, trying to be warlords setting up their own little kingdoms based on smuggling and extortion, while enjoying the support of neighboring governments. They fight for control of territories, villages, and people, often with cruelty and brutality which disrupts lives and leads people with no choice but to take sides or flee.

Guerrilla wars can last for decades when the guerrillas are not strong enough to take over and the government forces are not strong enough to crush them. The level of violence can flare up and then die down for years before re-emerging. Even when they come to an end or are brought to an end by the intervention of the great military power states, societies are often scarred by the violence, their peoples untrusting of one another, and casualties continue to occur as old scores are settled, or old landmines left over from the war are triggered by accident, and some holdouts keep fighting.

How effective are terrorists and guerrillas? The answer to that depends on what they are trying to achieve. Some possible motives include:

- Making their opponents hurt and pay for their alleged wrongdoings. Al Qaeda operatives sometimes act like this is their primary motive when they kidnap, torture, and kill people in particularly gruesome ways. We are paying you back for what you have done to our people.

- Giving themselves the self-respect of standing up to their oppressors after years of keeping quiet and doing what they were told. Young men caught up in the "Arab awakening" in Libya and Syria speak of taking up arms in this way, to feel free and to feel like men again.

- Merely surviving as a symbol of opposition and as a nuisance to those they oppose. For decades, members of the Irish Republican Army, the Palestine Liberation Organization, and ethnic movements in the Shan states of Burma concentrated on avoiding being killed and keeping their organizations in being.

- Merely surviving as a money-making proposition. Surviving requires resources to pay, feed, and equip those who fight and their leaders. Sometimes terrorist and guerrilla groups seem to lose sight of their original objectives and to concentrate on supporting themselves. For example, the IRA ran taxi services and extorted money from local businesses, and the FARC in Colombia gained control over some of the local trade in drugs.

- Creating a new state or gaining control of an existing state. Many guerrilla and terrorist movements have their eyes on a prize at the state level. ETA, the Basque radical nationalist movement, wants an independent Basque state separate from Spain. The IRA seeks a united Ireland. The Free Syrian Army, in contrast, wants a new political order inside Syria as it presently is. The Chinese Communists under Mao Zedong in the 1940s succeeded in transforming a guerrilla campaign into a conventional civil war which captured the Chinese state.

- Changing the way a region or the whole world is organized. Nihilists in the 19th century and Al Qaeda today want to destroy the existing global order so that their respective ideas about a better order might replace it. ISIS provides an interesting hybrid example for it tried to set up a state of its own on the territory of Syria and Iraq and ignoring the border between them, it operates an international terrorist network, and its rhetoric suggests it wants a world-wide Caliphate (an Islamic form of political organization).

Terrorist and guerrilla movements are quite successful at surviving even though counter-terrorist and counter-insurgency methods have become more sophisticated. By simply surviving, they make their point, attract support, and embarrass their opponents. Success in the form of killing terrorists, however, can be a two-edged sword as it may encourage more people—their brothers, sisters, and friends—to join the cause. Indeed, guerrillas and terrorists sometimes try to provoke governments into taking harsh measures which will make the governments unpopular. As noted in Chapter 4, for example, the failure of ISIS in the Middle East has resulted in it launching more attacks in Western European states with some of its people returning home. It has also encouraged unhappy individuals in the US, Europe, and elsewhere, to launch attacks of their own, so-called "lone wolf" terrorist attacks.

Terrorists and guerrillas both struggle if they have no external help with funding and arms. Al Qaeda obtains much of its financial support from some conservative Sunni Muslims in the Arabian Peninsula. The IRA was backed by private American citizens and Libya's Muammar Gaddafi. The fortunes of Kurdish guerrillas in Turkey, Iran, and Iraq in the 1970s, however, rose and fell as these states turned on and off their support for those Kurdish guerrillas fighting the governments in their neighboring states. On occasions, terrorists and guerrillas can greatly weaken their opponents and keep them weak. They have helped prevent the return of an effective central government in Somalia since 1991, and the outcome of the struggles in Afghanistan, Iraq, Syria, and the Yemen remains in doubt. Terrorists can also inflict a great inconvenience on their opponents. Think of the costs in time and money of anti-terrorist measures such as increased policing and the security checks at airports. They can contribute to big political changes, for example, in Algeria in the 1950s and possibly in Syria today. These movements do not seem to have decisive effects, however, until they take on state-like characteristics of their own. As noted above, the Chinese Communists in the 1940s, for example, first succeeded as a guerrilla movement among the peasants. To gain victory over the government, however, they had to develop a parallel state with its own conventional army. Hezbollah in southern Lebanon has tried to grow from a combination of political party, militia, and terrorist group into an organization with its own army which controls territory, provides social services, and stands up to the Israelis, and claims to do all of this more effectively and efficiently than the Lebanese state. Its fighters even intervened effectively in the Syrian civil war in 2013. ISIS, in contrast, appears to have failed despite spectacular early successes in 2013–14.

WMD and nightmares about terrorists

What if a terrorist group acquired weapons of mass destruction? And what if that terrorist group believed that destroying the world was a price worth paying to put an end to sin and was prepared to launch martyrdom (suicide) operations with such weapons? They might not even bargain like a James Bond villain or Dr. Evil after they highjacked nuclear weapons. They might just smuggle them into a state and detonate them.

Documents were captured in Afghanistan which suggested that Al Qaeda was trying to get help with WMD and to develop them itself. What if a "rogue" state with nuclear weapons transferred one to the terrorists? This concern was put forward by George W. Bush as a reason for attacking Iraq. He wanted to make it clear that by even thinking about transferring WMD to terrorists, a state could bring down a preventive war upon itself. No WMD were found in Iraq, and its links to anti-Western terrorists barely existed. However, Libya, a state with a record of supporting terrorists, gave up its limited efforts to develop WMD shortly after Iraq was defeated.

It is hard for states to develop WMD or the normal means of delivering them. It would be harder for terrorists who lack resources and spend much of their lives on the lam. No state has transferred WMD materials to a terrorist group so far. The people who develop WMD seem too interested in power and wealth in this life to hand over WMD to fanatics who do not care about getting themselves or anyone else blown up or poisoned.

Suppose Iran succeeds in developing nuclear weapons, and suppose on facing defeat in a war against it, Iran's leaders transferred them to terrorists who used them. If this nightmare occurred, and a large Western city was destroyed by a hidden nuclear, chemical or biological weapon, the consequences in human terms would be just as devastating as the attacks on Hiroshima and Nagasaki. In terms of political and military power, however, the consequences would remain unclear. The targeted state would still be there. The people who detonated the bomb would be no nearer to their objectives. However, they and anyone thought connected with the attack would be much closer to meeting their own Maker as the target and its allies prepared to retaliate against those suspected of being involved. Some terrorists might be fanatical enough and wicked enough to use WMD at any cost, but the people in a position to help them do so seem to be far more cautious.

Today, the armed forces of the great military power states and states under attack spend more time fighting terrorists and guerrillas than fighting the forces of other states. Much of this "fighting," however, involves little combat. When monitoring the efforts of terrorist groups to acquire WMD materials and to deploy weapons of mass destruction, for example, it involves activities more like police work—surveillance, building up information by monitoring social media, patrolling, creating good community relations, and making arrests. Much of this work is undertaken by the normal authorities like the police, the immigration service, and customs agencies, especially along states' borders and at their ports of entry. A number of factors have increasingly drawn the regular armed forces of some states into these duties, however.

- Problems like illegal immigration, drug smuggling, human trafficking, illegal fishing, protected species game poaching and, of course, terrorism have been seen as becoming larger, more important, and requiring urgent attention.
- The agencies which usually deal with these issues have been undergoing cuts in budgets and personnel because of economic difficulties and government austerity policies.
- The criminal gangs have become better equipped with, for example, aircraft, fast boats, surveillance systems of their own, and heavier firepower.
- The armed forces and police of some so-called "narco" or "rogue" states are heavily involved in the illegal activities of gangs and terrorists, as are corrupt members of some states trying to fight these activities.[9]

Increasingly, as a result, soldiers patrol borders to prevent illegal crossings, warships patrol some of the oceans to prevent pirate attacks on commercial shipping and pleasure craft, while military aircraft patrol the air space to identify boats and planes involved in smuggling. Sometimes, the wars on drugs, terrorists, and guerrillas are completely bound up with each other. In Afghanistan, for example, soldiers, diplomats, agronomists, engineers, and educators work to persuade farmers to stop growing poppies which produce the heroin the Taliban and corrupt officials smuggle abroad and sell. They try to get them to grow legal crops instead. In recent years, thousands of people have made the crossing from North Africa to southern Europe across the Mediterranean looking for a better, more secure, life. Many have drowned, a very few have turned out to be terrorists or terrorist sympathizers, and the warships of several European states have helped local coastguard and police services both to rescue people and to catch those with hostile intentions.

Key terms

Al Qaeda   An Arabic term which loosely translates as "The Base" and was the name of the association of small groups (cells) of radical Islamic terrorists which acted under the guidance of Osama Bin Laden in the first decade of the 21st century. Recently, and especially since Bin Laden's death, the name has served as an umbrella for a number of groups in the Middle East and North Africa which see themselves continuing his fight to transform the world of Islam and to rid it of the influence of unbelievers. ISIS is a spin off which became more important than its parent organization.

guerrillas   People, usually not professional soldiers, who use terrorism, hit and run military operations, ambushes, assassinations, propaganda demonstrations like road blocks and document checks, in guerrilla wars to fight the professional armies of states often as part of broader nationalist or revolutionary political campaigns.

terrorists   People who use violence and threats of violence to destroy and/or intimidate their opponents by creating a feeling of fear or terror. Terrorism is the use of terror in this way to gain power and influence.

Key takeaways

- Terror is an emotional state brought on by the imminent prospect of losing something of very great importance. It is associated with pain.
- Terrorists use terror, but other people also do things which create terror.
- Terrorists' use of force is widely seen as illegitimate, but just who is a terrorist is not always easy to answer.
- Terrorism is a strategy by which terror is intentionally used to hurt, weaken or dismay an opponent.
- The word *guerrilla* means small war by irregular fighters (guerrillas) who rarely try to hold territory or directly fight the armed forces they oppose.
- Guerrillas and terrorists fight for a wide range of political, economic, social, and religious objectives.
- Terrorists and guerrillas are hard to defeat but struggle to be successful without external help.
- No one knows how big the threat of terrorists with WMD is, or how to stop it if it exists.
- The armed forces of states spend more time fighting terrorists and guerrillas than the armed forces of other states, and some of what they do looks like the work of police, immigration officials, and customs agencies.

Exercises

1. Why do some people have difficulty defining terrorism and terrorists?
2. Who is most likely to use terrorism and guerrilla warfare? Why?
3. What are the strengths of terrorism and guerrilla warfare?
4. What are the weaknesses of terrorists and guerrillas?

7.6   The future of military power and war in an era of uncertainty

What is the future of military power and war? Wars will continue to be about the fastest with the mostest—that is, delivering the right amount of destructiveness—be it an assassin's bullet; an improvised explosive device; a precision-guided "smart" shell; a bunker-busting massive ordnance penetrator; or, if things go very badly wrong, a thermo-nuclear device—to the right place at the right time. Just who will fight wars is more uncertain. For now, asymmetric wars will continue to predominate, although the hybrid experience of the Islamic State in Iraq and Syria (ISIS) as part state and part terrorist movement is an interesting and worrying development. The possibility of interstate wars as in the 20th century remains remote for now, at least between the great powers. Owing to the tensions emerging between China and many of its American-backed neighbors, and the tensions between NATO and Russia over Ukraine and the Baltic states, however, it seems a little less remote than it did until recently. Elsewhere, for example, between Armenia and Azerbaijan, Eritrea and Ethiopia, Pakistan and India, North Korea and South Korea, and, more recently, Saudi Arabia and Iran, interstate war remains a possibility.

The rise of ISIS: from asymmetrical war to hybrid war?

One of the most troubling consequences of the second American-led war against Iraq in 2003 and the way it was fought was the rise of the Islamic State in Iraq and Syria (ISIS, also known as just the Islamic State and as the Islamic State in Iraq and the Levant or ISIL) in 2014. This movement emerged from various Sunni groups in Iraq who were opposed to the mainly Shia Iraqi government and its US and Iranian supporters. It combined with other Sunni groups which were opposed to the mainly Alawite government in Syria backed by Iran and Russia, and it was aided by several thousand radical Muslim fighters who came from other parts of the world.

ISIS combined elements of a state (it gained control of territory, an economy, and people and had a fairly centralized government), with elements of a terrorist organization (it used brutal violence to intimidate people and provoke their governments into overreaction), and elements of a guerrilla force (it used ambushes and bombs), plus elements of a criminal operation (it extorted, stole, and smuggled). It managed to defeat the conventional armies of two states and gain control of large amounts of territory and several big cities. Expert opinion was surprised by its success and did not expect it to last as ISIS was surrounded by enemies and had little direct support from other states. Iraqi troops and Kurdish militia, with American support and supplies have recently recaptured territory and towns in both Iraq and Syria. ISIS appears to be in decline and transforming into a conventional terrorist network for now, but the hybrid character of its operations, part state, part terrorist movement, and part crime syndicate, may be a model for some wars.

Technical capabilities in terms of information about targets and accuracy in hitting them will continue to improve. The US, for example, is working on a Prompt Global Strike capacity which will allow it to deliver precision attacks on any point of the globe within one hour. These capabilities will also become more expensive and beyond the means of all but the most technologically advanced and rich states, at least until the knowledge diffuses and the technologies become cheaper. Some wars will be swift and appear decisive. Most will be long and settle nothing on their own, until the prospect of failing to win looks more attractive than carrying on to one or both the antagonists.

States, or those states which can afford it, and those in dispute, will continue to prepare their armed forces to fight the armed forces of other states, but they will continue to face problems posed by economic difficulties and shrinking budgets. How much should they spend on tanks and high-performance combat aircraft, for example, as opposed to lightly armed assault forces and helicopters? How much dare they try to save by relying on a few Special Forces and outsourcing other military tasks like truck driving, providing armed escorts, and even some combat roles to private companies? Should they risk the political costs of re-instituting some form of draft to keep the number of soldiers up and the costs down? How much of their budgets should they continue to spend on weapons of mass destruction and keeping them up to date, and how much should they divert to the rapidly-growing competition in information networks—so called cyber warfare—and satellite-based mapping and targeting systems in space?

Land power in the form of soldiers will remain crucial for those who wish to control territory and people, or wish to avoid being controlled by others. Sea power will continue to be important as an adjunct to land power, providing platforms from which raids, bombardments, and invasions can be mounted and forces supplied. Blue water sea power will continue to appear as a public good from which all benefit, at least until there is more than one state capable of maintaining a strong blue water navy on the high seas. Air power will face the strongest challenge in terms of whether the very best for fighting the air forces of other states remains necessary, at least in the short term.

Power in all three dimensions will continue to face the "David and Goliath" challenge. Can cheaper, simpler systems within the price range and social capacity of poorer, weaker states and other actors offer short cuts to military success against the most powerful and best equipped states? In particular, can a variety of relatively cheap rockets armed with a variety of conventional, nuclear and possibly chemical and biological warheads shoot down the expensive aircraft, destroy the expensive armored units, and, above all, make the hugely expensive aircraft carriers, or even cities, of the powerful states vulnerable? The historical record suggests that "Davids" can achieve surprising successes in the short term, but that, by definition, the rich, powerful, and technologically advanced Goliaths can come up with countermeasures and restore their advantage faster. That is, if they don't bankrupt themselves in the process.

Above all, wars will continue to be dangerous, painful, and wasteful affairs in which the innocent suffer, glorious deeds are performed, crimes against humanity occur, and a few warriors and leaders obtain gratification. They will continue to occur because most people believe that there are things for which it is worth fighting, whether they do the fighting themselves or have others fight for them.

Recommended reading (and playing)

John Baylis, *Strategy in the Contemporary World: An Introduction to Strategic Studies*, Oxford, 2010.

James Turner Johnson, *Morality and Contemporary Warfare*, Yale, 2001.

Elinor C. Sloan, *Military Transformation and Modern Warfare: A Reference Handbook*, New York, 2008.

National Security Strategy report, December 2017 accessed at https://www.whitehouse.gov/wp-content/uploads/2017/12/NSS-Final-12-18-2017-0905.pdf

The Operational Art of War, Talonsoft, Matrix Games.

Notes

1 Karl Von Clausewitz (J.J. Graham, A. Rapoport eds.), *On War* (abridged), Harmondsworth, 1968.
2 Barry Posen, "Command of the Commons: The Military Foundation of US Hegemony," *International Security*, 28, 1, Summer, 2003.
3 John Keegan, *The Price of Admiralty*, Harmondsworth, 1988.
4 A.T. Mahan, *The Influence of Sea Power on History*, Cambridge, 1890.
5 Stanley Baldwin, "A Fear for the Future" speech to the House of Commons, 10 November 1932, *Hansard* vol. 270 cc525–641.
6 Lawrence Freeman, *The Evolution of Nuclear Strategy* (3rd edition), Basingstoke, 2003.
7 Albert Wholstetter, "The Delicate Balance of Terror," 1958, *Rand Objective Analysis: Effective Solutions*, accessed at http://www.rand.org/about/history/wohlstetter/P1472/P1472.html.
8 Colin S. Gray, *Modern Strategy*, Oxford, 1999.
9 "Rogue state" is a term used extensively by politicians and some academics to refer to states which treat their own people badly, violently threaten other states, seek to acquire WMD, and fail to abide by or respect international law. Iran, North Korea, and Iraq under Saddam Hussein were routinely referred to as rogues. The US and Britain have been referred to as rogues. The use of the term is often controversial and always has political connotations. See, Paul Sharp, *Diplomatic Theory of International Relations*, Cambridge, 2009.

8   International law, international organization, and human rights

We concluded in Chapter 7 that war and violent conflict are not likely to disappear from international relations anytime soon. As we shall see in Chapter 8, this is not for want of people trying either to get rid of war completely or to re-arrange the international system in such a way as to make it less likely. This has been attempted in three ways: by establishing laws to regulate the relations of states; by setting up organizations where states can resolve their disputes and deal with other problems non-violently; and by attempting to insist that states and peoples accept certain basic principles regarding how human beings should treat each other and what they should be able to expect from life. While the key actors in each of these three areas have historically been states, a major development has been the growing involvement of a wide range of other actors.

Law is usually seen as a system of enforceable rules about human conduct which people accept as legitimate and right. Sovereign states claim that there is no legal authority above them that can tell them or their citizens what to do with the force of law. So how can there be such a thing as **international law** in a system of sovereign states?

Some Realists say there can't be.[1] States talk about international law, but they obey it only when they want to or are forced to, and they try to ignore it when it clashes with their national interests.

Liberals say international law is proper law, even if its enforcement mechanisms are weak. They note that more and more international relations are law-governed, and that most states obey international law most of the time. That is why we can see the growth of international organizations, the increasing efforts to uphold human rights, and the rise of global governance as a way of handling the affairs of the world.[2]

Constructivists say it all depends. If people think about, talk about, write about, and say they are acting in accordance with international law, then clearly there is such a thing as international law. Equally clearly, though, people see international law as different from domestic law.[3]

How they see the relationship between international and domestic law influences the way people and states see international organizations like the United Nations (UN), international campaigns like the ones to make governments respect the human rights of their people, and global management processes like the ones to make states control their levels of borrowing, spending, and polluting. Are we steadily building our way toward a world whose politics and economics will be organized by international law on a global scale? Are we feeling our way toward more regulation by international law in some areas, like human rights, and less in others, like national security? Do international law, international organizations, and global governance reflect a growing concern with the ethical dimension of international relations and questions of right and wrong, or do they remain simply weapons and battlefields in the ongoing struggle for power and influence between states?

8.1 International law

Learning objectives

1. Explain how international law differs from domestic or municipal law.
2. List the different sources of international law.
3. Describe the two main areas of international relations originally covered by international law.
4. Provide examples of how international law works.

International law is primarily a set of rules for the conduct of states and their relations with other states. International law also provides rules for how the law itself is to be interpreted, how disagreements about it are to be handled, and how it is to be enforced. In the past, only states and the organizations created by them could be the subjects of international law. An individual person could not bring a case against someone in international law or have a case brought against them. Today, international law is developing in a way which makes individual people—and especially powerful people accused of crimes against humanity—subjects of international legal procedures. Treating human relations in a law-based way is different from treating them in other ways—for example, political, economic, diplomatic, or personal. It involves the explicit application of rules according to a distinctive process of reasoning to decide whether a particular act is or is not lawful. International law is generally treated as being different from domestic law in three ways:

- It lacks a single, final authority like a sovereign state-based system of government and law which is universally accepted as legitimate and having precedent in all cases.
- It lacks a single, effective, and universally accepted mechanism for enforcement and punishment like a sovereign state-based system of courts and police.
- It depends to a higher degree than a sovereign state-based system of law on its subjects agreeing to place themselves under it and abide by it in advance.

We can think about the sources of international law in two ways: first, in terms of its origins or nature; and second in terms of how international laws are actually created. People have debated its origins and nature for centuries as part of broader arguments about law, politics, and religion. Does law reflect rules that come directly from God or the gods in the way, for example, many Christians, Jews, and Muslims believe Moses brought the Ten Commandments down the mountain on stone tablets? If not, where does it come from?

We can trace a development in Europe from the time of the Reformation and the fragmenting of Christian unity away from the notion of God's law directly revealed, to the idea that God's rules about right conduct were somehow inherent in our nature. Since God had created the natural world, it seemed reasonable to suggest that we were simply born with an ability to recognize or to reason our way to rules like the Ten Commandments as natural law, and thus what is right. With the failure of Catholics and Protestants to reconcile and the emergence of an increasingly science-based understanding of human beings and their world in 17th-century Europe, however, the case for natural law was challenged. People were governed, it was argued, by the law of nature, derived not from God's will, but from their needs and wants as animals in a world which conformed to the laws of physics, chemistry, and biology. In this conception, the right and wrong aspect of law was not very strong compared to laws of nature about survival and avoiding pain. The right and wrong aspect did not come from God either—there probably wasn't a god. It came from the practical experience of living with each other and finding that we were all better off if we could agree on some basic rules.

This conception was especially important in thinking about international relations. One of the oldest questions about laws—especially about the treatment of other people—concerned to whom they applied. Was it to believers only, to "our people," or to all people—no exceptions? The anthropological and historical records show that this is an important question for every group or society which sees itself as distinctive and different. Hugo Grotius, a Dutch lawyer writing in the 17th century, addressed this question by arguing that a set of laws applied to all people, but that the laws which governed relations between peoples (in the form of states and nations) were different from the laws which governed relations between people (as individuals). In particular, he stressed how in the former, the requirements of peace and co-existence were often more important than doing the right thing as this might be conventionally understood. Grotius had seen how the contending conventional moralities of Catholics and Protestants had led to savage warfare and terrible bloodshed in the Thirty Years War (1618–48), because both sides believed their own conception of God's will applied to everybody—no exceptions. He still made his argument in terms of God's will expressed in a natural law which people could recognize by thinking it through.[4] By the 19th century, however, certain thinkers had dispensed with God and natural law altogether. In their **positivist law** conception, international law was simply those rules which states had found it possible to agree to on grounds of mutual convenience and practicality. It did not reflect any more profound or divine moral code governing the affairs of people or states. As we shall see, these old issues between proponents of revealed, natural, and positivist views of law about the origins of international law and to whom it applies are alive and well today.

There is more agreement about the origins of international law in the practical sense of how it gets created. **Treaties**, the most formal level of agreement negotiated between sovereign states, provide a major source of international law. According to the Vienna Convention on the Law of Treaties, a treaty is "an international agreement concluded between States in written form."[5] When states register a treaty with the UN, they then commit themselves to fulfilling its obligations under international law (there are other, less formal agreements between states like conventions, declarations, and understandings which do not have this force). Treaties can be bilateral (between two states) like the nearly 300 bilateral treaties which exist between the US and Canada. They can be multilateral (between more than two and perhaps many states) like the treaty binding the twenty-eight members of NATO, and they can be universal (every state, or nearly every state signs them) like the UN Charter. Typically, the representatives of states sign a treaty, and then it is confirmed or ratified back home. In some states, the US, for example, this involves approval by a legislative branch of the government, but not in all states. Other states may later accede to, or join, a treaty already in existence. Treaties are regarded as binding for as long as they are in force on those who signed them and their successors. Often treaties have time frames or review processes written into them which give a state an out if it follows the right procedures, like the anti-ballistic missile treaty between the US and the Soviet Union (later Russia). Sometimes states argue that treaties are only binding so long as the circumstances in which they were signed have not radically changed. Occasionally, a state will simply break a treaty on grounds of national interest. Since this hurts their future reputation as a treaty partner, however, states will go to great lengths to explain why breaking their commitment is either justified or how they are not really breaking it. Historically, treaties were used to create alliances, to end wars, and settle territorial claims. Today all the big issues of international relations on Earth, as well as the Moon and Outer Space, can be the subject matter of treaties.

The US-Soviet Anti-Ballistic Missile Treaty 1972

The US and the Soviet Union signed a treaty in 1972 committing both sides to restricting the number of defensive missiles they would deploy for destroying incoming ballistic missiles armed with nuclear warheads. At the time, both states agreed that deploying these defensive systems would be very expensive, that they probably would not work, and that they might be de-stabilizing (see Chapter 7 on stable deterrence). There were opponents to the agreement in both countries who said the technology might be made to work and that, if so, the defensive missiles would be worth the expense. These opponents also thought the other side could not be trusted and that the stability argument was wrong.

The treaty had built into it procedures for review, amendment, and unilateral withdrawal from it after six months' notice. It was amended in 1974, and the US gave notice before it withdrew unilaterally in 2002. President

George W. Bush's administration argued that times had changed. The US wanted to work on developing anti-ballistic missile defenses because the technology had improved, and it was now worried about a few missiles launched from Iran or North Korea which would be easier to stop than an unlikely strike with lots of missiles from Russia or China. There continue to be big arguments about whether this was a smart military policy. There were also arguments about whether the US's pullback, although within the terms of the ABM treaty, would hurt its reputation as a signer of arms control treaties. Subsequent agreements with Russia on missile levels suggest this has not been the case.

Custom is regarded as another source of international law, especially by those states and legal experts with a common law tradition and a positivist view of law. The Vienna Convention on Diplomatic Relations (see p. 193) of 1961 provides an example of how the ways in which states conducted their diplomatic relations with one another grew from habits of convenience, to practices involving rights and duties, and then to a system of law over time.

General principles of law are also regarded by states and legal experts as sources of international law. If it's wrong in a system of domestic law, then it's likely to be wrong in a system of international law. Thus Joshua Goldstein cites theft and assault as standard principles which transfer from domestic law to international law.[6]

Notions of equity and fairness may also provide sources of international law. Of course, just like in domestic law, in international law general principles provide the starting points—not the finishing points—for arguments. Compare Argentina's invasion of the Falkland Islands (Malvinas) in 1982, Iraq's invasion of Kuwait in 1990, and the US invasion of Iraq in 2003. The attacker in each example made their case in terms of self-defense, righting a wrong, and restitution. The defenders in each case declared themselves to be the victims of unprovoked, unjustified, aggressive, and violent assaults.

The final source of international law is found in the advice and opinions of international legal experts based on their research and reasoning. This source tends to work indirectly, however, as arguments placed by states and others before those who make judgments on cases, or as principles which states introduce into their treaties or customary practices. It is argued, for example, that the research and reasoning of legal experts is playing a role in getting international law to accept a modified understanding of the rights of sovereign governments. Those rights, it is being suggested, should not be fully recognized where governments extensively violate the human rights of their citizens.

There are different types of international law pertaining to all the big issues of public policy and to all the different types of international actors to be found in the world today. Two big traditional areas of great importance to states, however, have been the **international law of diplomacy** (or diplomatic law) and the **international law of war**. Most of the international law of diplomacy is to be found in the Vienna Conventions on Diplomatic Relations (1961)[7] and on Consular Relations (1963).[8] These formalize key principles which have been established by state customs, practices, and previous agreements such as those reached at the Congress of Vienna in 1815. They assume a diplomatic system of resident missions, usually embassies staffed by diplomats under the leadership of an ambassador or head of mission. They spell out the rights, duties, and privileges of these missions and their staff, as well as the rights and duties of the receiving states to which they are sent. They also spell out the procedures by which the sending state suggests (accredits) diplomats and the receiving state agrees to accept them. Diplomats are not supposed to become involved in the internal affairs of the receiving state, especially its internal politics, and they are not supposed to engage in espionage. The big arguments over the role of Sergey Kislyak, Russia's former ambassador to the United States, during the American election campaign in 2016 reflect this concern. Was he just doing his job in talking to people from the election campaigns, or was he interfering? In return, the receiving state grants diplomats accredited to it immunity from prosecution in its legal system, refrains from entering the embassies without permission, and does not interfere with communications between the mission and its own government through what is known as the diplomatic bag or pouch (which can be as big as a shipping container).

States can have no diplomatic relations with each other (and thus have neither embassies nor diplomats in each other's countries). The US and Iran have no official diplomatic relations and their affairs are handled by the interests section of another embassy in each other's capital. Until diplomatic relations were restored between the US and Cuba in 2015, a large US mission was maintained in Havana, the Cuban capital, as an interests section of the much smaller Swiss embassy which "protected" it. States can be in diplomatic relations without necessarily opening embassies and exchanging their diplomats, but it is more usual for states in diplomatic relations to have embassies and diplomats in each other's capital city.

The diplomatic corps is made up of all the accredited diplomats at the different missions in a capital city and tries to ensure that the rights, privileges, and duties of both the government and the diplomats are being respected. The status of diplomatic relations is often seen as a measure of how good the relationship is between states. States will call their ambassadors home for consultations, declare particular diplomats *persona non grata* and ask them to leave, or break relations completely and close an embassy as signals of disagreement. However, professional diplomats tend to regard anything which reduces communications in times of tension as a bad idea.

The strange case of Julian Assange

Most of us only hear about diplomatic immunities and privileges when a story surfaces in the press about diplomats not paying parking fines, being allowed to go home without penalty after having killed someone, or when a mission is attacked, as happened to the US consulate in Benghazi, Libya, in 2012. Immunities and privileges used to be justified by the idea that the ambassador stood in place of his sovereign (king or queen) and should be treated the same. More recently, they have been justified on functional grounds. Diplomats cannot do their jobs if they can be the subject of private lawsuits or police officers bursting in to conduct searches of their missions. Diplomatic asylum is a practice by which embassies may offer protection, based on their own inviolability, from the law to a fugitive who is believed to be in great danger of unjust punishment. Political asylum is a convention by which a state can refuse to return the citizen of another state who is wanted for legal proceedings, if those proceedings are for so-called political offenses.

WikiLeaks is an Internet organization which specializes in making secret information public on the Internet. From 2010 onwards, it began uploading secret diplomatic cable traffic from US embassies to the US Department of State. An American soldier—Bradley (later Chelsea) Manning—was subsequently charged with leaking information. The actual content of the cables ranged from boring and routine to funny and embarrassing, although some of it caused short-term damage to US relations with states whose leaders US diplomats had been rude about, or whose cell phone conversations had been listened in on. The US also maintained the leaks caused major security problems, putting people's lives at risk, for example. The leader of WikiLeaks, Julian Assange—an Australian—was in Britain when the Swedish government announced it wanted him to come to Sweden to answer questions about accusations of rape and sexual assault. Assange appealed to a British court, saying the charges were just a pretext to get him, so the Swedes could extradite him to the US to face charges of espionage and a possible death penalty.

After a long process, the British denied his request and Assange fled to the embassy of Ecuador in London and requested asylum. South American states have a long tradition of offering political asylum to each other's political opponents. Ecuador and the US had poor relations, and Ecuador had already considered offering Assange asylum. Its London embassy let him in. British police were stationed outside the embassy, ready to arrest him for breaching the conditions of his bail, if he stepped out. Under the Vienna Convention, no one can enter an embassy without the ambassador's consent. The British government threatened to enter the embassy in accordance with a law passed when one of its officers was shot dead by a gunman from the Libyan embassy 28 years before. After another long delay, the Ecuadorian government decided to grant Assange political asylum. In 2017, the Swedish courts dropped their charges, but the British police said they still had a warrant for Assange's arrest. At the time of writing, he remained stuck in the Ecuadorian embassy in London and has been there for over five years. Some people have asked why don't the British police just break into the embassy and arrest him. Others, especially diplomats, answer because we don't want to provide an excuse or precedent for others breaking into our embassies.[9]

The international law of war focuses on the justness of war. As we saw in Chapters 6 and 7, nearly all people accept that wars are bad, but most people accept that there are some things for which it is worth fighting. In addition, most societies have tried to establish rules or principles about when going to war can be seen as the right thing to do and how to fight wars. These rules often have their roots in the religious beliefs of societies. Islam, Judaism, and the spiritual beliefs of many Native American tribes, for example, all set out these sorts of rules. In Europe, Christian—and mainly Catholic—thinkers ranging from Saint Augustine to Thomas Aquinas developed a tradition of thinking which came to be known as Just War Theory.[10] This divides the issue into two parts: the right to go to war (*jus ad bellum*); and the right conduct in war (*jus in bellum*). Some of the circumstances in which going to war might be regarded as just were as follows:

- in self-defense; and so long as there is a prospect of success;
- to stop an aggressor who is about to attack (pre-emptive war);
- to right a wrong, when the evil created by the war will be less than the evil created by failing to fight.

To these it might be added that wars should be undertaken only by legitimate authorities (states). They should not be fought for gain, glory, or the conversion of souls. They should be fought as a last resort when all other options have been exhausted, and they should not be expanded from the original just cause to accomplish other things.

According to Just War Theory, wars had to be fought justly as well. Thus, Just War Theorists argued as follows:

- Non-combatants should not be specifically targeted, and every effort should be made to spare them suffering as a result of military operations (soldiers who surrendered should not be harmed either).
- The violence used should be proportionate to the offense it was intended to correct.
- Unnecessary violence causing unnecessary suffering should not be used.

As you can see, there is plenty of scope for disagreement about these principles, what they mean, and how they are to be applied. A notable difference between cultures, for example, exists in regard to the treatment of prisoners. Are they to be treated like citizens with individual rights, or are they to be treated as dishonored soldiers enjoying few rights? The distinction between combatants and non-combatants has broken down in a number of ways. In World War II, the British and the Americans justified area bombing of German and Japanese cities as revenge, and because German and Japanese families provided emotional support to the soldiers (and future soldiers), and civilians living around the factories built the guns and tanks and ships which would be used in the fighting. Some theologians have argued that the destructiveness of nuclear weapons makes their use incompatible with any conception of just war. They argue that these weapons fail the test of maintaining any meaningful distinction between combatants and non-combatants, and that they fail the test of proportionality. In guerrilla wars and anti-terrorist operations, soldiers find themselves fighting civilians, often helped by their own communities, who might appear as friendly non-combatants at one moment, while being ready to attack as combatants at another. As the question of how to treat the Taliban and Al Qaeda fighters held for years by the Americans at Guantanamo illustrates, these are problems which we still face. Are these people prisoners of war, alleged criminals, or something else entirely?

In spite of these great difficulties, however, states and legal experts have devoted great efforts to codifying the reasons for which wars may be justly fought. As we saw in Chapter 6, acceptable reasons have steadily been reduced to fighting wars of self-defense and, as we shall see below, fighting wars mandated by the UN Security Council to counter threats to international peace. At the Hague Conventions of 1899 and 1907, states worked in great detail on rules about the mechanics of warfare—for example, "dum dum" (hollow nosed) bullets, incendiary ammunition which burns, and saw-edged and corkscrew bayonets were all outlawed because they would cause unnecessary suffering. Ironically and sadly, a third Hague Conference scheduled for 1914 had to be postponed because of the outbreak of World War I. Nevertheless, states have continued to work on the challenges of reducing suffering in war. The Geneva Protocol banning chemical and biological warfare was added in 1925 to agreements reached at The Hague Conventions, and a whole series of conventions at Geneva, from 1864 to 1949, established how prisoners of war should be treated. The latest protocol to these, on identifying symbols which non-combatants doing medical work in combat zones might use, was adopted in 2005.

In addition to concerns regarding when to fight (*jus ad bellum*) and how to fight (*jus in bellum*), a third concern for Just War Theory has developed in recent years. This is concerned with the treatment of defeated states when they are occupied by the forces of victorious states (*jus post bellum*). Are the occupying power and its soldiers simply under obligation to behave themselves, or do they have greater obligations, for example, to repairing the damage they have done or to building a good political system, however that might be defined?[11] This line of inquiry has its origins in historical experience, for example, the Allied occupations of Germany and Japan at the end of World War II, the Israeli occupation of Arab territory after 1967 and, more recently, the American-led coalition presence in Iraq and Afghanistan. However, it can also be related to a broader challenge to Just War Theory which rejects the claim that the moral standards by which we judge conduct concerning war should be any different from the standards by which we judge any other human conduct. How, for example, was assassinating Osama bin Laden different from killing someone else? How is using drones to strike at people believed to be terrorists and anyone who happens to be near them justified in peace time? And can soldiers escape all blame for fighting unjust wars on the grounds that their governments ordered them to do so? Driving these questions is a sense that the claim of states to be sovereigns to which normal moral principles and laws do not always apply is becoming harder to defend.[12]

How then does international law work? This question is best answered by looking first at how domestic law works and why most of us obey it most of the time. We obey a particular law for a number of reasons:

- It may be obviously in our self-interest to obey the law.
- It may be a law which we think is right and just.

- Leaving aside what we think of the law, we may believe that the source of the law is legitimate and has a right to make the law for us.

- We may be afraid of punishment if we disobey the law, especially if we have a high expectation that the law is going to be enforced.

To these we can add that people accept that in general laws should be obeyed; that is to say there is a law-about-laws principle operating inside us. Think in the terms above about why you obey the law to stop at red lights and go on green when driving, but only keep close to the speed limit, and why you pay your taxes, but may try to ignore laws about the consumption of alcohol. Now think about why you do not commit murder.

States respond to international law in the same way, although with three important differences. The first is that enforcement procedures are less effective in international law, while practical and moral arguments about the possibility of not obeying the law for reasons of national interest and responsibility are currently stronger. The second is that states see themselves as contracting into international law—they agree to abide by it—in a way that citizens do not agree to abide by domestic law. They are just born into being subjects of it. You would think that this might make international law stronger, in the sense that states choose to abide by it. Rightly or wrongly, however, this process of contracting-in gives states a sense that they might at some point contract out again. The third difference is that states are a lot less sure about the legitimacy of the sources of international law than most citizens usually are about the legitimacy of the sources of domestic law. International law comes from other states just like them, and so the impulse for states to say "who the heck do you think you are?" to international legal authorities—especially when those authorities are saying "no" to them—is much stronger than it is for most citizens receiving a domestic court notice or unfavorable finding. Taken together, these differences suggest that acceptance of the law-about-laws principle—that the law should be obeyed because it is the law—is weaker in international law than domestic law.

Nevertheless, states comply with a great deal of international law because—like red lights and green lights on traffic signals—it is in their obvious self-interest. Think about how states make sure their air traffic and air traffic control systems comply with international regulations about air travel. They also comply with international laws because they want other states to comply with them too. This is the principle of **reciprocity**. We won't enter foreign embassies in our capital and foreign governments won't enter our embassies in their capitals. We will make our citizens and companies respect laws about contracts with foreigners and other states will do the same with their citizens and companies. States also abide by a great deal of international law because they think it just and because they want to be seen as law-abiding when others (especially their own citizens) see the law as just, for example complying with laws about protecting wildlife or the environment. States also do worry about the enforcement of international law. Both Iraq and Iran faced crippling sanctions on their ability to engage in international trade and finance because of their non-compliance with their commitments under the Nuclear Non-Proliferation Treaty and subsequent demands from the UN to allow full inspection of sites suspected of being involved in researching and developing WMD. With enforcement, however, it is critically important that large numbers of states agree that a law has been breached and that enforcement or punishment is appropriate. In the absence of this broad agreement, enforcement operations can look like Wild West posses, or even lynch mobs with a few states taking the law into their own hands.

Finally, states find international law very useful—some would say indispensable—as a way for talking to each other about disputes, for resolving them and, where necessary, deciding who is at fault, who should be punished and who should make restitution. The International Court of Justice (informally the World Court) and the International Criminal Court are the two primary institutions of the international legal system in this regard (Figure 8.1).

Two courts of international law

The International Court of Justice (http://www.icj-cij.org/) was established by the UN Charter in 1946 as a successor to the Permanent Court of International Justice of the League of Nations. It attempts to resolve disputes between states and provides rulings on issues brought before it by other UN agencies and organs. It is composed of fifteen judges elected to nine-year terms by the UN General Assembly and the UN Security Council. Judges from permanent member states and representing the main legal traditions of the world—common law, civil law, and post-communist law—are represented by judges. Extra judges can be added when parties to a dispute do not have a judge of their own nationality on the Court. These judges are supposed to be impartial, but the impartiality of individual judges can be challenged. The judges can express collective and individual opinions on a case, and a Court decision or opinion is determined by a majority.

The Court works best when both or all the states in dispute agree to bring the dispute before it. Some states have signed an Optional Clause which commits them to accepting its decisions, although this acceptance can be qualified on certain policy issues and in certain circumstances. For example, in 1986, the US qualified its commitment to the Optional Clause after the Court ordered it to pay compensation for military activities in Nicaragua. The Court works less well when only one state or side in a dispute asks it to decide. The other state may simply refuse to cooperate, as did Iran when the US took its detention of US diplomats in Teheran to the Court in 1979–80, or as China did in rejecting the Court's support for the Philippines' case against it in the South China Sea in 2016.

When there is non-compliance with a decision of the International Court of Justice, the matter can be referred to the UN Security Council. However the Council may be unwilling or unable to do anything about it. The International Court of Justice can act slowly and be expensive. Even where it is unable to secure compliance with a decision, however, the state whose position it supports gains some moral and political satisfaction, the losing state is embarrassed and placed on the defensive, while the rest of

Figure 8.1 The Peace Palace at The Hague, Netherlands, home to the International Court of Justice and the Permanent Court of Arbitration

(Source: mauritius images GmbH/Alamy Stock Photo)

the world now views the dispute in the light of the Court's decision about who was right.

The International Criminal Court (ICC) (http://www.icc-cpi.int/menus/icc/) is a newer institution established in 2003, and based in The Hague. Its establishment followed the setting up of a number of ad hoc International Criminal Tribunals focused on specific cases of mass killing: Rwanda; the former Yugoslavia; and Liberia. Their proceedings sometimes appeared on television news when infamous leaders like the Bosnian-Serbs, Radovan Karadžić, and Ratko Mladić, or former Liberian president Charles Taylor, were brought to trial. The ICC's focus is not on states, but on individual human beings who are accused of having committed war crimes or acts of genocide (killing large numbers of people simply because of their national, ethnic, racial, or religious-cultural identity). It has eighteen judges and has heard cases concerned with human rights violations in the course of civil wars, government repression, and unrest in a number of African states. Its highest profile case involved it issuing an unsuccessful arrest warrant in 2008 for Omar el-Bashir, the president of Sudan, in connection with human rights violations committed by his government's troops in the province of Darfur. Its focus on Africa has been a source of criticism, but cases from elsewhere have also been brought to its attention. It functions when state legal systems either refuse to handle a case, or look like they are unable to do so impartially.

Most states have ratified the treaty establishing the ICC, but a few, including the US, have not. The US worries that what it regards as frivolous or politically motivated charges will be brought against its generals, admirals, and leaders by opponents of American military operations around the world. Although it cooperates with the ICC on occasions, the US also tries to get countries in which its armed forces operate to sign Bilateral Immunity Agreements (BIAs) promising they will not refer US personnel to the ICC. For most Americans, this reflects the US's special role as the world's policeman, plus the fact it has its own, honest legal system for handling such cases if they arise. Much of the rest of the world is not impressed by this claim to be special, and does not like it when the US Congress demands pressure on states which will not sign BIAs.

We tend to associate international law with international courts. However, it is important to remember that the national courts and legal systems of states are often engaged in handling disputes which involve international law. In 2012, for example, the British bank, Standard Chartered, agreed to pay the State of New York's banking regulatory agency $340 million to drop charges that it had violated UN-sponsored international agreements curtailing relations with Iran's banks as part of the campaign to stop Iran developing its nuclear industry.

In 1993, Belgium claimed **universal jurisdiction** for its courts, among other things meaning that people could bring violations of the Geneva Conventions from anywhere around the world before it. Again, there are big arguments about this sort of international judicial activism, especially when it originates in a particular state. Opponents argue that anyone with an axe to grind can launch lawsuits against perfectly respectable, law-abiding leaders who have been involved in military operations which enjoy the support of the UN and the international community. Several former American generals and statesmen, for example, are possibly now more careful where they travel abroad than they used to be, because they are worried about being held on such a charge. Supporters argue that no one should be exempt from answering serious charges if the grounds for these exist, and that anything that makes potential war criminals more cautious about killing, brings some war criminals to justice, and makes the lives of other war criminals more fearful and inconvenient is worth doing. Belgium modified and eventually repealed its law on universal jurisdiction in 2003, accepting some of the criticisms about frivolous and impractical cases and suggesting that the ICC would better perform this role once it was established. However, Belgium and several other states claim some jurisdiction regarding human rights violations by their own citizens no matter where, and against accused citizens of other states who happen to be on their territory.

Key terms

international law   A system of potentially enforceable rules about state conduct and more recently, the international conduct of non-state and individual actors, which states and people regard as legitimate.

international law of diplomacy (diplomatic law)   The law which regulates the official, peaceful relations of states and the conduct of those who represent them.

international law of war   The law which sets out who may go to war (states), the reasons for which they may go to war, the way in which they may fight wars, and, latterly, how they should conduct the occupation of defeated states.

law   A system of enforceable rules about human conduct which people regard as legitimate.

positivist law   A view which sees law as the product of practical agreements between states or human beings, rather than as a system of rules reflecting the will of God or timeless and universal moral principles.

reciprocity   A principle in agreements which involves parties to those agreements treating each other and being treated by each other in the same way.

treaties   Formal and binding agreements between states. They can be bilateral, applying to two states; multilateral, applying to three or more states; and universal, usually multilateral in practice but aimed to apply to all states.

universal jurisdiction   A claim for a national or international legal system that specified actions of states and people anywhere in the world may be regulated by it or judged within it.

Key takeaways

- A growing and important body of international law helps regulate the conduct of states.
- States obey international law for much the same reasons that individuals obey domestic law.
- The enforcement of international law between states is weaker than the enforcement of domestic law within states, and the sense that international law ought to be obeyed by states can be weaker.
- The sources of international law are: treaties, custom, general principles of law, and international legal experts.
- Two key areas of international law are the international law of diplomacy and the international law of war.
- Two key institutions of international law are the International Court of Justice (for states) and the International Criminal Court (for individuals).
- Courts within states may also attempt to use and enforce international law.

Exercises

1. What is international law and what does it do?
2. When do states obey international law and when might they ignore it?
3. How does the International Criminal Court differ from the International Court of Justice? Why has the US Senate refused to ratify the treaty-making the United States a party to the International Criminal Court, and why has Canada been an enthusiastic signatory?

8.2	International organization and the United Nations

Learning objectives

1. Explain what **international organizations** are and why states create them.
2. List the main organs of the **United Nations**.
3. Provide examples of how the United Nations contributes to international peace and security.
4. Provide examples of how measures to protect state security may negatively affect human security.
5. List the reasons which may be given to explain the ineffectiveness of the **United Nations Security Council**.

A domestic system of law has institutions: legislatures for making the law; executives for carrying out the law; courts for interpreting the law; and police for enforcing the law. Institutions provide specific regular patterns of ways in which people ought to act, together with reasons and incentives for them so doing. They exist when people accept that they do, act in accordance with them, and provide resources for their maintenance and operations. Institutions operate as sets of rules, expectations, and justifications. These may result in complex social organizations and extensive material dimensions like buildings, equipment, and assigned people. However, they may simply exist in the minds of a set of people. Think of the institution of marriage as an example of an institution in all of these terms.

As we learned in Chapter 3, many Liberals saw war resulting from the weakness of the institutions and law possible in an international political anarchy of sovereign states. They argued by domestic analogy that less war and more peace would result if international politics were made more like domestic politics—the politics inside states. Stronger international law would need stronger international legal, political, and economic institutions. Some argued for a world government to operate like the governments of sovereign states, but over them.[13] Other Liberals were not sure this was practical, but they all agreed that stronger institutions needed to be organized and that international relations in general needed higher levels of organization. As a result, international organizations like the League of Nations were created. However, the idea of international organization (with no "s" on the end) was also developed as an alternative to the idea of international anarchy. As Liberals pointed out, even the political anarchy constituted by sovereign states had a great deal of organization. Think of the laws of diplomacy and war examined above. More organization, they argued, would mean better institutions, stronger law, less war, and more peace.

Attempts to organize and institutionalize international relations can be found wherever state systems exist or have existed in the past. Most people most of the time and in most places are attracted to the idea of making the relations between the political communities in which they live more predictable, stable, and peaceful. The ancient Greek city states and the tribes of the Iroquois, for example, organized leagues which were more than just alliances against others. In addition, they regulated relations among the members on the assumption that the members ought not to fight each other if at all possible. Big, more powerful states are also attracted to the opportunity for organizing international relations on terms which favor their ways of seeing things, while small, weaker states are also attracted by the possibility that more organization and law will offer them better protection from the big, powerful states.

European diplomatic history is full of stories of efforts to create such leagues. The Concert of Europe, for example, was established in the early 19th century at the end of the Napoleonic Wars. Through it, leaders of the victorious Russian, Prussian, and Austrian empires attempted to operate as a great power club which regulated relations between themselves and directed the way relations between everyone else ought to be conducted. They also tried to dictate relations within states faced by revolutions which threatened both peace and the imperial principle of government (the British were founder members of the club, but disagreed with this counter-revolutionary policy and stopped attending meetings of the Congress).

The League of Nations, established in 1919, diluted the influence of the great powers and reflected the concerns of the smaller, weaker powers in line with the democratic and national principles of representation favored by the United States and its president, Woodrow Wilson. We examined the fate of the League of Nations in Chapters 2 and 3. As the Realists expected, support for its rules was not strong enough to prevent states using force when their national interests suggested that they should, nor was it strong enough to compel states to use force for collective security when their national interests suggested they should not.

Twenty-one years after the League of Nations was set up, World War II started, but the international organization idea was only briefly discredited. Indeed, with the passage of time, the failure of the League of Nations becomes less and less remarkable. What catches the eye instead is the determination of the capitalist United States, the communist Soviet Union, the imperial powers of Europe, and just about every other state in the world to have another go at creating an international organization—the United Nations (http://www.un.org/en/)—which would build on and improve upon the unhappy experience of the League. No one was prepared to give up on the arguments that more peace needed more international law, and that more international law needed stronger international institutions.

The United Nations (UN) was established in 1945 at the end of World War II. Its headquarters is in New York, although some agencies are elsewhere—especially in Geneva, Switzerland, the site of the old League of Nations. The institutions, or organs in UN jargon, of the UN system mirror those of the League and have the look of a government in embryo. There is a senior council (the UN Security Council) which looks like an executive, an assembly (the **United Nations General Assembly**) which looks like a legislature, a set of committees for making policy, a secretariat which looks part bureaucracy and part executive, and, as we have seen, a court for interpreting law and settling disputes. Member states sign on to the rules and obligations of a universal treaty, the UN Charter, instead of the League's Covenant. Of course, neither the League nor the UN actually is a government since both international organizations are composed primarily of sovereign states (imagine if the US was composed of 50 states which claimed sovereignty and sent their representatives to Washington to act as if they were a federal government).

Despite these similarities between the League and the UN, however, they differed in one very important respect. As we shall see, the UN gave more influence than the League did to the great power states. The lesson of the League had seemed to be that without the great power states involved, nothing could be accomplished, but the great power states would not be involved unless their own interests, influence, and power were protected. In this, the UN represented a compromise between the democratic universalism of the League of Nations and the more exclusive great power "country clubbyness" of the Congress of Europe.

The primary purpose of the UN is to maintain international peace and the security of states, and, as its Charter says, "to save succeeding generations from the scourge of war." At the heart of the UN system is the UN Security Council. The Security Council consists of five permanent members (the P-5 in UN jargon): the US, China, Russia, France, and Britain, each of which can block any substantive action agreed to by the rest of the Security Council, plus ten other

Figure 8.2 A UN Security Council meeting in 2014, chaired by US President Obama. It is unusual for a head of state to chair these meetings
(Source: White House Photo/Alamy Stock Photo)

members elected from the General Assembly for two-year terms. Thus while all states are equal, in the UN some states are more equal than others. Each state on the Security Council is represented by an ambassador, the head of the state's permanent mission at the UN, although others including foreign ministers, prime ministers, and presidents may attend and speak.

The members of the Security Council may consider any issue they agree to, providing the issue has some bearing on international peace and security. They can also be asked to consider similar issues brought before them by the **United Nations Secretary General** (see p. 211). They may simply talk, or they may debate and vote on resolutions which express the Security Council's opinion, request a member state, several member states, or all member states to take specified actions, or set out what the members of the Security Council themselves, or some of them, are going to do. The Charter makes the Security Council very powerful. It can determine threats to peace, and it can order member states to engage in or support economic sanctions and military operations under the Security Council's direction against aggressor states. To take action, however, requires a majority vote of at least nine members in favor and none of the P-5 voting against (although the resolution carries if a P-5 member abstains or does not participate in the vote). (See Figure 8.2.)

The Syrian Crisis and the UN Security Council

In 2010, the Syrian government was faced with protests which it tried to repress with violence while promising reforms. The government was a dictatorship dominated by a single family—the Assads—and their close relations. They were members of the Alawite minority, a Shia sect of Islam in a country with Christian and Druze minorities, but with a Sunni Muslim majority. At one level, the protests and what followed were part of the great "Arab awakening" of peoples against their governments which had taken place in Tunisia, Egypt, and Libya, as well as elsewhere. At another level, they were and are part of an older struggle for power between the Sunni majority and the rest, and between clans, families, and regions in the state. At still another level, they were part of a struggle for power and influence between different states in the Middle East, some interested in leading a wealthier and more influential region, others looking to lead Arabs and Muslims in general in an Islamic revolution which will restore their understanding of what God and Mohammed would have regarded as a pious and just political and religious order.

The Syrian government's repression did not work. The protests continued and fighting developed, waged with great brutality. The issue was brought before the UN Security Council in accordance with the UN Charter because it posed a threat to peace between Syria and its neighbors. Humanitarian concerns with the killing and power political concerns with influence in Syria also played a part. All the members of the Security Council agreed that the Syrians should stop killing each other and start talking to each other. All the members of the Security Council agreed that outsiders should stop interfering with guns and money. And all the members of the Security Council agreed that steps should be taken to encourage all the parties to start talking. A special negotiator (former UN Secretary General Kofi Annan) and a small number of soldiers as a peace observation (see below) mission were sent to Syria to help.

However, the Americans, the British, and others saw the Syrian government and its repressive tactics as the main problem. They wanted the UN Security Council to acknowledge this was so and to adopt economic sanctions which would make it harder for the Syrian government to carry on. The Russians and Chinese, in contrast, saw the rebels as the main problem. They opposed taking steps against the Syrian government, saying that taking sides like this was wrong and would make things worse, causing the country to collapse and become a base for terrorists. The Americans and the British accused the Russians and Chinese of shielding the Syrian government. They condoned its massacres, the Americans and British said, because Syria was a Russian ally, and because both Russia and China were afraid that UN Security Council pressure on Syria would set a precedent for pressure on them regarding how they treated their own peoples in the future. The Russians and the Chinese accused the Americans and British of wanting to destroy a regime which was not all that bad and that treated its people better than some of the rebels who were trying to replace it probably would. They "vetoed" the resolutions proposing strong action by the UN Security Council by casting opposing votes. For critics of the "veto" this looks like a return to the days of the Cold War when the USSR stopped the UN from taking collective action on numerous occasions.

On paper, the collective security mechanisms of the UN Charter look very strong, but they depend on the P-5 all agreeing about what should be done. What is the point of them, the critics say, if one P-5 member can simply bring everything to a standstill by voting against it at the very moment when strong UN action is needed? For supporters of the veto, the Syrian episode proves its continuing value. With no veto, the UN Security Council could simply become a weapon to be used by whoever had the most votes on a given issue. Thus, it might make war between the great power states more likely, rather than less likely. Supposing, for example, a veto-less UN Security Council had agreed to strong measures against Syria over the objections of Russia and China and had started to take them, how would Russia and China have responded? Suppose a veto-less UN Security Council had agreed to strong resolutions against Israel for holding on to Arab territory, how might the US have responded?

For critics of the membership of the UN Security Council, the Syrian episode illustrates a different set of problems. The P-5 are the states which were the big players of the winning alliance in World War II nearly three-quarters of a century ago. France's international position was not very strong in 1945 and Britain's has declined since then. Why either of them should be still on the UN Security Council, capable of pushing it to act on issues like Syria or vetoing measures they don't like is not clear to the critics. Nor is it clear why they should be able to veto being voted off the Council or new members like India, Japan, Brazil, Germany, or Indonesia being voted on to it.

Hardly anyone defends the present composition of the Council. The US, for example, supports Indian membership. Everyone is stumped by how to change it, however, and worries about the arguments to which trying to change the membership will give rise. China does not want Japan. Pakistan does not want India, and if Germany is let on, then there will be three permanent members from Western Europe. Meanwhile, Britain and France note that it is a *security* council, and that they still have military capabilities which some of the new contenders for membership do not. Why mend something that isn't broken they argue, and why risk breaking something by expanding the club and having big arguments about who's to be let in when it already works fairly well?

During the Cold War, therefore, the UN Security Council did not perform as the UN Charter envisaged in regard to security measures because the permanent member states could not agree. During the Korean War in 1950, it managed to act—sending an international force to help the South Koreans turn back a North Korean invasion. This was a one-off, however, made possible by the Soviet representative's instructions to boycott the meeting (the Chinese seat on the Council was still held by the anti-communist Nationalist government on Taiwan at this time and its representative voted in favor). The "police action" which followed was successful. Americans tend to remember it as a rare UN success. Much of the rest of the world, however, was uneasy with the UN flag being used in what was clearly a US-led and dominated operation against an ally of its superpower rival, the Soviet Union.

More success was obtained in the **peacekeeping** and **peace observation** missions that started being improvised during the same period. Instead of using large UN armies to defeat aggressors in the manner of the Grand Alliance against Germany, Italy, and Japan in World War II, these used much smaller forces to help newly independent states to end fights they wanted to stop and keep out of, and to preserve order while these new states established themselves. Some of these missions were very small—a few soldiers observing and reporting from the lines separating former adversaries, like the group on part of the India-Pakistan border which has been there since 1949. A few had tens of thousands of soldiers like the forces sent to the Congo to help end a civil war in 1960. Most, however, had between five- and fifteen-thousand soldiers who would be placed between antagonists, or would patrol and administer an unsettled piece of territory. The soldiers usually came from states which were not great powers and which did not have a big interest in the dispute in question. The missions could last for just a few weeks and months or for decades, and their operations depended on the consent of the host state. UN peacekeepers do not fight their way in.

After the Cold War, it was hoped that the UN Security Council would begin to function as envisaged in the Charter. With the major exception of the first American-led war against Iraq in 1990–1, however, this has not been the case. Instead, peacekeeping operations have been greatly expanded with more missions and larger forces operating principally in Africa and, to a lesser extent, in the Middle East. Indeed, the term "peacekeeping" is sometimes replaced by the term "peace-building" to suggest a more ambitious role for international forces in developing war-torn societies. However, the recent difficult experiences with peace-building in Iraq and Afghanistan may have dampened enthusiasm for peace-building for now.

Some peacekeeping forces are not under UN direction, for example, the Multinational Force and Observers deployed in the Sinai between Israel and Egypt since 1982 and the African Union forces deployed in Sudan and Chad. Some are undertaken by other groups on behalf of the UN, for example the NATO and EU forces in Bosnia, and NATO forces in Kosovo. Some peacekeeping forces continue to be placed between antagonists—Lebanon and Israel for example—but most of these peacekeeping forces are deployed to maintain order, to protect human rights, and to assist in the construction, repair, and maintenance of infrastructure such as roads, schools, and water supplies. The international forces in Iraq and Afghanistan have engaged in war-fighting, peacekeeping, and peace-building (through the activities of what are called Provincial Reconstruction Teams), all at the same time.

Peacekeeping operations are not without controversy. Soldiers, even ones who wear the blue helmets of the UN, are soldiers, and some UN peacekeepers have been accused of rape, arms smuggling, and human trafficking. Some soldiers of the peacekeeping force in Haiti probably introduced cholera to the local population by accident in 2010. It is sometimes claimed that peacekeeping forces prop up the status quo instead of pushing for solutions to disputes. There have been UN peacekeepers in Cyprus since 1964, for example, and on the Golan Heights between Israel and Syria since 1974. It is sometimes claimed they are too weak to be of any use. The 2012 UN observer mission to Syria, for example, merely watched the country disintegrate into civil war, then returned to its bases, and was finally withdrawn by the UN Security Council for its own safety. Certainly, the injunction to "first do no harm," makes peacekeeping operations appear cautious. However, the UN Security Council and states in general seem to find them very useful when states are failing, people are being harmed, and there is enough agreement on the ground for peacekeepers to be sent in without a big fight resulting. China, long a skeptic about peacekeeping, is becoming a major contributor. As of 2017, there were fifteen UN peacekeeping operations around the world involving well over 100,000 soldiers, police officers, and other staff from 124 states.

If there is a sense that the UN Security Council has underperformed, there is a sense that the second major organ of the UN, the UN General Assembly, has functioned as it was intended. It can be seen as the parliament or legislature of the world for every member state of the UN has a seat and one vote in the UN General Assembly. It is a parliament with few powers, however, other than those concerned with running the UN itself, its agencies, and its programs. In particular, it approves the UN's own budget and how much each member state should pay towards the budget. The image which most of us have of the UN General Assembly comes from the media coverage of its Plenary Session each autumn. This is a general debate lasting several weeks in which each state has a chance to say its piece about the condition of the world. The media focus in each state tends to be on what its own president or foreign minister has to say. Sometimes there is theater, as when the Soviet leader, Khrushchev, took off his shoe and banged it on the lectern to emphasize a point, or when the Palestinian Liberation Organization Chairman, Yassir Arafat, made sure that an empty gun-holster could be seen beneath his jacket as he spoke. Sometimes there are arguments, especially in the US itself when people like the former Cuban leader, Castro, or the former Iranian president, Ahmadinejad, come to New York to speak. Opposition politicians in the US especially like to complain about letting enemies of America into the country.

The General Assembly also meets in special sessions to consider issues of current importance. It can meet in emergency session, although the Security Council is generally the first responder to emergencies like wars breaking out or states collapsing. The General Assembly passes resolutions with a two-thirds majority and no state has a veto. In addition to allocating the UN's own budget, it decides questions of membership, and it administers through its **Economic and Social Council** (ECOSOC) a large number of committees, commissions, and programs. ECOSOC has 54 members elected from the General Assembly. They deal with issues which come under the label of human security (see Chapters 13 and 14). These range from economic, agricultural, and industrial development and trade to issues like general health, population management, the wellbeing of children and women, and drug control (for a full list of programs and agencies access the UN website at http://www.un.org/en/aboutun/structure/index.shtml).

There are also some very important autonomous agencies like the World Bank. The World Trade Organization and the International Monetary Fund are formally linked to the UN through ECOSOC, but operate independently (see Chapter 10).

While the delegations from the member states working together supervise these programs, the actual work is undertaken by the **United Nations Secretariat**, a bureaucracy of about 15,000 people mainly in New York and Geneva, plus experts like engineers, scientists, financiers, doctors, educators, business people, and soldiers working in the agencies or in the field in countries with UN programs.

The head of the UN Secretariat is the United Nations Secretary General. The Secretary General is the manager-in-chief of the UN bureaucracy but, as we have seen, the position has other powers. The Secretary General can bring threats to international peace to the attention of the UN Security Council for its members to discuss, can make reports to them which may influence their decisions, and can provide discreet mediation services (good offices) between parties in dispute.

Does the UN work? Most, but not all people support the ideas behind it. The exceptions range from those who do not trust governments to have people's best interests at heart and those who regard governments as incapable of handling any important issue effectively, to those who think that no foreigner should be able to tell their own government what to do. For the UN is, first and foremost, a government sort of organization composed of other governments. The doubts are worth noting, nevertheless, because they receive fairly strong expression in the United States, the most powerful state in the world and the biggest single financial backer of the UN. Most criticisms of the UN relate to its performance, especially when it fails to prevent or end a war as in Viet Nam, a genocide as in Rwanda, or some other sort of human catastrophe. The UN was strongly criticized, for example, for its "failure" to take tough action against the Bosnian Serbs to prevent the slaughter of Muslim men at Srebrenica in 1995.

People also get upset with it when the UN is critical of their own state, which they tend to assume is on the right side of any argument. Many Americans, for example, found it much easier to like the UN in the 1950s when the US could count on strong support for its policies in the General Assembly, but became impatient as the new members of the expanded General Assembly became increasingly critical of Israel and US support for it.

It is important to remember, however, that the UN is just barely an actor in its own right, usually when the Secretary General launches an initiative. More often, it acts in the way the 193 member states can agree to permit it, and sometimes it is just a meeting place where they talk or an arena where they argue. Permanent members can veto UN decisions. Big budget providers like the US and Japan can severely restrict its operations by withholding their GNP-based financial contributions for which each member is assessed every year. And even quite small and weak states can sometimes simply ignore its resolutions, in which case the members of the UN have to decide if they can agree to exert more pressure—as in the case of sanctions on Iran, North Korea, and, in the past, Iraq. There have been problems with corruption and inefficiency at the UN, although the scale and significance of some of these is not clear. However, arguments about the ineffectiveness of the UN—especially over sanctions—tend to have a half-full/half-empty character to them. Doubters note that North Korea and Iran have yet to be stopped by sanctions. Supporters note how life has been made incredibly difficult for both states, how their nuclear programs have been slowed, and how other states—even sympathetic ones—are very cautious about helping them.

Finally, whatever sense of underperformance exists regarding the UN's contribution to international security between states is more than matched by a sense of its success in the less glamorous, less headline-grabbing fields of economic development and **human security**. Thanks to the UN-directed efforts of the World Health Organization, for example, smallpox has been all but eradicated and AIDS is being brought under control. Even gains such as these can be threatened by reduced contributions, however, resulting from the economic difficulties of member states or political pressure from those who object to government interference in matters of health and wellbeing on religious or ideological grounds.

Key terms

Economic and Social Council (ECOSOC)   The primary body of the UN General Assembly concerned with the economic and social development of its members and their citizens.

human security   A concept which focuses on reducing physical, social, and economic threats to human beings, often contrasted with state security, especially when the measures states take to secure themselves make human beings less secure.

international organizations   Associations of primarily of states, but increasingly also other actors which come together to advance their interests and values on a wide range of issues.

peace observation   Usually small missions of soldiers and police officers tasked with monitoring ceasefires between warring parties and reporting on them.

peacekeeping   Military missions of various sizes tasked with supervising, maintaining, and, sometimes, imposing ceasefires between warring parties.

United Nations   The primary, universal international organization established in 1945 and based in New York.

United Nations General Assembly   The primary assembly of all UN members providing them with opportunities to discuss and take action on a wide range of issues either directly or through the UN committee system.

United Nations Secretariat   The UN bureaucracy based primarily in New York and Geneva.

United Nations Secretary General   The UN's chief executive officer with responsibility for carrying out resolutions of the Security Council, for drawing its attention to threats to international peace and security, and for managing the UN Secretariat.

United Nations Security Council The primary UN body with responsibility for maintaining international peace and security.

Key takeaways

- International organizations exist to strengthen cooperation between states and reduce conflict.
- International organizations are not new and they work on the domestic analogy of making relations between states more like relations within states.
- International organizations have traditionally been concerned with the security of states. Their institutions generally have a security component which great power states try to dominate and a democratic component in which all states participate.
- The UN has a security component in its Security Council and a democratic component in its General Assembly.
- UN collective security has disappointed, but UN peacekeeping and peace observation missions have been more successful, if less ambitious.
- The UN General Assembly focuses on human security through fostering economic development, health improvements, population control, and the protection of human rights.

Exercises

1. How does the UN differ from its predecessor, the League of Nations?
2. Why are the P-5 members of the UN Security Council permanent, and why do they have the veto?
3. How do the purposes, membership, and operations of the UN General Assembly differ from those of the UN Security Council?

8.3 Human rights

Learning objectives

1. Define the idea of **human rights** and list the possible sources of human rights.
2. Explain the differences between **negative rights** and **positive rights**.
3. List the ways in which human rights may be established, defended, and extended.
4. Give examples of the way in which the idea of human rights can become controversial in international relations.

Human rights are one of the key issues with which international law and international organizations are concerned. The idea is that all human beings have certain rights recognized by others regarding how they should be treated and how they should be able to live their lives. There are negative rights which take the form of saying that all people should be free from, for example, torture, exploitation, or unjust imprisonment, and there are positive rights which take the form of saying that all people should be entitled to, for example, food, shelter, employment, and a fair trial. Human rights can also be distinguished in terms of **civil and political rights** and **economic and social rights**. Some of them can also be distinguished in terms of rights pertaining to particular categories of human beings, for example, women, children, the elderly, gay people, and indigenous peoples.

All human societies have some ideas about how their people should be treated which we could recognize as rights. Historically, many societies have regarded the proper treatment of their people as reflecting the will of God, a god, or gods. Others have suggested that human rights are intrinsic to us as human beings, whether or not these rights reflect a divine will. Detached observers, in contrast, have stressed how some sort of conception of people's rights is a necessary condition of any social order. Even slaves have to be given something in terms of their conditions of work if they are to continue to produce, and they develop expectations, for example, about breaks and quitting time which their owners cannot ignore without cost. In a sense then, people claim rights on behalf of themselves and give them to other people.

As an international issue, however, individual human rights are relatively new. This is so for two reasons. First, the way they are presented today reflects a particular tradition of thought about human rights developed in Europe and exported to the rest of the world from the 18th century onwards. Second, they become an issue because the idea of rights which all human beings enjoy—**universal human rights**—can collide head on with another Western European idea, that of the sovereignty of the state. The sovereign state, it was argued, recognized no legal authority over it. The sovereign state looked after the rights of its citizens. When it didn't, according to the sovereignty argument, it was usually because the interests of the state were more important than the individual rights of its citizens. And it was no one else's business but the state to determine whether violating its citizens' rights was justified.

Ever since the genocides of World War II, this argument has taken a terrible battering. States have committed to reaching agreement among themselves on a list of basic human rights. They have committed to upholding the human rights of their own citizens. And an increasing number have committed to exerting pressure on the governments of other states which extensively violate the human rights of their citizens. As we have seen, the US and its allies have begun to argue that the sovereign right of states to be free from interference in their internal affairs should be treated as conditional on their respecting human rights. Thus the NATO armed interventions in the former Yugoslavia (1995) and Kosovo (1999) were justified in terms of a new doctrine affirmed in 2005, "the Responsibility to Protect," know in UN jargon as R2P. According to this, not only might states which persistently violated human rights forfeit the protections of sovereignty, but also other states might be regarded as under some obligation to put an end to these violations.

The **Universal Declaration of Human Rights** passed by the UN General Assembly in 1948 is the foundation of efforts to establish and uphold human rights around the world (at http://www.un.org/en/documents/udhr/index.shtml).

Preamble to the Universal Declaration of Human Rights, 1948

"Whereas recognition of the inherent dignity and of the equal and inalienable rights of all members of the human family is the foundation of freedom, justice and peace in the world,

Whereas disregard and contempt for human rights have resulted in barbarous acts which have outraged the conscience of mankind, and the advent of a world in which human beings shall enjoy freedom of speech and belief and freedom from fear and want has been proclaimed as the highest aspiration of the common people,

Whereas it is essential, if man is not to be compelled to have recourse, as a last resort, to rebellion against tyranny and oppression, that human rights should be protected by the rule of law,

Whereas it is essential to promote the development of friendly relations between nations,

Whereas the peoples of the United Nations have in the Charter reaffirmed their faith in fundamental human rights, in the dignity and worth of the human person and in the equal rights of men and women and have determined to promote social progress and better standards of life in larger freedom,

Whereas Member States have pledged themselves to achieve, in co-operation with the United Nations, the promotion of universal respect for and observance of human rights and fundamental freedoms,

Whereas a common understanding of these rights and freedoms is of the greatest importance for the full realization of this pledge,

Now, Therefore THE GENERAL ASSEMBLY proclaims THIS UNIVERSAL DECLARATION OF HUMAN RIGHTS as a common standard of achievement for all peoples and all nations, to the end that every individual and every organ of society, keeping this Declaration constantly in mind, shall strive by teaching and education to promote respect for these rights and freedoms and by progressive measures, national and international, to secure their universal and effective recognition and observance, both among the peoples of Member States themselves and among the peoples of territories under their jurisdiction."

This preamble is followed by 30 articles listing rights.

The Convention has since been reinforced by a number of international treaties. These target special areas of human rights concern, for example and as noted above: racial and gender discrimination; economic and political rights;

torture; the rights of children; and the rights of migrant workers. As with other treaties, which states sign them and which states' legislatures ratify them are important questions. Domestic political issues have prevented, for example, China and Saudi Arabia signing the Convention on Civil and Political Rights, and the United States and Somalia signing the Convention on the Rights of the Child.

In addition to the UN treaties and conventions, pressure on states to respect human rights comes from several other sources. Regional systems like the European Union have their own network of agreements. Individual states can blow the whistle on violators. The US State Department, for example, keeps a scorecard on how other states respect human rights and issues a report each year (http://www.state.gov/j/drl/rls/hrrpt/humanrightsreport/#wrapper). As we have seen, the International Court of Justice and the International Criminal Court also attempt to play important roles in this regard.

The most striking development, however, has been the rise of civil society actors and nongovernmental organizations like Human Rights Watch (http://www.hrw.org/) and Amnesty International (http://www.amnesty.org/). These two are large and well known, with networks of supporters, reporters, and lobbyists around the world. They are respected, or at least treated with respect, by most states. Other groups can be very small, however, situated in one country and sometimes operating covertly against governments which want to shut down their activities and arrest them; for example, the Bahrain Center for Human Rights (http://www.bahrainrights.org/en). In common, however, they all seek to publicize human rights abuses, to embarrass and expose those states and organizations which engage in these abuses, and to lobby and put pressure on international organizations, transnational corporations, other states and their peoples to take action against the violators.

The issue of human rights is controversial. Looking at those rights listed in the Universal Declaration it is hard to imagine why this should be so. This is especially the case if you are a citizen of a Western democracy. Nevertheless, there are a number of problems.

First, states generally react very badly when they are accused of violating human rights or tolerating their violation by others. They may flatly deny the charge like the Chinese do when criticized about their repression of Tibetan or Uyghur nationalists. They may offer justifications in terms of special circumstances, as do the Americans regarding their detention of prisoners at Guantanamo and their delivery of detainees to other states for interrogation under the process of "extraordinary rendition." And when all else fails, states may play the sovereignty card and try to deflect accusations by complaining about the unwarranted interference of mischief-makers in their internal affairs.

Second, there seem to exist genuine differences between cultures about how to view human rights and how to rank the ones which are most important. The Chinese, for example, emphasize the collective rights of human beings to a certain level of economic welfare and the development that delivers it. Many developing states are sympathetic to the argument that individual rights, as these are understood in Western states, should be subordinated to the challenges of delivering economic development for all. Western states, in contrast, see individual rights as the foundation on which all else ought to be built. Without individual freedom, they argue, any economic development will be flawed, unjust, and vulnerable to collapse.

Thirdly, there is the old "Westphalian" perspective referred to in Chapter 1. This said that a big point of treating states as sovereign was to take a lot of arguments—about religion, politics, and society, for example—off the international political table. Putting human rights on the international political table, in this view, just gives states more to argue about, and provides them with sticks with which to beat each other. When the Americans object to how the Chinese treat their political dissidents, in this view, they don't really care about the dissidents. They just want to put the Chinese government on the back foot in negotiations. Likewise, when the Europeans object to America's treatment of captured terrorists and retention of the death penalty, or when the Chinese point out the huge gap which exists between the lives lived by America's richest and poorest citizens. And, of course, every military intervention for human rights reasons involves a dreadful balance between the human rights of those secured by military operations and the human rights of those killed by those same military operations and the disruptions which follow.

Whatever the merits of the Westphalian view, however, there is little prospect of disputes about human rights being taken off the international political table. Governments may be cynical about human rights. Human rights may be currently defined in "Western" terms, and Western states may enjoy most of the advantages of media power for deciding who are the violators of human rights and who are the upholders of human rights. Nevertheless, most governments have to work with populations who care about human rights (if only their own). These populations have ever easier access to information about violations occurring around the world. And they are informed, educated, and mobilized by growing numbers of individuals, groups, and organizations that strongly believe in the cause of advancing human rights everywhere.

Key terms

civil and political rights Rights concerning the terms on which human beings live as subjects of law and government.

economic and social rights Rights concerning the access of human beings to material wellbeing, social status, and respect.

human rights Expectations about how all human beings should be entitled to live.

negative rights Expectations about what threats or harms human lives should be free from.

positive rights Expectations about what goods all human beings should be entitled to.

Universal Declaration of Human Rights A declaration adopted by the UN General Assembly in 1948 listing human rights which members of the UN committed themselves to upholding and extending.

universal human rights   Rights which all human beings agree all human beings should enjoy (although they may disagree about what these rights are and their order of importance).

Key takeaways

- Human rights are concerned with the sort of lives people ought to be able to live and the way they ought to be treated.
- All human societies have understandings about what to most of us look like human rights even though they may not use this phrase.
- People and societies disagree on where rights come from. Do they come from God, the gods, or do we simply grant them to each other?
- Human rights can be distinguished in terms of positive and negative rights, social and economic rights, and civil and political rights.
- People and societies disagree about which rights are most important.
- States criticize each other's human rights records and do not like to have their own record criticized.
- A growing number of individuals, groups, and organizations are concerned about promoting human rights.
- The activities of these groups plus the increasing availability of information about human rights violations to general publics suggest that human rights will be in an international issue of increasing importance.

Exercises

1. Why do human rights exist?
2. Why do different states emphasize the importance of different types of human rights?
3. Why are human rights an issue of growing importance in international relations?

8.4   The future of international law, international organization, and human rights in an era of uncertainty

International law, international organizations, and campaigns by states and citizens to advance human rights have existed for centuries. However, there is a growing sense among many governments, diplomats, academics and citizens, especially in Western, developed states, that the world is changing. The way it is changing, however, is one of the major sources of the present international uncertainty.

There are at least three stories to be told. The first is of the emergence of a liberal world order through the course of the 20th century in which international law developed and was given more respect, international organizations were established through which states increasingly conducted their relations, managed their disputes and solved their shared problems, and in which a concern for human rights became increasingly important. Think of how most governments now say they agree with the doctrine of "Responsibility to Protect" with all this implies for the sovereignty of all states including their own. The second story, however, is of a perpetual tug of war between those who wished to create this liberal world order on one side, and those who either did not want it, or saw it as an impossibility given the nature of sovereign states, on the other. In this story, the attempts to develop international law, build international organizations, and strengthen respect for human rights habitually overreach themselves creating their own problems. Think of how the Realists said that focusing on the League of Nations left democratic states poorly equipped to meet the challenges posed by the dictators in the 1930s, or how opponents of the wars in Iraq, Afghanistan, and Syria say that great powers use the human rights argument as an excuse to intervene. Now, however, there seems to be a third story emerging in which newly powerful states like China and India do not challenge the principles of developing international law, building international institutions, and strengthening human rights. Rather, they have their own preferences about what those laws, institutions, and rights should emphasize, and they are trying to advance them.

From a state-centric perspective, the argument is between those who see state sovereignty as an obstacle to the effectiveness of international law, international organization, and human rights and who seek to extend them all at the expense of state sovereignty, and those who see state sovereignty as the foundation for effective international law, international organization, and human rights, and who want to protect their internal affairs from what they see as outside interference. From a transnational perspective, the argument is between established centers of power—sometimes, but not always, states—and ordinary people who have higher expectations about how they live and better information about the obstacles to this better life than they had in the past. The result is a paradox in which international laws, international organizations, and concern for human rights appear to be greatly on the rise and yet greatly threatened at the same time. The diplomatic challenge is to manage the growth of international law, international organizations, and respect for human rights, plus arguments about what kind of law, what kind of organizations, and which rights, plus those who say there is too much law, too much organization, and too much emphasis on rights, all at the same time.

Recommended reading and viewing

Gerhard von Glahn, *Law Among Nations: A Guide to International Public Law*, 10th edition, Upper Saddle River, 2012.

Margaret P. Karns and Karen A. Mingst, *International Organizations: The Politics and Processes of Global Governance*, Boulder, 2009.

Thomas G. Weiss, *What's Wrong with the United Nations and How to Fix It*, Cambridge, 2016.

The United Nations at a Glance, at http://www.un.org/en/aboutun/index.shtml

Michael Haas, *International Human Rights: A Comprehensive Introduction*, New York, 2008.

Obama Presides at UN Security Council Summit on Nuclear Disarmament (2009) on YouTube at http://www.youtube.com/watch?v=gTB-LDWoETA&playnext=1&list=PL359D95450DA 81454&feature=results_main

Notes

1 H.J. Morgenthau, *Politics Among Nations* (4th edition), New York, 1948.
2 R. Keohane and J. Nye, *Power and Interdependence*, Boston, 1977.
3 Alexander Wendt, "Anarchy Is What States Make It: The Social Construction of Power Politics," *International Organization*, 46, 2 (Spring, 1992), pp. 391–425.
4 Hugo Grotius, *De Jure Belli ac Pacis* (translated by F.W. Kelsey), Oxford, (1646) 1925.
5 *The Vienna Convention on the Law of Treaties*, 1969, accessed at http://untreaty.un.org/ilc/texts/instruments/english/conventions/1_1_1969.pdf
6 Joshua S. Goldstein and John C. Pevehouse, *International Relations* (10th edition), Boston, 2010.
7 *The Vienna Convention on Diplomatic Relations*, 1961, accessed at http://untreaty.un.org/ilc/texts/instruments/english/conventions/9_1_1961.pdf
8 *The Vienna Convention on Consular Relations*, 1963, accessed at http://untreaty.un.org/ilc/texts/instruments/english/conventions/9_2_1963.pdf
9 Brian Barder, "The FCO Seems to have Lost the Plot: Here's What to Do" on *Ephems* accessed at http://www.barder.com/assange-the-fco-seems-to-have-lost-the-plot-heres-what-to-do/
10 Michael Walzer, *Just and Unjust Wars* (4th edition), New York, 1977.
11 Helen Frowe, *The Ethics of War and Peace: An Introduction*, Abingdon, 2011.
12 Jeff McMahon, *Killing in War*, Oxford, 2011.
13 Hidemi Suganami, *The Domestic Analogy and World Order*, Cambridge, 1989.

9 International trade and international production

The last chapter shifted us away from the state-centric approach in that it focused on ways in which states themselves and others have worked to regulate and restrict the exercise of state sovereignty through international law, international organizations, and by elevating the importance of human rights. This chapter continues that shift by beginning our examination of issues—in this case, economic ones—in which states historically had little direct interest. Just as with international law, international organizations, and human rights, however, we will see that in international trade and international production, state priorities, state interests, and, above all, state power, continue to play critical roles.

Economic activities involve the production, exchange, and distribution of goods (material things like food and housing) and services (like banking and healthcare), together with the creation and the investment of the finance often necessary to make this activity possible. International economic relations occur when these activities take place across the borders of states. Economics refers to the study of these relations and the economic systems or economies to which they give rise. Historically, most economic activity took place within states and the political communities which preceded them. This is still the case, but the proportion of economic activity which crosses borders to all economic activity has risen since the 16th century.

How does international economic activity differ from the economic activity which takes place within states? In many respects it does not differ at all. Human and material resources still have to be organized for production, and the resulting products have to be traded in markets. The obvious difference, that economic activity crosses international boundaries, used not to be regarded as particularly important.

Economies were thought of in national or state-based terms, for example, the US economy, the Chinese economy and so on. The important things for a state were to make sure that it did not import goods and services from abroad to the extent that others could take advantage of its dependence on them, and that it did not import goods and services worth more than the goods and services it exported. This gave rise to a general sense that exports were good and to be encouraged, while imports were bad and to be discouraged.

Since the Industrial Revolution, however, more and more states, firms, peoples, and individuals have come to realize that they could become rich and powerful more quickly and more efficiently if they had access to the goods, services, natural resources, markets, investment capital, technologies, and populations located and produced in other states. Almost no states have been able to resist the temptation and the pressure to engage more in international trade, production, and finance. Doing so presents a number of problems, however.

First, if states and the people who live in them become more and more dependent on goods and services from abroad, will this reduce their independence? It may not matter, for example, that the US no longer mass produces its own televisions, but does it matter that it now imports nearly all its rare earths—elements used in the production of military equipment? States which depend on other states for military equipment or military-related materials have to think carefully before putting their relationships with these states at risk.

Second, if states import more of the things their consumers want, then what becomes of the people who used to produce these goods at home? Chinese people are very happy to get jobs exporting electronic goods to the United States, but how should they feel when their companies start importing the components for those goods from states like Viet Nam where they can be made even more cheaply? As consumers, we all like cheap goods even if they are made abroad. As producers, however, we are not so sure, especially if it is our jobs which are put at risk by cheaper imports of the things we are employed to make.

Third, what happens when big corporations, banks, and economists start telling us to stop thinking in terms of state-based economies which must be safeguarded and invite us to think in terms of a single global economy in which we are all competing for a part? We live as citizens of our own states, paying taxes, obeying their laws, and being prepared to serve in their armed forces because we feel that we belong to these states and believe they have our best interests at heart. How willing are we to make these sacrifices, however, to make sure that a global economy remains open and efficient, and that it continues to grow? (See Figure 9.1.)

We think of international economics as a new issue in the study of international relations. This is partly because of the rate at which it has become more important since the end of the Cold War. However, it is also partly a result of the way the study of international relations has traditionally been focused on or privileged the political and military relations of states, leaving economic relations in the periphery of our vision.

The study of **political economy** draws our attention to the ways in which this separation of economics and politics is artificial. As we shall see, some political economists lean in the direction of economics. Think about how people sometimes say that politics and government are all shaped by "the bottom line" or "the almighty dollar." What they mean is that no matter what people say, one of the biggest motivators is acquiring money and nothing much happens—from raising families to raising skyscrapers—without money to finance it. Other political economists lean towards politics. Think how people comment about big economic decisions, like locating a new factory or football team, that "it's all politics" which shapes the choice. What they mean is that power, rather than, for

Figure 9.1 The harbor at Singapore with shipping containers stacked in the foreground (Source: Ivan Nesterov/Alamy Stock Photo)

example, efficiency and profit-making or even fairness and justice, often decides how money gets spent.

Either way, however, political economists and international political economists agree that we increasingly run into trouble when we ignore how economic factors shape international political relations, and how political factors shape international economic relations. In this chapter, we will apply this insight to international trade and production. In Chapter 10, we will apply it to international investment and the global financial system.

9.1	Trade theory

Learning objectives

1. Explain the Mercantilists' understanding of gold.
2. Explain the Mercantilists' emphasis on achieving national self-sufficiency.
3. List the advantages of free trade according to Liberals.
4. Explain how the theory of **comparative advantage** provides a role for less efficient producers.

Mercantilist theories originated in Europe in the late 15th century and dominated economic thought there for the next two hundred years. Mercantilist practice, in contrast, predates that period, and its assumptions continue to influence economic decisions in most states today. As with all social theories, the key assumptions of Mercantilism about what is important shape its views of economic relations, how international trade is conducted, and how it ought to be conducted.

The most important thing for Mercantilists was the state. Historically in Europe, states were assumed to be possessions of their governments (usually a king or queen), which were viewed as sovereigns governing by the grace of God. These sovereigns were interested in preserving and increasing their independent power, both for themselves and to safeguard their people, and this was primarily accomplished by maintaining the biggest armies and navies they could afford. To do this, these sovereigns required gold to pay for their armed forces, and other resources for equipping, transporting, and feeding them.

As a consequence, according to Mercantilists, sovereigns ought to be interested in trade at home because they could tax it to raise money which could be converted into gold with which to maintain their armies and navies. The pre-revolutionary French government, for example, treated internal movements of goods and services in much the way that it treated foreign imports for tax purposes. Duties (taxes) were levied on economic transactions taking place between different places within the state.

International trade, however, was another matter. Mercantilists argued that the import of goods from other states should be kept to an absolute minimum to reduce the outflow of gold which paid for them, and to avoid becoming dependent on foreign goods which would reduce the independent power of the state and its sovereign. They viewed the export of goods so foreigners could buy them more positively as a source of gold from taxable income. Even exports should be restricted, however, if they benefited the state to which they were going more than the state from which they were being exported.

Mercantilists argued, therefore, states should strive for self-sufficiency. They should produce as much as possible of what they needed at home and engage in as little international trade as they could get away with—seeking a favorable balance of trade in which they exported more than they imported. Indeed, where the resources which they needed lay beyond their borders, Mercantilists argued that states should pursue a policy of expansion to gain control of the territories in which the resources were located. Since Mercantilists and the governments which followed their recommendations believed that they lived in a world of finite resources, and thus finite wealth, it was doubly important to gain control of resources, for their own use and to deny them to their rivals.

Jean-Baptiste Colbert (1619–83): a French Mercantilist statesman

"It is simply, and solely, the abundance of money within a state [which] makes the difference in its grandeur and power."

Colbert was France's Minister of Finances under King Louis XIV between 1665 and 1683. Louis wanted to build up the power of the French state so that it could defeat the other great powers and become the leader of Europe. On one occasion he is famously said to have declared, "l'état, c'est moi" (loosely translated as "I am the state"), and he liked to be known as the Sun King—like the sun, the main source of power, wealth, and life in general for everyone.

The foreign wars which Louis' policy involved France in crippled its economy, and when Colbert was appointed Minister of Finances, the state was bankrupt. Colbert pushed through a series of economic reforms to increase economic efficiency, develop French manufacturing industries, improve the quality of French goods, and boost exports. He wanted to improve the economy both for its own sake and to improve public finances so that France could afford Louis' policies and wars. Colbert's approach was Mercantilist for the following reasons. First, the state directed the economic revival saying what was to be produced where and how. Second, imports of certain goods—for example, glass from Venice—were banned so that French industries could develop without competition. Third, experts from abroad were invited into the state—for example, textile-makers from the Netherlands—to improve the quality of French goods while French experts were prevented from emigrating. Finally, Colbert supported both foreign wars and some trade deals skewed in France's favor to secure from overseas what France could not produce at home.

As absolute monarchies gave way to more representative governments after the English, American, and French revolutions between the 17th century and the 18th century, Mercantilist arguments were modified. Building state power remained important but, as the state was no longer said to belong to the king or the government, building up the economic welfare of the people or the nation was added as a reason to work for self-sufficiency or favorable trade balances.

In the 20th century, Mercantilist approaches to economics were increasingly challenged by Liberal critiques which we will examine below, and radical critiques which we will examine in Chapters 13 and 14. The United States and all other Western states gradually rejected Mercantilist theories. The Soviet Union and its communist allies attempted a form of Mercantilism based on state control of the economy but, after an early period of spectacular growth, this contributed to their eventual stagnation and collapse. Many developing states attempted their own version of a Mercantilist strategy when they became independent after World War II, but with much the same results eventually (see Chapter 13).

Today, Mercantilist theories of economics are almost completely discredited in the Western world, but Mercantilist practices and assumptions can still be found in every state. To understand the reasons for the decline of Mercantilist theory, the reasons for the survival of Mercantilist practices and assumptions, and the reasons why Mercantilist theory itself may be undergoing a revival, it is necessary to look at the Liberal critique of Mercantilism and the rise of **Liberal political economy**.

Liberal theories originated in Europe in the 17th century. Like Mercantilist theories, they were a product of the Enlightenment, which replaced the idea that human beings lived in a God-ordained, ordered, and essentially mysterious universe, with the idea that through the use of their own reason, people could come to understand the world and improve their lives within it.

Mercantilists worried about how to maintain political order once people no longer accepted the claim that sovereigns acted as God's representatives and were carrying out God's will. Their answer was to build up the state and loyalty to it. Liberals, in contrast, like John Locke (1632–1704), maintained that it was individual human beings, not states, which actually existed in a physical sense. To this they added that there could be no grounds in reason for denying that all human beings had equal rights to their lives, to their liberty, to property, and to the chance to pursue their interests. These interests they defined primarily in economic terms, although Liberals acknowledged that what an individual's interests were was largely up to the individual.

Rather than defend states, sovereigns, and order, therefore, Liberals asked what moral, legal, political, and economic arrangements would give people the best chance of living secure, free, and happy lives. In economic terms, Liberals stressed the right which individuals had to owning property which was exclusively theirs, the importance of **free markets** where people could trade their property, the goods and services their labor had created, or their labor itself, for what they wanted from others. In political terms, Liberals stressed the importance of small governments in terms of power, since governments always infringe on the liberties of some individuals, even when upholding the liberties of others, and they advocated governments which were accountable to the people affected by their decisions.

According to Liberals, all that was needed from governments was as follows:

- they should uphold the laws which protected the lives and property of their citizens;
- they should uphold the laws which enabled free markets to operate;
- they should protect their citizens from foreign attacks and invasions.

Unlike Mercantilists, therefore, Liberals did not have the interests of any particular state or its citizens at heart. American Liberals or French Liberals, for example, did not care much about the fate of the United States, France, or their respective citizens when they were thinking as Liberals (although they might feel quite different as citizens or nationals of their states). They liked states which upheld Liberal principles, and they recognized that the citizens of some states were stronger supporters of Liberal principles than were the citizens of some other states, but that was about it for Liberals as far as particular states were concerned.

Instead, Liberals sought fair competition in free markets encouraging efficiency—the most effective use of resources and labor to create the most goods and services—and innovation—the application of new techniques to creating goods and services more efficiently and developing new sorts of goods and services—in economic production. In an economic system where these conditions existed, more goods and services, and more goods and services which people actually wanted, would be created than under any other kind of economic system. Don't worry so much about which state you live in and whether it is big and powerful, Liberals suggested. Worry about whether it has established the sorts of laws and is pursuing the sorts of policies which will let you live freely, achieve the level of prosperity you desire, and pursue what will make you happy.

Mercantilists, monarchs, and many ordinary people worried about this advice, and their equivalents continue to do so today. They were all concerned with the consequences of losing the competition which free markets were supposed to provide to producers. Mercantilists asked, what happens to the balance of payments of states if all the money flows away from the states with the least efficient producers to the states with the more efficient producers to buy their goods and services. Monarchs (and governments) asked, what happens to the independent power of our state if its economy fails to compete with the economy of more efficient states who are consuming the resources of the world, making money and growing more powerful as a result. And ordinary people asked what happens to my livelihood if the economy of my state is not competitive and the industry we work in has to close down.

The Liberal responses to these concerns were based on the arguments of three great Liberal thinkers, David Hume (1711–76), Adam Smith (1723–90), and David Ricardo (1722–1823), and continue to be so today. Mercantilists should not worry about the balance of payments problem, Liberals argued, because it would correct itself over time. In his essay on foreign trade, David Hume claimed that the foreign gold flowing into the most competitive state to buy its exports would eventually force prices to rise in that state.[1] This would eventually make goods produced in that state more expensive, and this would allow formerly uncompetitive, but now cheaper, producers in other states back into the market. If one of these other states came to dominate the market, then the same self-correcting process would operate again.

Monarchs or governments should not worry about their independent power being wiped out, Liberals argued, because that independent power had no intrinsic value. It was valuable only so long as it contributed to maintaining an open economy and free competition. If monarchs and governments simply used wealth to build up their independent power and greatness, then they would be a drag on efficiency and possibly a threat to both the accountability of governments and the openness of economies. The tragedy of international relations for many Liberals was that a state which focused on Mercantilist priorities might force other states to do likewise just to neutralize the threat it posed.

Ordinary people should not worry about losing their livelihoods, Liberals argued, because the amount of wealth in the world was not fixed and a truly open economy would encourage the creation of new wealth and new economic opportunities. As Adam Smith argued in his *Wealth of Nations*, an open international economy would permit the creation of more wealth in two ways. It would allow greater economies of scale because the cost of producing individual units becomes cheaper with the more units produced. It would allow a more efficient **division of labor** because the economy of each state could focus on making what it was best at, rather than making everything it needed, and then trade what it was good at making for other things it needed.[2]

Even if your state was the most inefficient producer in the world of everything, there would still be something to do in a properly open market. David Ricardo argued, suppose we have two states both making cars and bicycles (he used different examples), and the first state is more efficient than the second at making both cars and bicycles. People worry that the less efficient state will be driven out of both the car business and the bicycle business under conditions of free trade. Not so, said Ricardo, at least if people are smart. Suppose the first state is more efficient at producing cars than bicycles. It has a comparative advantage in cars. Thus, Ricardo, argued, it would make sense for the first state to concentrate on cars, get out of the bicycle-making business and leave that to the second state. If people were sensible, there was a place for every state and its people, even the least efficient, in a liberal, open, international economy.[3]

As we have noted and will examine below, Liberal theories of political economy, trade, production, and finance, triumphed over their Mercantilist predecessors. Hume, Smith, and Ricardo all lived at the very beginning of the industrial age, just as the application of science and technology to the creation of wealth was greatly accelerating the growth of production and consumption. This process of acceleration has generally increased ever since, deepening the involvement of national or state-based economies in the wider regional, international, and global economies in which they are situated.

The relationship between the emergence of new technologies, fast rates of growth, and the application of Liberal ideas to economic policy is a complex one. By 1945, however, all the developed capitalist states were in agreement that Liberal principles of political economy should be applied and followed *whenever possible*. By 1990 and the end of the Cold War, nearly all former communist states and developing states had joined the Washington Consensus that free market economies and political democracies offered the only way of achieving sustained economic growth, although they too employed the same caveat, *whenever possible*.

Key terms

comparative advantage   A situation in which a producer can produce one type of goods more efficiently than another type of goods.

division of labor   The idea that efficiencies are gained when producers specialize in producing some good rather than a full range of goods.

free markets   Markets where the exchange of goods and services is unrestrained by factors other than the wishes of those who trade and the resources available to them; the term is associated with free trade.

Liberal political economy   An approach to political economy which focuses on individuals or private actors rather than states, plus free markets, efficiency, competition, and limited accountable governments.

Mercantilist theories   Political economy theories which stress the finite character of wealth, the importance of gold as a source of political and military power, and the need to make either self-sufficiency or favorable balances of trade an objective of state policy.

political economy   The idea that political and economic activity, and political and economic systems, are very closely related to each other and should be studied together rather than separately.

Key takeaways

- International economic relations are becoming increasingly important.
- International political economists study the way international political relations and international economic relations affect each other.
- Mercantilist political economists focus on the state, gold, self-sufficiency, and favorable trade balances.
- Liberal political economists focus on individuals, efficiency, free markets, and competition for trade, and the limited role of the state and government in upholding the laws and protecting citizens from foreign invasion.
- Liberal political economy has come to dominate economic thinking in the developed and developing states, but this domination has been threatened in the past and might be under threat again.

Exercises

1. Why have economic issues become more important in international relations?
2. Why did Mercantilists think gold was so important?
3. Why do Liberals think free markets are so important?

9.2	Trade practice

Learning objectives

1. Provide examples of the sorts of goods which are exchanged in international trade.
2. List reasons why people in states trade with the people of other states.
3. Describe the sorts of trading agreements into which states can enter.
4. Explain the ways in which states and others try to maintain open markets.
5. List the ways states avoid free trade obligations and explain why.

Trading involves the exchange of goods and services between people. Anything that people value may be traded. In the distant past, trading within communities was achieved by a simple process of exchange known as barter. As we shall see in Chapter 10, the invention of first money and then credit greatly expanded opportunities for trading, as did the development of technologies which allowed the movement of ever greater amounts of goods over ever greater distances more cheaply.

Trading within communities is one of the oldest of human activities, but trading between communities, what we would want to call international trade, is nearly as old. We have archeological records, for example, of societies exchanging raw materials which they regarded as sacred or magical, human beings for labor and sacrifice, and women, in particular, for breeding purposes.

We conventionally categorize the types of traded goods into the following: agricultural products like wheat and raw materials like iron ore; semi-processed materials like steel plates, molded plastics used in the production of finished goods, and components of finished goods like car engines and computer chips; and finished goods like cars and computers themselves. To these can be added trade in land, buildings, sources of energy like oil and gas, ownership shares in companies, production and distribution rights, and, as we shall see in Chapter 10, trade in forms of money and debts.

It is harder to categorize the services which people trade with one another. Rather than exchanging a concrete good, these usually involve performing a desired task or providing important information. However, these tasks can range from simple services like feeding someone with a hamburger or giving them a haircut which most of us could manage, to performing delicate brain surgery, staging rock concerts, or portraying movie roles, which most of us cannot. And information can range from simple advice about, for example, which school to attend or getting the house painted, to recommendations on complex matters like the performance of the stock market and hard-to-get intelligence about conditions in foreign markets.

We can similarly categorize the reasons why people trade. They trade goods and services which they do not want or need for those they cannot produce themselves, those they do not want to produce themselves, those which they cannot produce as cheaply themselves, and those which they cannot produce at the same level of quality themselves.

The same reasons for trading which apply to individuals within states, also apply to trading which crosses the borders of states. Historically, the relative value of the international trade in which states have engaged has been small when compared to their gross national products (GNP), and this remains the case for many states today. However, the value of international trade as a proportion of all world production has generally been rising quickly since the industrial revolution and the drastic lowering of production, transportation, and communication costs which resulted from it (Table 9.1).

Table 9.1 Value of international trade (imports and exports combined) as a percentage of the GNP of selected countries, 1978, 1988, 1998, and 2008

Country	Year			
	1978	1988	1998	2008
United States	9.8	9.9	11.8	15.2
S. Korea	29.7	31.1	37.6	53.5
Germany	20.1	23	28	44.1
Ireland	51.6	54.5	81.1	79.3
Mexico	10.7	17.5	29.9	29.4

Source: Table compiled from data presented country-by-country in the *OECD Factbook 2010: Economic, Environmental and Social Statistics* accessed at http://www.oecd-ilibrary.org/sites/factbook-2010-en/03/01/01/index.html?contentType=/ns/StatisticalPublication,/ns/Chapter&itemId=/content/chapter/factbook-2010-24-en&containerItemId=/content/serial/18147364&accessItemIds=&mimeType=text/html

Data like this always have to be treated with care, but even so a number of patterns in the value of international trade as a proportion of the value of all economic activity can be identified:

- the upward trend in all states, big, small, developed, and developing
- the generally higher figure for smaller states
- the generally lower figure for developing states
- the generally lower figure for big states.

It is also worth noting that the United States is relatively less dependent on international trade than are many other states, that the value of international trade for some small, open, developed states can match and even exceed the value of their GNPs, and that when the world economy slows down, so too does the general trend noted above. During the great financial crisis which began in the US and spread to the rest of the world after 2008, for example, the value of imports and exports (international trade) as a proportion of world GNP ceased to grow and actually declined for a time. So far, however, as the economies of states and the world economy have recovered from slowdowns, the rising trend has resumed but remains weak.

Trading between states is generally different from trading within them. It does not have to be. As we have seen above in the case of France, in the past trade within states often faced the same sorts of controls and obstacles that international trade between states faces today. And Liberals argue today that trade between states ought to be as open as trade within them. All it needs is an authority to make and enforce the same rules for everyone about fairness in competition and openness, respecting property, keeping contracts (promises and agreements), and maintaining standards of quality and safety.

However, as we shall see, there are important factors which make it easy and tempting to engage in discrimination against foreign goods and services. Historically, therefore, international trade has rarely just happened on its own—at least not for long. Once foreign goods showed up, agreements had to be reached between the state from which they originated and the state in which they had appeared about the terms on which goods could be traded. These terms generally concerned the type, the quality, and the quantity of goods to be traded, together with the duties (taxes)—for example, no duties at all (free access), similar duties to domestic goods, or additional duties—which would be levied on them. Typically, a state would enter into **bilateral trade agreements**, one on one with another state.

The Treaty of Windsor, 1386

The Treaty of Windsor confirmed the Anglo-Portuguese alliance, claimed by both parties to be the oldest alliance still in existence today. It was primarily a military alliance with both sides promising to help the other in the event of an attack. However, there was an important commercial

> component by which English traders were allowed to establish warehouses in the Portuguese city of Porto. Through these they shipped English cloth and codfish caught by English fishermen in exchange for Portuguese wine, cork, salt, and oil. The military component of the alliance has been superseded by the NATO membership of both states and the commercial component has been superseded by their membership of the European Union. However, the alliance and the many treaties which sustain it have never been terminated.

Far more common today are **multilateral trade agreements** which multiple states try to reach about the terms on which specific goods and services, or goods and services from whole sectors of the economy, will be traded. These agreements are usually based on the assumption that more open trade is better and apply the principle of **Most Favored Nation** status. By this, states commit to treating the goods and services from other states the same as the goods and services from the state to which they offer their best trading terms. These multilateral agreements are often set up on a **regional** basis. Thus the thirty-one states of the European Economic Area (EEA) are committed towards creating an open market in which goods and services from each participating state are treated the same as their own goods. The North American Free Trade Area between the US, Canada, and Mexico involves similar commitments, as does the Association of South East Asian Nations (ASEAN) between Indonesia, Singapore, Malaysia, Thailand, the Philippines, Brunei, Viet Nam, Burma (Myanmar), Cambodia, and Laos. Negotiations for a Trans-Pacific Partnership by many of these states plus others, including the US, were well advanced until President Trump withdrew the US from them. Talks were underway about creating a Transatlantic Trade and Investment Partnership (TTIP) between the US and the EU but these are presently stalled (2017). Similar agreements between ASEAN and China are being negotiated which would not include the US.

Just about every part of the world is covered by a patchwork of bilateral and regional trading agreements based on the principle of making trade freer and fairer, if not exactly free and fair. More important, in principle at least, however, are the global or **universal trade agreements** negotiated under the General Agreement on Tariffs and Trade (GATT) and between the members of the **World Trade Organization** (WTO) after this was set up in 1995. Progress has generally been greater on freeing up trade in goods than trade in services, and trade in manufactured goods rather than agricultural products.

These agreements are based on three assumptions. First, if free trade and free trade agreements are good things, then agreements which involve more states (or all states) and cover more goods and services (or all goods and services) are better. Second, global or universal agreements are consistent with the Liberal view that a world of states with multiple jurisdictions is itself a source of economic inefficiency. In principle, at least, one authority would do. Third, bilateral and regional agreements—even if designed to make trade free and fair—have a way of giving preferential treatment to states which sign them and are, therefore, "unfair" to states which do not. Suppose, for example, the US had signed a free trade agreement with Canada but not with Mexico; then Canadian exporters of car parts to the US would have an advantage over Mexican exporters of car parts.

From Geneva to Doha: the rounds of the GATT and the WTO

One of the international institutions which the US and its allies attempted to establish at the end of World War II was a World Trade Organization (WTO) as a sub-unit of the UN. Fears about having trade regulated from abroad—especially in the US—resulted in the WTO not being created for another forty years. As a substitute, leading developed states agreed to a series of multilateral negotiations known as "rounds," starting in Geneva in 1946 by which **tariffs** (duties or taxes) on whole sectors of goods would be reduced between the states which signed on. These were very successful. More and more states joined the rounds. Tariffs were greatly reduced especially on manufactured goods. Many non-tariff barriers and other preferential techniques were reduced, and mechanisms for dealing with trade disputes were developed.

However, by the time of the last round (to date) which began in Doha, the capital city of Qatar, in 2001 much had changed. Developing states wanted the progress achieved in manufacturing sectors to be extended to agricultural sectors so they could export their produce to the developed world. Developed states, however, were very reluctant to open their markets for agricultural products or to remove subsidies which protected their own farmers and agricultural businesses. In addition, they wanted free trade to be extended to service industries like banking and insurance, and to see new rules regarding copyright infringements and intellectual property rights.

The WTO attempted to address these problems by strengthening the institutions which managed negotiations and heard disputes. A ministerial conference was established which generally meets every two years. Considerable progress appeared to be made in a series of follow-up meetings as part of the Doha round, especially on agricultural subsidies, but then developing states began to worry that opening their markets to the big agribusinesses of the developed world would harm their small scale and subsistence farmers. Developing states accused the developed states of trying to preserve their advantages. Developed states accused the developing states of wanting the concessions to be all one way. And everybody accused the newly industrial states like Brazil, China, and India of simply ignoring the rules they had signed on to. As a result, the negotiations proceed, but only very slowly.

Nearly everybody agrees that free trade and fair competition are good things, at least in principle. In practice, it is a different matter. Competition is said to increase efficiency and productivity, but not everyone wants to be more efficient and more productive (which often means, working harder), and no one likes to lose to competition. The argument is that, with competition, more wealth is created and we are better off in the long run. As the famous economist John Maynard Keynes is supposed to have said, "however, in the long run we are all dead." The person who loses their job or their business, particularly if they are older, takes little comfort from the claim that short-term pain delivers long-term gain. Similarly the person working on a zero-hour contract or for commission only has few grounds for celebrating the lower costs of doing business which result. Who experiences the costs and who experiences the gains of such measures? These are political questions, and politicians are very sensitive to their voters experiencing the pain while someone else, possibly even a foreigner, experiences the gain. As a result, when companies close plants in one part of the world because they are uncompetitive (see Figure 9.2) and especially if they move the production abroad where labor is cheaper, more productive, or both, then fierce political arguments occur in legislatures and protestors often take to the streets. This can also happen when free trade agreements are being negotiated which may result in these sorts of changes.

In addition, the governments and some of the economists of developing states argue that under conditions of free trade, whichever state has the most competitive industries has a built-in advantage which is very hard for the newcomers to challenge. It may be pointed out, for example, that when Britain outperformed and outproduced the rest of the world because it was the first to industrialize, it became a big supporter of free trade. However, when it surrendered its competitive edge to states like Germany and the US, it lost its interest in free trade and developed a system of imperial preference favoring trade between members of the British Empire. In the late 20th century, governments of newly industrializing states like China and Brazil used to argue that they needed to build up their

Figure 9.2 Closed and abandoned steel plant in Duisburg, Germany
(Source: blickwinkel/Alamy Stock Photo)

"**infant industries**" behind the **protection** of tariff barriers until they became competitive with the industries of already developed states. Moreover, they pointed out to Americans and Europeans giving them lessons on the virtues of free trade, that the US and Germany had both pursued policies of building up some of their industries at least behind tariff walls in the 19th century.

Since free trade and open competition necessarily create winners and losers, governments—even those that say they strongly support the principles of free trade and fair competition—are always under pressure in certain circumstances to depart from these principles and pursue policies of protection. They can attempt to give their own citizens, or some of them, an advantage in a number of ways.

The most established way is tariffs. These are duties or taxes raised on imported goods by the unit to raise government revenue and to raise the price or lower the profit margin on the imported goods. International agreements have made tariffs harder to impose except in emergency circumstances or as retaliation. For example, in 1964 the US placed a 25 percent tariff on imported light trucks known as "the chicken tariff," in response to European tariffs protecting German poultry farmers from US poultry imports. Tariffs have the advantage of letting the importer still try to be competitive despite the price disadvantage their goods face as a result of the tariff.

Quotas limit the number of units which can be imported, usually over a specified period of time. For example, in the 1980s, the US asked Japan to limit the number of cars it was importing into the US until American carmakers mastered the skills involved in producing competitive, smaller, front-wheel drive vehicles. Quotas, it is argued, do not let importers try to be competitive since they can only sell a set number of units. Nevertheless, in this case, quotas arguably had the unintended consequence of forcing the Japanese to shift from making small cars for export to the US. Instead, they began to master the skills of building bigger, more luxurious cars which were more expensive and had a greater profit from each vehicle. This also allowed them to "invade" an area of the market where the US previously held an advantage. The South Korean motor car industry is currently making this transition from exporting small, cheap models to larger, more luxurious and expensive ones.

Technical and safety certifications may be used to prevent goods being imported until they meet certain standards. For example, the European Union has resisted the importation of hormone-injected beef and chicken washed in chlorine from the US on safety grounds, and the US prevented the import of Soviet-built Lada motor cars and ended the import of the original Mini cars from Britain for the same sorts of reasons. It is hard to determine how genuine safety arguments are. Americans point out that they eat hormone-injected beef and chlorine-washed chicken without ill effects, while Ladas and Minis were successfully sold all over the world.

Bureaucratic bottlenecks are informal ways of protecting home producers. Importers usually have to obtain import licenses, for example, and government bureaucracies can simply drag their feet about issuing them, or insist that all processing of import requests takes place at an understaffed office at a single port of entry. India, in particular, enjoyed a reputation for employing this "informal" approach to protection.

Ignoring copyrights, intellectual property rights, and licensing requirements have become increasingly important techniques of protection. Manufacturers of global brands of medicines, food and clothing, innovative software programs, music and movies, for example, complain when their products are "pirated," and copied, and the results marketed in developing states without any compensation for the original developer of the product.

In addition to protecting producers in their own markets, states can try to give their exporters advantages which are now generally regarded as unfair. They may, for example, provide government subsidies, public money to help an export-oriented industry develop its products, lower their price, and help pay for workers in the industry. The European Union has been accused of helping the aircraft manufacturer Airbus in this way (see p. 236). States may engage in dumping, selling goods at a loss abroad—either to get rid of surplus goods or to knock out competitors and capture market share before raising prices again. China has been accused of dumping cheap steel in foreign markets because of the slowdown in its own economy. Saudi Arabia has been accused of selling oil cheaply to drive its Iranian, Iraqi, Russian, and American competitors out of business before putting the price up again. Or states may develop producer cartels (groups) with other states and companies which agree to maintain a set price for their goods rather than compete with and undercut one another. Again, it is often difficult to establish whether unfair practices have intentionally been pursued.

Logs, planes, and oil

Toward the end of the 20th century, Canada and the US got into a big argument about the lumber trade between them. American forestlands are typically privately owned, and US lumber companies either own the land or make competitive bids for the right to harvest lumber. Canadian forestlands, in contrast, typically belong to the state. Canadian lumber companies pay a stumpage fee to the government to harvest the lumber on these Crown Lands. The American companies complained that they were facing unfair competition from cheaper Canadian lumber because Canadian companies got sweetheart deals from the Canadian government for cutting trees on Canadian Crown Lands. The Canadians maintained they had simply modernized their industry quicker than the Americans and besides that, the Crown Lands approach was the way they had always done things in Canada and they weren't about to change.

In the mid-20th century, European governments began to integrate their civil aviation industries to achieve the economies of scale and technical innovation necessary to make competitive commercial aircraft. American aviation companies complained that the resulting new Airbus Industrie Company enjoyed the unfair advantage of government support and subsidies. Now Airbus makes aircrafts which compete successfully and profitably with the last surviving American manufacturer of large civilian aircraft, Boeing. Americans still complain that Airbus was built with public funds which it never had to repay. The Europeans reply that Boeing has benefited from massive US government defense purchases from Boeing's suppliers which they call indirect subsidies. Besides, they say, what would be competitive or fair about leaving just one company, Boeing, to monopolize the long-haul jet business.

The Organization of Petroleum Exporting States (OPEC) was established in 1965. In 1973, in the middle of the "Yom Kippur" war, its members agreed to cut off oil supplies from states which had failed, in their view, to criticize Israel sufficiently. They also agreed to manipulate the price of oil until it quadrupled and, later in the decade, doubled again by cutting back production. Oil consumers, especially the developed states, called OPEC a cartel engaged in unfair price fixing, rather than letting competition between producers establish the "true" or fair price of oil. OPEC members responded that in the past, the price of oil had greatly fallen against the price of other goods as oil companies and foreign governments bullied and threatened individual producers. Only by working together, they argued, could they get the price up to a fair level and, besides, they were doing the world a favor by guaranteeing a reliable supply at a stable price and building themselves up to be importers of goods from the developed world.

In each of these cases, one can identify "sharp practices" in terms of ideas about free trade and fair competition. At the same time, however, one can also identify special or particular circumstances which provide a plausible and, in some cases, powerful reason why states engaged in these practices. The World Trade Organization and other trade regulating and monitoring groups have a difficult time settling some of the disputes which arise because of argument complexity resulting from the different assumptions of the parties, plus the difficulty of establishing evidence and agreeing about its significance. Disputes sometimes take years to resolve, and sometimes the resolutions are ignored or come too late to matter.

So far, we have examined how states attempt to avoid commitments to free trade and fair competition in order to provide their own producers with protection from imports or an export advantage in the markets of other states. As we saw in Chapter 5, however, states also use some of these measures, known as **sanctions**, in support of the political objectives of their foreign policies.

There are two principal trade methods used by states and international organizations. First, an embargo is when a state or states refuse to export any goods or a particular class of goods to another state. In 1979–80 the US imposed an embargo on grain exports to the Soviet Union for invading (the Soviets called it intervening in) Afghanistan. Second, a boycott is when a state or states refuse to import any goods or a particular class of goods from another state. Boycotts can also be organized by private citizens as a protest against the foreign policies of another state or the way it treats its people. Some Americans, for example, were televised pouring Russian vodka into the gutter at the same time as the grain embargo, and many Europeans used to refuse to buy oranges from Israel and apartheid South Africa in protest at their policies.

Sometimes embargos and boycotts are combined, as in the case of the former US policy toward Cuba, used both to punish and to weaken its communist government. Sometimes, trade measures are combined with financial measures. States may, for example, freeze financial assets in the way the US stopped Iranians accessing bank accounts they had in the US after the seizure of the American embassy in Teheran. They may also punish other states and traders who seek to ignore sanctions by taking similar steps against them. For example, by the Helms Burton Act of 1996 the US threatened legal action and commercial retaliation against the companies of other states trading with Cuba, and legal action against anyone buying Cuban assets which had originally been nationalized after the Cuban revolution.

All these measures are popular, because they are coercive measures which fall short of actually killing people or destroying property. It was far easier for the US and its allies to threaten Russia with embargos when it annexed the Crimea in 2014, for example, than to threaten it with the use of military power. These economic sanctions are also controversial, however, because they still hurt people. The poor, old, and weak are disproportionately vulnerable when supplies are cut off and prices go up. In contrast, the rich, well-connected and the elite manage to find alternatives, and the target government may even be strengthened by becoming the sole supplier of scarce goods. And, as the US has found out in its increasingly lonely policy of sanctions against Cuba, all such measures face collective action problems. Where some refuse to trade, there is money to be made by those who are willing to take the risks for principle, profit, or both.

Dumb, smart, and selective sanctions

Economic sanctions have always been an instrument of foreign policy, but their importance increased with the rising importance of trade and the ability of states to control trade. The use of economic sanctions rose at the end of the Cold War as the UN and big, liberal trading states used the latter's economic muscle to get weaker states to treat their people better and to abandon attempts to acquire weapons of mass destruction (WMD). Iraq (until 2003) was a target of such sanctions, while North Korea and Iran continue to be so at the time of writing (2017), although the sanctions against Iran were to be relaxed after the successful negotiation of an agreement on its production of nuclear fuels in 2015. Russia is also a target of sanctions after its invasion of the Crimea noted above. China may become a target if it is judged not to have reduced its links with North Korea sufficiently.

Despite their popularity, however, economic sanctions became controversial in the 1990s. In the Caribbean state of Haiti sanctions resulted in great price rises in staples like cooking oil, which hurt the poor, while the rich and the families of the military government were said to fly over to Miami on shopping expeditions bringing back contraband for themselves, their friends, and to sell at a profit. Similarly, restrictions on imports of food, medicines, machinery, and machinery parts for Iraq were said to have devastating effects on the health care and diets of babies, children, sick people, and the elderly. Even an attempt to allow controlled sales of Iraqi oil in return for food and medicine collapsed in accusations of corrupt deals between Iraqi officials and foreign contacts, one a close relative of the then UN Secretary General. And, of course, the target governments always ensured that maximum media exposure was given to the suffering in their states "caused" by the sanctions.

Accordingly, foreign policy experts, UN officials, economists, and other specialists developed so-called "smart" sanctions designed specifically to hurt the elites, rather than the ordinary citizens, of targeted states. The main guinea pigs for these smart sanctions to date have been Iran and North Korea in an effort to restrain their nuclear programs. Iran has been subjected to several rounds of progressively tighter smart sanctions designed to target the finances, influence, and lifestyles of its political elite, especially senior members of its Revolutionary Guard Corps, an armed group which controls many financial institutions and economic operations. The smart sanctions target the international financial assets of senior Revolutionary Guard members, threaten them with arrest if they travel abroad, and impose huge penalties on banks, companies, and individuals caught doing business with them.

The hope is that these sanctions hurt those who deserve it, rather than ordinary people, and can change policies. The assumption is that the elites in the target states really like the wealth, power, and privileges which their positions of influence bring them and will be sensitive to this sort of pressure. As the argument during the 2012 presidential campaign between the Obama administration and supporters of Governor Romney over whether sanctions were working suggests, this is not clear. Iran's economy has been crippled by what Vice President Biden called the strongest set of economic sanctions ever but, as Governor Romney pointed out, the centrifuges used to achieve purer grades of uranium were still turning. The 2015 agreement with Iran provides some evidence that economic sanctions can work, although how effective the agreement is remains a matter of controversy.

Smart or dumb, the sanctions on Iran and North Korea face the problems confronted by all sanctions. Everybody has to be on board with the measures, and sanctions always create an economic incentive for someone to "bust" them. Once established, they inevitably hurt innocent people and, as in the case of Cuba, they may generate support for the target government as it seems to stand up to the whole world. Sanctions are usually slow to work. Indeed it is hard to tell if they are working in terms of producing the desired outcome, as opposed to simply hurting the targets. And, as the North Koreans have shown, the carrot and stick game of rewarding good behavior and punishing bad behavior can be played by both sides, not just the sanctioners. In their argument with Russia over the Ukraine, the US and its allies can do more economic damage to Russia than it can do to them. Nevertheless, the Russian ability to retaliate, by reducing or stopping supplies of natural gas for example, has made the Europeans, in particular, very cautious about putting pressure on President Putin. This fear of retaliation may also partly explain why the US and the EU imposed only "smart" sanctions on Russian leaders, rather than general sanctions on Russian goods and investments at the start of the Ukraine crisis.

Sanctions beat going to war, however, especially when people are not convinced that going to war is absolutely necessary, that it will not make the problem bigger, or that it will even work. In the Iran case, for example, no one was sure if an attack would bring a halt to its nuclear programs. The fate of Saddam Hussein's Iraq provides the best clue to how economic sanctions work. Alone they could not bring him down. The short war and his quick defeat in 2003, however, showed just how damaging years of sanctions had been to his economic, political and, above all, military position.

Key terms

bilateral trade agreement   An agreement between two states regarding the types and quantities of goods they will trade with each other, and the terms in which their companies will be allowed to conduct business in each other's economies.

infant industries   Infant industries are newly established ones and the term is used in arguments for protection from foreign competition until they have had a chance to grow and become competitive.

Most Favored Nation status   A status in a trade agreement where states promise to offer each other terms as good as the best terms they offer to any other state. This has evolved from a discriminatory principle by which special trade partners were identified and rewarded to a general principle which should normally apply to all trading partners.

multilateral trade agreement   A similar agreement between more than two states.

protection   Measures like tariffs which are imposed by a state to increase the costs to foreign competitors with its own industries.

regional trade agreement   A similar agreement between more than two states generally located in the same geographical region or each possessing a coastline on the same sea or ocean.

sanctions   Measures taken to harm the economy of a state in an attempt to get it to change its behavior.

tariffs   Sometimes called "duties," these are a tax placed by governments on goods entering a state from abroad.

universal trade agreement   A trade agreement applying to all or most states usually negotiated at the international level through the UN or one of its affiliated organizations.

World Trade Organization (WTO)   Established in 1995 as the successor to the General Agreement on Tariffs and Trade, the Geneva-based WTO provides assistance for member states engaged in trade negotiations and mechanisms for resolving disputes between them. It is based on the principles of free trade and fair competition. States have to commit to its principles to become members. Not every state is a member, but the formal expectation is that they will be eventually.

Key takeaways

■ International trade has become increasingly important both as a proportion of all international economic activity and as a proportion of the economic activity of individual states; but the importance of trade to different states varies.

■ Free trade and open markets involve the absence of barriers to foreign goods and services and their being treated the same as domestically produced goods and services.

■ Fair competition involves free trade and states not providing their own producers subsidies to lower costs or protections like tariffs to raise the costs of goods and services produced elsewhere. Fair competition also involves private companies avoiding measures like dumping their goods below cost to drive competitors out of business, stealing intellectual property and copyrights, or other forms of law-breaking.

■ Nearly all states say they are committed to the principles of free trade and fair competition, and the World Trade Organization exists to help them reach agreements and settle disputes, but all states will try to avoid their commitments to these principles, usually, but not always, in exceptional circumstances.

■ States may seek to protect their economies or hurt the economies of other states to get them to change their behavior for political, military, and moral reasons as well as economic ones.

Exercises

1. What sort of things get traded between the economies of states and why has international trade increased?
2. Why might a state impose tariffs on goods imported from a particular state?
3. In what sorts of ways are economic sanctions an attractive foreign policy option, but why they are sometimes ineffective?

9.3   Trade trends

Learning objectives

1. Discuss the arguments for and against protectionism.
2. Examine the reasons why bilateral and regional free trade agreements may both help and hinder free trade and fair competition.
3. Explain the ways in which production is being internationalized.

Liberal political economists look at the way states sometimes try to avoid obligations arising from their commitment to free trade and fair competition, and make three points.

First, they argue, the temptation to go back on these commitments is always present because the benefits of free trade in terms of it generating more wealth are distributed across the board and are thus hard for people to identify. What does it mean for a person or family that the economy of the state in which they live has gained billions of dollars or grown by one percent as a result of a particular measure to liberalize trade? The costs of free trade, in contrast, are concentrated and clear for all to see in the form of closed businesses and unemployed workers. The reverse is the case for attempts to protect economies from free trade. The costs in terms of less efficiency, productivity, and wealth are distributed across the board and are hard for people to identify. The gains, in terms of a plant and jobs saved when, for example, import duties are imposed on competing goods from abroad, or a company is threatened with the withdrawal of government support if it closes a plant and sends the jobs abroad are clear for all to see. Politicians do not like to be associated with closures, but they do like to be associated with saving jobs (Figure 9.3).

Second, however, Liberal political economists argue that breaking these commitments is both morally wrong (you should keep your promises) and practically mistaken. It is mistaken because the gains made from tariff and dumping policies are not sustainable. Eventually, even a protected industry will fail. It does not need to compete and therefore will become more inefficient. Why prop up a failing car company like General Motors in the US or Peugeot Citroën in France,

Figure 9.3 President Donald Trump speaking in Ypsilanti, Michigan, in 2017
(Source: 506 collection/Alamy Stock Photo)

for example, if they are only going to be back in a few years' time looking for more help from the government and the taxpayer? Plus, the longer this failure takes to happen, then the greater will be the wealth lost and missed opportunities as a result of the subsidies that have been given to keep inefficient domestic industries going and as a result of the extra money consumers have paid for foreign cars with a tariff built into their price. Governments, Liberal political economists say, should encourage their electorates to stop thinking in terms of the small picture of **relative gain**. Instead of worrying about how we are doing compared to the other fellow and how to hold on to our piece of the pie, governments should be getting us to think in terms of the big picture, the **absolute gain** to be achieved when trade is freer and competition made fairer. Concern with relative gain gets you into the sort of bad economic relations and angry political relations that contributed to World War II. Concern with absolute gain contributes to the sort of fast-paced growth and rising living standards which characterized the developed world in the 1950s.

Third, Liberal political economists believe protectionist practices to be unsustainable because they argue that all the big pressures of what science and technology let us do, and the evidence of what free people actually want, is pushing the world steadily in the direction of an interdependent, integrated, global economy. And they believe that people are smart enough to figure this out and, provided with the right incentives, are capable of accepting and acting in accordance with demands for more efficiency, productivity, and flexibility in the way they work.

It is very difficult to argue with this general claim about the direction the world is moving, or has been until fairly recently. Certainly, as the Liberal political economists note, Mercantilist alternatives were experimented with in the fascist dictatorships but these flamed out in the destruction of a world war for which they were responsible. Socialist alternatives were attempted by the Soviet Union and China, but the former collapsed and the latter is scrapping the old system as fast as it dares. Neither could compete with Liberal capitalism for delivering peace, growth, and higher standards of living.

Liberal economists also note that progress toward freer trade and fairer competition is neither uniform nor guaranteed. Sometimes the world economy or parts of it slow down. When this happens as for periods of time in the 1970s, the 1990s, and the first decade of this century, the rising level of world trade may slow down, stagnate, or even reverse. And the temptation to protect economies may increase when people are feeling the consequences of an economic slowdown in terms of lost jobs and lowering living standards. However, these slowdowns are generally part of a **business cycle**. During a downturn in the economy, the Liberal political economists argue, markets adjust expectations about earnings, investment returns and economies start growing again. Even if the economic difficulties are **structural difficulties** and involve the way economies are set up to produce and trade, runs the argument, sooner or later societies adjust and growth returns. The general direction is still towards more open economies and fairer competition.

Thus where global negotiations like the Doha Round to open up economies are stalled, we see the effort transferred to the regional level—between Europe and

Africa, for example, or among the states surrounding the Pacific Ocean. Where regional agreements stall, we see the effort transferred to a new generation of bilateral free trade agreements like those between the US and Australia, Chile, most recently, Colombia, and possibly post-Brexit Britain.[4] We can see a global economic system in which all states are moving in the same direction, even if at different speeds. Gradually, they evolve up the ladder from producing crops, animals, and raw materials, through the so-called metal-bashing industries like ship-building and car making, to service economies engaged in banking, financing, and knowledge-production. As they do, economies become more open and integrated to the point where no longer is it just financing and trade taking place on an international scale. We can also see the **internationalization of production** emerging.

What is an American (Japanese) (British) car?

Historically, the production of cars was organized on the basis of companies with clear national identities. For example, Chevrolets were thought of as American, Land Rovers as British, and Volkswagens as German. Things were never quite what they appeared from very early on. General Motors (GM), the parent company for Chevrolet, always had extensive operations in Canada, Land Rovers often used a heavily worked over GM engine, and Volkswagen built many cars in South America. Even so, the national idea held up very well with cars and it worked both ways. Some people found the idea of owning a foreign car "exotic," while others found the idea of owning cars built in their own state "patriotic."

As car companies expanded their operations abroad, however, national identities were eroded in four ways. First, car companies would sometimes keep the names of the local operations they had bought. Thus, GM cars made in Germany were called Opels and in Britain were called Vauxhalls. Second, car companies would start moving cars around their international networks. After the 1970s oil crises, for example, American companies started shipping cars from their foreign subsidiaries which had more experience with small cars and small engines into the US. Third, car companies created production chains where different parts of the same cars were made in different states, thus Ford cars purchased in the US from the 1980s on might be 100 percent US, or they might have German engines, Spanish tires, Mexican electrical wiring and, in the case of the Ford Fiesta, British windshield wipers. Production would be allocated on the basis of factors like the skill levels required, how intensive the labor component was, and the availability of resources. Fourth, by the start of the 21st century, car companies were entering into alliances with each other to reduce the costs of research, development, and production. Fiat and Chrysler, Mazda and Ford, GM and Peugeot Citroën are examples of such alliances.

Place still matters, but in strange ways. Thus, people think of Jaguar as British. For now, it builds its cars in Britain (although it is opening a plant in China), but it was owned by Ford for many years, some of its cars were based on Ford designs and all used Ford parts. The company is now Indian-owned. Minis, another car thought of as British, are built in Britain but by BMW, a German company. And in Britain, GM tried to sell small sports utility vehicles built in South Korea as Chevrolets in the hope that Britons might like the idea of owning an "American" car. Meanwhile the British think they have "lost" their car industry because most of their famous companies went bankrupt, even though they have one of the largest and most successful car industries in Europe building Japanese cars under license for the British market and to export to the rest of Europe!

The car industry provides examples of two big trends in the global economy. The first is known as the **"disembedding of production."** This refers to the idea that most things can now be made anywhere and to a lesser extent that it does not matter where they are made. The second is the **"dematerializing of production."**[5] This refers to the idea that we are more interested in the symbolic effects of owning goods—a Jaguar, the latest iPhone, or a Coach bag, for example, than in what the goods actually do. This is generally associated with consumerism in the developed world, but it can be found in the developing world also. In Malaysia, for example, the cars of Japanese and South Korean companies have more status than those produced by Malaysian companies.

As we shall see in Chapters 13 and 14, this benign view of economic development through freer trade and fairer competition on an increasingly global scale has always had its critics, generally from sources associated with the political left and, more recently, in the developing world. Since the financial crisis which began in the US in 2008 and spread to the rest of the world, however, old Mercantilist arguments have resurfaced which cast their own shadow of uncertainty on this sense of progress, at least for now. They have done so for the following reasons.

First, concerns grew about the US economy and the ability of its government and society to address its problems. Growing government deficits, persistent trade imbalances, and a banking crisis precipitated by a combination of social policies affecting the way loans were made and deregulatory policies affecting the way their liabilities were distributed and hidden, shook confidence both in the US economy and in the ideas about free markets and fair competition which had fueled its success in the past.

Second, these difficulties suggested that the resulting global economic crisis was not just part of the business cycle, but had deep structural causes which might not be easily fixed. Capital from fast-growing parts of the developing world like China and resource producers like Saudi Arabia was flowing into the US in the form of loans to sustain borrowing which financed the US consumers' purchase of foreign imports. These loans were premised on an eventual US economic recovery as in the past, but what if the US didn't recover? A similar crisis of confidence developed in the European Union (EU) in regard to how rich states, like Germany, provided loans to poor states, like Greece, in order to maintain markets for German exports.

Third, a sense developed that a large and accelerating shift of power and wealth was underway from developed parts of the world like the US and the EU to developing states like Brazil, Russia, India, China, and South Africa, the so-called BRICS (although Russia's position in this grouping is highly questionable).

As a consequence, many people began to look at familiar developments in a new light. Should, for example, free trade agreements—either bilateral or multilateral—be viewed as the building blocks of a global freer trading system which was gradually growing bigger—the conventional view? Or should they be viewed as signs that big, regional trading blocs were emerging through a process of trade diversion which encourages trade between the member states inside them at the expense of trade between the members and outsiders? As we shall see in Chapter 11, this question has long been asked of the EU because it is a customs union with a common tariff levied on goods and services flowing into member states from outside. However, could it be now asked about the maneuvering for a Pacific free trade area where the parties argued about it including the US or China, but not both?

Perhaps the most important "new look" to what was happening after the 2008 crisis concerned China. The conventional argument in the developed world was that China's fast growth resulted from some simple market reforms which allowed it to take up the slack caused by decades of communist-inspired inefficiency and misallocation of resources. This was the easy part, however. If China was to progress further it would have to undertake much more difficult reforms. It would have to privatize the big sectors of the economy which remained under state control. It would have to abandon state trading, especially with states which violated human rights. Above all, the Chinese Communist Party would have to relax its own grip on power and allow its people the freedoms which are necessary to the success of a highly developed economy in the information age of disembedded and dematerialized production.

The continued growth of the Chinese economy—together with the prosperity and power it has generated—has called some of these claims into question. The Chinese are certainly less inclined to listen to this sort of criticism, especially from states whose economies are stagnant or shrinking, while theirs continues to deliver growth rates of eight percent or more. Beijing is currently engaged in carving out a larger role for itself in international trade by creating an Asian Infrastructure Investment Bank, promoting its One Belt One Road initiative across Asia, its "16 plus 1" initiative in Eastern Europe, and new investment partnerships in Africa. These schemes seek to attract capital to match Chinese capital for regional development. In addition, the One Belt One Road initiative seeks to restore and greatly improve the old sea and land trade routes from China across Central Asia all the way to Western Europe, with new harbors, highways, and high speed rail links (Figure 9.4). Perhaps a command economy with state-managed production, trade, and monetary policy can deliver wealth and power, and Mercantilist political economy still has something to offer. The Chinese government seems to think so, and there are many other governments around the world who seek the fast and sustained economic growth promised by Liberal political economy, but fear the disruptions to their societies and their own power and privileges which seem to come with opening up to free trade and fair competition.

Figure 9.4 Chinese President Xi Jinping addresses a forum on China's "One Belt One Road" initiative in 2017

(Source: ITAR-TASS Photo Agency/Alamy Stock Photo)

Key terms

absolute gain   The sum of all actors' gains. There are big moral, political, and economic arguments about the extent to which human beings are and ought to be concerned with relative gain and absolute gain.

business cycle   The idea that the economy expands and contracts as growth leads to more goods being produced than can find buyers. This overproduction leads to a drop in prices and a contraction of the economy until there is a scarcity of goods relative to buyers. Prices begin to rise, attracting more producers. The economy begins to grow again until the cycle starts again.

dematerializing of production   The ideas that the production, distribution, and exchange of services are becoming more important relative to the production, distribution, and exchange of concrete goods, and that the symbolic significance of goods is also becoming more important relative to their function.

disembedding of production   The idea that goods and services can be produced anywhere and that the place of origin of goods does not matter for purposes of exchange and consumption.

internationalization of production   A process by which not only the movement of goods and capital takes place across international borders, but also the production of a good or service takes place in different states.

relative gain   The size of one actor's gain in comparison to another actor's gain.

structural difficulties   Economic difficulties arising from problems like productivity differences, the inflation/deflation of currencies, or shortages of capital for investment which lie outside the fluctuations of the business cycle and are therefore less likely to be self-correcting or easy to fix.

Key takeaways

- The general trend in the world economy since the mid-20th century has been toward more free trade and fair competition, yet states are always under pressure to take measures to protect parts of their economies from foreign competition and to give them advantages in foreign markets.
- Multilateral and bilateral free trade agreements (as opposed to universal ones) are generally regarded as steps on the way to creating more free trade and fairer competition across the globe. However, if they divert trade rather than create more trade, multilateral and bilateral free trade agreements can be seen as evidence of emerging trade blocs.
- Liberal political economists regard protectionist measures as immoral, irrational, and unsustainable except in the very short term. Mercantilist political economists and others note that establishing free trade and fair competition can impose crushing economic and political burdens on states and their people in the short term.
- Production is increasingly being internationalized, disembedded, and dematerialized through transnational networks between big companies and within big transnational companies.

Exercises

1. Who can more free trade benefit and who can it harm?
2. Why is China's economic rise a puzzle to many people?
3. In what ways does the rise of international trade in smartphones illustrate the internationalization and dematerialization of international production and trade?

9.4   The future of international trade and production in an era of uncertainty

The key theme of this text, that we live in an era of uncertainty, is no better illustrated than by how people are arguing about what is happening to the international or global economy. The points about trends in this chapter suggest an economy facing structural difficulties and great imbalances between states whose economies are growing and becoming more productive, and states whose economies are stagnant or shrinking, uncompetitive, and deeply indebted. Problems in one part of this economy quickly create problems in another part of it, and the whole system confronts the challenges posed by increasing automation and the rise of what is sometimes called the "internet of things" to societies historically organized around work.

The G8 (currently G7 as Russia was expelled in 2014) group created by developed states in the 1980s and led by the US looks like being overtaken by a G20 group in which BRICS states join with the original G8 and attract much attention. Especially in the aftermath of Britain's vote to leave it in 2016, the members of the EU worry whether they can hold together and look for investments from and markets in the newly developing states. Meanwhile China's economy is on track to overtake the US economy in the next few years, at least by some measures, and the Chinese government has let it be known that it has little interest in joining a G2 with the US to manage the rest of the world.

And yet this picture of a changing world can be called into question. It is based on incomplete information about possible trends and these are sometimes talked up by political and economic interests which would be served by people accepting that they are happening (just as the arguments for free trade and fair competition favor some political and economic interests more than others). China faces increasing competition from other newly industrializing states as its labor costs go up. Its population is aging and wanting to work a little less hard while enjoying a greater piece of the pie. Experts worry about the consequences of how quickly it has created its new infrastructure of buildings, roads, railways, and communications. Its government has to keep providing cheap loans in increasing amounts to secure a rate of growth which keeps slowing. And no one knows whether its Communist Party can remain in control or, if not, what would be its replacement. The BRICS can suddenly look vulnerable when their dependence on high prices for the raw materials they export is exposed by the economic slowdown in the markets they sell to. Indeed, some commentators are already suggesting they are past their peak. Meanwhile, the US remains the largest and most innovative economy in the world. It has mainly continued to recover from the worst point of its own economic crisis in 2009. And the new techniques of "fracking" to release deposits of oil and gas which were previously inaccessible on a commercial basis hold out the possibility of energy self-sufficiency and even a surplus in oil in the next few years—that is, if its new producers can survive periods when the price of energy is low (see Chapter 12).

Perhaps the best sense of how complex the picture has become is provided by Greece, at the heart of the monetary and debt crises through which the EU has been struggling (see Chapter 11). With its debts and government spending growing to unsustainable levels in 2009, Greece was offered loans on condition that it instituted reforms which cut public spending by the government, raised taxes, and privatized the large parts of its economy publicly owned by the state. This is standard free market advice, but when the Greek government attempted to sell off some of its state-owned businesses, the first bids did not come from private investors but from Chinese and Russian state-owned corporations!

The important point here is not to ask, "so what is really happening to the world economy?" It is too early to tell. The important point is to note the way in which more and more people are paying attention to the claims that the international economy is changing and are arguing about what is happening and why it is happening. It is these arguments which will require skillful diplomatic management. They constitute, in a sense, the political side of political economy, and the political arguments are fiercest around making sense of changes in the international financial system which we will examine in Chapter 10.

Recommended reading and viewing

J. Freiden and D. A. Lake (eds.), *International Political Economy: Perspectives on Global Power and Wealth*, New York, 2000.

Adam Smith, *The Wealth of Nations*, London, 1776.

Susan Strange, *The Retreat of the State*, Cambridge, 1996.

Benjamin J. Cohen, *International Political Economy: An Intellectual History*, Princeton, 2008.

Barry Eichengreen and Bokyeong Park (eds.), *The World Economy After the Global Crisis: A New Economic Order for the 21st Century*, Singapore, 2012.

Robert Gilpin and Jean M. Gilpin, *Global Political Economy: Understanding the International Economic Order*, Princeton, 2001.

J. M. Gieco and J. Ikenberry, *State Power and World Markets: The International Political Economy*, New York, 2003.

Economics is Fun, Part 13: International Trade, Adam Smith Institute, YouTube at http://www.youtube.com/watch?v=MvvFwqeLCoE

Notes

1 David Hume, *Essays, Moral, Political and Literary*, London, 1752.
2 Adam Smith, *The Wealth of Nations*, London, 1776.
3 David Ricardo, *On the Principles of Political Economy and Taxation*, London, 1817.
4 See The Office of the United States Trade Representative at http://www.ustr.gov/trade-agreements/free-trade-agreements
5 Chris Brown and Kirsten Ainley, *Understanding International Relations* (4th edition), Basingstoke, 2009.

10 International and global finance

Preamble

In the previous chapter we examined the growth of international trade. Here we look at international and global finance. It is with finance that using the word "global," as opposed to "international," is perhaps most justified, because the case can be made that we increasingly have a single, growing, and fast reacting system of financial movements around the entire world. Further, it is a system in which many actors operate, but in which no one seems to be in control. Indeed, the possibility of controlling this global financial system has been called into question by some. As with international trade, however, the origins of the present conditions lie long in the past with the emergence of the idea of a **medium of exchange** instead of direct barter.

Where we find exchange or trade in human societies, we also soon find money. Where we find money, we soon find loans, and later the ideas of credit and investment. When thinking about money, loans, credit, and investment in international relations, it is useful to think about the roles of those ideas in a domestic economy—that is to say, the economy inside a state. This is certainly how the people first involved in international trade and exchange thought about these ideas. However—and just like with international trade itself—the division of the world into separate political groups with separate economies soon presents different sorts of problems with which states, traders, financiers, and the people who study their activities have wrestled with ever since.[1]

One set of problems emerged as soon as money replaced barter, the direct exchange of goods and services for other goods or services in foreign trade. Foreign traders were paid in the money of the state or political community into which they were importing goods. How much was that money worth in the money or currency of their own state or political community? Could they even spend it back home, or were they stuck with buying things in the local economy?

A second set of problems concerned international loans and investments. Is it any different when the money used to finance or buy firms is "foreign" money coming from abroad as opposed to money raised at home? Could foreign loans and investments in its economy somehow weaken the independence of a state and the freedom of its people? Could the state from where the loans and investments were sourced use them, and the possibility of stopping them, as a way of influencing the policies of the state benefiting from them?

Finally, in addition to these old problems, a new set of problems has emerged. What happens when the source of foreign loans and investments is a bank or firm which is not based in one particular state, but is a transnational actor with no particular home, its organization spread around the world, and its operations dwarfing the economies of many of the small states with which it deals? And what happens when the amount of money moving around the world looking for loan and investment opportunities in states begins to dwarf the total value of trade or the financial resources of any single state or group of states? Who then, if anyone, is in charge?

10.1	Money and international relations

Learning objectives

1. Describe the ways in which money is useful as a medium of exchange.
2. Explain the **exchange rate** problem for traders working in different currencies.
3. Explain the reasons states abandoned the **Gold Standard**.
4. List the advantages to a state of possessing a **reserve currency**.

Money is not only nice to have, it provides a far more convenient way of trading than by the direct exchange of goods and services through barter. Human beings replaced lugging around all their goods for trading, first with artifacts like beads and shells, then with coins made out of precious or valuable metals, then with paper notes which promised payment in coins or precious metals, and more recently with instruments like your debit card which can be used to transfer money between electronically connected bank accounts.

(For an account of the origins of money see the beginning of the Adam Smith Institute's video, "Economics is Fun, Part 6: Money" at the following link http://www.youtube.com/watch?v=pwja18iG_iI)

The effectiveness of money depends on people having confidence that other people will accept it as a medium of exchange for goods and services. They will be prepared to accept money—instead of other goods and services—in return for their goods and services. They will use money—instead of goods and services—to acquire other people's goods and services. Normally today, the governments of states have a monopoly over making coins, printing paper notes, issuing both through their **central banks**, and insisting that people in their states accept their currency as legal tender for exchange. They have also had a monopoly over issues of virtual or electronic currency until recently.

It does not have to be this way. In principle, anybody could issue currency unless prohibited by law. In the past, simple currencies, like the shells system in the Polynesian Islands, predated the existence of states. As late as the early 19th century in the borderlands between the US and British North America (Canada), US dollars, British pounds and Native American scrip circulated in parallel. Today, Panama and Ecuador use the US dollar, issuing only their own coins, and the euro is the official currency of nineteen European Union member states in the Euro Area, even though no single state issues it or guarantees its value. Six other small states also use the euro, and "bitcoin" has had some success as a virtual currency recently.

Since the early 19th century, however, the norm has been one state-one market-one currency. This has been justified on grounds of economic efficiency and as part of the political project of building developed and independent states referred to in Chapter 1. As we shall see, issuing their own currency has also been a source of both economic and political power for governments. It is this fact, that there are multiple currencies circulating, which has given rise to the problem of valuing currencies for purposes of international trade. When, for example, an American medical equipment company exports diagnostic devices to India, it knows what they are worth in US dollars. However, what are these devices worth in the Indian currency (rupees) in which the Indian buyer wants to pay the American company for them? Or, to put it another way, what are Indian rupees worth in terms of US dollars and vice versa? How is the exchange rate between the two currencies, and between them and other currencies, to be determined?

There are a number of ways to attempt this. Back on the old Canadian-American border, traders simply tried to make deals about what they thought pounds, dollars, and scrip were worth in relation to each other. Over time, the relative values of the currencies could be seen to "float" up and down against each other in response to several factors. A Montreal-based trader from British North America, as Canada used to be called, would be more interested in getting pounds to take back and spend in Montreal, while a Saint Louis-based trader from the US would be more interested in getting dollars for much the same reason, and both would be reluctant to accept scrip which was only traded locally. Factors like these would affect the exchange rate between the currencies in each transaction. When it became clear after the Treaty of 1818 that the British were clearing out of the border area and that the Americans would have exclusive control, traders and native Americans alike tried to get rid of their pounds and acquire dollars, causing the value of pounds (which no one wanted) to fall against the value of dollars (which were soon to be the only legal tender).

This system of floating exchange rates might work on the margins of the world economy, but during the 19th century it was increasingly thought to be too clumsy and unpredictable for increasing levels of international trade between quickly developing industrial economies. Instead, governments borrowed on the old system by which they had tried to maintain confidence in their currencies at home. Originally, the coins issued by a state's central bank had been made of precious metals like gold and silver which are highly valued for their beauty and durability, and which hold their value over time. The value of the coins matched their weight in the precious metal of which they were made.

Gold, in the form of bars, is often kept by the states to maintain confidence in the value of their currencies, and to allow them a safe store of value when the prices of other assets are unstable or falling (Figure 10.1). Individuals and financial organizations also hold onto gold in smaller amounts but for the same reasons.

Coins in gold, silver, and other metals, have a long history, the value of the coin matching the value of the weight of the metal in the coin (Figure 10.2). There

Figure 10.1 Gold bars owned by the US Government
(Source: Kristoffer Tripplaar/Alamy Stock Photo)

Figure 10.2 Old Arabian silver coins
(Source: imageBROKER/Alamy Stock Photo)

were problems with coins made from precious metals, however. Over time and through use, some of the metal would wear away or be chipped, sometimes deliberately. More importantly, governments and citizens would want more coinage in circulation than their stock of precious metal would allow. Accordingly, they made coins of cheaper metal and paper notes, promising that their central banks would pay anyone who showed up with either an equivalent and fixed value in gold. The idea was that once people knew this and believed that their coins and paper notes were "as good as gold," they would not show up at the central bank to trade them in.

The same principle was extended to international finance with states and their central banks committing their currencies to a "Gold Standard" or "silver standard."[2] If foreigners showed up with a state's currency at its central bank, they were promised the same deal, payment in an equivalent and fixed amount of gold or whatever precious metal in which the state's commitment was made. Fixing the value of a state's currency in terms of the price of gold was intended to inspire confidence abroad just like at home.

However, it also provided a way of valuing the different currencies of different states on the Gold Standard in terms of each other. If the US Federal Reserve Bank "pegged" its currency at $35 to an ounce of gold, for example, and the British Bank of England "pegged" its currency at £9 to an ounce of gold, then traders and others would know that a British pound was worth about four US dollars in their exchanges. They would also be able to plan their future transactions on the assumption that this exchange rate would hold up over time.

Supporters of the Gold Standard say its advantages are as follows. First, it creates confidence in national currencies because they are either based on the circulation of gold coins or backed by gold reserves held by central banks. Second, it provides a way of valuing currencies against each other. Third, it does so over an extended period of time. All these contribute to a more predictable trading environment and thus add to economic confidence.

However, the Gold Standard also has disadvantages and poses problems for states and their governments. As we shall see in the section below on credit, states are often tempted or come under pressure to issue more currency than the value of the gold coins and gold bars (bullion) they possess. In times of difficulty, they may want to stimulate the economy by spending or making credit available. In times of war, they may need to be able to spend on expanding their armed forces at fairly short notice. Today, issuing far more currency than is covered by gold reserves is the norm.

Most economists would say issuing more currency than is covered by gold is a good idea since not everyone is likely to show up at the central bank demanding gold for their non-precious metal coins or paper notes at the same time. However, the trick is in knowing how much currency can be issued without making the people who hold the currency worry and show up at the central bank demanding gold or the currency of other states.

They may do so for two basic reasons. First, they may worry about inflation where the amount of currency in circulation increases relative to the amount of goods and services being produced. In such situations, prices rise, the value of savings declines, and these developments may contribute to, or make worse, an economic slowdown. An economic slowdown in turn creates balance of payments problems for the government. It struggles to pay its own bills when the slowdown causes a reduction in the money it gets from taxation. It also may create a broader balance of trade problem for the economy as a whole as exports decline relative to imports.

This leads to the second problem. People who hold the currency now begin to worry about the state of the economy and about whether the state will be able to maintain the fixed "peg" between its currency and the price of gold. Some of them start bringing the currency to the central bank and asking for gold or for other currencies. The central bank keeps its promise, running down its reserves of gold and other currencies to buy back its own currency at the fixed rate.

The central bank hopes that this will restore confidence, but for how long can it keep using up its reserves? The more it uses, the more other holders of the currency worry that there will be no gold left by the time they go to the central bank. Besides, both the government and the currency holders know that the state will be under huge pressure or temptation to break the link with gold before it uses up all its reserves.

In the short term, a state may simply stop trading its currency. It may also devalue its currency, offering less gold or a smaller amount of foreign currencies in return for a fixed amount of its own currency. Devaluing will ease the immediate problem and it might help with other problems like the balance of trade because it will make a state's exports cheaper for foreigners to buy and make imports more expensive for its own people temporarily. If a state devalues its currency, then all the holders of it have lost out. Gold that cost £9 per ounce today may cost £18 per ounce tomorrow if the state devalues. The result of all these fears and pressures may be what is known as a **run on the currency** as holders of it, fearing a **devaluation**, try to cash it in for gold, thereby making the very thing they fear more likely.[3]

Throughout the 19th century, the Gold Standard (and to a lesser extent a silver standard) was regarded as the best policy, and a world where all states adhered to the standard was seen as ideal. As a matter of practice, however, some states never established the policy while others would abandon it when they needed to spend quickly under the pressure of economic difficulties or when they needed to finance a war. The great departure from the Gold Standard came in 1914 with the outbreak of World War I. Many states never re-established it after the war was over, and even those who did eventually abandoned it during the Great Depression when their gold reserves were depleted with no sign of recovery in sight.

In the absence of a Gold Standard, states have a number of options for solving the problem of foreign exchange. One thing they can do is set and manage an exchange rate against other currencies which their central bank believes is the best rate for their economies. These fixed exchange rates are usually set by several states committing their central banks to trading their currencies at pre-negotiated values against one another. This offers more flexibility in terms of borrowing and spending when compared to the Gold Standard, but does not inspire the same confidence, for the values of the different currencies are not backed by gold, merely by the commitments of each state to one another. An important variation of the fixed exchange rates approach operated for some thirty years after World War II, in which the US dollar was pegged to gold, and other currencies were pegged to the US dollar (see text box p. 259–260).

Where the commitment to peg currencies to gold or to each other is absent, however, variations of the floating system of exchange discussed above appear. A pure or clean float involves the central bank of a state stepping back and letting the value of its currency be determined by the price at which it trades on foreign exchange markets. Supporters of this approach note that currencies can be treated as a commodity to be bought and sold in the marketplace just like any other commodity. One advantage of this approach is that the price at which a state's currency trades serves as a signal of what traders think of the health of its economy. Consider the slow decline in recent years of the value of the US dollar against the rising value of the Chinese renminbi in these terms, and consider the more recent strengthening of the US dollar against the euro and the British pound. A disadvantage is that fluctuating currencies make for a less predictable trading and investment climate over the middle to long term. It is hard to commit to long-term purchases, sales, or investments abroad when you cannot be sure what they will be worth in your own currency in the future.

Another problem with floats is that states and their central banks are rarely content to let them stay clean. They intervene by buying and selling currencies to produce a desired exchange rate. When a central bank uses its gold or foreign reserves to buy up its own currency on international money markets, it hopes to raise its value by reducing the supply of the currency. When a central bank sells its own currency in exchange for gold or foreign currencies on international money markets, it hopes to reduce its value by increasing the supply of the currency. Sometimes, the central banks of several states will coordinate their interventions (buying and selling currencies) in an attempt to drive up or down the value of one or more of their currencies. When they do this over time to maintain the stability of the value of their currencies in relation to each other, this is known as a monetary system.

With managed floats, governments and their central banks usually make a public declaration that they have a desired range or band within which they are content to see their currency fluctuate against other currencies. They intervene only to keep it floating above the bottom of the range and below the top. With dirty floats, central bank interventions are less public and sometimes even undertaken secretly, and the practice is regarded as unfair. In the 2012 presidential election campaign, for example, Governor Romney accused China of being a "currency manipulator" buying up foreign currencies with renminbi to keep the latter's exchange value down and thus Chinese exports cheap and competitive. Donald Trump renewed this accusation during his presidential campaign in 2016. The question of whether a float is clean, dirty, or managed is always a difficult one with political implications. The Chinese could have pointed out that the US has pursued economic policies which have allowed, or encourage, the value of the dollar to fall for several years.

Today, the monetary systems of the world present an increasingly complex picture. In exchange rate terms, there are weak currencies and strong currencies.

There are hard currencies like the US dollar and the Swiss franc which float, are trusted to hold their value and are easily exchanged. There are soft currencies like the Zimbabwe dollar which no one wants (even in Zimbabwe), and which governments protect by trying to control currency trading and by keeping the exchange value of the currency at an artificially high rate. There are formal international monetary systems where the member states try to manage the value of their currencies relative to each other, and informal monetary systems where several states try to track the value of a particularly strong currency without saying they are actually doing this. And there is at least one monetary union—the euro system—where several states have abandoned their own currencies in exchange for a single currency which they all use (see p. 273 and Chapter 11).[4]

The problems posed by money and its international exchange raise difficult technical questions concerning economics and economies. As political economists remind us, however, there is a highly political dimension to nearly all of them. To be able to create money and insist on its use as a medium of exchange usually involves possessing political power. Creating money which is accepted as a medium of exchange is also a source of political power. This is why states have nearly always sought a monopoly when it comes to money used by their citizens in their territory. A useful example of the relationship between power and money is provided by the fate of the Confederate dollar in the American Civil War. Almost from its creation it lost value against the US dollar, and when the South was finally defeated, it lost any remaining value it had overnight.

The dynamic of absolute gain versus relative gain also plays its part in the attitude of states to money. On the one hand, they all share an interest in a common store of value which maintains its value and is universally accepted. It is good for the economic activity from which states and their people benefit. On the other hand, states seek particular advantages for themselves and their own people over others, and they resent it when others gain the same sort of advantage over them.

In wartime, this dynamic can play out quite crudely. The Germans considered a plan for parachuting fake British banknotes into Britain during World War II to cause both inflation and chaos. Rich and powerful states routinely insist on payment in their own currencies and try to drive enemy currencies out of neutral marketplaces as a medium of exchange. They can also use exchange rate policies to control their allies. In 1956, for example, Britain and France joined Israel in invading Egypt. The international financial markets judged that Britain and France could not afford a war and began selling off pounds and francs anticipating devaluations. The British and French used up their gold and foreign exchange reserves trying to maintain the value of their currencies, and they asked the US to join them in buying pounds and francs to maintain their value. The US refused because it disapproved of the attack. The pound continued to decline. Within forty-eight hours of the attack being launched and facing bankruptcy, the British called the operation off and the French were forced to follow suit.

A strong currency can be seen as an indicator of national power. It can make easy the pre-emptive buying of scarce strategic materials abroad to deny them to an enemy with a weaker currency. The US and Britain followed this practice in World War II to deny scarce minerals to Germany. A strong currency can also draw other states into an economic sphere of influence by offering them high prices for their exports and easy loans which they cannot obtain elsewhere. The Germans followed this policy in South Eastern Europe during the 1930s. Particularly when they get into economic difficulties, some people in southern Europe argue that the euro still works this way and to Germany's benefit.[5]

Even a weak currency can provide an advantage on occasions by making a state's exports cheaper and its imports more expensive in order to ease its balance of payments problems. However, the big economic lesson of the Great Depression in the 1930s was that devaluing a state's currency to make its exports more competitive and its imports more expensive did not work. It invited competitive devaluations by other states which left everyone worse off and postponed a general recovery. Nevertheless, states today are still tempted to engage in informal devaluations to ease their immediate balance of trade problems and to avoid job losses which will be politically costly.

The politics of money: the case of the Bretton Woods system

The political nature of international monetary problems is well illustrated by the case of the Bretton Woods monetary system, which was established at the end of World War II and lasted for over thirty years. Possessing a strong currency can give a state a number of advantages. One of these occurs when other states find the strength of its currency and the stability of its value so attractive that they want to acquire and use it in some of their transactions. For much of the 18th and 19th centuries the British pound enjoyed this status as what is known as a reserve currency. The attractiveness of the pound reinforced itself, making the pound stronger, Britain better able to afford its imports, and British banks and financiers better able to invest in the economies of other states. The reserve status of the pound also made other states very sensitive to British economic policy, and slow to do anything which might hurt the value of the many pounds which they, their banks, and their companies had acquired.

Through the course of the 20th century, as the US acquired the status of a global economic power, the US dollar steadily replaced the British pound as the primary reserve currency. In 1945, the Americans and their allies decided to use the US dollar as the foundation of a new international monetary system which would foster growth and make the economic disasters of the Great Depression less likely to occur. A full return to the Gold Standard was not politically possible, so they decided on the next best thing. The US dollar would be pegged to gold at $35 an ounce—that is the Federal Reserve, in theory, would trade gold and dollars at that rate—and other currencies would be pegged to the US dollar with room for a one percent variation above or below the initial rate of exchange.

One problem of the old Gold Standard noted above had been that in times of economic difficulty like during a balance of trade or balance of payments crisis, pressure would build on the currency of the state in difficulty as holders of it tried to sell its currency before it lost value. In the new system, these pressures were eased by setting up the International Monetary Fund (IMF) with money provided by members available to provide short-term loans to states facing balance of payments crises. Knowing that a state under pressure would be helped out by the IMF, holders of its currency would be less scared that a sudden devaluation might happen and less likely to try to sell off its currency in a hurry. At the same time, an International Bank of Reconstruction and Development (the World Bank) was established to help finance postwar recovery in the war-damaged economies of the developed states. In short, an international monetary system designed to deliver stable exchange rates and to help states maintain the values of their currencies when under pressure was established. It was a great success, and it depended on the US alone being willing to shoulder the burden of having its currency pegged to gold.

Political interests played their part in Bretton Woods from the start, however. The US rejected the idea of a world currency pegged to gold, reserving that role for the US dollar. By the late 1960s, the US was increasingly printing dollars to pay for the war in Viet Nam and its Great Society social reforms at home. It could do so without hurting the value of the currency because it was pegged to gold. Other states began to worry about the increasing gap between the dollars in the circulation and the amount of gold the US possessed to cover them. The unofficial price of gold began to exceed the pegged value in US dollars, and on one occasion, the French actually announced they would bring their US dollars to the US Federal Reserve and ask for gold.

Other developed states, especially after they recovered from the war and became richer, resented the US ability to print money with little inflation. However, they were afraid to press the US too hard in case it ended the dollar gold link and left everyone with greatly devalued dollars. Nevertheless, their fear came true in 1971 when, without warning, the Nixon administration broke the link, suspended the ability to trade dollars and gold temporarily, and then let the dollar lose value against gold as part of a package of measures to deal with the US's own economic problems. While the Bretton Woods system had clearly served US economic interests, the US had born the strain of maintaining it. Once that burden became unsustainable, however, the US pulled back unilaterally to fix its own problems.

The Bretton Woods system never recovered from the "Nixon shock" as it was called. Instead, the system was replaced with a series of less formal managed floats supervised by the big central banks of states and international financial institutions. They cooperate to avoid sudden shifts in exchange rates and to help states through the sorts of economic difficulties which tempted or forced them to devalue in the past. The system is not always successful and the challenges which it faces are made increasingly complex by two factors.

First, while the dollar is still the world's most important reserve currency (the US dollar still accounted for over 63 percent of global currency reserves in 2016), it has shared in the relative decline of the US economy and no longer dominates the international financial system as it did in the second half of the 20th century.[6] The Japanese yen and the EU's euro have both taken on regional reserve currency roles. The Chinese renminbi looks like it might become a reserve currency in the future, and the Chinese have suggested that the US dollar be replaced by a unit comprised of what is known as a "basket" of the world's leading currencies. Thus, with no one state and its currency dominating the world economy, exchange rate policy has to be coordinated between many centers of power, each with its own interests as well as shared interests.

Secondly, not all these centers of power are states. As we shall see below, the growth of international finance, investments, and capital movements relative to international trade has increased the number of private, and often transnational, actors that can have an impact on exchange rates and exchange rate policies. No longer are central banks always the key players in managing exchange rates. Indeed, on occasions, and even acting together, they can seem dwarfed by the scale of the capital movements and the power of the private financial actors which they try to manage.

Key terms

central banks Public banks like the Federal Reserve or the Bank of England charged with issuing and withdrawing money, monitoring its value, and setting interest rates.

devaluation Where the central bank of a state reduces the value of its currency making it cheaper to buy and sell in exchange for gold or other currencies and making gold and other currencies more expensive in terms of the devalued currency.

exchange rate The price at which the money of one state trades against the money of other states or gold. The rate can be fixed, managed, or floating.

Gold Standard A situation where the central bank of a state guarantees to trade gold for its own currency at a fixed rate.

medium of exchange Something, usually a form of money, used for trading for goods and services, rather than trading them directly.

reserve currency A currency whose value is so strong and so stable that other states, plus the banks and firms of other states, like to acquire it and conduct much of their trade and investment in it.

run on the currency A situation in which many holders of a currency become worried that it is about to lose its exchange rate value and seek to sell it back to the central bank or to other people.

Key takeaways

- Money performs the same role in international economic relations as it does in the economies of states.

- Its role in international economic relations is complicated by exchange rates, the values of different currencies when compared to each other or to a precious metal like gold.

- Currencies can be traded like other goods, usually between central banks and private actors for gold or for other currencies, and their exchange value can rise and fall.

- Traders and states usually have a shared economic interest in currencies which are easily exchanged and maintain stable values against each other.

- Stable values for currencies can be maintained by fixed rates or by managed rates where central banks allow currency values to change only slowly or by small amounts.

- States sometimes have a relative political interest in their own currency being strong or weak. A very strong currency can become a reserve currency. A very weak currency can boost a state's exports and reduce its imports.

Exercises

1. Why do the currencies of states have to be bought and sold?
2. Why might the values of currencies fluctuate against one another?
3. What did the US find were the advantages and disadvantages of having a strong currency (highly valued) after World War II?
4. Why has the US government suggested that China might be a currency manipulator?

10.2	International credit and investment

Learning objectives

1. List the reasons why individuals, firms, banks, and states borrow and lend money.
2. Explain the differences between foreign direct and foreign indirect investment.
3. List the reasons why most states work so hard to attract foreign investment.
4. Describe the processes by which capital flows have increased in proportion to trade flows in the last twenty years.

In trade, people exchange one good for another or for money. In addition to being a medium of exchange, in the trading of produced goods and services, money has two other uses. It can be lent, and it can be used to purchase the firms which produce goods and services, or a share in those firms.

In lending, people provide the use of something for a limited time, usually without getting anything in return. You might lend a new neighbor a lawn mower to cut his grass because his has not arrived yet, or you might lend a friend a sharp suit or prom dress because theirs is out of fashion or has become too small and/or they are broke. All you expect back are what you originally loaned to somebody, although, if you do not know them well or trust them, you might ask for something as security. If you run out of gas, for example, the attendant might ask you to leave your wristwatch or phone until you bring back the spare gas tank he has loaned you after putting the gas in your car.

Lending changes when lenders expect more back than they lent. Filling the borrowed mower with gas or getting the borrowed suit or dress dry cleaned before giving them back might be seen as a nice touch. It might also be seen as compensating for "wear and tear" which cannot be replaced or restored. If prices go up between the time you lend someone twenty dollars and the time you get it back, you might expect a little more back—say twenty-one dollars, if that's what it costs now to buy what twenty dollars would have bought when you made the loan.

Things really change, however, when loans are made with the express purpose of getting more back—interest on top of the value that was originally loaned. They change so much that in some of the great cultures of the world interest-based loans are seen as wicked and lazy—making money off lending money without actually doing any work. Islam rejects anything more than "wear and tear" notions of paying back more than was borrowed.[7] Christians in medieval Europe used to feel so uneasy about interest-based loans for profit that they used to leave it to Jews and others they regarded as outsiders to engage in banking. And even today, we are quick to get angry at people who we see charging too much interest—whether they be criminal loan-sharks and "pay day" loan operations exploiting people in difficult circumstances, or respectable banks catching foreclosed homeowners, bankrupt businesses, or unwary students with tough penalty clauses when they cannot pay their bills.

Nevertheless, organized systems of interest-based lending for profit have played a critical role in creating the modern international economy and the high standards of living and consumption associated with it. For them to be successful, three key elements need to be present.

First there need to be producers with good ideas about what consumers would like them to produce and workers with the ability to create those goods and services, both of whom lack the money—known as **capital**—to set up production and support themselves until the goods and services they produce return an income plus a profit. It usually takes some time before a new business sells enough to make a profit, and established businesses often need more money than they are presently generating, for example, to replace worn out or old-fashioned equipment.

Second there need to be holders of capital who are willing to support the ideas of the producers and the labor of the workers with their money, in the expectation of obtaining a share of the profits made possible by their **investments**. We often think of these people as capitalists, people with money over and above what they need to survive or wealth tied up in their own property. It is perfectly possible, however, for someone to make a living completely out of lending money, and many people of quite modest means in the developed world get part of their income from interest—a savings account, for example, or a pension plan to which they contribute—invested in **stock markets** or bonds issued by governments (see below).

The whole process of investment involves risk, the possibility that the idea is one which fails to make money. The producers and the workers risk their livelihoods. They will be out of a job if things go wrong and no one wants their goods at the price they have to sell it. The investors risk their capital. If the project does not work out, they lose some or all of their money. Generally, the greater the risk that a project will not be successful, the greater the return investors expect on their capital. Thus, there are relatively "safe" investments with a high probability of success, but low returns, and there are relatively more risky investments with a higher probability of failure but a promise of greater returns if they are successful.

Risk also exists at another level, however. Like central banks issuing paper money whose value is greater than the gold covering it, commercial banks and investors often provide credit to borrowers in greater amounts than the money or gold they actually have covering their loans which they have received from depositors. They do so by borrowing from other sources, and by trying to ensure that the income from investment loans and loan principals being paid back will exceed the losses from loans that are not repaid.

This gearing, as it is called, of bank or investor assets to loans made becomes a problem if too many loans go bad. Then people worry if the bank or investor in question can meet its own obligations to those depositors whose money it has effectively borrowed at one interest rate to lend out at another. Nevertheless, it is widely agreed that the relaxation of gearing requirements in 17th- and 18th-century Europe greatly expanded the amount of cheap credit available to borrowers.

It was this cheap credit which funded many of the merchant companies which established themselves in the New World. These companies borrowed money to pay for the people, supplies, and ships which would create new wealth-creating communities in the Americas. The banks, private investors, and, sometimes, governments which lent them the money did so in the expectation of being paid back and receiving a regular income, once new colonies were established and making money. Many of these companies and colonies succeeded. Others collapsed in spectacular failures brought on by combinations of bad luck, bad ideas, and corruption.

The Darien Scheme/Disaster

At the end of the 17th century, Scotland was still an independent state, although it faced increasing economic difficulties. Like other states at the time, and conforming to the logic of mercantilism, it tried to solve its problems by creating a new colony abroad, this one in the Isthmus of Panama. The new colony would provide a flow of luxury goods and possibly provide access for Scotland to the markets of and supplies from the Far East across the Pacific.

The financial resources of the wealthy Scottish landowners were not enough to fund the project, and so the middle classes were asked to contribute their savings and to borrow money to invest in shares so they could take advantage of this opportunity. Meanwhile, poor people from the town and countryside were recruited to settle and work the new colony. The Darien Scheme, therefore, was not just an economic proposition. It was billed as a national project which would be the making of Scotland and its economy.

The project faced difficulties from the start. The climate in the Isthmus made it a hard place to live. The Spanish, who were already there, besieged the Scottish settlement. The English—who shared a joint monarch with the Scots—in nearby Jamaica refused to help with either military or humanitarian assistance. They had no interest in a successful Scottish colony and were scared of annoying the Spanish. After two attempts at a settlement, the Scots gave up in 1700. Their state was bankrupt. When the Scottish parliament voted for a union with the English parliament in the new state of Great Britain in 1707, the Darien disaster was widely seen to have played an important role in weakening Scotland's economic strength and political confidence. Or as the Scottish poet Robert Burns more forthrightly declared, "We're bought and sold for English gold, such a parcel of rogues in a nation."

The Darien project was funded by a combination of loans and the sale of shares in the project which would provide profits to investors. The anger at bankers and others who arranged its financing is familiar today in the aftermath of the banking crisis which developed in 2008. Then a combination of unwise loans to people unlikely to be able to pay them back, loans which went bad (were not repaid), and fears that banks lacked sufficient reserves to cover their losses, created a crisis throughout the international system. It should be remembered, however, that the system of relatively easy credit which made these disasters possible, also funded the ideas, technical innovations, and operating costs of enterprises which brought about the agricultural and industrial revolutions of the 18th and 19th centuries. Since then, money crossing state borders in the form of loans, direct investment, and indirect investment, has continued to play an ever-increasing role in financing economic activity all around the world.

Foreign investment occurs when money, usually from a foreign company, flows into a state. This money may be used to buy shares in a company, for example, in the way the Brazilian Company 3G Capital now has a majority stake in Burger King, and the Italian Fiat car company has a nearly 60 percent share in the ownership of the Chrysler Motor Corporation through a merger of the two companies. It may be used to buy a company completely in the way General Motors used to wholly own the German car company Opel which, in turn owns the former British car company Vauxhall. And it may be used to add to an already existing stake in a company to improve or expand that company's operations.

Foreign direct investment is undertaken for much the same reasons as investments at home. Companies need to expand and grow if they are to remain competitive and make profits. Mergers or takeovers give them better economies of scale, greater market share, and access to the technical know-how of former rivals. A hostile takeover can result in a rival being purchased so it can be closed down or absorbed.

In addition, foreign direct investment by companies from rich, developed states in companies from poor, developing states may simply reflect the relative economic power of the two. In the 19th century, for example, rich British companies and individuals saw better returns on their capital if it was invested in South American railroad construction and Texas cattle farming than if it was invested back in Britain. In the 20th century, roles changed and US companies became heavily involved in making direct foreign investments.

Finally, companies may engage in direct foreign ownership as a way of getting around tariffs which penalize their exports to a state. Many US companies set up operations in Western Europe after World War II as a hedge against the Europeans becoming more protectionist, for example, as did Japanese companies in the US beginning in the 1990s. However, this fear of protection suggests a number of problems with foreign direct investment tied to Mercantilist and nationalist assumptions about what is good for an economy.

Foreign direct investment (FDI) may be politically sensitive because it hurts national pride in the target state. When the American food giant Kraft (now Mondelēz International) bought the British Cadbury's chocolate company in 2010, there was uproar in Britain. Cadbury's had a long tradition as a successful company, a good corporate citizen, and as a specifically British success story. To see it sold to a company known in Britain for making processed cheese and from a state whose chocolate enjoyed a bad reputation hurt. Like the idea of Burger King being owned by Brazilians rather than Americans, it just seemed wrong to some people.[8]

People also worry about FDI in terms of whether a foreign owner will have the best interests of "their" state's company at heart. Where will General Motors make new investments or use new technologies first in good times or cut jobs in bad times: Michigan or at its Chinese plants? The same question can be asked about Toyota and its plants in Japan, Kentucky, and Australia (scheduled to close in 2017). The fear is that a company will take care of its home base first and put its foreign plants second. Economists tell us that companies weigh many factors when they make these decisions, but they also suggest that considerations such as these can play a part in their deliberations.

FDI can also raise questions about military security and political independence. In 2005, for example, a state-owned Chinese oil company, the Chinese National Offshore Oil Corporation (CNOOC) made a bid to buy the American-owned Union Oil Company of California (UNOCAL). The US Congress asked the Bush Administration to review the bid on national security grounds. Did the US really want state-owned companies from communist China buying up the US oil industry? Sensing that its bid would go nowhere, but at a great cost in both legal fees and Chinese-American relations, CNOOC withdrew its bid and UNOCAL merged with the US oil company, Chevron, shortly after.

Economists suggest that opposition to FDI based on national pride and fears about independence, security, and neglect are overplayed. These arguments may be a smokescreen for companies, politicians, and citizens who want to be protected from foreign takeovers which may result in more efficiencies and increased competitiveness and, therefore, smaller operations and lost jobs. As noted in Chapter 9, the British-owned car industry all but disappeared at the turn of the century with huge loss of jobs and a big blow to British pride. Thanks to FDI, however, more British people than ever before are employed today in building and assembling cars for both the home market and export. The economists say that having an efficient, competitive industry which creates jobs is far more important than the question of whether the industry is owned by the British or foreigners.

Realists and Mercantilists, on the other hand, are not at all surprised when FDI creates controversy. They note that even states with the most pro-free market and fair competition ideologies, like the US and Britain, find it much easier to argue for why their FDI should be allowed into the economies of other states than for why foreigners' FDI should be allowed into the US and British economies. In most cases, the argument for FDI and the economic benefits it brings, wins, especially if a company or plant will close without investment which is only available from abroad. When national security issues are flagged however, as in the CNOOC/UNOCAL case, even very good FDI deals in economic terms may be heavily modified or even called off.

Investments create jobs. Generally speaking, therefore, the citizens of small states, and states in general when times are bad, welcome any investment and are not overly concerned with its source unless it is competing with a locally owned company and threatening to drive it out of business. However, when economic times are difficult, concerns about FDI may be raised in the state from which capital is flowing abroad. "Why invest in jobs for foreigners, when you should be investing in jobs at home" is an easy question for politicians to ask. As we shall see below, this is especially the case when a company looks like it wants to shrink or close its operations at home so that it can move offshore to places where the costs of production are lower.

Concerns about FDI have contributed to its decline relative to another way in which money is moved from one state to another to finance economic operations—foreign indirect investment, sometimes known as foreign portfolio investment. The basic idea behind foreign indirect investment (FII) is simple. Instead of investing in a company or a share in a company, foreigners invest in the stock market or the **bond market** of a state.

On stock markets, shares in the ownership of companies are bought and sold. The value of shares in a company rises and falls in accordance with the economic performance of the company and judgments about its future prospects. These shares may yield a dividend, a proportion of the profits paid out to shareholders at regular intervals. They may yield no dividend but be attractive to buyers who hope they will increase in value. They may be bought in sufficient quantities by a single buyer to establish a controlling stake in a company. Shares are often traded many times over as the fortunes of companies and the economies in which they operate rise and fall.

Bonds are promises issued by companies and, more importantly, by governments, as a way of borrowing money which will be paid back with interest after a specific amount of time. Some bonds can be issued for a matter of months, while others are offered for longer periods like ten or thirty years. Some bonds may cost the buyer a fraction of the face value (the amount on the bond), but they will get the full face value of the bond if they hold on to it for a specified period of time before trading it back to whoever issued it. Other bonds are auctioned off at the lowest interest rate the issuer can obtain. Bonds, like shares, can be traded multiple times, with the interest rate and price at which they are traded rising, and occasionally falling, beyond the rate at which they were originally issued (see the US Treasury website for more information at the following link: http://www.treasurydirect.gov/indiv/research/indepth/tbonds/res_tbond_rates.htm).

Many of the advantages of FII are the same as those applying to indirect investment undertaken inside a state. The buying and selling is usually undertaken by an agent or broker working for a financial institution. These agents may have more financial expertise and time to study the markets than the people whose money they are managing. The prices and interest rates at which shares and bonds respectively trade can be seen as signals about how well a company, government or state's economy is performing. And, in addition, FII is generally more anonymous and diffuse than FDI. When foreign investors try to buy a company, everyone usually can see what's going on. When they invest in the stock markets or make purchases on the bond markets indirectly through a financial institution, their money just adds to the general flow of money in these markets.

At least that used to be the case. Historically, in the larger states with the most developed economies, FII represented a small amount of money relative to locally owned capital and the size of the economy as a whole. Capital flows in and out of states could have big effects on occasions. After World War I, for example, it was vitally important that US dollars flowed into Germany to enable the Germans to maintain the economic activity which allowed them to pay the reparations (fines) that they were ordered to pay Britain, France, and others by the Treaty of Versailles. These reparations then enabled the British and French to pay off debts they owed to the US. When the flow of dollars from the US was interrupted, the whole system broke down.

And as we have seen, the eventual accumulation of US dollars overseas during the Bretton Woods period created concerns about inflation and devaluations which brought an end to the system of fixed exchange rates. On the whole, however, the central banks of the bigger developed states were able to establish controls on the flow of currencies when they were concerned that too much capital was flowing out of their economies and, besides, moving large amounts of money was not always easy or quick.

Since the early 1990s, however, the amount of capital moving across international borders has increased massively in proportion to the value of international trade and the size of national economies. By the end of 2010, it was estimated that the value of foreign exchange traded on a given day exceeded the value of goods traded by sixty times.[9] This growth has occurred for two main reasons.

First, the end of the Cold War was accompanied by a sense that the principles of Liberal political economy had triumphed over those of other systems just as much as the US and its allies had triumphed over the Soviet Union. The push to make international trade more open was accompanied by pressures for **financial deregulation**. The more capital was put into the markets, it was argued, the better this would be for growth and for profits. Instead of relying on state pensions, national health services, and unemployment benefits funded by taxation and, increasingly, government borrowing, ordinary citizens would be freer, more responsible and better off, if these services were paid for by their own money invested in the market. As a result, all sorts of new actors became involved directly or indirectly in financial markets both at home and abroad. In addition to working for themselves and their traditional customers, for example, banks and other financial institutions became engaged in managing the investments of pension funds, university endowments, and investment clubs of ordinary people on a much greater scale than ever before.

Second, this ideological shift was greatly enabled by developments associated with the revolution in information and communication technologies. It became ever easier to transfer electronically ever larger sums of money ever more quickly around the world to take advantage of investment opportunities or to avoid investment dangers. By the start of the 21st century, stock markets and bond markets around the world, and those who invested through them, were all part of a network transferring capital nearly instantaneously at the push of button, and running twenty-four hours a day.[10]

The advantages and disadvantages of this new and ever-growing financial system are hotly debated. What nearly everyone agrees, however, is that the power of states and their central banks to control their national financial and economic systems had been greatly reduced. Indeed, as we shall see, it began to look like international financial markets often had greater influence over the kind of economic policies states could pursue than did their own governments and peoples.

Figure 10.3 Wall Street, New York City, home of the New York Stock Exchange
(Source: Simon Davis/Alamy Stock Photo)

The Great Financial Crisis of 2008 and beyond: Part 1, the US

In 2008, a major US financial services company, Lehman Brothers, went bankrupt. Fearing it could not cover its debts and was exposed to bad loans, people had withdrawn their money from it, and the US government refused to rescue it with public funds. A general loss of confidence quickly spread to the rest of the US financial sector and then around the world. The immediate causes of the crisis are still hotly contested.

Critics of the financial sector pointed to the way financial deregulation had made it possible for financial institutions to make vast amounts of money by issuing far more risky loans than in the past. The risky loans had then been divided up, combined with other loans, and sold on to other buyers. No one, from other big financial institutions to ordinary workers whose pension schemes were invested in the market, knew how exposed they were to the risky part of these bundled loans.

Defenders of the financial sector noted that no one had complained while stock markets were soaring, increasing many people's earnings and property values, enabling them to borrow and spend more money. If people over-borrowed in the good times, that was their problem. Besides, they argued, many of the bad loans resulted from government-mandated programs to enable poorer people who would not have qualified for loans in the past to buy houses.

There was more agreement about the long-term problems which lay behind the immediate causes of the crisis. The world economy was changing with manufacturing goods industries shifting to quickly industrializing states with cheaper labor costs like China and Brazil from developed states like the US which concentrated increasingly on services and high technology and high-end goods. However, the US and most European states were increasingly buying more from and selling less to states like China, creating balance of payments problems which they funded by public and private borrowing encouraged by very low interest rates. These problems worsened, particularly in the US, where they were made more complicated by the costs of the wars in Iraq and Afghanistan.

In the case of the US, much of this borrowing was made possible by the willingness of other states and foreign financial institutions to continue buying US government bonds. They were willing to do this for several reasons. First, they assumed that the US, still the largest, richest, most productive economy in the world, would recover in the medium term. If it didn't, then everybody would be in terrible trouble. Second, they needed the US to keep buying their exports or their own economies would slow down. Third, they had large amounts of dollars from their previous sales to the US for which they had no better investment options, and which they were worried would lose their value if the US economy failed. And, of course, the more states like China loaned to the US, the greater their stake in the US not failing.

By the time the Obama administration took office in 2009, the financial crisis had grown into a general economic crisis with banks and major companies at risk, unemployment rising, and people losing their homes to foreclosures because they could not make their mortgage payments. For the first time since the 1960s, the benign cycle which encouraged foreigners to keep lending to the US was called into question. Why keep lending to the US if its economy was going to shrink and the value of the dollar collapse no matter what?

The Obama administration acted quickly, if controversially. It announced that it would rescue major banks and other financial institutions by providing them with public funding to restore confidence that they could meet their obligations. The administration said it would buy majority shares in some major businesses (notably carmakers) putting them into public ownership, but keeping them in business until they reduced their operations to a level at which they would be profitable again. And it said it would accomplish all this by creating money and by encouraging investors to continue to buying US bonds and investing in US financial markets. After all, what alternative did they have if they did not want to see their existing markets and stake in the US economy disappear?

In the short term, the gamble worked. The catastrophes of massive bank failures, company closures, and soaring unemployment in the US were avoided. The US government and the rest of the world were betting on an eventual US economic recovery on a new, more competitive basis. A return to faster growth and revived exports would ease many of the US's economic problems by increasing tax receipts, reducing the deficits in government spending, and improving the trade balance between imports and exports. It would also ease the concerns of all the central banks and financial institutions which have loaned or invested great sums in the US, and the states which depend on it as a market for their exports.

The US economic recovery has been very slow, however. Some of the methods by which it has been achieved remain controversial. Low interest rates are maintained to encourage borrowing for investment, but borrowers are not spending or investing sufficiently in the US economy, as opposed to abroad. Money is kept plentiful by a technical process known as quantitative easing. The Federal Reserve (the US central banking system), creates money—not by printing, but electronically—and uses this to buy back bonds from those who have loaned it money. This causes fear of inflation where the ratio of money to goods increases and money begins to lose its value, although this has not occurred significantly at the time of writing (2017).

Defenders of the policy say its negative effects in these terms are small compared to the positive effects—exposing ordinary American people to as little economic pain as possible and speeding the recovery which will eventually come around. Critics say it encourages more debt and inflation. A big challenge will occur, the critics argue, as the US and other states like

Japan and Britain which took similar approaches start reducing the amount of money they are pumping into their respective economies. US trade balances, especially with China, are not responding. The critics argue that the policy is only postponing the evil day when the US will have to make even more painful adjustments to restore its finances and competitiveness. By 2017, the US had completed its quantitative easing programs and was beginning to raise interest rates, while the EU launched its own program in 2015. Raising interest rates without killing off growth or precipitating another economic crisis is the next big challenge, but living without quantitative easing appears to be one too. Fears about Brexit caused the British to launch a new round in 2017. Nearly everyone around the world agrees that the old days of the US borrowing on the strength of the fundamentals of its economy to consume the exports of the world are over. Nearly everyone also agrees, however, that a healthy US economy remains critical to the health of the world economy.

Political scientists, economists, politicians, bankers, and business people all talk a great deal about the idea of economic interdependence we examined in Chapters 1 and 3. The key feature of modern economies and the technologies which make them possible, we saw, was the mutual need they create between different states and peoples. The US cannot maintain its living standards without cheap Chinese imports. Neither China nor other developing states can maintain their fast economic growth rates without the US and the rest of the developed world being able to pay for their exports. And no one can manage without secure, affordable supplies of oil and gas to power their economies. However, it takes a big eruption like the financial crisis of 2008 and beyond to expose the sinews of this interdependence. Mutual need does not always create warm, loving, and peaceful relations. Like individuals, states and their people can also experience interdependence as a trap from which there is no escape, or as an unfair relationship which they think is doing them harm but to which there is no alternative.

China wonders why the US will not let it have its economic place in the sun after how hard the Chinese have worked to become a successful economic power. Americans wonder why the world is so angry at the US after decades in which it served as the world economy's locomotive and protector. And as we shall see in Chapter 13, developing states have complained for decades that the odds of achieving sustained and balanced growth seem stacked against them.

Just like individuals when their relationships go sour, states and their peoples start thinking about changing some relationships and getting out of some altogether. As the case of the European Union (EU) shows below, however, it is then that the full force of what it means to be interdependent hits them.

Figure 10.4 The symbol of the euro outside the European Central Bank in Frankfurt, Germany

(Source: Zoonar GmbH/Alamy Stock Photo)

The Great Financial Crisis of 2008 and beyond: Part 2, Europe

The European financial crisis emerged in 2009, a year after its US counter-part. It had two components. The first was fear among creditors that the sovereign (government) debt of some European states was becoming too large. They worried that these governments would soon be unable to afford the regularly scheduled interest payments on their debt, never mind paying down the principal on their loans. The second was that many European banks were exposed to bad loans just like their US counterparts, especially in the housing sector.

The Europeans liked to blame the Americans for their difficulties. The US economic difficulties, they argued, had slowed down their own economies. This had reduced their takings from taxes which, in turn, made it hard for them to make their debt payments. In a similar way, the crisis over American financial institutions had shaken confidence in banks in general, and this contagion had spread across the Atlantic to pose doubts about European banks. Americans (and many Europeans) said nonsense. Europe had plenty of problems of its own capable of causing a crisis, not the least of which was a structural (long-running) trade imbalance between more and less competitive states in the European Union.

The situation was greatly complicated by the existence of the EU (which we will examine in Chapter 11), and the Euro Area or Eurozone, a single currency system of which seventeen out of the then twenty-seven members of the EU had joined. The European Union's origins were in a plan for many states to participate in a single market protected by a single system of tariffs. This union would achieve economies of scale, help poorer states and regions catch up with richer ones, and allow a system by which relatively generous social benefits could be financed by a higher rate of tax than that to which Americans, for example, were used.

A logical extension of this idea was an attempt to manage the exchange rates of the different currencies along the lines of the Bretton Woods system, but on a regional scale. By the end of the 20th century, this had grown into a single currency—the euro—with a central bank in Frankfurt, Germany. The euro was designed to achieve efficiencies (no more exchange rate costs for trade between its members) and a stable price environment (its central bank had safeguarding against inflation as the first priority in its charter).

While the Eurozone had a single monetary authority responsible for creating money and setting interest rates, however, there was no single financial authority. The member states preferred to retain the power of setting their own taxing, borrowing, and spending policies. However, they were supposed to stay within European-wide targets for how much they borrowed and how much they would allow inflation measured as proportions of their respective GDPs.

In times of economic growth and easy credit, the system seemed to work well. Poorer states like Greece, Spain, and Portugal were able to attract loans which they would have not obtained had they been outside the Eurozone, since they were seen as part of the same system as strong and rich states, like Germany and the Netherlands. Money was invested in modernizing their economies, and many of their people's living standards made great gains. Much of the money was not productively invested, however. Some was lost to corruption. More went into property and caused prices to rise in property markets. In the case of Cyprus, big investments were made in Greek bonds which lost much of their value in a deal to fix Greece's economic problems. Very often the new capital was used in the form of low interest loans to sustain living standards, often through buying imports from the states like Germany and the Netherlands, whose banks were lending the poorer states more euros.

All the while, however, the public and private debts of these poorer states were increasing while the economic competitiveness of their exports both to the strong European states and poorer states outside the EU was declining. In the spring of 2012, the Greeks, then the Portuguese, the Spanish, and the Italians all felt the pressure of doubts about their economies. They could only raise loans in bond markets by offering higher and higher rates of interest which it was feared would be impossible to repay.

In the old days, these states could have eased the pressure by simply devaluing their national currencies—drachma, escudos, pesetas, and lire—and possibly defaulting on all or some of their debts. In the euro, they could no longer devalue to gain relative advantage, and defaulting risked the contagion of a debt crisis and bank failure spreading quickly to the rest of the European Union. The European Union, the European Bank, and the International Monetary Fund all offered money to the states in difficulty provided that they carried out very painful economic reforms associated with the policy of **austerity**.

Political instability followed. Democratically elected governments in Greece and Italy fell and were replaced by new leaders backed by technical experts. These committed their states to undertaking the reforms, and money was gradually released to them to service their debts and keep the financial system from collapsing. By the end of 2012, the crisis had eased although, as noted above, the EU undertook its own program of quantitative easing from 2015.

Nevertheless, opponents of the agreement in the states in trouble were asking, who rules us, our own governments or European and international financiers and technocrats? Are we still sovereign? In 2013 the Italians voted their technocratic prime minister and his government out of office. Meanwhile, opponents of the agreement emerged in the strong states like Germany and the Netherlands. They asked, why are we risking inflation to bail out people who work less hard than us and who do not pay their taxes? They might be better off with their old currencies, and we might be better off with our old ones, deutschmarks and guilders. In short, the difficulties of modern economic and financial interdependence had produced stresses and strains which not only threatened the existence of the EU and Eurozone. They also threated to revive old nationalist concerns and ugly passions which had been dormant for decades. By 2017, these difficulties had been eased by economic recoveries but, critics note, the underlying problems remain unsolved and the long-term consequences of quantitative easing remain uncertain.

Key terms

austerity   A policy by which a government addresses economic problems by stabilizing public finances, usually by a combination of increased taxation and reduced expenditure resulting in cuts to public services and the jobs which provide them.

bond market   A market where investors can purchase bonds which firms and governments issue as a way of borrowing money; bonds may be purchased directly or traded in secondary markets.

capital   Goods and money which can be used in production to create value; often used to mean the money invested in companies and economies to pay for and support economic activity.

financial deregulation   A policy favored in developed states from the late 1990s by which some rules restricting the operations of banks and other financial institutions were relaxed or scrapped to allow more efficiencies and more money to be made.

investments   Resources, usually money, committed to production in return for a share in the profits from the wealth created by that production; investment can be direct or indirect, domestically sourced, or sourced from abroad.

stock market   A market where shares in firms and other enterprises are traded.

Key takeaways

■ Loans and investments from abroad play an important role in financing economic activity in nearly every state.

■ Foreign investments can be direct (investment made to generate economic activity in companies) or indirect (investment in stock markets).

■ Loans are provided to companies and states through bond markets.

■ The international movement of capital has greatly outstripped the international movement of goods and services because of deregulation and technical developments which have allowed for almost instantaneous transfers of capital through electronic networks twenty-four hours a day to nearly everywhere in the world.

■ International financial networks make the creation of great wealth possible, but also quickly transmit crises of confidence about the security of loans and the sustainability of government policies involving high spending, taxes, and debt.

Exercises

1. Why do investors living in a state send money abroad, and why does foreign capital in the form of investments and loans come into a state from abroad?

2. What criticisms were made of US financial institutions in the great financial crisis of 2008, and what criticisms were made of the financial policies of the US government?

3. How do the financial relationships between China, the US, and the EU illustrate that we live in an interdependent world, and how do they show that interdependence can be stressful and cause conflict?

10.3 Transnational corporations

Learning objectives

1. List the reasons why states seek investments by **transnational corporations**.

2. Explain the ways in which transnational corporations influence the economic policies of states.

3. Examine the reasons for claiming a democratic deficit exists in the governance of international trade and finance.

Investment, trade, and production increasingly take place on regional, international, and, some would say, global scales (see Chapter 1). This expansion has delivered fast economic growth and rising living standards to much of the world. It has also brought great changes in the way many societies and their politics are organized.

People often welcome some of these changes—longer lives with more consumption, for example. They regret other changes—for example, the disappearance of a slower, more relaxed pace of life, but see them as a necessary price to be paid for progress. And some changes they flat out resent and resist; for example, a loss of jobs, pensions, and benefits. At the center of the process by which these positive and negative changes have been delivered are three actors or institutions: transnational corporations, international financial institutions, and international financial regulatory institutions.

Transnational corporations (TNCs) are sometimes referred to as multinational corporations or international corporations. They are big businesses which are usually, but not always, privately owned by a few people or many shareholders. Sometimes they are partly or wholly owned by a state. Their key characteristic is that they undertake economic operations in two or more states.

The terms transnational, multinational, and international can be used interchangeably. However, some observers suggest that the term "multinational corporation" is best used for a company headquartered in one state from which it directs its operations around the world—for example, the McDonald's Corporation. The term "transnational corporation," they suggest, is best used for a company that is not particularly anchored in one state. The Ford Motor Company, for example, likes to present itself as a global collection of operations, even though its main headquarters remains in the US. On the other hand, the big oil company BP presents itself as a transnational corporation in markets where its British background will not help it sell more gasoline, and as a British company in those markets where this background will help it sell more petrol.

TNCs are not new. The early ones developed in 17th century Europe to create trading posts overseas and to ship goods and supplies between states and their colonies. Some of them were highly developed. By the 18th century, for example, the Dutch and British East India Companies both owned fleets of armed warships, owned trading posts, operated armies, and conducted diplomatic relations with local rulers. They were companies which looked a bit like states.

Modern TNCs began in the US in the late 19th century, however. Like the Singer Sewing Machine Company, for example, they were based on the latest mass production techniques and incorporated the latest technologies into their products. They were able to beat their competitors at home and grow larger. The resulting economies of scale increased their competitiveness, and finally they expanded into the economies of other states where they repeated the process. Many TNCs have been so successful that their financial and technical resources exceed those of many sovereign states although, to date, they lack the guns or the legitimacy of sovereign states.[11]

The reasons why governments seek to attract TNCs are much the same today as when the British government welcomed Singer's decision to open a sewing machine plant in Scotland in 1867. They bring investment and technical knowledge which create jobs, further local economic activity, and hold out the possibility of exports to other economies. Generally speaking, they also do all this on a scale which local producers are unable to match.

All this looks very attractive to governments, especially when the alternative is that the company will enter your market with imports from its home state which will destroy companies and jobs in your economy without creating any new jobs or providing any new investment. As a result, governments usually work very hard to attract transnational corporations and the foreign direct investment they bring. They see themselves in competition with the governments of other states for this investment and offer a variety of incentives.

Ireland's policy for attracting direct investment

Ireland provides an excellent model of the sorts of things states can do to attract foreign direct investment. Its government allows TNCs very low tax rates and sometimes allows them to pay no corporation tax at all for a limited time. It offers special deals, for example on land, equipment, and energy purchases for TNCs' operations. In addition, it aggressively advertises Ireland in business and trade magazines as a great place to do business. The state has a modern transport infrastructure with good links to the rest of Europe and open access to the markets of the EU states. Its population is young and highly educated, especially in the information, natural, and mathematical sciences. And the Irish speak English—the language of global business and American investors.

The strategy, pursued since the 1960s, has been highly successful in transforming Ireland from a stagnant economy with high levels of emigration into a successful exporter of goods instead of its own people. It became one of Europe's major producers of pharmaceutical chemicals and computer software for companies based abroad. For a time, Ireland was known as the "Celtic Tiger." By some measures its citizens enjoyed a higher standard of living than many others in the EU, including those in the United Kingdom, although, as we shall see, it fell on very hard times after the financial crisis of 2008.

However, TNCs also attract a great deal of criticism both in the **host states** which receive their direct investment and the home state from which they operate. Many of these criticisms are related to the problems with direct foreign investment noted above. Whose interests do they put first when facing difficult choices or new opportunities—the economy of the host state or the economy of the home state? The response of TNCs is that they put their own interests as a company first, but this does not comfort those who see their branch plants operating under directions from head offices thousands of miles way.

There are other objections to their activities. First, they are often said to drive local companies out of business and put their employees out of work. Second, especially in the developing world, they are accused of heavily marketing unsuitable or unnecessary products, for example, baby formula which lacks the chemicals found in mothers' milk which strengthens their babies' resistance to local diseases (see Chapter 13). Third, they are said to force states into a "race to the bottom" as they compete by lowering taxes, relaxing work and safety conditions, and making the rest of the population pay for the benefits which the relatively few managers and workers hired by the TNC enjoy. This is an argument made not just in states competing for investment from TNCs, but also in their home states, especially the US, by people who see jobs disappearing overseas.

Finally, TNCs are said to take cynical advantage of the incentives provided by governments to attract their investment, leaving as soon as the incentives are withdrawn. In the Irish case, for example, a European company gained notoriety for shipping bottled pickles from their home state to put labels on the jars in Ireland before shipping them back home. This was done just so it could gain access to Ireland's tax breaks, grants, and other incentive payments, without providing the economic activity these incentives were designed to create. All the real production was undertaken elsewhere. Some companies—so called "brass plate companies"—have moved just their addresses and a small office which they call their headquarters just to take advantage of tax concessions. TNCs tend to shrug their shoulders at these criticisms. You can't blame us for putting our profits and the interests of our shareholders first, they say. And judging by the lengths to which governments and people still go to attract direct foreign investment, they seem to think that its benefits still outweigh the costs of these types of problems.

These arguments work well in good economic times. In bad times, however, the criticisms sharpen and receive a broader hearing. For example, it became more difficult for British coffee drinkers in 2012 to accept that a US company, Starbucks, paid little or no taxes in Britain at a time of austerity when the British themselves were being asked to pay more and face cuts in public spending. A boycott of Starbucks briefly flourished, and the coffee company agreed to pay more tax. It also became harder to know that TNCs were routinely moving profits generated in all the states in which they operated to the one with the lowest taxes before declaring them and engaging in **transfer pricing**—artificially low prices—to reduce taxes on internal transactions.

TNCs today are engaged in a wide range of activities beyond investing in production overseas. An increasing number, for example, are engaged in providing security services formerly provided by states in places like Iraq and Afghanistan. It is unclear whether the US withdrawal from some of its military commitments around the world will reduce or increase the use of private security firms, but a return to heavily armed operations like the East India companies seems unlikely. Modern TNCs are generally reluctant to provide a broad array of public goods, as opposed to the one, for example, security, in which they specialize. As the criticisms associated with tax avoidance and transfer payments suggest, however, TNCs have been drawn into performing like international financial institutions by the massive expansion of international finance relative to international trade. In some situations, it is the capital and technical "know how" they can provide which is more important than any goods they produce.

We have seen how international financial institutions like large banks and investment brokerages have become important as a result of increasing deregulation and the emergence of the technologies which made possible 24-hour global currency markets. They have generated great economic growth, especially in developing parts of the world and have enriched the increasingly wider circle of shareholders which has been created in the developed states. We have also seen how this process of deregulation has been associated with the financial crisis which emerged in the US in 2008. One result of that crisis was great anger at the banks, brokerages, and mortgage lenders associated with it. At one moment, they seemed to be presiding over perpetual growth with shareholders' earnings, pension plans, and property values always rising. People were encouraged to borrow more with low interest rates in order to provide more capital for the markets to invest. At the next moment, all the new wealth seemed to disappear as the value of share portfolios evaporated, firms closed, jobs were lost, and debtors defaulted.

This anger was sharpened by a sense that only a very few of the big bankers, brokers, and captains of industry who had presided over the disaster were actually hurt by it. Their living standards, like those of other chief executives of TNCs, seemed to remain untouched, no matter how badly their organizations performed. Their lives were not destroyed, and the headlines soon noted that they were commanding big salaries and bonuses once again.

Not only that, but the first steps at easing the crisis never seemed to be on the backs of the financial institutions widely seen as responsible for the mess. Ordinary people had to lose their homes and savings, or had to pay more taxes and lose more benefits to restore public finances to the point where the bond markets would lend their governments more money to service previous debts.

It was the way markets made and unmade governments in the EU, and the way its central bank staked out a claim to overseeing and approving the national budgets of member states that prompted some citizens to talk of a "democratic deficit" when it came to the people's control of their own economic destinies. A second result of the crisis, therefore, was a call in all the developed states for a return to more financial regulation.

Key terms

host states   States in whose economy direct or indirect investments are being made, in contrast to home states from where the investment is sent; it is possible and common for a state to be both a host state and a home state at the same time.

transfer pricing   Where a TNC engages in internal trade between its operations in different states, it may under-declare the price of the components being transferred to avoid paying taxes; TNCs may also declare earnings from around their international operations in the host state with the lowest tax rate.

transnational corporation   A publicly operating private business with operations in more than one state.

Key takeaways

- TNCs often possess competitive advantages over firms based in one state resulting from their size, wealth, and level of technical development.
- States provide incentives to attract TNC direct investment into their economies, but critics say their operations can be damaging in terms of economic, social, and political corruption, disruption, distortion, and exploitation.
- International financial institutions provide indirect investment in stock markets and loans in bond markets.
- Both TNCs and international financial institutions played controversial roles in the recent debt crisis leading to calls for more regulation of both.

Exercises

1. Suppose a foreign TNC that made aircraft components was proposing to build a plant in your town. What would be the advantages and disadvantages of them doing so?
2. Why did British coffee drinkers get angry at Starbucks in 2015, and what did they do?

| 10.4 | The future of international finance in an era of uncertainty |

International finance, and the politics and economics which surround it, are complex issues. The importance of international finance relative to international trade and production has expanded hugely since the 1990s. This is partly due to the triumph of free market capitalist democracies under the leadership of the US in the Cold War, and partly due to the role of the information revolution in making a global network of instantaneous and cheap information transfers possible. The consequences of this expansion remain uncertain. A massive deregulation and some quickly rising living standards were followed by the global financial crisis of 2008 onwards. This brought calls for the re-regulation and re-ordering of the international financial system. However, the questions of what is to be regulated, to what extent, and by whom remain fiercely argued over.

These are not new questions, but the intensity with which they are argued over, especially in developed states, is new. At one end of the continuum are those who call for a system of global finance which is not based on the currency of any particular state. It is unlikely that states and their people are ready for such a system. At the other end of the continuum are those like the people who wanted Britain to leave the European Union in 2016 and argued that Britain should make its own decisions about regulating finance and much else. In the British case, the government and its supporters wanted less regulation, but movements for putting control back in the hands of states and their governments are often seeking more regulation. Until recently, the diplomatic challenge was a two-step one: first, how to get states and others to agree to certain principles for regulating the international financial system and actors operating in it; and second, how to get them to act consistently with those principles. Now the challenge is far more complicated. The processes of international and global financial integration are paralleled by processes of disintegration along political, national, racial, religious, and—in the arguments about the widening gap between rich and poor—class terms. They are also increasingly paralleled by proposals for alternative international and global financial arrangements but forward by the rising powers, notably China. The relationship between the first two processes is hotly contested. Do we need more financial integration to overwhelm with prosperity the divisions still existing between peoples, or is this integration exacerbating or even causing those divisions? In Chapter 11, we shall see how these arguments play out around the world, but especially in Europe and the European Union.

Recommended reading

Eric Helleiner, Stefano Pagliari, and Hubert Zimmermann, *Global Finance in Crisis: The Politics of International Regulatory Change*, London, 2010.

Ayse Everensel, *International Finance for Dummies*, Hoboken, 2013.

Richard J. Barnet and Ronald E. Muller, *Global Reach, the Power of the Multinational Corporations*, New York, 1976.

Charles P. Kindleberger and Rober Z. Aliber, *Manias, Panics, and Crashes: A History of Financial Crises* (6th edition), Basingstoke, 2011.

Notes

1 Chris Brown and Kirsten Ainley, *Understanding International Relations* (4th edition), Basingstoke, 2009.
2 Susan Strange, *States and Markets*, London, 1998.
3 Paul Krugman, *Currencies and Crises*, Boston, 1995.
4 Julian Knight, *The Euro Crisis for Dummies* (Kindle edition), New York, 2012.
5 Simon Shuster, "Germany Finds Itself Cast as Villain in Greek Drama," *Time Magazine*, July 16, 2015.
6 Timothy Taylor, "Conversable Economist," January 3, 2013 at http://conversableeconomist.blogspot.com/2013/01/will-us-dollar-lose-its-preeminence.html
7 Brian B. Kettell, *Introduction to Islamic Banking and Finance*, Chichester, 2011.
8 Deborah Cadbury, *Chocolate Wars: The Hundred and Fifty Year Rivalry Between the World's Greatest Chocolate Makers*, New York, 2010.
9 Scott Burchill, "Liberalism," in Scott Burchill et al., *Theories of International Relations* (4th edition), Basingstoke, 2009.
10 Richard Langhorne, *The Coming of Globalization*, Basingstoke, 2001.
11 Alfred D. Chandler Jr. and Bruce Mazlish, *Multinational Corporations and the New Global History*, Cambridge, 2005.

11 International and regional integration and disintegration

Preamble

In the last chapter, we looked at international finance and, in particular, the emergence of an integrated global financial system. In this chapter, we look at integration and disintegration more broadly as they operate in other dimensions of international relations. Integration suggests a process by which separate parts appear to be merging into a single whole. Think about two high schools merging to save money and cope with declining enrollments. Disintegration suggests a process by which a single whole is breaking up into parts. Think about when a high school's social group breaks up during the summer vacation or go their separate ways on graduating. **International integration** suggests processes by which the politics, economics, cultures, and societies of separate states are merging into one another. **International disintegration** suggests processes by which the politics, economics, culture, and society of a single state or group of states are breaking into separate parts or simply breaking down.

We tend to focus on international integration—the pulling together or merging of states or parts of states—for a number of reasons. Rightly or wrongly, many people tend to assume integration is both a good thing and the wave of the future. The way European states have merged many of their institutions and processes in the European Union (EU), for example, is seen as a step up or away from the system of feuding sovereign states which gave us two world wars in the 20th century.[1] The way Canada, the United States, and Mexico have used the North American Free Trade Area (NAFTA) to open their markets to one another and coordinate their economic policies is as seen as evidence of the need for bigger economic actors in an era of globalization.[2]

We should remember, however, that there is also a great deal of disintegration going on in the world. Many of the old ties of empire between the European states and their former colonies, for example, weaken year by year, as do the old communist-era ties between Russia and some of the former Soviet republics. War, civil war, and, as we shall see in Chapter 12, environmental stress can all contribute to the disintegration of states and regional state systems. Indeed, we might say that integration and disintegration are two sides of the same coin. Wherever we find integration, for example the coming together of the American colonies in the 18th and 19th centuries to form the United States, we also find disintegration, the pulling apart of ties to the British Crown, the destruction and assimilation of native political systems and societies, and the erosion of settler loyalties to their individual colonies.

As this last example suggests, processes of international integration and disintegration are not new. As we shall see, we often think of them as new because we associate them with the EU and globalization. These are both sources of great and recent change in international relations. The forerunner to the EU was established in the 1950s, and despite the financial crisis which developed in 2008 and Britain's decision to leave in 2016 ("Brexit"), it remains widely assumed that globalization will continue to gather steam once the recovery from that crisis takes hold. If we could run a speeded-up film of the way groups of people have lived throughout human history, however, we would see a constant process of multiple mergings together and pullings apart undertaken by tribes, empires, states, unions, leagues, and other associations. Right now, processes of integration seem to dominate, at least in the developed parts of the world, but this has not always been the case and we need not assume it will always be so in the future. Indeed, there is some evidence to suggest that at the time of writing (2017) forces of disintegration are becoming stronger, although how strong remains uncertain.

| 11.1 | Theories of integration |

Learning objectives

1. Describe the processes of integration and disintegration.
2. Explain why Mitrany's functionalist argument targeted the sovereignty of states.
3. Distinguish between contractually based and identity based conceptions of loyalty.

Processes of integration vary by what gets integrated and to what degree. Think of two people getting married or entering a committed partnership. They may decide to live under one roof, but keep separate bedrooms. They may decide to set up a division of labor on household chores and expenditures and have an agreed standard of how clean the bathroom needs to be and how much should be spent on food while keeping their bank accounts separate, or they might clean the house together and have a joint bank account. At some point, they might declare that for some purposes, taxation for example, they want to be regarded as a single household rather than two separate people. And, of course, when relationships go bad, the way they disintegrate varies along the same dimensions. Some people keep certain parts of their relationship integrated, sharing a house for example, but separate finances. Others go for complete separation, although children and memories may make this difficult.

States and other political communities go through similar processes of integration and disintegration. During the Cold War, for example, the Soviet Union organized the states it had occupied in World War II into a military alliance, the Warsaw Pact, and an economic organization, the Council for Mutual Economic

Assistance or Comecon.[3] Military policy in the Warsaw Pact was supposed to be completely integrated to the point where the armed forces all used the same equipment and, under Soviet leadership, operated almost as a single force. Economic policy, in contrast, operated on a division of labor principle in which different states specialized in different kinds of manufacturing, again under Soviet leadership. In one sense, these are bad examples because of the extent to which they depended on coercion from Moscow. In another sense, however, they are useful for they illustrate intense processes of integration and disintegration taking place over a period of less than 50 years.

More benign processes of integration and disintegration are widespread, however. The members of the North Atlantic Treaty Organization (NATO) joined together willingly. NATO has a Council where the representatives of its members seek to come up with common policies, but only on matters of joint concern. It has divisions of labor with regard to who is primarily responsible for directing certain military tasks, common policies for training its soldiers up to shared standards of proficiency, and, while NATO members do not all use the same military equipment, they try to make them interoperable (for example, using the same sizes of ammunition and running on the same types and grades of fuel).[4]

Northern Ireland and the Republic of Ireland are politically separate. The former is a province of the United Kingdom as a result of which the two parts of Ireland currently use different currencies—the euro and the British pound sterling. Nevertheless, both sides have worked to make their border "invisible" and to integrate policies on issues like transportation, health care, and emergency services. They have done so because most people believe that these services can be delivered more efficiently by integrated providers, and because some people hope this integration will lead to Ireland becoming united once again. Examples of benign disintegration include the breaking up of Czechoslovakia into the Czech Republic and Slovakia, two independent states, in 1993, and Norway breaking its union with Sweden in 1905. In both cases, the breakaway party (the Slovaks and the Norwegians) wanted to be independent and believed it would also be better off economically. Meanwhile, both parties that were left (the Czechs and the Swedes) believed the costs of trying to hold things together outweighed the costs of letting their partners go.

While we have a good idea what processes of international integration and international disintegration look like, our sense of why they occur or where they are going is not as clear. Most of the theoretical work which has been done in this area has until recently focused on European experiences since World War II. It is sometimes charged with political preferences and agendas, and it gets heavily used by both supporters and opponents of European integration. Nevertheless, we can identify two basic theoretical approaches which it is important to know: **functionalism** and **neo-functionalism**.[5]

Functionalism has its intellectual origins in the structural-functionalist approach used by sociologists and anthropologists. This suggests that we should study institutions like the family, the legislature, or the state in terms of what they do, asking what parts they play in keeping individuals and societies running. The functions of the family are to nurture its members, for example, particularly the younger ones, and to provide the first level of socialization in the process of transforming them from simply human beings into members of society and citizens.

Functionalism in the study of international relations, however, is used a bit differently, in an argument which is particularly associated with David Mitrany.[6] Functionalists argued that the failure of Liberal Internationalism and the League of Nations system in the 1930s was not, as the realists maintained, that they had asked too much of states and were too idealistic. The problem was that they had not asked enough.[7] States, functionalists argued, should be gradually stripped of their sovereign authority in international relations and especially international economic relations. The production, exchange, and distribution of goods and services should be organized on grounds of technical efficiency and satisfying human needs from which the narrow political concerns of states and nations should be excluded. Also, these activities should no longer be run by governments and politicians, but by managers, technical experts, engineers, and scientists—people who knew how the real world worked and could make it work better. Ordinary people would transfer their loyalties from sovereign states to scientific-technical-administrative authorities as they saw them work better than states at securing economic goals and satisfying human needs.

As so often with international theorists, Mitrany's work was deeply influenced by a particular development—the inability of states to collaborate and be less self-centered in their attempts to find their way out of the Great Depression of the 1930s. And as so often is the case with international theories, functionalism got its big chance because another disaster—World War II and its destructive consequences in Europe—made governments and people there unusually open to the possibility of big changes in the way they did things. The war left Europe devastated, its people traumatized, its economic infrastructure smashed, and its governments discredited.

What the people of Europe needed and as soon as possible, the functionalists pointed out, was food, shelter, heat, and light. To provide all these, coal mining, the iron and steel industries, agriculture, and the railway network had to be restored as quickly and as efficiently as possible. The way to do this was not on a national basis, with each state making its own effort and competing with one another for resources, but on a functional basis which ignored states' national boundaries.

In Western Europe, a movement grew to integrate the coal and steel industries of the German Federal Republic (West Germany), France, Belgium, the Netherlands, and Luxemburg. Normally, it would have met fierce resistance from the existing owners, unions, and those who realized that if their coal and steel industries were integrated, France and Germany would no longer have the basis for independent armaments industries. They would find it much harder to go to war—especially against each other. If they lost that ability, would they still be independent, or even sovereign, states?

Two factors temporarily favored the functionalists' argument, however. First, French and German citizens had seen their states fail the test in the most basic obligation of any state to its people—to provide for their security. Both had just been defeated in a disastrous war. An independent war-making capacity had not done France much good in 1940 and had eventually led Germany into catastrophe in 1945. Second, the US had promised to invest in postwar European reconstruction to restore the confidence which would attract other investors into what still looked like a very risky and difficult project. The US made it clear, however, that there would be no money forthcoming unless the Europeans ceased to argue among themselves and began to cooperate along functionalist lines.

The European Coal and Steel Community (ECSC) was established in 1951 by the Treaty of Paris with Italy joining the original five states. It was based on a **common market**, had an executive for making policy, a judiciary for settling disputes, an assembly for discussing policy, and other administrative bodies. It was confidently expected that the Community would expand into other areas of European policy, and that it would serve as a model of development which would be adopted in other parts of the world. In 1956, the European Economic Community (EEC) and the European Atomic Energy Agency (Euratom) were established by the Treaties of Rome. It seemed as though Mitrany's vision of a world which would shift from organizing economies on sovereign state principles to integrating them on functional necessity principles was coming to pass.

There were three big problems with functionalism, however. The first concerns people's loyalty. Would people transfer their loyalty from their states to the managers and experts of the new transnational agencies established on the functional principle? This depends on the extent to which people's loyalty to political authority is contractually based, or identity based. In the **contract-based loyalty** view, states promise to protect citizens from criminals, foreign invasion, and extreme economic distress. In return, citizens promise to pay taxes, obey the laws, and fight for the state if necessary. The citizen can be loyal to whoever provides the services and, arguably, can transfer that loyalty if a new provider is established or a better deal comes along. In the **identity-based loyalty** view, citizens feel that they belong to the state or the country it represents at a much more emotional level. Being American, Chinese, or Nigerian is a part of who they feel they are. In this view, transferring loyalties is much more difficult and, indeed, impossible for most people. In the European case, as the horrors of war receded and economies recovered (partly thanks to the success of economic integration), the identity-based conception of loyalty seemed to win out over the contractually based one. The Germans remained Germans, for example, and the French remained French in their primary political loyalties.[8] Neither Germans nor French became Europeans in the sense of citizens of the European Community with strong feelings of loyalty towards it.

The second problem for functionalism was with the idea that politics, and especially national politics, could be taken out of the processes by which goods and services are produced and allocated. The trouble with this is that whoever makes the decisions about what gets invested in and produced, and how it gets distributed, has power whether they are experts, governments, or politicians. Experts might be less concerned with the national interests of states, but other political interests besides these might influence their decisions. For example, they might want to distribute resources more fairly to poorer states and regions. Or they might want to allocate them to people who were more likely to be helpful—for example, providing coal first to those who are best able to produce electricity which the provider can use, rather than those who are merely cold. And even if a decision is made purely on technical grounds, it is invariably seen as political by others, particularly those who lose out as a result of it. Functionalism might squeeze the politics of national interests and state-based rivalries out of decisions about how goods and services are produced, exchanged, and allocated, but it could not squeeze all political considerations out of them, and it might inject them with new ones.

Finally, as you may have noticed already, the first great success of functionalism, the ECSC, was established *by* states, not in spite of them as functionalist theory expected. French Foreign Minister Robert Schuman introduced the idea, and the governments of the other European states responded to it. The same was the case for the flood of integration measures which followed this and established what eventually became known as the European Union (EU). It was the governments of European states which made the running in this regard.

This gave rise to the second basic approach to understanding the processes of international integration among international theorists known as neo-functionalism. While neo-functionalism stressed the state-driven character of these processes, however, it was far less clear about why they were occurring and in what direction they were taking Europe and possibly the rest of the world. We can best understand what was going on by looking in more detail at the development of the EEC/EU on which the observations of the neo-functionalists were largely based.

Key terms

common market   A trading system in which the member states are committed to removing all barriers, such as tariffs and quotas, to trade between the members.

contract-based loyalty   A conception of loyalty based on an agreement between governments of states and their citizens by which governments protect and help their citizens in return for which citizens obey and support their governments.

functionalism   A theory of how the sovereignty of states and their power might be eroded by organizing the production, exchange, and distribution of goods and services on grounds of technical efficiency and satisfying human needs.

identity-based loyalty   A conception of loyalty in which citizens obey and support the governments of their states because the citizens feel that being a member of the state is an important part of who they are.

international disintegration   Processes by which the politics, economics, culture, and society of a single state or group of states break into separate parts or simply break down.

international integration   Processes by which the politics, economics, cultures, and societies of separate states merge into one another.

neo-functionalism   An account of how international integration is usually undertaken by states rather than those who want to reduce the power and independence of states.

Key takeaways

- Processes of international integration and international disintegration are always occurring in international relations.
- Processes of international integration seem more prominent than processes of international disintegration and are associated with increasing levels of economic interdependence and globalization.
- The European Union provides the most prominent example of international integration.
- Functionalists see international integration as way of reducing the power of states and replacing them with institutions more focused on efficiency and human need, rather than national interests.
- Neo-functionalists note that more international integration is actually initiated and undertaken by states.

Exercises

1. What reasons can be given for thinking international integration is a good thing?
2. What problems does the functionalist theory of international integration face?
3. Do you see your loyalty to your own country in contract-based or identity-based terms?

11.2	Neo-functionalism and the European Union

Learning objectives

1. Describe the principal institutions of the EU.
2. List the main common policies pursued by the members of the EU.
3. Explain how intergovernmental and federal conceptions of the EU differ.
4. List the difficulties created by the enlargement of the EU and the deepening of its relations.

The European Union is a complex and at times confusing set of processes and institutions. It seems to be continually evolving through a series of treaties which commit its members to pursuing more integration and creating new institutions. At the same time, however, it often seems to be running on the spot, revisiting the same issues over and over again. This is for two reasons. First, the member states and EU officials are very much feeling their way forward in uncharted territory. Think of the EU as a big experiment or a work in progress. Second, the member states often do not agree among themselves about what the EU should be doing or where it should be heading. Indeed, there are often sharp disagreements inside each member state on these issues.[9] At present, the future of the EU looks more uncertain than it has for a long time with the British voting to begin the process of leaving ("Brexit") in 2016, political parties who want to leave becoming stronger in some other member states, and some EU leaders arguing that the pace of integration should be accelerated although disagreeing about the direction in which everyone should move (for a brief history of the EU see "European Union: 50 Years in 5 minutes" at the following link: http://www.youtube.com/watch?v=sO75ZsvMkc8).

The European Union consists of a number of key institutions. The **European Commission** in Brussels, the capital of Belgium, looks like a set of government departments and agencies known as directorates (Figure 11.1). These directorates are organized on functional principles around particular policy areas—for example, agriculture, finance, and justice. However, political realities are reflected in how each member state gets a commissioner in charge of a directorate, and each commissioner is backed by a bureaucracy of civil servants under a director general. Under the direction of its president, the European Commission is responsible for the day-to-day running of the EU and for advising the member states. Unlike most bureaucracies, however, the European Commission also enjoys the formal right of initiative in regard to new EU policies.

The principal target of the Commission's advice is the **Council of the European Union** (formerly the Council of Ministers). The Council mainly meets in Brussels and remains the central decision-making body for EU policy. Like the Commission, the Council also blends functional principles with political realities. The members of the Council are ministers of the member state governments who travel to Belgium to meet to discuss policy. However, the Council has a shifting membership depending on what functional issue is being discussed. Thus, finance ministers attend for financial matters, agriculture ministers attend when farm policy is being considered, and when the issue is judged sufficiently important, the political leaders of each member state—presidents in some and prime ministers in others—will attend.

The Council decides policy by **unanimity** on issues of vital national importance, simple **majority voting** by member state on some issues and, increasingly **qualified majority voting** on others. Qualified majority voting is weighted according to complex formulae to reflect the different population sizes of member states. This makes sure that a coalition of several states with small populations cannot outvote a few states with big populations, but also that two or three states with big populations cannot outvote the rest. On the issues where unanimity operates, taxation for example, all the members have to agree before a proposal is accepted, effectively giving each member state a blocking veto (for information about the Council of the European Union and images of its meetings follow this link http://www.consilium.europa.eu/en/press/audiovisual/).

Decisions of the Council are sometimes forwarded to the legislatures of member states and always to the **European Parliament** which meets in Strasbourg, France, and Brussels. Originally, the Parliament was appointed by the governments of member states and had very little power, primarily that of overseeing legislation and especially delaying acceptance of the EU budget. Since

Figure 11.1 European Union flags before the Berlaymont Building, headquarters of the European Commission in Brussels, Belgium

(Source: Arterra Picture Library/Alamy Stock Photo)

1979, however, it has been directly elected every five years, and the political parties of the member states make alliances in the Parliament with other parties which share their general political outlook. The European Parliament now shares budgetary and legislative power with the Council of the European Union. It also elects the President of the EU Commission, appoints the Commissioners and can force them all to resign (for a lively debate in the European Parliament in 2012 in which British Eurosceptic MEP, Nigel Farage, criticizes the President of the European Commission, José Manuel Barroso, and is criticized in turn, follow this link http://www.youtube.com/watch?v=8_24J5SZ6SA).

The European Union also has the following institutions. The **European Court of Justice**, based in Luxembourg, was originally concerned with interpreting European Union legislation, ruling on its application, and settling disputes which arose as a result. In addition, however, it has developed a role in insuring that the policies and the laws of member states conform to EU legislation which is regarded as superior to their own state legislation. It also hears appeals from firms and individual citizens of member states against the legal decisions of their own states, especially on human rights issues (for a short film, *en français*, but with subtitles, "How It Works: Luxembourg, the European Capital of Justice," follow this link: http://www.youtube.com/watch?v=KIa47M8rSfM).

The European Court of Auditors monitors and audits expenditures undertaken by other EU bodies. The **European Central Bank** (ECB) (see Chapter 10) was established in Frankfurt in 1998. It is charged with maintaining price stability among the currently nineteen out of twenty-eight EU member states which use the euro (called the Eurozone), monitoring the monetary and financial policies of those states and, increasingly, providing assistance in the form of loans to member states facing financial problems. It acts like the central bank of a state in terms of monetary policy (issuing currency, setting interest rates, managing currency reserves, and monitoring exchange rates) but has little direct control of the financial policies (borrowing and spending) of member states. There is a big debate at present about whether monetary and financial policy can be kept separate like this and, if they cannot, whether the ECB should get more control over the financial policies of states in the Eurozone.

Who is the President of Europe?

Henry Kissinger, US Secretary of State 1973–77, is reputed to have asked, "Who do I call if I want to call Europe?" He has since denied ever asking the question but maintains it is a good one. In the event of an international crisis, to get the US's views, you would try to reach Washington DC and the American president, but who would you contact to get the EU's views: Brussels, Berlin, Paris? The question suggests that until it has a clear answer, the EU would not be taken seriously as a powerful international actor.

The EU has tried to answer that question, but its efforts show the problems it faces and have in some ways made things worse. From the mid-1970s, the Council of the European Union (then the Council of Ministers) developed something called the European Presidency or Presidency of the

Council of the European Union. Each member state chaired the Council's meetings for a six-month period and hosted the last one in their own national capital. A six-month presidency with hardly any staff, especially when held by one of the smaller member states, did not produce an impressive world leader, however, even when the staff of the previous, current, and next presidents began to work together to provide some continuity. To be fair, the Presidency of the European Council, as it began to be called was never really intended to play such a part, even though many people, especially in the media, expected it to try.

To complicate matters, there were already two other presidents. There was the President of the European Commission elected by the European Parliament. This president was, in a sense, just the head of the EU civil service. Several very active presidents, however, parlayed the Commission's right of legislative initiative into a powerful role in forcing the pace of European integration. In the 1980s it looked at times as if there were two European presidencies competing with each other for influence and often with quite different visions of what the EU ought to be. And there was the President of the European Parliament, a minor position to begin with, but one which grew in importance as the Parliament itself became more powerful on appointments, budget, and legislation.

In 2009, the problem of getting Europe to speak with a single voice was addressed by establishing a European Council. This was composed of all the government leaders of member states, plus the President of the Commission, who together would elect a President of the European Council for a two-and-a-half-year term if approved by the European Parliament. This President was intended to be the external voice of the EU. At the same time, the Office of High Representative of the Union for Foreign Affairs and Security Policy was also created. However, the other presidents were not scrapped. In other words, no answer to Henry Kissinger's question has yet been found.

For Eurosceptics like Mr. Farage in the video link above, this is precisely the sort of mess you get when you leave politicians and bureaucrats in charge. They simply create more jobs to serve themselves without regard for cost, efficiency, or effectiveness. To a degree, the proliferation of presidents does reflect turf wars and struggles for influence. However, it also reflects what a complex organization the EU really is. It cannot simply bulldoze all its members into line around a single voice or viewpoint. Nor, in the view of many of its members with a keen sense of European history and its wars, should it even be trying to do so.

The European Union pursues a number of **common policies**. The overarching purpose of many of these policies is to create a single economic, social, and political space within the EU. Thus in economic terms, producers of goods and services in one member state should have access to the markets and resources of other member states on the same terms as home producers. French trucks and locomotives, for example, should be sold on the German market on the same terms as German ones, while French purchasers should not be able to favor French trucks and locomotives over German ones simply because they are made in France and support French jobs. In social terms, individuals from one member state should be able to live in another member state on the same terms as the locals. For example, a German should be able to work, vote, and have access to health care, education, and unemployment benefits in France on the same terms as a French person.

Other common policies are designed to secure the benefits of increased cooperation like those delivered by the integrated coal and steel industries. For example, the operating procedures of the legal systems, law enforcement agencies, and educational institutions of member states are increasingly harmonized with one another. New legal statutes are written up to be consistent with one another. Police forces cooperate in the sharing of information and the conduct of cross-border operations against drug smugglers and terrorists. And eventually it is intended that a high school diploma, bachelor's degree, and professional qualifications in, for example, law, medicine, or engineering obtained in one member state will be recognized in all of them.

Other common policies are designed to advance specific preferences and principles. For example, the EU uses some of the tax revenue collected for it by member states as a result of the customs union around them all, to advance infrastructure projects or job-training schemes in economically disadvantaged areas. It is not unusual to see big signs with the EU flag on them near new bridges and highways, or restored buildings and monuments declaring that they were made possible with funds from the EU. The Common Agricultural Policy (CAP) attempts to maintain a secure food supply and family farms by a controversial, but now much reduced, system of price supports. The Common Fisheries Policy allows all members to fish in each other's waters, but in a regulated way which maintains fish stocks. And, of course, there is a common monetary policy which eventually resulted in the euro in 2002, a common currency justified on grounds of efficiency, designed as a barrier against inflation, and promoted as a way of creating a common European identity.

All of these policies can be presented as reasonable measures undertaken on apolitical, functional grounds. Yet all of them are capable of generating political controversy. Some of this controversy is present in ordinary independent states. The beneficiaries of farm price supports, for example, by which farmers and agribusiness get guaranteed prices for what they grow and produce, will always argue with those who have to pay higher prices for food as a result. The controversy is sharpened, however, when the split falls along the national lines of member states, for example, when British taxpayers believe they are subsidizing French and German farmers, or the underdeveloped Irish fishing industry sees large, well-organized Spanish and Portuguese trawling fleets over-fishing Irish waters.

The controversies are deepest, although not always most noticeable, when not every member state participates in a common policy, or a common policy struggles to develop. We have already considered arguments surrounding the euro (see Chapter 10). Only 19 of the 28 member states are actually in the Eurozone. Most of those outside it want to join as soon as possible and are committed to do so, but Britain, Denmark, and Sweden have not joined for a variety of reasons ranging from national economic interests to popular fears that the euro threatens their national sovereignty.

The most obvious area in which a common policy has struggled to develop is in foreign and defense policy. After an early attempt by France to create a European army was voted down by its own legislators, defense policy was deliberately left to the member states all of which at that time were members of NATO. It was agreed that the European Community was intended to be primarily an economic and political organization. Nevertheless, the attempt to create a Common Foreign and Security Policy (CFSP) never completely disappeared. The French, and to a lesser extent the Germans, saw it as the only way that Europe could exercise global influence. In addition, the French and the British saw it as a way of diluting American influence in Europe, a development to which the French were attracted and which the British opposed.

The French and Germans have experimented with joint military formations. There have been plans for a European intervention force (Eurocorps) of 50,000 troops.[10] The EU frequently presents itself as a single diplomatic actor speaking with one voice, especially at the UN, and it has developed an External Action Service (in addition to the system of diplomatic representation the Commission already has). On the whole, however, concrete results have lagged far behind the rhetoric of European foreign and security cooperation. The French, for example, one of its strongest enthusiasts, say "hands off" when anyone suggests a European nuclear force superseding their own nuclear *force de dissuasion*.

To understand why this is so, it is necessary to look at some of the arguments about what the EU is supposed to be, where it is supposed to be going, and how it is supposed to get there. Keep in mind two processes which are captured by Tables 11.1 and 11.2. The first process concerns the expansion of the European Union from the original six members in 1957 to 28 in 2013 with the promise of more to come, although one, Britain, looks like leaving following its referendum on membership in 2016. The second process concerns what is sometimes known as "deepening" institutional cooperation or, in other words, increasing the powers of the EU institutions relative to the power of the individual member states.

Membership of the EU is, in principle, open to all the states of Europe provided they meet certain political, economic, and legal standards known as the

Table 11.1 Enlargement of the EC/EU (in addition to original members: France, Germany, Italy, Belgium, The Netherlands, and Luxembourg)

Date of Enlargement	States joining on that date
1973	Britain, Ireland, Denmark
1981	Greece
1986	Spain, Portugal
1995	Sweden, Finland, Austria
2004	Latvia, Lithuania, Estonia, Poland, Hungary, Czech Republic, Slovakia, Slovenia, Malta, Cyprus
2007	Romania, Bulgaria
2013	Croatia

Note: Turkey, Serbia, Iceland, Montenegro, and Macedonia are official candidates, and there are several other potential candidates. The application is a long and arduous process. Turkey, although an exceptional case, first applied in 1987.

Table 11.2 Major treaties of the EEC, EC, and EU

Treaty Name	Date Signed	Details
Rome Treaties	1957	Established a customs union and committed members to the creation of a common market and establishing other common policies
Merger Treaty	1965	Merged the ECSC, EAEA (Euratom) and EEC under the Commission and Council of the EEC
European Council	1975	Established regular two or three days meetings between the heads of member governments initially three times a year, but now between four and six meetings
Solemn Declaration	1983	Confirmed members' commitment to a "common destiny," "European identity," and progress toward "an ever closer union" among peoples and member states of the EC
Schengen Agreement	1985	Reduced cross-border checks originally between five member states. Superseded by Schengen Convention in 1999 which committed all but two members (Britain and Ireland) to open borders and a common visa policy
Single European Act	1986	Amended the Treaty of Rome to commit members to a common market by 1992, established European Political Cooperation as a process for member states to reach common positions on international issues, extended majority voting in the European Council of Ministers on some issues, and gave the European Parliament more influence on new policies
Maastricht Treaty	1992	Established the European Union with three "pillars," the EC, the Common Foreign and Security Policy, and Justice and Home Affairs, and committed members to a monetary system and eventual single currency
Amsterdam Treaty	1997	Strengthened the role of the European Parliament and the EU's role in regard to making laws regarding individual rights and policing policies
Nice Treaty	2001	Reformed the European Commission, the European Parliament and voting procedures in the Council of the European Union in anticipation of a major enlargement of the EU membership
Constitutional Treaty	2004	Replaced original treaties between member states with a constitution, but abandoned when the French and Dutch electorates voted against it
Lisbon Treaty	2009	Introduced more qualified majority voting in the Council of the European Union, further strengthened the powers of the European Parliament, created a new President of the European Council and High Representative of the Union for Foreign Affairs and Security Policy and made the EU's Charter of Fundamental Rights legally binding in member states

Source: This table is based on information on the treaties provided at the *europa.eu* website of the European Union at https://europa.eu/european-union/law/treaties_en.

Copenhagen criteria. States that wish to join the EU need to be democracies with free market economies and respect for the rule of law. While committed to enlargement, however, members of the EU have had to deal with the problem of effectiveness, in terms of getting things done. The more states are allowed into the

EU, the bigger the collective action problem of getting them all to agree to doing anything becomes. A "one state one vote" system becomes more vulnerable to one state objecting. On the other hand, a simple majority system becomes more vulnerable to alliances of small states outvoting a few big ones. As the list of treaties (Table 11.2) suggests, therefore, considerable changes have been made to how the EU makes decisions through the systems of qualified majority voting.

In addition to problems of effectiveness, more EU members also means less homogeneity. Can states with very different histories, cultures, and levels of development integrate with one another successfully? The EU's position is that they can once they satisfy the Copenhagen criteria. Thus the formerly communist states of Eastern Europe have all had to undergo an extended period of extensive reforms to harmonize their domestic policies and practices with those of the EU. Some, like Latvia, Lithuania, and Estonia, accomplished this fairly quickly. Others, Croatia and Bosnia Herzogovina (not yet a member), for example, have found becoming members much harder. And still others, like Ukraine and Serbia, have had fierce internal arguments about whether they want to make the necessary reforms. Indeed, in 2014 these arguments became so heated in Ukraine that a government was overthrown and the population badly divided between those who saw their future in the EU, those who wished to maintain ties with Russia, and those who wanted to have few ties with either (see Chapter 2). A more difficult problem has been posed by Turkey. While it has spent many years undergoing reforms, Turkey still has not been able to join the EU. Opponents argue that it is not actually in Europe (only a small, but important, part of it is). They also point to its political difficulties—a long-running rebellion on the part of Turkey's Kurdish minority, for example, the failed military coup in 2016, and the increasingly dictatorial tendencies of the Turkish government. Supporters suggest with some justification that the real objection is that Turkey is a Muslim country with many poor people who would enjoy open access to the rest of the EU once it became a member. More embarrassingly, it is now occasionally asked whether less developed states like Greece, Cyprus, and Malta, and possibly even Spain and Portugal, should have been let in in the first place.

The problems with effectiveness and homogeneity which EU enlargement highlights are also prominent in the second process, the commitment of the member states to deepening their relations in what the Solemn Declaration of 1983 called "an ever closer union" (see Table 11.2). As the treaties and agreements listed here suggest, the EU is supposed to be evolving and developing and, as they also suggest, the process of growth has been difficult, controversial, and not always successful.

One vision of where the EU is heading is to see it as an **intergovernmental organization** where member states collaborate ever more closely when they can agree to do so, but go their separate ways when they judge this to be in their national interests. Another, more ambitious, vision—**federalism**—sees the EU growing into a United States of Europe—something like the United States of America—through the development of **supranational institutions** which exercise more and more authority over the member states. Power, authority, and legitimacy have been steadily shifting from the member states to the EU, to new regional authorities and to local ones too.

The arguments about what is actually happening are complicated. They are made even more complicated by three factors. First, member states do not line up clearly on one side or the other. Britain, for example, is seen as a Eurosceptic state, while Germany and France are both regarded as strong supporters of the *acquis communautaire*, the EU principles which have already been established. Nevertheless, there are arguments inside all three states between people who want more EU integration, those who say there has been enough already, and those who want less.

Second, arguments about the EU often track mainstream political and economic arguments, which people elsewhere would quickly recognize, about the role of government intervention, taxation, and the regulation of private enterprise. In a sense, the EU is just another political arena in which the international dimension adds more heat to the arguments. Sometimes, these arguments look like the ones between liberals and conservatives inside a state, but it can be more complicated than that with members of the same political party arguing with one another about what should be happening to the EU.

Third, the term federalist is more often used by opponents of the EU who maintain that the EU's supporters have a hidden agenda to get rid of Europe's nation states, while supporters of the EU accuse their opponents of having hidden nationalist, socialist, or American-style neo-liberal capitalist agendas. In practice, nearly everyone involved in the arguments accepts some measure of intergovernmentalism, some measure of supranationalism, and some measure of **subsidiarity** (letting issues be handled at the lowest level possible). What they disagree on is the right balance between the three. That said, the EU did appear to reach a tipping point in the aftermath of the global financial crisis that began in 2008. As the list of treaties shows, from the 1980s onwards a sustained effort was made to strengthen the EU's institutions at the expense of its member states. One consequence of this was the emergence of the so-called "democratic deficit."

The political elites of most member states generally supported the shift towards more integration and stronger EU institutions, although they might resist it in specific areas like taxation, foreign policies, and defense policies. Many ordinary people, however, were not so enthusiastic, often seeing the EU as a distant, interfering body which acted as if "it knew better." One consequence was a series of embarrassing rejections of some the EU treaties when they had to be voted on by electorates in France, the Netherlands, and Ireland. On two occasions, the Irish government simply held another referendum. Supporters of the EU argued it was wrong that a very small percentage of the EU's population could hold up progress on such vital and important issues for the rest. Opponents of the EU accused it of forcing the Irish to keep voting until they "got it right," yet more evidence, to their mind, of the EU elites' "we know better" undemocratic attitude. There is a possibility of a second referendum in Britain too on the terms it manages to negotiate for its departure from the EU. Those who wished to remain in the EU argued that their opponents had misled the British public on the dangers of leaving the EU and that the vote had been only advisory and only narrowly in favor. Those who wished Britain to leave presented this call for a second referendum as evidence that the EU is undemocratic and does not care what the citizens of its member states think.

This "democratic deficit" left the EU in a weak position when it came to dealing with the economic crisis discussed in Chapter 10. Some people in the Mediterranean member states like Greece, Cyprus, Italy, and Spain started to see the EU as an instrument of German policy and its northern European supporters, imposing harsh economic austerity on them to pay for the mistakes of the banks. People in Germany, Finland, and the Netherlands started to see the EU as a conduit transferring the wealth created by their hard work to the "lazy southerners" who enjoyed an EU living standard but were not prepared to work for it. Both views were caricatures.

Underneath these populist politics, however, a real choice appeared to be emerging. Either the EU pressed on with further integration, especially with supranational regulation of the monetary and finance policies of member states by the European Central Bank to prevent these problems re-occurring, or some states would have to exit the Eurozone and re-establish independent currencies. Most experts have agreed that the EU will have to move in the direction of more integration or less integration, and that it cannot stand still. Beyond securing some of the weakest banks and re-negotiating some of the biggest debts of member states, however, not much has happened, and the future looks uncertain for the time being, especially as a consequence of "Brexit." Since the British referendum, pro-EU parties have won elections in the Netherlands and France, but anti-EU parties have made electoral gains.

Further integration looks politically impossible, at least for now. This may change when/if Britain finally leaves. France and Germany say they support further integration, for example, but cannot agree on what functional principles it would be based. France wants a system in which the rich and successful provide assistance to the poor and unsuccessful—a real community operating in the way, for example, the federal governments of the US and Canada help their poorer states and provinces respectively. Germany, in contrast, wants strong rules which prevent individual states from taking on debts they cannot afford and makes them responsible for the difficulties they get into. Members like Greece, Italy, and Spain look enviously at how non-Eurozone EU members like Britain, Sweden, and Denmark can ease their problems by letting their currencies depreciate (see Chapter 10). However, they know that actually pulling out of the Eurozone would be a terrible blow to the idea of working for "an ever closer union."

The EU and most of its member governments are probably waiting for a global economic recovery which will ease these problems and let them carry on without having to make the tough choice between more or less integration. This is still probably a shrewd position reflecting the neo-functionalist character of the EU as a state-driven and state-limited project. Waiting, like the Dickens character, Mr. Micawber, for "something to turn up," however, looks less shrewd at the time of writing (2017) than it did in previous years. A global economic recovery is developing, but one which does not look strong enough to ease economic stagnation and unemployment in many of the EU member states.

Key terms

common policies Policies adopted by all EU member states, although members may negotiate derogations which let part or all of a common policy not apply to them for a period of time.

Council of the European Union Formerly the Council of Ministers (not to be confused with the European Council or the Council of Europe), the executive decision-making body of the EU comprised of EU member state government ministers relevant to the issue being acted on.

European Central Bank Bank of the EU with responsibilities for issuing the Euro, setting interest rates in the Eurozone (EU member states which use the Euro), and monitoring spending and borrowing policies throughout the EU.

European Commission The bureaucracy of the EU, although a bureaucracy with the important right of legislative initiative.

European Court of Justice The court of the European law presiding over the constitutionality, application, and enforcement of Community Law, and the compliance of EU member state policy making and legal systems with Community Law.

European Parliament The legislature of the EU with powers over budget, legislation, and appointments which have increased over time.

federalism A conception when applied to the EU which presents it as a system in which power is at least shared between the EU institutions and the EU member states, and in which power is shifting from the EU member states to the EU institutions possibly to create a United States of Europe.

intergovernmental organization A conception when applied to the EU which presents it as a system which makes it easier for governments to cooperate with each other and coordinate their policies when they agree it is in all their interests.

majority voting Procedure by which a measure is adopted if more EU member states vote for it than against or abstain.

qualified majority voting Procedure by which a measure is adopted if supported by a specified number of EU member states with a specified percentage of the EU's total population. More issues are now decided by this process than in the past.

subsidiarity An EU principle by which decisions ought to be taken at the lowest or most local level possible.

supranational institution An EU institution above EU member state institutions with authority over them in the way, for example, the EU legal system is said by EU member states to have authority over their own legal systems.

unanimity Procedure by which all EU member states have to agree before a measure can be adopted. Fewer issues are now decided by this process than in the past.

Key takeaways

■ The European Union is an example of the state-led integration envisaged by neo-functionalism.

■ The institutions of the European Union look like the institutions of a sovereign state government and have considerable powers over member states.

■ The membership of the EU has greatly expanded, and relations between EU member states have "deepened" (become more integrated).

■ EU member states retain considerable powers over their own affairs, and the larger member states of the EU have considerable influence over the operations of the EU.

■ The EU can be viewed as both an emerging new federal super state and as an exercise in intergovernmental collaboration. Either way, it faces great economic and political challenges.

Exercises

1. Which EU institutions best reflect the federalist view of the EU, and which best reflect the intergovernmental view?

2. What are the arguments for and against simple majority voting (one state, one vote) in the EU?

3. If you were a citizen of a small EU state like Ireland or Portugal, would you be more likely to be a Europhile (pro-EU) or a Eurosceptic (suspicious of the EU)?

11.3 Integration and disintegration beyond the EU

Learning objectives

1. Describe the ways in which information technology might contribute to integration.

2. Describe the ways in which information technology might contribute to disintegration.

3. Explain how pluralist and solidarist views of integration differ.

The EU experience dominates discussions of integration. It does so for several reasons. First, it is the most developed example of its kind. As already noted, there are other trading and economic associations—for example, Mercosur and the Andean Community (Andean Pact) in South America, the Association of South East Asian Nations (ASEAN), and the Caribbean Community and Common Market (CARICOM). None of them have expanded as far or developed as deeply as the EU, however.

Second, Europe is still one of the richest and most powerful regions of the world. If the EU developed into a United States of Europe, it would, by several measures, be the largest, strongest, superpower, outstripping the US in population and China in GNP. What happens in and to Europe affects everyone else.

Third, Europe gave the rest of the world—or thrust upon it—the Westphalian system of sovereign, territorial states. Whether as a new superpower, therefore, or as a complex and ambiguous system of overlapping authorities and jurisdictions, perhaps Europe is once again serving as a pathfinder to the future for all of us in an era of uncertainty.

The EU integration story, however, is a story about what is happening to states. Are they coming together, merging and disappearing and, if so, how are they doing it? Examining integration outside the European context gives us a different picture, especially when we link it to the big changes associated with the communication and information revolutions, particularly the rise of the internet and other high-speed communication networks.

In the past, information was scarce, expensive, and travelled slowly. If knowledge was power, then the political structure of social organizations like states tended to reflect this. Since information was expensive and scarce, it was hoarded by the few who were rich or powerful enough to acquire it. The operations of states' diplomatic and intelligence services were directed at acquiring and controlling information in such a way as to enable firm boundaries to be maintained between different groups of people who knew relatively little of each other. What then are the consequences of information becoming plentiful and cheap?

One consequence in international finance, which we have already considered (see Chapter 10), is the emergence of integrated capital markets operating 24 hours a day. Bad economic news in one part of the globe—disappointing data about slowing industrial production in China, for example, travels almost instantaneously to another part causing stock markets to slide in Singapore and London, bond spreads to increase in Rome and Madrid, and the dollar to gain value against the yen and the euro on US currency markets. In so doing, it also affects the financial fortunes of all the individuals and organizations whose savings are invested in stocks and bonds.

Another consequence on a regional scale is that in East Africa, a micro-banking system has emerged within the cellular phone network which, because it is relatively cheap, East African states and people have been able to afford. The phone network not only communicates transactions, it has become a place where accounts are established, while deposits and withdrawals are made.[11] Meanwhile you and I can buy clothes, download music, place bets, and study for a college degree all by transactions on the Internet.

It is easy to see who has lost control as a result of these integrated markets—for example, the central banks of sovereign states, the local producers of goods and services, retail malls, or shopping centers, and the enforcers of local rules about gambling. It is less easy to see who, if anyone, has gained control. There is no new "they" in charge, no matter what radical right wing and left wing groups may want to say about the very real power and influence of groups like the **Trilateral Commission**, Bilderberg meetings, and private holders of vast amounts of capital, plus big new online retail companies like Amazon. And while local producers of goods and services may see their markets raided from the other side of the world, they are, in principle, just as free to raid the markets of their rivals right back. In some industries at least, the **collapse of distance** seems to have occurred and all markets seem to have become more like local markets.

The integrated capital markets operating on a 24-hour cycle are matched by global news networks operating on a 24-hour news cycle. The **"CNN effect"** where George Bush senior and Saddam Hussein appeared to be watching each other's moves as reported in real time by a private television news service was first noted in 1990.[12] Not only could governments no longer keep secrets or hide bombings and massacres from the media, they seemed to need the media as a source of information and way of communicating with their counterparts. After the revelations in 2012 and 2013 of Private Bradley/Chelsea Manning and Edward Snowden of masses of information about US military and diplomatic actions it may be possible to speak of a WikiLeaks effect.

More impressively, even the big media corporations seemed to lose control of the news cycle as the Internet, camera phones, and **social media** groups allowed small groups of people and individuals not only to take over reporting in difficult and dangerous spots, but also to blur reporting the news with making the news by organizing and covering demonstrations and even military operations. The new media played a vital role in organizing and reporting on demonstrations after the Iranian elections in 2009 with the support of sympathetic governments and telecommunications companies abroad.

Social media has played a similar role in organizing and reporting on protests connected with the Arab Spring or Awakening, especially in Egypt during the campaign to oust President Mubarak in 2012. And a principal source of information on the civil war in Syria—the Syrian Observatory for Human Rights—is a one-man operation run from a suburban house in Coventry, England. All you need, it seems, is a cell phone and a lot of contacts on the ground willing to call you, and a reputation for honest and fair reporting. An example of the influence of social media is the You Tube clip showing the death of Neda Agha-Soltan during protests following the Iranian election 2009. It came to symbolize the regime's brutality and the courage of the protestors, becoming a rallying point for opponents of the Iranian government. The protests and the publicizing of Agha-Soltan's death did not reverse the outcome of the election but, arguably, they contributed to a process of steady pressure which has caused the Iranian regime to soften some of its positions (note: some may find the images in this link disturbing http://www.youtube.com/verify_controversy?next_url=/watch%3Fv%3D76W-0GVjNEc).

Notice how in both cases integration at one level or in one dimension—the globally integrated capital markets and the globally integrated media markets—produces disintegration at another level. State-based capital markets merge into a market on a global scale with the prospect that they and the state-based economies which they finance may one day effectively disappear. State-based news media and information systems merge into a global media network with the prospect that the state-based political orders which they help to reproduce may one day effectively disappear.

Solidarists (see Chapter 3) see processes of integration and disintegration moving us away from a world divided into lots of different human communities and toward a single global economy, global polity, and global civil society. Parts of the world move fairly smoothly in this direction either because they do well out of the changes which this sort of integration is bringing about, or because it is taking place on their terms. People who work for big competitive corporations, for example, and people who make a living servicing and supplying them, can face this sort of future fairly calmly. It threatens neither their livelihood nor their sense of who they are. Others, however, are dragged kicking and screaming toward a future in which both their livelihoods and their identities have no place—people in labor-intensive industries in high wage developed states, for example, or those whose identity, status, and power depends on traditional tribal and religious structures.

To be sure, solidarists argue over who these integrative trends favor in a general sense. Do the social media-assisted and amplified protests in the Iranian capital of Teheran and the Egyptian capital of Cairo demonstrate that the age of dictators and powerful governments ruling over their peoples is coming to an end, because ordinary people are empowered by the leveling and opening influences of the Internet, cell phones, and smart devices all over the world? And what are we to think when social media is used by the unscrupulous and fanatic to mobilize alienated and unhappy people to do terrible things in the name of spreading Islam or saving the white race? Or do the patterns of integration we are witnessing still favor the big battalions—states elites, global financial institutions, and transnational corporations—all collaborating and integrating their activities in the interests of maintaining a global economy out of which they do well at the expense of the rest? However they line up on the answers to these questions, solidarists agree that the game of global politics is shifting in terms of the players and the levels they play on. In this world, nationalist dictators, socialist state planners, religious ayatollahs, protectionist trade unionists, and old-fashioned patriots are the deadenders, holdouts from a previous era who sooner or later are going to be swept aside.[13]

Pluralists (see Chapter 3), in contrast, would disagree with this solidarist concept of new integrated global politics and for the following reasons. First, they would say it underestimates how deeply rooted people's sense of their collective, but separate identities actually is. The political map may change over time. New states and groupings of states have come into existence to be sure. Nevertheless, old identities which have formed over centuries lie just beneath the surface. We see this in the Americas and Africa, where supposedly long-vanished pre-European societies keep exerting their influence on the way many peoples think about themselves and their relations with other groups of people.

We have also seen it in the EU in periods of stress, with Greeks feeling less that they and the Germans are Europeans together and remembering rather World War II and the German occupation. Even in happier times, however, outsiders underestimate how Poles, for example, think of their membership of the EU not in terms of leaving their history behind them, but in terms of what it does for their tricky position as a Catholic nation wedged between the Protestant Germans on one side and Orthodox Russians and other Slavs on the other. And even if some particular identities change over time, the pluralists argue, the habit of thinking in terms of separate identities itself has deep historic and prehistoric origins which are not easily uprooted.

Secondly, pluralists note, the patterns of integration which attract our attention today do not erode all separate identities in favor of a single global, human, cosmopolitan one. They erode some identities to be sure, but they produce many new ones too. If the EU succeeds, pluralists note that it is more likely to be as bloc or super state with its own way of seeing things and its own interests. It is not likely to be as one of the building blocks in a new globally integrated political and economic system. Secretary of State Hillary Clinton probably assumed that in pursuing what the State Department called "digital diplomacy," keeping Egyptians connected with each other and the rest of the world by protecting their links to the Internet and cellular networks during the Arab Awakening in 2011, she was creating allies for political democracy and open markets.[14] However, she was also helping to sustain and strengthen groups uninterested in either of these principles as she understood them. When people talk to each other, they develop their own collective identities and priorities based around what matters to them, for example, concerns about faith, race, generational preoccupations, and gendered priorities.

Thirdly, pluralists note, processes of integration like those outlined, do not simply erode established centers of power like sovereign, territorial states. It has long been assumed, for example, that once the Chinese people had the sort of easy and affordable access to large amounts of information provided by the Internet and cell phones, the Chinese Communist Party would no longer be able to exert tight control over them. It would have to reform or disappear in much the same way the eastern European communist parties did once their people had large-scale access to information from the West. This may still be the case eventually. What we see at the present, however, is that access to this sort of information does not automatically and uniformly generate popular hostility to Chinese Communist Party rule. What we also see is that the information revolution operates in more than one direction. It has provided old power centers like state security and intelligence agencies with access to more information about their citizens' lives than was dreamed possible until fairly recently. It has also provided them with the new means of "cyber warfare" with which to conduct old rivalries, with states stealing each other's national security and, increasingly, commercial secrets, for example, making public embarrassing private communication by politicians, and disrupting the operations of any state or organization which relies on information technology to perform key functions.[15]

Key terms

CNN effect   An idea based on the novel impact that CNN 24-hour real time news coverage was said to have on international relations in the 1990s. The speed and depth of news coverage made possible by developments in information technology, it was suggested, had transformed the media from a source of reports on the news to an active participant in making the news.

collapse of distance   An idea associated with Walter Benjamin and Paul Virilio. It is commonly taken to suggest that developments in the technologies of communication and information transfer decrease the importance of the effects which distance has on human relations.

social media Internet-based communication networks and sites such as weblogs, forums, wikis, and podcasts which permit various forms of direct and real time communications and exchanges of ideas for various purposes between multiple parties who may or may not come to regard themselves as groups or communities.

Trilateral Commission A non-partisan, non-governmental think tank or discussion group of influential people from Japan, Europe, and North America established in 1973 to consider and advise on major economic and political issues. Along with the Bilderberg Group and the World Economic Forum, it is often criticized by nationalist groups on the right and anti-capitalist groups on the left for exerting undue influence on the policies of democratically elected governments.

Key takeaways

■ Processes of integration are not restricted to the European Union; they occur in other parts of the world at the global, regional, and local levels.

■ Processes of integration today appear to be generated by developments in the technologies of information generation, distribution, and exchange.

■ Solidarists emphasize how contemporary processes of integration erode the independence of existing sovereign states and reorganize politics, economics, and social life into transnational interactions on a global scale.

■ Pluralists emphasize how processes of integration and disintegration erode the independence of some existing communities while strengthening the independence of other existing communities and creating new ones.

Exercises

1. How do 24-hour global capital markets influence the economic policies of states?

2. How do solidarists say the "CNN effect" influences the relations of states with one another?

3. How do pluralists say social networking may have influenced political protestors during the Arab Spring or Awakening?

4. Have you ever participated in international relations by social networking?

11.4 The future of integration and disintegration in an era of uncertainty

How important the new sorts of actors and new forms of action made possible by integrated information networks may become is uncertain. The demonstrators in Cairo's Tahrir Square played a vital role in bringing down President Mubarak, but the Egyptian state and its old elites remain in place for now. Likewise, how well old-established actors like states will be able to exploit these networks for old ends like controlling their people or competing with rival states is by no means clear. The Chinese Communist Party seems at one moment supremely confident in the way it acts, yet at another absolutely terrified that the smallest challenge from uncontrolled media sources will threaten the Party's power unless it is crushed.

However, all these developments are not easily squared with any simple assumptions about how the technologies of integration will lead to any single conception of a globalized future. They might produce competing versions of such a future or they might result in a measure of disintegration as new groups with new identities pull back from or resist the future which appears to be on offer. The popularity of Donald Trump and Bernie Sanders in the US presidential nomination process, the results of the British referendum on EU membership, and the rise of nationalist political movements in other parts of Western Europe, can all be presented as "push backs" in response to the pressures of living in an increasingly integrated and globalizing world. And, as pluralists note, even the most universal claims about where the world is heading in terms of integration and globalization are always based on the particular views of some people at a particular time and a particular place about what is important. Truths about life, liberty, and the pursuit of happiness which seem self-evident and universally applicable to most, but not all, Americans, for example, may seem like very American priorities—or covers for them—to many people elsewhere. Claims about the inevitability and desirability of the expansion of the Dar es Salaam (or Abode of Peace), in which everyone lives according to the teachings of Islam, until it covers all the world remain unattractive to non-Muslims, and even most Muslims accept these claims as a pious and weakly held aspiration.

However, two things are clear. First, we seem to be moving into a world in which the diplomacy of negotiating the interests of actors like states is being hugely complicated by the need to negotiate the identity of states and others. What does it mean, for example, to be an American, a European, a Citizen of the Global South or, for that matter, a man, a woman or trans? These are questions to which the answers are no longer as settled as they once were. Second, there may be one claim which does have universal validity, whether people accept it or not. It is the claim that the ways in which most of us live are not environmentally sustainable. If this is true and we do not change our ways, then all our arguments about politics, economics, societies, states, and international relations will not matter. We will be too busy trying to survive an environmental and human catastrophe. It is this claim we examine in the next chapter.

Recommended reading

John Pinder and Simon Usherwood, *The European Union: A Very Short Introduction*, Oxford, 2007.

Official Website of the European Union, http://europa.eu/

Christopher Hill and Michael Smith (eds.), *International Relations and the European Union (New European Union)*, Oxford, 2011.

Borzel Tanja (ed.), *The Disparity of European Integration: Revisiting Neofunctionalism in Honour of Ernst B. Haas (Journal of European Public Policy Special Issues as Books)*, London, 2006.

Philip Seib, *The Al Jazeera Effect: How the New Global Media are Reshaping World Politics*, Lincoln, 2008.

Eric Schmidt and Jared Cohen, *The New Digital Age: Reshaping the Future of People, Nations and Business* (Kindle Edition), New York, 2013.

Eric Helleiner, Stefano Pagliari, and Hubert Zimmermann, *Global Finance in Crisis: The Politics of International Regulatory Change*, London, 2010.

Ayse Everensel, *International Finance for Dummies*, Hoboken, 2013.

Richard J. Barnet and Ronald E. Muller, *Global Reach: The Power of the Multinational Corporations*, New York, 1976.

Notes

1 Mark Leonard, *Why Europe Will Run the 21st Century*, London, 2011.
2 Julie-Anne Boudreau and Raul Hinojosa-Ojeda (eds.), *The Role of the New NAFTA Institutions: Regional Economic Integration (Conference Proceedings)*, United States Department of Labor, June 19–20, 1998 at http://www.dol.gov/ilab/media/reports/nao/ucla.htm
3 Vojtech Mastny and Malcolm Byrne (eds.) *A Cardboard Castle? An Inside History of the Warsaw Pact, 1955-1991*, Budapest, 2006.
4 Peter Duignan, *NATO: Its Past, Present and Future*, Stanford, 2000.
5 Charles Pentland, *International Theory and European Integration*, London, 1973.
6 David Mitrany, *A Working Peace System*, Oxford, 1944.
7 Chris Brown and Kirsten Ainley, *Understanding International Relations* (4th edition), Basingstoke, 2009.
8 Anthony D. Smith, *National Identity*, Reno, 1993.
9 Paul Taylor, *The European Union in the 1990s*, Oxford, 1996.
10 Jolyon Howorth, *Security and Defence Policy in the European Union*, Basingstoke, 2007.
11 World Bank, *Information and Communications for Development 2012: Maximizing Mobile*, Washington, 2012.
12 Piers Robinson, *The CNN Effect: The Myth of News Media, Foreign Policy and Intervention*, Abingdon, 2002.
13 Vice President Cheney used the term "deadender" in reference to Saddam Hussein before the war which removed him, suggesting that dictators like Saddam belonged to a previous era and had no future. Cheney's own close relations with the oil industry might qualify him as a member of the global elite produced by patterns of integration, while his unilateral, nationalistic approach to foreign and defense policy would make him a "deadender" in these terms.
14 Alec Ross, "Digital Diplomacy and US Foreign Policy," in Paul Sharp and Geoffrey Wiseman, *American Diplomacy*, Leiden, 2012.
15 See "China and Cyber War," *The New York Times*, May 7, 2013 at http://www.nytimes.com/2013/05/08/opinion/china-and-cyberwar.html?_r=0

12 Natural resources, population, and the environment

Preamble

Some issues threaten to make everything else examined so far unimportant or even irrelevant. When the fate of the planet is at stake, arguing about who is rich, powerful, or secure in the world and the best ways to avoid poverty, weakness, and vulnerability may seem like arguing over deck chair arrangements on the Titanic. We also shift away from thinking about international relations in conventional political and economic terms. Instead of asking how we solve problems and gain advantages with the sort of politics and economics we have available to us, we ask how do people change their ways of doing politics and economics so that they can address the sorts of problems the whole world faces in common. And in examining these problems, we rely less on the wisdom of the humanities, the arguments of the social theorists, and the research of the social scientists. Instead, we have to look at what a majority, but not all, of the world's natural scientists and technical experts are telling us about what is actually happening to the planet, why it is happening, and what needs to be done to avoid a series of catastrophes. It is as if the functionalist perspective on European integration outlined in Chapter 11 is finally triumphing out of necessity on the environment at the global level. We shall examine three very broad issues: natural resource extraction, processing, and consumption; population growth and movements; and environmental degradation and environmental sustainability.

In some respects, these issues are not closely related to one another, but in one important respect they are. They can all lead us toward thinking in terms of the interdependent character of our relations both with other human beings and with the physical world we all inhabit. As we shall see, however, whether this sort of thinking actually leads to a global society based on functional principles, or whether we should want it to do so, remain open questions.

12.1 Natural resource extraction, processing, and consumption

Learning objectives

1. List some of the main **natural resources** which are critically important to human life.
2. List some of the main natural resources which are critically important to modern, industrialized life.
3. Describe why the extraction and consumption of these natural resources takes on an international dimension.
4. Explain how concerns about getting access to natural resources differ from concerns about the need for access to natural resources and concerns about how they are used.

Throughout human existence, people have used land and water to obtain and produce food and drink. They have also used the resources in the earth, seas, and rivers as tools, weapons, fuel, things of beauty, and as objects of religious significance, or to produce all of these. Natural resources like stone, wood, bone, copper, tin, and iron have long been important in terms of their practical uses as the **raw materials** people make into other things, while, as we saw in Chapters 9 and 10, silver and gold have been valued for other reasons in addition to their practical qualities. We tell stories of peoples in terms of changes in the way they produce and reproduce their lives, for example, from hunter-gatherers to subsistence farmers; from subsistence farmers to agrarian societies; from agrarian societies to industrial societies; and from industrial societies to post-industrial or service societies. We also characterize peoples by the resources which we believe are most important in shaping the way they live; for example: Bronze Age, Iron Age, the Age of Coal and Steel, and today, the Information Age. It is sometimes now suggested that we live in the Anthropocene Age, one in which human activities significantly impact the ecological systems of the planet. Throughout human existence, people's need for natural resources has given rise to a constant set of questions. Where are resources located? Who has access to them? Who owns or controls them? What consequences result from their being extracted, their being used, and their being used up? None of these are new questions, and the answers to them are shaped by many factors which have also remained constant.

Resources tend to be distributed unevenly in finite concentrations. Water is to be found in one place, for example, and iron ore in another. Resources are, therefore, not equally accessible to all peoples. Acquiring resources for use has costs in terms of effort—the work to prepare a field, for example—and it has costs in terms of the consequences of acquiring them: exploiting a food source like wild cereals and grasses will affect the availability of other food sources like rabbits which depend on them, for example, and techniques for getting gold from a creek might harm the stream as a source of drinking water.

The process of acquiring access to resources has long played a part in international conflicts, producing local struggles for oases and good farmland, for example, and it has played a part in helping to produce great migrations of peoples when their habitat has undergone severe changes. However, resources have not played a big part in our understanding of international relations until relatively recently. The principal reason for this was that building and maintaining political communities placed relatively low demands on resources. Land, soil, and water were necessary. Certain minerals—copper and iron, for example—were very helpful. If they were lacking, however, the odds were they could be obtained by migrating and resettling, or by trade. Given what was needed in terms of natural resources, there was often enough to go around and little incentive for trying to corner supplies other than to deny them to enemies and rivals. Thus natural resources were seen as occasional assets in the struggle for power, wealth, and glory. They were rarely seen as determining factors which shaped the course of international relations.

This began to change with the Industrial Revolution in Britain in the late 18th century. Improvements in the technologies of production greatly increased people's appetite for natural resources. They did so in three ways. First, more raw materials were needed for the goods produced. In the textile industry, for example, more cotton and wool were needed to feed machines that spun fibers into threads and wove threads into cloth. Second, more raw materials were needed to produce the machines which processed the raw material. Again, in the textile industry, more wood was needed for the frames and more iron for the machine parts of the power mules and power looms which spun and wove the cotton and wool. Finally, more raw materials were needed to provide the motive power by which these machines operated—for example, iron for the hearths, cylinders, and pistons of the steam engines that did this work, plus wood and coal to provide the energy to fuel them.

Even so, natural resources were not in themselves a big international issue in the 19th century. Industrialization occurred first where there were accessible supplies of coal, iron ore, and water. Even those less well off in these regards usually could find access to all three, especially as canals and railways were developed to transport bulk goods. Access to coal, iron ore, and water, for example, were not issues in either of the world wars until territory containing them was lost in the course of fighting.

Nevertheless, the international significance of natural resources did increase through the 20th century for two reasons. The first was industrialization's success in expanding both the capacity to produce goods and the demand for those goods on an unprecedented scale. The second was the development of new technologies of production and transportation requiring natural resources which were not widely distributed but concentrated in certain parts of the world, most importantly oil. Throughout the 20th century, these trends sharpened the international competition for natural resources. At the same time, they also gradually raised concerns about how increasing demand for natural resources was straining sources of supply, and how increasing consumption of natural resources was affecting other aspects of the way people live, notably the wellbeing of the environment which makes their lives possible.

The growing importance of natural resources in the 20th century world wars

States cannot fight wars any more than they can do anything else without natural resources. Modern armed forces need fuel, food, and processed materials produced on an industrial scale. A naval blockade on all traded goods, including natural resources, played a part in Germany's collapse at the end of World War I. For the governments of the participating states, however, the war was not about access to and control of natural resources. They saw themselves fighting for more generalized concerns about the balance of power, spreading their influence, acquiring status and prestige, improving the world and, ultimately, their own survival.

Word War II was different. All these factors were in play, but governments of the participating states also thought much more explicitly in terms of access to natural resources and control of them. The British focused on the Middle East for the old reason that it provided the most direct route to their empire in India, but also because of the growing importance of the oil fields around the Persian Gulf. The Americans used the "oil weapon" on the Japanese, organizing an embargo on oil exports in an attempt to get Japan to withdraw its armies from China. The Japanese regarded this as an existential threat which not only committed them to war, but to war in the Pacific to secure oil supplies, rather than in North Asia to help their German allies destroy the USSR.

The Germans also took natural resources very seriously, although in what was becoming an old-fashioned way. Hitler invaded the USSR to gain land for agricultural production and colonial settlement. On one occasion he insisted that his armies prioritize the capture of a target of primarily symbolic value, the city of Stalingrad, rather than seize control of oilfields, even though Germany was short on oil supplies. By the end of the war, however, Germany was weakening its own defenses in a desperate attempt to hang on to oil fields in Romania and Hungary which supplied fuel for its tanks, aircraft, and submarines.

Today, it is widely assumed that oil and, to a lesser extent, natural gas, are two of the primary causes of military conflict. Americans, for example, tend to agree that the two US-led wars against Iraq were in part, at least, about oil. They only argue over whether or not this was an appropriate reason for fighting. Politicians and pundits, especially in the developed, oil-consuming world, often bemoan the fact that all the oil seems to be located in trouble spots around the world. Many of these troubles, of course, are actually caused by the oil and competition for it. The Middle East, Nigeria, Venezuela, the Central Asian former Soviet republics, and even Russia itself all seem to have big political problems and lots of people who seem hostile to the US and its allies. Oil is one of the principal sources of conflict as states and political interests where the oil is located, plus multinational oil companies and oil-consuming states from far away compete to control or secure oil supplies.

The most obvious natural resources issue today, in the developed world at least, is the sources of the energy which powers economies, transportation systems, and which provides the light, heating, and cooling on which people have come to depend. In 2010, 80 percent of the energy consumed by the world came from fossil fuels like oil, coal, and natural gas, which are for practical purposes **non-renewable**. The remaining 20 percent came from biomass (12.4 percent), nuclear energy (2.7 percent), with several innovative sources accounting for the rest.[1] By 2015, fossil fuels still led (78.4 percent), and although wind and solar power had made gains, they still represented a very small share of the total.

We can note a number of trends.

- First, world energy consumption from all sources is going to increase in both absolute and per capita terms for the foreseeable future. There have been considerable developments in the efficient use of energy. Consider, for example, improvements in car miles per gallon and techniques for heating and cooling buildings. However, these improvements are swamped by the rising demand for energy in industrializing states like China, India, and Brazil.

- Second, the fossil fuel share of all energy supplies has declined in recent years as new sources of energy have been, and continue to be, developed. The share of coal has declined within that, while the share of natural gas has continued to rise. The overall decline may not continue because of new sources of oil and gas which are being developed. Even the decline in the use of coal may slow given its place in India's plans for economic development, and given President Trump's promise to revive the industry. Whether this overall decline continues or not, however, fossil fuels will continue to provide the lion's share of the world's energy supplies for the foreseeable future. And, since energy consumption from all sources is projected to rise for the foreseeable future, oil, coal, and gas production will continue to rise in absolute terms.

- Third, the developed world consumes the lion's share of world energy production on both a per capita basis and in absolute terms. Within the developed world, the US consumes a great deal more than, for example, the members of the European Union in both gross and per capita terms. However, energy consumption by industrializing states, China in particular, is increasing very quickly. In 2009, China probably replaced the US as the largest consumer of energy, although it is still far behind in per capita terms.[2]

The long-established issues associated with natural resources are still with us. In strategic terms, the big consumers worry about the security of the supply of oil, for example, because of its location in potentially unstable areas of the world controlled by potentially hostile governments. Note that the presence of oil and other energy sources in politically unstable or troubled areas is often a source of the instability and trouble. As noted in Chapter 7, some 20 percent of the world's oil passes through the Straits of Hormuz (a higher percentage in the case of some individual states like Japan), and threats by Iran to interfere with shipping there can send oil prices and shipping insurance rates soaring.

Over 30 percent of EU member states' oil imports and nearly 40 percent of their natural gas imports come from Russia.[3] Between 2005 and 2009, Russia and Ukraine became involved in a price and payments dispute during which Russia would interrupt or reduce supplies of gas to Ukraine. Ukraine allowed these interruptions to affect the flow of gas to Europe across its territory, leaving Europeans feeling vulnerable to Russian energy policy. The dispute between Russia and the US and EU over Ukraine which developed in 2014 has resulted in the Europeans trying to reduce their dependence on Russian gas and Russia seeking to diversify its gas exports with sales to China.

In addition, states worry about how increasing demand for oil and gas will increase the competition for both. A new customer, like China, raises the demand, and thus the price, and puts a further strain on existing supplies. To counter these problems, states and oil companies cooperate to find new supplies in more secure and friendly areas like Alaska, northern Canada, the Caspian Sea and its surrounding states. They also look for more secure and friendly supply routes along which oil and gas can travel through new pipelines, or by new roads and railways and shipping routes. Often, however, even the attempt to explore for possible new sources of supply worsens relations between interested parties, for example, in the South China Sea between China, Vietnam, the Philippines, Malaysia, and Taiwan, and in the South Atlantic around the Falkland Islands/Malvinas between Britain and Argentina. And new routes seem no more secure than the old ones, generating tensions and rivalries between supplier states, consumer states, and transit states. Russia, for example, has worked hard to ensure that new gas pipelines to Europe avoid Ukraine and Turkey and are laid across the Black Sea and Baltic Sea, while the US has tried to make sure that oil and gas supplies to Europe from Central Asia and the Caspian Sea avoid Russian territory (for a map of Russian gas pipelines to Europe see "Gazprom pipelines" at the following link, https://eegas.com/fsu.htm).

The demand for oil has resulted in price instability in the short term and increasing costs over the long term. In the first decade of the 21st century, for example, the price of a barrel of oil fluctuated between \$40 and \$140. It soared in response to crises in oil-producing areas and tumbled when economic slowdowns in the developed world reduced the demand for oil. Such fluctuations create uncertainties which discourage business investments and can turn profitable projects—including the household economies of individuals and families—into money-losers in a matter of weeks. Regarding the long term, in 1973, the Organization of Petroleum Exporting states (OPEC) succeeded in quadrupling the price of oil and, six years later, after the Iranian Revolution, its price doubled again. The end of the era of cheap energy in which this resulted contributed greatly to the economic difficulties of the developed world in the 1970s and early 1980s known as "stagflation." In addition, it resulted in the accumulation of a great surplus of dollars, known as petrodollars, in the Middle East. These were invested by governments and rich families from the Middle East in economic activities in the developed states which often left their governments and public feeling very uneasy.

Manchester City FC, Sheik Mansour, oil money, and the future of British football

Manchester City FC (City) is a famous football (soccer) club in the English Premier League (EPL). It has a long history of occasional success, spectacular implosions, and long-running underachievement with which any fan of the Chicago Cubs or New York Mets would be immediately familiar. Like both these baseball clubs, City has had to live in the shadow of a more successful and famous club based in the same town, in its case, Manchester United. Over the years, however, City has retained the loyal support of a large fan base which mostly lives in or near Manchester, plus sympathy from football fans elsewhere who have admired its style of play while sympathizing with its failure to deliver sustained success.

To compete in the EPL requires not just success in England, but also in European competitions, and this requires a great deal of money to develop, purchase, and retain world-class players and to attract world-class coaching staff. In 2007, City accepted a takeover by a Thai businessman and former prime minister with a questionable human rights record. He greatly increased spending on players. A year later, in 2008, an Abu Dhabi-based company from the United Arab Emirates (UAR) replaced the Thai investor. The company was owned by Sheikh Mansour bin Zayed Al Nahyan, a member of the Abu Dhabi royal family and UAR government. He began to spend unprecedented sums of money on players, coaches, the playing facilities, and development projects like a hotel and shopping mall. Abu Dhabi has successful financial service and tourism industries, but the foundation of its wealth is large oil reserves. In less than half a century from 1965, oil discoveries transformed it from a quiet backwater known for pearl fishing into a sophisticated and expensive urban area with large investments in the developed world.

City's supporters are delighted with the influx of oil money, which has brought the club success. Other football fans are not so sure. While other clubs have benefitted from oil money, City faces the charge that it has bought success. Some of its players cost more than the entire squad of some of the lesser clubs in the EPL. How can other clubs compete with City's resources, other supporters ask, and what will happen when its Middle Eastern owners lose interest in their hobby? Now City's owners want the club to be a global brand. They have a Gulf airline sponsoring it. The club has entered into a partnership with the New York Yankees to co-own a new professional soccer team in New York, and it is building a fan network in the Middle East and Asia. Some things don't change. For all the oil money invested in it, there is still a sense that City can spectacularly implode on the field of play. Some things do change. City and its supporters no longer enjoy the sympathy of the football world when things go wrong for them, and they are not used to being disliked and envied.

A fierce debate has emerged about energy supplies and the problems associated with them. In the past, most people assumed that since energy was so important to a modern life, then states should do whatever it took, and whatever was in their power to maintain a secure and sufficient energy supply. After all, none of the difficulties outlined above are particularly new. Human communities have always had to struggle with nature and compete with each other for at least some of its resources. From the mid-1970s, however, a new set of arguments began to emerge associated with the Club of Rome, a think-tank of politicians, international civil servants, economists, scientists, and business leaders from around the world who met in the Italian capital. They and others made projections about future increases in the demand for natural resources, compared them to information about known, accessible reserves of these resources, and concluded there were going to be "**limits to growth**" in the future.[4] It was no use to the rest of the world imagining that one day it would develop to the point that its peoples could consume like Americans and Canadians. There were not enough resources in the world for that, or even for the rich to keep consuming at their present rate.

The Club of Rome and other like-minded groups took a broad approach to the resource-demand balance, but media and public attention, already shaken by the disruptions to oil supplies as a result of the 1973 Middle East War, fastened onto the idea that the world was running out of oil. It wasn't, of course, for the simple reason that the amount of accessible oil reserves fluctuates with the price of oil. As oil becomes more expensive, reserves which were previously too expensive to exploit, for example in the Gulf of Mexico or the Siberian tundra and, more recently in the Bakken field of North Dakota, become commercially viable. The world may run out of oil one day (although people may simply stop using it long before then), but not for a long time to come.

Despite this false start (which was not entirely the Club of Rome's fault), however, we can see a change of general attitudes begin to develop from this time. Instead of simply asking what it takes to secure the energy supplies which maintain our way of life, people in the developed world began to grasp the other end of the stick. They started asking, is keeping our way of life unchanged worth the sorts of costs we are being asked to pay for it. To maintain secure energy supplies seemed to involve dependencies in unstable parts of the world and wars with the peoples there. It involved risks of economically and environmentally damaging oil spills from tankers and pipelines as oil was obtained from more inaccessible places further and further away. It required oil companies to take ever greater risks to obtain oil from places like deep under the ocean where, if something went wrong, it would be expensive and perhaps impossible to fix. In 2010, for example, an explosion occurred on a BP oil platform drilling in the Gulf of Mexico, killing 11 workers. As a result, oil poured from the seabed for 87 days. An estimated 4.7 million barrels damaged fisheries, wild life habitats and the Gulf Shore tourist industry. And even if the world is not running out of oil and is prepared to take on the risks and costs involved in getting it from difficult locations, what would happen if it reached **peak oil**, the tipping point at which the maximum rate of extraction is reached while demand continues to climb? All these problems, it was widely assumed, could only get worse.

Others argue that the price remains well worth paying. By the standards of the past, they say, the US-led wars in the Middle East have been small, controlled, infrequent, and fought for other very good reasons besides securing energy supplies. Oil companies go to extraordinary lengths to clean up the pollution caused by accidents, and to compensate those whose livelihoods have suffered as a consequence, and are constantly improving their extraction techniques to reduce the risk of future accidents. In addition, huge efficiencies and reductions in pollution have been achieved in the way oil and other energy sources are used. For example, it would take over twenty present Ford Fiestas to produce the same amount of pollution as the original version of the car from the 1970s. In addition, coal, which is dirty to burn and dangerous to mine, seems to be on the way out, at least in the developed world, while the use of clean, cheap natural gas is on the rise.

It is very difficult to pick a way through these arguments without being an expert. And even the experts disagree among themselves. Their scientific judgments, preferences about the way we all live and, sometimes, professional and economic interests seem bound up with one another. There is no better issue than the future of fossil fuels to illustrate the theme of uncertainty around which this textbook is built. On the one hand, we have an image of a world which is becoming increasingly and unsustainably hooked on a declining source of fossil fuels with damaging consequences for the health of its people and the environment in which they live. On the other, we have an image of a world which is using fossil fuels more efficiently, developing new techniques for extracting existing reserves, and managing a careful transition to a post-carbon future without disrupting the good life which is becoming increasingly available to more and more people. Then into the debate comes induced hydraulic fracturing ("**fracking**"). This is a process by which high-pressure jets of water and sand are directed into the cracks or faults in shale rocks to release oil and natural gas which collects there. This is not a new process. However, improvements in fracking techniques coupled with the rise in price of energy have made vast reserves of previously inaccessible oil and gas commercially viable, especially in the US (a CNN video clip explaining fracking may be viewed at the following link: http://www.youtube.com/watch?v=LAxsTJd7VCA).

Its proponents say that fracking changes the terms of the global energy debate. The pressure to move beyond fossil fuels in a hurry may now be much reduced. Fracking may also change the international balance of power by reducing the dependence of the US on foreign supplies, making it self-sufficient in oil in the next few years and, possibly an oil exporter later in the 21st century. This development raises a number of interesting questions. How might it affect US policy in the Middle East, for example, and how might it affect the policies of states like Japan which still depend on oil from the Middle East?

Its critics, on the other hand, argue that the fracking process is expensive and only viable when oil prices are high. Some fracking companies have been driven out of business recently by Saudi Arabia pumping lots of oil, thereby increasing the global supply of oil and lowering its price. The benefits of fracking, the critics say, are only short-term. A huge amount of financial investment is required to create well heads with only a very short life span. The process of creating rock fissures or making them bigger may create local earthquakes. Most importantly, its critics argue, it illustrates the crazy lengths to which our appetite for energy takes us, because it puts at risk the most precious natural resource of all. Fracking uses large amounts of water—bad enough in itself. After it has been used, however, the critics maintain that this same water, now sludge mixed with sand and petroleum, may flow into neighboring water tables, contaminating them and making them unusable. If this is the case, then the quest for more energy has produced a direct threat to another older and more important natural resource, water. However, many experts argue that these fears are exaggerated since fracking takes place at levels far below the water table (for a critical view of fracking see Link TV's "Fracking Hell" at the following link http://www.youtube.com/watch?v=dEB_Wwe-uBM).

People have always been concerned about gaining access to a secure supply of water. Some of the oldest international disputes have been over water. A memorable, fictional, scene from the film of Arthur C. Clarke's *2001: A Space Odyssey*, depicts very early people learning how to fight with weapons (animal bones), but they are fighting over access to a water hole (see the video clip at the following link, http://www.youtube.com/watch?v=qtbOmpTnyOc). As noted in Chapter 7 water in the form of lakes, rivers, and seas provides a medium for communication, travel, and trade, but it can also serve as a barrier to all three. Accordingly, controlling bodies of water and denying them to opponents have long been objectives of conflict. Water is not only a medium, however. It is also a resource which, once accessed, can be used and consumed. The fictional struggle for the waterhole above has its counterparts today. Ethnic conflicts, for example, often have a resource component to them. The tensions between Tutsis and Hutus which exploded into the Rwandan genocide in 1994 were caused in part by land shortages and water shortages. So were the tensions between different ethnic and culture groups in Sudan's Darfur province.

Rivers also continue to provide sources of conflict, principally as a result of people downstream objecting to the uses made of rivers flowing through their lands by people living upstream from them. Dams which interfere with the flow of water and the nutrients in it, irrigation schemes which take water out of rivers, and industrial and farming practices which put pollutants into them through dumping and runoff are the chief causes of concern. Thus Iraqis worry about the uses made of the Tigris and the Euphrates by Syria and Turkey before these two rivers cross the border and flow into Iraq. They also worried about the neglected condition of big power dams located in areas controlled by ISIS in northern Iraq and north eastern Syria. Mexicans (and US downstream states and counties) worry about the use of the Colorado's waters by people upstream from them. And Jordanians worry about the use Israelis make of the Jordan River, while Israelis worry about what Syrians and Lebanese might try to do with it.

Quarrels over Jordan

For the Israelis, the wars and military operations against their Arab neighbors in 1948, 1949, 1956, 1967, 1973, 1978, 1982, 1993, 1996, 2006, and 2008 have been about survival and security. For Arabs, these same conflicts have been about justice and dignity. For all the parties to the conflict, however, access to water supplies has also provided a source of tension and obstacle to peaceful relations.

The Jordan River rises in the southern hills of the Lebanon and Syria (although much of the Syrian territory has been controlled by Israel in the Golan Heights since 1967). It flows along the old Israeli-Syrian boundary through Israeli-controlled territory to the Sea of Galilee. Just below the Sea of Galilee it becomes the border between Israel and Jordan and flows south to become the border between the Israel-controlled West Bank and Jordan. It then flows into the Dead Sea from which there is no outflow.

Israel, Jordan, and Syria began arguing about the use of water from the Jordan River in the 1950s, basing their positions on estimates of how much water tributaries in their own territories contributed to the system as a whole. In the early 1960s, Israel, not wanting to negotiate with states with which it had fought and which did not yet accept its right to exist, completed a system of canals, tunnels, and pipes to transport water from the Sea of Galilee to populations in the center of the state and farming areas in the south where water was scarce. This was followed by Syria and Jordan beginning diversion projects on the headwaters of the Jordan River which would have greatly reduced its flow before it reached the Sea of Galilee. The Israelis bombed Syrian construction in 1967 and later captured the area where much of the diversion work was being undertaken.

Since that time, water disputes in the region have been exacerbated by claims that the Israelis are taking most of the water from the aquifers—great natural reservoirs of water—which lie under the West Bank, the area mainly populated by Palestinians who are thus prevented from getting access to their fair share of this water. In addition, scientists and environmentalists note that everyone is taking water at beyond the natural replacement rate, and that the Jordan River has been so over-used that its southern portion, along with the Dead Sea, may simply drain and evaporate away.

These disputes have all arisen out of concerns about access to water. Who gets it and how much? Just as with sources of energy, however, concerns about why people need the water they say they do, and concerns about how people use it, have emerged. Historically, everyone has agreed that water, and especially fresh or sweet water as opposed to sea or salt water, is important as the basis for life. Where it has been scarce—in desert areas like the Arabian Peninsula or the South Western United States, for example—water has been regarded as a matter of life and death. Where it has been plentiful, in contrast—areas like Western Europe, for example—water's importance has translated into the idea that everyone should have free access to do with it more-or-less as they wish. As with energy and the limits to growth idea, however, a sense has grown that even where water is plentiful there are limits to its supplies and consequences from how it is used. This sense of what is known as **water stress** has emerged from several sources. It has long been known, for example, that when water is taken from a river in large quantities, the quality of the remaining water declines. As in the case of the Colorado River and the Jordan River above, it may become so salty that it is unusable for agricultural purposes. It may become unusable because the run off upstream contains dangerous chemicals. And the water may simply disappear.

The end of the Aral Sea

The most spectacular case of the overuse and misuse of water is the Aral Sea which lies between Kazakhstan and Uzbekistan in the former Soviet Union. The Aral Sea used to be one of the four largest lakes in the world.[5] In Soviet times, the tributary rivers which fed the Aral Sea were diverted to irrigate cotton crops. This had the unintended, tragic, and spectacular consequence that the lake more or less dried up (Figure 12.1). All lakes, as the geographers and geologists tell us, are temporary features. Dried-up lake beds are as plentiful as actual lakes as geographic features, and some lakes have a permanently temporary existence dependent on seasonal rains. Nevertheless, the disappearance of the Aral Sea is important because of the speed and the scale of the event, and the fact that it resulted from what people had done. A natural habitat, a fishing industry, and a way of life were destroyed (Figure 12.2). The land and remaining water supply were contaminated. A local climate system was changed. And it had all been undertaken to transfer water in an inefficient and wasteful way to build a cotton industry which was never particularly successful. In recent years, engineering projects re-diverting waters have led to some recovery, but the Aral Sea is unlikely ever to be restored to its full extent.[6]

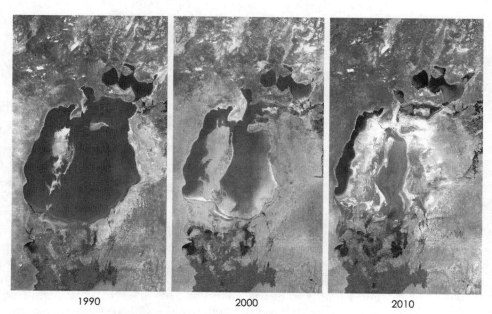

1990   2000   2010

Figure 12.1 The Aral Sea shrinking between 1990 and 2010

(Source: Universal Images Group North America LLC/Alamy Stock Photo)

Figure 12.2 Abandoned fishing boats on what was once the seabed of the Aral Sea
(Source: Theodore Kaye/Alamy Stock Photo)

As in the energy industries, great efforts have been made to be less wasteful and more efficient with the use of water. Many of the techniques and measures adopted have been very successful. For example, not all industrial processes require fresh water. Dirty and polluted water can be used and reused for some of them. Water which is used in cooling processes that work by transferring heat can then also be used as a heat source in other processes rather than be just left to stand in huge cooling towers. More effective and efficient irrigation schemes have been developed which drip water on plants and crops rather than spray them with it. And, if agriculture in one particular location requires extensive and ongoing irrigation, then people are increasingly suggesting that it be moved to where it rains more. Even more so than with global energy sources, however, there is a sense that the increasing use of water is still far outstripping any savings made by increased efficiency and, more importantly, the natural rate of replenishment of water sources. People think of their water coming from the skies as rain or out of rivers and lakes. As a practical matter, however, most of it comes from underground. Hydro-geologists speak of the water table, where water pressure equals atmospheric pressure and below which aquifers are saturated with groundwater. This is where most of people's water is directly drawn from, either through simple wells or complex pumping and purification processes. Many of these aquifers are being depleted at a rate far greater than their rate of natural replacement. This is particularly the case in those states which are currently undergoing industrialization and experiencing fast rates of growth like China, India, and Mexico.[7] In some cases, aquifers which accumulated under different climatic conditions from those existing today, in the Sahara for example, are being drawn down with no prospect of replacement. In others, aquifers are said to be threatened by polluted irrigation water seeping back into the earth or, as noted above, by chemicals from processes like fracking.

In the last fifty years, the world's population has more than doubled while the supply of water has remained much the same. Modern diets and modern lifestyles entail that people today use more water than people fifty years ago. Many parts of the world have moved beyond water stress to what is known as **water crisis**. Crop yields have fallen in parts of China and India, for example, because of water shortages. Eight hundred and eighty billion people in the world do not have access to safe potable (drinkable) water. A further 2.5 billion have inadequate access to water for sewage and sanitation purposes.[8] Many people did not have access to safe water in the past. The prospect now, however, is that many more never will. In spite of huge improvements in access to water for people in the developing world, many still face water shortages resulting from depleted and spoiled reserves, competing demands from industry and agriculture and, of course, competing demands from other people.

So far we have framed the problem in terms of the resources. How can they be accessed? Are there enough of them to go around? What happens when they are depleted? What, however, if the problem is not resources but people themselves—their multiplying numbers, their relentless expectations, their insatiable appetites, and their increasing demands on each other and the world? We examine people in the next section.

Key terms

fracking A process by which oil and gas deposits are recovered by injecting a mixture of water, sand, and chemicals into rock faults. "Fracing" or "fraccing" are the preferred terms in the energy industry.

limits to growth The idea that since natural resources are either finite or only very slowly replaceable, economic development for all people can only occur to a certain level or at a certain rate beyond which resources necessary to development are depleted.

natural resources Liquids, gases, rocks, minerals, and plants occurring naturally which can be used by people.

non-renewable A natural resource which is not replenished once used, for example oil, contrasted with a renewable resource like timber which can be replaced by fresh growth or solar power and wind power which are not always available but cannot be used up in any meaningful sense; the rate of renewal relative to the rate of use is important.

peak oil A situation in which new oil reserves are being discovered and developed at the same rate at which oil is being used; with the implication that the rate of discovery and development will fall behind the demand for use.

raw materials Components of a production process which are naturally occurring and have been channeled, captured, mined, or harvested for use.

water crisis A situation in which existing and projected supplies of water are insufficient to meet existing demand either temporarily or permanently, and in which the management of existing supplies is already causing major harm to people and irreparable damage to the environment.

water stress   A situation in which existing and projected uses of a water supply make the future of that supply in sufficient quantities uncertain.

Key takeaways

- People have always depended on natural resources to provide raw materials to consume directly or for producing the things they need.
- People have always worried about the security of the supply of these resources and have travelled, traded, and fought to obtain and use them.
- Before the Industrial Revolution, the chief security of supply concerns for people were caused by the uneven distribution of some resources.
- Since the Industrial Revolution a growing security of supply concern has emerged regarding the imbalance between consumption rates and replacement rates of natural resources.
- The demand for energy and water is growing worldwide; supplying that demand has become more expensive, and meeting current projected demands will be difficult and, in some cases, impossible.

Exercises

1. Why did security of supply concerns shift from problems of access and production to problems of consumption after the world industrialized?
2. List the reasons for being optimistic about the future of global energy and water supplies.
3. List the reasons for being pessimistic about the future of global energy and water supplies.
4. Name two items vital to your everyday life which depend on natural resources from abroad.

12.2   People and population

Learning objectives

1. Describe the growth curve in the world's population before and after the early 19th century, and identify where most of the growth has taken place since the 1960s.
2. Explain why the populations of states start to rise and then eventually stabilize.
3. List the population policies pursued by states and international organizations.

Students of international relations used not to think much about people and populations. Things of concern to most people were thought to go on inside states, not between them. Most people were not supposed to be interested in international relations and were not expected to understand them. As far as the subject of International Relations was concerned, populations were only important as attributes of the power of states, or when they had to be transferred from one state to another, at the end of a war, for example. This changed for two reasons. First, from the time of the great political, social, and industrial revolutions at the end of the 18th century it became increasingly accepted that people and their wellbeing ought to matter. States should serve people and not the other way round. Second, from around the same time, there began a massive expansion in the world's population which, though with a slightly slower rate of growth, continues to this day. According to the UN, there are now over 7 billion people in the world and this figure grows by 80 million a year, with over 90 percent of that growth taking place in the global south (see Table 12.1).[9]

Of course, throughout human history and for long before it was recorded, biological drives, conscious self-interests, and moral codes combined to suggest that more and more people were a good thing. Parents liked large families of children who would look after them when they grew old. Kings liked large populations which would provide wealth, taxes, and soldiers. Priests liked more worshippers who could honor the gods. And since life itself was regarded as good then, all things being equal, more people experiencing life or living lives was regarded as better. Things were not always equal, of course. Natural disasters like floods and locusts, diseases like bubonic plague, and crop failures resulting from blights could create situations in which populations exceeded available supplies of food

Table 12.1 Population in millions, by selected states

State	1900	1960	2000	2011
China	419,920,000	682,024,000	1,262,645,000	1,344,130,000
India	271,000,000	431,463,000	1,053,818,107	1,241,491,960
USA	76,212,000	179,323,175	282,162,411	311,591,917
Indonesia	42,746,000	92,701,000	213,395,411	242,325,638
Brazil	17,984,000	70,281,000	174,425,387	196,655,014
Pakistan	19,759,000	49,955,000	144,522,192	176,745,364
Bangladesh	29,012,000	51,586,000	129,592,275	150,493,658
Nigeria	15,589,000	42,739,000	123,688,536	162,470,737
Russia	132,000,000	214,000,000	146,303,000	142,960,000
Japan	43,000,000	93,418,000	126,870,000	127,817,277
France	38,000,000	44,772,000	60,910,922	65,433,714
Paraguay	715,000	1,774,000	5,343,539	6,568,290

Note: 1900 figures for India (whole of British India), Pakistan, and Bangladesh are pre-independence, pre-partition (1947) and pre-Bangladesh independence from Pakistan (1971). 1900 figures for Indonesia and Nigeria also pre-independence. 1960 figure for Russia is the USSR including fourteen now independent former Soviet republics. All figures are intended to provide rough guides.

Source: 1900 and 1960, *Populstat* website: Jan Lahmeye at http://www.populstat.info/Asia/indiac.htm by continent, and 2000 and 2011 from *World Bank* at http://data.worldbank.org/indicator/SP.POP. TOTL and drink, or even land and water. Natural aging, a temporary shift to smaller families, migration, and the occasional war or natural disaster, however, would, sooner or later bring populations and resources back into a better balance in which more people were to be desired.

At least so it was thought until the political economist and early student of **demography**, Thomas Malthus (1776–1834), argued that populations always increased at a rate in excess of the resource base which sustained them.[10] People were unlikely to exercise self-restraint in regard to sexual activity. It was almost impossible for others to restrain them. This being so, Malthus argued only famines, epidemics, and wars would limit populations. They were not unfortunate and occasional acts of nature or God visited on humankind. They were its destiny at frequent intervals. Malthus' gloomy predictions might have been right in the details of specific situations. As we can see from population increases in Table 12.1, however, they were wrong, or at least premature, when it came to the overall pattern of human development. Malthus vastly underestimated the gains in productivity which followed the agricultural revolutions and industrial revolutions. The same piece of farmland in most parts of the world now yields far more than it did in 1800. Land which was once inaccessible can now be used. Produce can be stored or be transported great distances without spoiling. In the two hundred years following Malthus' book, populations have increased, but so too has the quantity and quality of the food and drink which most of them consume. Indeed, when states begin to industrialize we see a very different pattern from that of population needs outstripping resource capabilities as envisaged by Malthus.

Instead, we see a process called the **demographic transition** associated with the demographer Warren Thompson.[11] Thompson identified four stages of demographic transition. Stage one is pre-industrial and characterized by high birth rates and high death rates roughly in balance. Birth rates and death rates are usually measured in terms of the number of people who are born and die per thousand of the population of a state in a given year. In stage two, states modernize their agriculture and develop their industry. Food supplies, simple health care measures, and sanitation improve. As a result, death rates begin to fall. More babies survive at birth. More children survive the first wave of childhood diseases. More adults survive illnesses which previously would have killed them. And more old people live longer. The population begins to grow quickly. In stage three, birth rates begin to fall as the improved status and education of women, increased use of contraception as a result of changing attitudes, plus **urbanization** with steadier and better jobs providing health care and pensions, leave families feeling more secure. Large families are no longer the best guarantee of support in old age. Finally, in stage four, birth rates and death rates both decrease, with birth rates often falling below the replacement rate, and the workforce shrinks as a proportion of the population as a whole. There are very few parts of the world today which completely correspond to any of the four stages, especially the first, or pre-industrial, stage. Western European and North American states moved into stage two in the 19th century, and the Western Europeans are now firmly in stage four. The US is not, thanks to relatively open immigration policies. Many states of the developing world, Egypt, India, and

Ethiopia, for example, are facing the rapidly expanding populations associated with stage two, while China and Brazil are arguably moving quickly into stage three with the first signs of stage four, population stagnation, on the horizon.

The demographic transition is a difficult, uncertain, and sometimes very costly process for any society to undertake. Those of us who live in developed states with stable populations and high standards of living should not forget the sacrifice and pain which many of our forebears went through without necessarily choosing to do so as their societies industrialized and modernized. It is not always a great comfort to people living through the demographic transition right now to be told that, with any luck, at some point in the future, their grandchildren may live better lives than they do, not least because it may not be true. In stage two, for example, the population starts to expand quickly. This typically results in **migration** from the countryside to quickly growing cities where people believe they will have better opportunities. This migration may take place in the same state through a process of urbanization. In China, for example, a mass internal migration from the rural interior of the state to the more developed and economically richer and faster growing coastal areas has been underway for the last forty years (Figure 12.3). In 1990, 26 percent of China's population lived in cities. By 2012, over 52 percent of the population (712 million) lived in cities, and the Chinese government expects this to rise to 70 percent in 20 years.[12]

Figure 12.3 Satellite image of Guangzhou and Shenzen, China

(Source: Universal Iages Group North America LLC/Alamy Stock Photo)

Note: Guangzhou has a population of 12 million and is just one of eight big cities situated close together in the biggest conurbation in the world.

If people have enough money and states are willing to let them in, cross-border migration may take place through a process of emigration (leaving)/immigration (arriving) in which they travel great distances to begin new lives in other parts of the world. The journey is often very difficult. People will spend their life savings to travel, and take great risks, when either emigration or immigration is illegal. They cross seas in flimsy boats or deserts with unreliable and often criminal guides to reach what they hope will be a better life. As we saw in Chapter 7, North Africans from states like Algeria, Morocco, Libya, and the states of sub-Saharan Africa, plus refugees from the Syrian civil war and the instability in Afghanistan try to reach Italy, Greece, and other states of the European Union by crossing the Mediterranean (Figure 12.4). Haitians and Cubans try to reach Florida across the Caribbean, while Mexicans and Central Americans take their chances crossing the difficult and dangerous borderlands between Mexico and the US.

Migrants have mixed feelings about leaving home, and they leave problems at home, for it is often the least able and least willing to travel who remain behind. When they arrive at their destinations, migrants may face discrimination and resentment on grounds of race, or because the local people believe the immigrants are stealing their jobs and welfare benefits. They may be badly exploited, especially if they have arrived illegally. They cannot go to the police to complain. And they may have unrealistic expectations for their new lives and become disappointed and angry, like the very few young men who have been radicalized and joined homegrown terrorists in France, Germany, Britain and other European states since 2015. Even internal migrants who stay in their

Figure 12.4 Migrants and refugees in the Mediterranean with an Italian warship
(Source: Michael Knowles/Alamy Stock Photo)

home state may face these difficulties. It takes many years, for example, for Chinese workers from the countryside to gain full residential status with its entitlements to accommodation, health care, and schooling in the big cities to which they have moved. Until then, they live as second-class citizens in their own state.

The demographic transition and its consequences are also associated with health issues and especially the spread of infectious diseases from one part of a state to another, and from one part of the world to another. When they spread on a large scale they are known as **pandemics**. These are not new. The last of a series of plagues, probably originating in Asia, spread through Europe in the 1660s. Europeans brought diseases like smallpox and measles to the Americas around the same time, and it appears that syphilis may have travelled in the other direction (see below). The consequences of these pandemics could be devastating.[13] Estimates range between 75 and 200 million deaths from plagues in the 14th century, with it taking 150 years at least for populations to recover the losses. It is also suggested that the resulting labor shortages contributed greatly to the end of the feudal system in Western Europe. The influenza epidemic in 1918–19 is estimated to have killed 40 million people, more than twice as many as the combat deaths from four years of the world war that had just finished.

It is unlikely that future pandemics could kill on the scale of the great plagues, reducing the world's population in absolute terms. However, in addition to the deaths, suffering, and misery they still cause, pandemics remain a source of concern for several reasons. First, infectious diseases can still be devastating at a local level. It is estimated that the **HIV/AIDS** epidemic, for example, infected a quarter of Botswana's population at its height, and that up to two million people a year were dying worldwide.[14] Second, in an era where travel has become fast and affordable for more people, infections can be spread more quickly and more easily. Third, the emergence of new threats like Ebola, the H5N1 and H7N9 ("bird flu") viruses, and the Severe Acute Respiratory Syndrome (SARS), together with the re-emergence of old problems like tuberculosis and malaria, call into question our sense (in the developed world, at least), that medical science is steadily solving our health problems. The Zika virus, which was first identified in Africa in the 1940s and achieved the status of a pandemic in South America in 2015–16, is but the latest of a series of sicknesses which cause widespread suffering and even more widespread fear and panic.

Perhaps most importantly in terms of international relations, the movements of peoples and diseases are full of political controversy. This is nicely illustrated by the continuing arguments over whether syphilis returned from the Americas with Columbus' sailors or was brought by them along with all the other "European" illnesses from Spain. Some Europeans took comfort from the idea that an "exchange" of harmful diseases had taken place between Indians and Europeans. Some Native Americans were relieved when it looked for a time like syphilis had originated in Europe after all, along with all the other diseases which had spelled disaster for their forebears. For many years, South Africa's former president maintained that HIV/AIDS was the result of a white plot to get rid of black people, since the virus originated in Africa and disproportionately affects black people. This was far easier for his electorate—especially men—to accept than the idea that their sexual habits were making the problem worse and needed to change. It is easy for politicians to blame "ignorant" and "dirty" immigrants when things go wrong. Ignorance and dirt, however, are not attributes of race, nationality, or ethnicity. They are consequences of economic deprivation, low social status, limited access to opportunity, and the absence of networks of support.

Notwithstanding the difficulties and dangers outlined, many people are prepared to move for the chance of a better life. More and more people seek out more and more contacts and connections with people elsewhere in the world. The lives of nearly everybody, whether they like it or know it or not, are profoundly affected by the processes associated with the demographic transition. As a result we can observe the emergence of a growing area of policy pursued by states and international organizations directed not at other states or even particular peoples. This population policy may have many objectives, but a common assumption is that populations—or the world's population as a whole—can be managed. In the past, population policies have been directed at getting rid of people—by killing them or forcing them out of a piece of territory—and acquiring people by capturing them or making them attractive offers to come to a piece of territory or reproduce more often. Today, there are powerful international norms against getting rid of people in large numbers, especially when it is attempted because of their racial, ethnic, or religious identity. However, it still happens—think of the Rwandan **genocide**, "ethnic cleansing" in the former Yugoslavia, and the campaigns against indigenous Indians in Guatemala in the late 20th century, for example. Today, the civil war in Syria and the campaign against Moslem communities in Myanmar/Burma could both grow into examples of this dark approach to reducing population or particular populations.

Genocide in the late 20th century

Genocide involves the deliberate destruction of a race, nation, ethnic group, or caste. It is one of the oldest population policies. It was practiced, for example, by both the Greek and Roman civilizations. When they defeated a people, they would often kill all its men and enslave the women and children (recall Thucydides' *Melian Dialogue* from Chapter 2). Genocide is based on the calculation that the best way to get rid of the problems posed by a people is to get rid of the people altogether. Acts of genocide are fueled by fear and anger, plus feelings of superiority and inferiority. They are also often accompanied by moral and religious justifications.

In the developed world, genocide is associated with the Nazis and their efforts to exterminate European Jewry between 1933 and 1945. There are arguments about how many people were killed. Six million Jews and over ten million other people—gypsies, homosexuals, communists, Soviet prisoners of war, and people with physical and mental disabilities, for example—are rough figures frequently cited. There can be no doubt, however, that the slaughter was on a massive scale and that Jews were easily the single largest group targeted.

In 1994 genocide took place in the central African state of Rwanda. Rwanda's politics took the form of struggle for power between the leaders of two ethnic groups, the minority Tutsi who historically had dominated and the majority Hutu who currently ruled. Tutsi groups were attempting a political comeback when the Hutu president was assassinated. Over the following 100 days, armed Hutu groups put into action a plan they had developed for killing the Tutsi and anyone opposed to the killings. Estimates suggest between 500,000 and a million people were shot, hacked, or burned to death.

In 1995 genocide took place in the former Yugoslav republic of Bosnia. Bosnian politics took the form of a three-way struggle between Bosnian Serbs who were seen as largely Orthodox Christians, Bosnian Croats who were seen as largely Roman Catholics, and Bosniaks who were seen as largely Muslims. Most of Bosnia's population had wished that Yugoslavia had held together and that Bosnia had not become independent. Once Yugoslavia did break apart, however, the Bosniaks wanted an independent state of the whole of Bosnia. The Bosnian Serbs wanted to clear non-Serbs out of their part of Bosnia by what they called "ethnic cleansing" so they could eventually join with Serbia. The Bosnian Croats went back and forth between aligning with the Bosniaks against the Bosnian Serbs and plotting with the Bosnian Serbs to break up Bosnia so their part could join with Croatia. The resulting civil war culminated in a massacre of approximately 8,000 Muslim men and boys who were taken prisoner by the Bosnian Serbs.

The 1948 UN Convention on the Prevention and Punishment of the Crime of Genocide (CPPCG) makes these sorts of mass killings illegal under international law. Since then, steps have been taken to broaden the definition of genocide and make it easier to punish those responsible for it, notably through the establishment of the International Criminal Court (ICC) in 2002 (see Chapter 8). These measures have involved painful arguments about what constitutes genocide. How many have to be killed? Can we treat 8,000 deaths and six million deaths as the same sort of thing? Do people have to be killed, or does taking the children of Australian aborigines and Native Americans and putting them in white boarding schools count? Do the killings need to have genocidal intent, or does the criminal neglect of African slaves on the passage to the Americas or ethnic Germans employed as slave laborers in Stalin's Gulag count? Does the massacre of your own people, as in Kampuchea in the 1970s, count? We may think of genocide as a population policy which is evil, barbaric, and belonging to the past. The historical record shows that civilized people can engage in genocide. The courts and tribunals which continue to meet in The Hague (Bosnia), Arusha (Rwanda), and Phnom Penh (Kampuchea/Cambodia) suggest that the possibility of genocide is very much still with us.

Of course, we do not usually think of population policy in terms of reducing the numbers of people by getting rid of them. It is usually presented in terms of achieving secure, healthy, free, prosperous communities of people who do not harm their environment, do not use their resources at a faster rate than they can be replenished, and live in harmony with each other and with their neighboring communities. Even this reasonable view of population policy, however, invites opposition from multiple religious, cultural and political perspectives, and reasonable population policies do not always produce reasonable results. Who should make population policy? One answer is that since it is a global issue: it should be addressed at the global level by the UN and its affiliated organizations such as the World Health Organization (WHO) and the UN Population Fund (UNFPA).

However, states (and sometimes their people) are very quick to take recommendations from these agencies about, for example, safe sex practices or avoiding smoking, as critical interference. Similarly, state and private donors to the agencies' budgets can get upset at population policies. For example, the US administration of George W. Bush withdrew financial support when the UNPFA advocated contraception and abortion as elements of its family-planning program. The US argued that the UN was supporting forced abortions and forced sterilizations in China. Funding was renewed under the Obama administration, and cut off again by the Trump administration. Agencies like the UNFPA undertake important work in gathering information and advocating policies regarding population management. The WHO played a critical role in the vaccination campaign which effectively eradicated smallpox worldwide in the 1970s. Nevertheless, the size of the WHO's total budget, $3.96 billion for 2011–12, is little larger than the budget for the health department of a major city in the developed world, circumstantial evidence at least of where states prefer to see population policies made and undertaken, namely at home.[15]

Even at the state level, however, population policy can be difficult and controversial. India and China shared a great fear in the 1970s (when they were entering stage two of their demographic transitions) that their populations would soon outrun their available resources. The Indians attempted a series of incentives, one being that they would provide free radios to men prepared to undergo voluntary vasectomies. The Chinese attempted a mix of incentives and strong disincentives. The most notorious was the "one child policy" by which families were rewarded with allowances and apartments if they kept to no more than one child. Families who had more than one child lost benefits and they faced considerable social sanction. Women who became pregnant a second time were put under very heavy pressure to have abortions.[16] The one child policy made people miserable. It encouraged the termination of female pregnancies (and possibly the murder of some baby girls) since boys were regarded as even more valuable now only one child was allowed. It created a generation of "little princelings" who did not always grow up to be well-adjusted young men, a shortage of young women, and a future population problem. Chinese demographers now worry about how distortions in China's demographic profile resulting from the one child policy will affect its ability to replace the current workforce when it retires. As a consequence, the Chinese government first relaxed many aspects of the one child policy and, in 2015, appeared to abandon it altogether.

Not all states want to reduce their populations or slow the rate of increase. A few, like Russia until recently, experience absolute decline. In Russia's case, the loss of the other Soviet republics combined with what might best be described as a collapse of national morale in which men drank too much and both men and women found it hard to see a good future for any children they might have. In 2006, President Putin called the demographic crisis the most urgent one facing Russia. A year later, a Russian regional government declared a "Day of Conception." It encouraged married couples to stay home and make love with chances to win prizes if they gave birth nine months later. Similar campaigns, both official and unofficial have been launched in Singapore, Japan, and South Korea.[17] Some states, like France and Britain, which are said to be in stage four of the demographic transition, worry about replacement rates rather than absolute decline. As a consequence, they look at the US example of pursuing a relatively open immigration policy to maintain their numbers. Just as in the US, however, immigration is a controversial policy. As noted above, people worry about the pressure which immigrants will exert on wages, housing, and health, especially in difficult economic times, and are not particularly appreciative of the contributions which immigrants make to the economy, the tax base, and the society's capacity to innovate. Fear about immigration played an important part in the British debates on staying in the EU. The members of the EU have open borders letting their people move around relatively freely. Brexit, some of its supporters argued, would let Britain close its borders or, at least, reduce the flow of immigrants. And in the US, the Trump administration has restricted immigration from states in the Middle East citing fears about terrorists slipping in among the migrants and refugees.

Immigrants themselves may no longer feel the same pressures to integrate with their host societies as they did in the past. Their links with their homelands are no longer completely broken. All but the poorest can afford at least the occasional trip back home provided it is safe for them to go. And nearly everyone can stay in touch with the homeland and the diaspora of others who have left through cheap phone calls, the Internet, and social media networks. Even if they are second and third generation—that is, the children of parents or grandparents who immigrated—the locals sometimes ask, "Are they really us? Do they want to be us?" Sometimes the young people of immigrant families, facing unemployment and suspicion, ask the same questions of themselves with devastating consequences. The terrorist attacks which have been occurring in Europe since 2015 have been undertaken by radicalized young Muslim men who were either immigrants or the children of immigrants from the Middle East and who identified themselves with ISIS.

Jihad in London, 2005

This is not, properly speaking, an immigration story. On July 7, 2005, four radical Islamic terrorists launched a series of suicide attacks in London, three on underground (subway) trains and one on a bus. Fifty-six people, including the four bombers, were killed and over 700 people were injured. Two weeks later a second wave of attacks occurred, but the bombs failed to detonate and the four bombers were quickly caught, although not before the police shot and killed an innocent man misidentified as one of the bombers.

In previously recorded statements, the attacks were justified as bringing the war home to the British people in response to the role of the British Army in Afghanistan and Iraq, where the bombers accused it of killing Muslim men, women, and children on behalf of the democratically elected British government. The bombers were admirers of Al-Qaeda but appeared to have no direct links with it.

All four had grown up around the northern English city of Leeds. The eldest was 30. The youngest was 18. Two were married with children. Three of the bombers were of south Asian origin and had Muslim names. The fourth had moved to Britain from Jamaica with his family when he was five. They were the children of immigrant families which had come to Britain from states which were former colonies of the British Empire.

The British government stressed that this had been a terrorist event pure and simple. Extreme right-wing political groups presented it as a consequence of lax immigration policies which allowed people of different races and cultures into Britain who did not belong and who had no loyalty to the country. Most people worried about how the four young men could grow up so disconnected and disaffected from life in Britain. Was it the majority population's racism and the lack of economic opportunity for young men of color which had made them this way, or was it the closed off nature of the ethnic, formerly immigrant, communities in which they had grown up? Should those communities have tried harder to integrate with the mainstream?

There are no simple answers to these questions. One simple answer "send people like this back home to where they belong if they don't like Britain," was a nonstarter. All four were British. They were already home.

One response to these difficulties with immigration is to attempt to be more selective about who gets in. Instead of admitting those who are poor, unskilled, and likely to become a burden on society, some politicians argue, the state should only admit people who fulfill a need or national priority. Australia pursues such a policy, and President Trump has suggested something similar for the US. When Hong Kong reverted from Britain to China in 1997, many of its people, fearing a communist government, wanted to leave. The British government, fearing an influx of up to five million Hong Kong Chinese claiming British citizenship had amended its citizenship legislation some years earlier to make sure this did not happen. However, both Britain and Canada made it possible for Hong Kong Chinese with lots of money to acquire full citizenship on the grounds that they would use their capital to create jobs. Many states have attempted policies which cherry pick immigrants on the basis of in-demand skills.[18] Developing states typically offer limited-term contracts to engineers, doctors, nurses, and educators, expecting them to go home eventually. Developed states are more likely to offer the opportunity of permanent settlement and eventual citizenship to the people they believe they want. The US offers a number of visas to foreigners by lottery each year. It is often argued that one of the great strengths of the US is its ability to attract the brightest and the best from around the world to its universities, research institutes, and private companies. They come. They want to stay, and Americans, generally speaking, make them welcome.

Even cherry picking has its problems, however. In Britain, the high proportion of doctors and nurses from South Asia in the publicly funded health sector is occasionally a source of resentment. In the United States, the call in the recent immigration debate to encourage and accept graduate students with training in the sciences and mathematics has been challenged on the grounds that, contrary to popular belief, there is no great shortage of Americans with these backgrounds. Perhaps most importantly, however, cherry picking can be challenged on moral grounds. When a developing state sends its brightest and best, in whom it has already invested a great deal of its own scarce capital, to the universities of the developed world, it expects them to come home once they have received training. Is it right that the developed states of the world should encourage a "brain drain" of those best equipped to do their own states and their own peoples the most good?

As the arguments over immigration in the US and other developed states suggest, population policy sometimes sounds like arguments over how to turn back the waves. As the terrible risk-taking of "boat people" in the Caribbean and the Mediterranean suggests, people seem to do what they will do and move where they will move no matter what policies are attempted. This is an exaggeration. There is some evidence that immigration flows respond to tough talk about future restrictions, and even stronger evidence that they respond to economic slowdowns in the states to which immigrants want to travel. It seems that policies like shipping home all illegal immigrants and building walls along the borders to keep the rest out will not work very well, not least because they raise difficult moral issues and because developed economies need the sort of labor at the sort of price which immigrants provide. Nevertheless, population policies have consequences, and some have enjoyed considerable success—the campaign against smallpox on a global level, for example, and the campaign to reduce the spread of HIV/AIDS in southern Africa and to reduce the consequences of infection generally. However, it is probably best to think of population policies in terms of managing problems which arise and need to be managed on a daily basis, rather than in terms of them providing long-term solutions. For the possibility of long-term solutions to population problems and other problems, we have to shift our focus away from natural resources, the people who use them, and the population policies which manage both, to look at what might be happening to the planet as a whole and the role of people in that.

Key terms

demographic transition The sequence by which industrializing societies experience falling death rates, fast population growth, and eventually falling birthrates and slowing population growth.

demography   The study of human populations.

genocide The intentional destruction of a people through large-scale murder, assimilation, and destruction of culture.

HIV/AIDS Human immunodeficiency virus/acquired immunodeficiency syndrome: a disease of the immune system which steadily reduces the body's ability to resist infections and tumors.

migration The large scale movement of peoples, internal migration within a state, or cross-border migration between states. Immigration refers to the movement of people into one state or place from another state or place. Emigration refers to the movement of people out of one state or place to another place or state.

pandemics Outbreaks of infectious diseases on a large scale which continue to spread and potentially affect everyone in a region or the whole world.

urbanization A process associated with industrialization by which people move from the countryside and employment in agriculture to the cities and employment (when they can find it) in manufacturing and services, in which the proportion of the total population living in cities grows relative to the population in the countryside.

Key takeaways

- The world's population has been growing since the early nineteenth century, with growth accelerating in the mid-twentieth century. It continues to grow but the rate of growth may be beginning to slow.
- Population growth is linked to industrialization, modernization, and the improvements in productivity and living conditions associated with them.
- Industrialization takes place at different rates in different places resulting in internal and cross-border migrations of large numbers of people.
- Population policies may seek to reduce and increase the size of the population of a state, region, or the world, improve the quality of life for members of a population, and ensure that their requirements remain in balance with available resources.
- Birth control, promoting bigger families, encouraging and discouraging emigration and immigration, and health programs such as immunization campaigns are all examples of population policies; so too is genocide although this is universally outlawed as cruel and evil.

Exercises

1. Describe ways in which industrialization initially encourages population growth.
2. Describe ways in which industrialization eventually encourages the rate of growth to slow.
3. List reasons why you might want to emigrate.
4. List reasons why a state might want to encourage immigration.

12.3   Environmental issues and perspectives

Learning objectives

1. Explain how increased carbon emissions are said to be warming the atmosphere.

2. List the ways in which climate change can affect the way we live.

3. Explain how an effective agreement on chlorofluorocarbons was achieved, yet an effective Convention on Climate Change has been difficult to reach.

4. Describe how an environmental perspective can change the way we think about international relations.

Until about fifty years ago, environmentalism was the preserve of scientists, technical experts and a few artists and writers. Today, concern for the **environment** is a major, and highly controversial, issue in nearly all states, affecting people's lives and the way they think about politics, economics, society, and international relations. As a result, most of us, in the developed world at least, have become familiar with ideas like **sustainability**, recycling, going green, carbon footprints (a measure of how much carbon the activities of each and every one of us produce), and **carrying capacity** (the capacity of a river, for example, to move or absorb the pollutants poured into it by human activities). Yet "environment" is one of those words which we find very useful and, at the same time is hard to pin down. The environment is our surroundings, but which bits? We start thinking of trees, forests, rivers, and lakes, but are gardens, houses, roads, schools, and factories part of our environment too? How about other people? How about everything around us? People concerned about the environment or who are simply interested in it have something more precise than this in mind. They have an idea of the environment as an ecological system of related and interacting parts. The operations of one part affect the operations of other parts and they do so in four ways.

■ First these processes can reproduce the ecological system, for example, in the way that water falls as rain, flows in rivers to the sea sustaining life as it flows, evaporates, and then falls again.

■ Second, these processes can change the system. For example, changes in rainfall can change forest to grassland and grassland to desert.

■ Third, these processes can cause the system, or parts of it, to break down. The shift from forest through to desert in a particular location with all its consequences for ending most life there, for example, might be regarded as a breakdown rather than a change.

■ Fourth, human beings and their activities contribute to the reproduction, change, and breakdown of the environmental system.

Most Liberal environmentalists take an **anthropocentric** approach.[19] They want to understand the processes of the environment so that people can use, shape, and exploit it without damaging it so much that we cause an environmental breakdown. Social environmentalists and biological environmentalists, in contrast, see this anthropocentric approach as a big part of the problem. We are not going to save the world by driving Priuses, composting, and sorting our garbage for recycling, they argue. We are going to have to completely rethink the way we live and relearn our humble place and role in the operations of the environment.

One thing all environmentalists and nearly all scientists agree on, however, is that human beings are changing the environment by the way they live and are causing parts of it to break down. If we are all a bit fuzzy about exactly what the environment is, we are absolutely clear about why we have started paying more attention to it. First, the Earth is warming up in a process known as global warming or climate change. Second, the number of species of plants, insects, and animals (biodiversity) is declining. Third, until recently, the ozone layer in the atmosphere was becoming thinner. These three developments have put concerns about global resources, population changes, and, potentially, the way we conduct international relations, in a new light.

Global warming and climate change

The average temperature of the atmosphere and oceans has risen by about 1.4°F (0.8°C) since the beginning of the 20th century. Two-thirds of this increase has occurred since 1980. The largest increases have been in the Arctic, the Antarctic, and in the oceans generally. As a consequence, the polar icecaps and mountain glaciers are retreating. As they melt, sea levels are rising and weather systems are changing. These changes result in increased rainfall and more frequent storms in some parts of the world, while in others heat waves, droughts, and desertification are on the rise. Scientists note that relatively small changes in temperature are capable of creating larger knock on effects which may occur more quickly than is expected. For example, it has been suggested that the North Atlantic Current which has brought warm water to the shores of North West Europe might cease to flow, removing its moderating effect on the climates of the British Isles and Norway.

It is true that the Earth's temperature has risen and fallen throughout its history, although it has been relatively stable for the last 2,000 years. It is true that even during that period, local temperature variations occurred. There was a medieval warm period, for example, followed by a series of cooler spells between 1550 and 1850. There appears to have been a slowdown in warming since the end of the 20th century, although there are arguments about this, and a recent reduction in the extent of annual seasonal retreat of icecaps. While the ice sheet in the Arctic has reached a point of critical collapse according to some experts, the ice sheet in the Antarctic has undergone a recovery. Some Himalayan glaciers also appear to be advancing recently. However, most scientists argue that these developments, at odds with what most of us would expect from global warming, are temporary effects of local conditions. The fact that some places get colder temporarily as a result of climate change, they argue, does not call into question the overall trend towards warming. Most climatologists expect this trend to resume, possibly at an accelerated rate.

Several causes have been put forward for this warming, including the heat given off by big cities, changes in the patterns of ocean currents, and sunspot activity. However, most scientists agree that global warming results from the buildup of "greenhouse gases" like carbon dioxide caused by the consumption of coal, oil, and gas, and is exacerbated by the destruction of carbon dioxide-consuming and oxygen-producing forests. These gases let in short-wave radiation energy from the sun, but trap long-wave energy reflected back from the Earth in the form of heat.

The consequences of global warming and the resulting climate change are important. The habitats of many species of animals may be changed to the point where they face extinction. Agricultural production in many areas will decline, although in some areas it may increase. Areas of human habitation, low lying islands and coastal areas for example, may be inundated or become prohibitively expensive to protect from rising sea levels.

Biodiversity

Biodiversity refers to the degree of variation of life forms and ecological sub-systems within an environmental system. On Earth, scientists tell us that this diversity is the result of 3.5 billion years of evolution with nothing but various forms of single cell organisms until 6 billion years ago. More biodiversity is generally regarded as better for several reasons: as a good in itself, because the existence of specific life forms is generally dependent on the existence of other life forms (think of the role of bees and wasps in spreading pollen); and because greater diversity may result in more robust, productive, and healthier sources of food, materials like lumber, and chemicals such as those in medicines.

Research reveals a series of mass extinctions of species since the emergence of life on the planet, with the possibility of a sixth one just beginning. Estimates suggest between one and three percent of the species that have ever existed are still around. The most recent extinction until now was that associated with the end of the dinosaurs. Estimates also suggest that forty percent of the species which currently are thought to exist are at risk. This reduction is mainly attributed to human actions which work in three ways: directly—hunting and fishing, for example; indirectly—habitat destruction through cutting down forests and polluting rivers and seas, for example; and systemically—habitat change through human activities leading to climate change.

The ozone layer

Ozone or trioxygen occurs in small quantities in the Earth's atmosphere. It has industrial uses as an oxidant. However, it can be harmful to plant tissue and the respiratory systems of animals and humans. It can contribute to the formation of smog and reductions in plant yields, and is a greenhouse gas contributing to global warming.

One way ozone is produced is as a result of the interaction of oxygen with ultraviolet light rays from the sun. This is why it exists in stronger concentrations in the stratosphere, sometimes known as the ozone layer. This interaction is beneficial because the ultraviolet rays it absorbs do not reach the Earth's surface where they can be harmful to plants and animals, including humans. It is the small amount that gets through which causes sunburn.

Since the 1970s, a steady drop in concentrations of ozone has been observed in the Earth's atmosphere, especially over the polar caps in their respective spring times. It has been demonstrated that this depletion is caused primarily by chlorofluorocarbons (CFCs) of the sort once widely used for coolants in refrigerators and air conditioning units, and as a stable propellant in aerosols. As the use of CFCs went up, the concentrations of ozone declined, leading to "holes in the ozone layer," especially one in the Antarctic. By 2000, the Antarctic hole had spread temporarily over southern Argentina, southern Chile, and the Falklands Islands, causing measurable increases in exposure to ultraviolet light. This created heightened fears among people there about skin cancer, cataracts, and damage to immune systems. Since the use of CFCs has declined, the ozone layer has recovered. Its current condition can be seen at NASA's "Ozone Watch," http://ozonewatch.gsfc.nasa.gov/. However, it appears that a major replacement for CFCs, hydrofluorocarbons or HFCs, contribute to global warming. Most states have pledged not to use HFCs after 2030.

In 1987, 22 states signed the Montreal Protocol on Substances that Deplete the Ozone Layer. They committed themselves to reducing the production of CFCs by 50 percent, with the wealthy states helping poorer states make the transition to safer refrigerants. Like the UN's immunization program for smallpox, the agreement was a success. More states joined the Protocol and accelerated the pace at which they would get rid of CFCs, and as the use of CFCs went down, the ozone layer recovered. The latest ozone treaty has been ratified by nearly all states and the ozone layer is expected to fully recover by 2050. It was successful for a number of reasons which are worth noting because progress in other areas has been much more difficult to achieve. First, there was strong consensus among experts that there actually was a problem. Second, there was a strong consensus among these same experts about what was causing the problem and how to fix it. Third, there was clear evidence that steps taken were actually making things better. Fourth, the steps that needed to be taken—scrapping CFCs—were not prohibitively expensive. Fifth, because the solution was not too expensive, rich, developed states were willing to absorb much of the cost to all states of undertaking it.

There has been much less progress on safeguarding biodiversity, but not for lack of international treaties. As early as 1946 a convention on international whaling emerged aimed at conserving stocks. In the 1970s, an agreement on preserving wetlands was established along with the Convention on restricting the International Trade in Endangered Species (CITES). A UN Law of the Sea (UNCLOS) was also negotiated with a conservational component. At the Earth Summit at Rio de Janeiro in 1992, a Convention on Biological Diversity was put forward. This focused on preserving the habitats of endangered species—forests, jungles, and wetlands for example—rather than particular species, but it also addressed the new issue of biotechnology. It employed the **precautionary principle** which said the absence of full scientific certainty should not be an obstacle to acting where a loss of biological diversity threatened.[20] It also used a similar formula to the Montreal Convention by which rich, developed states helped poor, developing ones, for example, by sharing the results of expensive genetic research on rare and potentially valuable forest products.

The problems generated by trying to safeguard biodiversity are large and complex. First, while there may be one problem, it shows up in multiple ways. Fishing, foresting, hunting, farming, genetic research, and patent law are all affected by addressing the problem. Second, some people do not care about preserving biodiversity. Ivory poachers, big game smugglers, and lumber companies (especially state-backed ones) specializing in hard timbers, find that the more treaties are signed to restrict their trade, the more valuable its products become. It is difficult and expensive to monitor big factory fishing ships and the size of their nets which scoop up all sorts of fish indiscriminately. Third, some people and governments say that other issues are sometimes at stake and other principles threatened by measures to preserve biodiversity. Norwegian and Japanese whalers, for example, say sentiment, and not science, determines the number of whales the International Whaling Commission says they can catch. Their governments sometimes agree and ignore parts of the whaling convention. The big drug companies in the US and American politicians say that the requirement to share the results of expensive research into the properties of rare flowers and plants from the Amazon, for example, violates their intellectual property rights. Finally, and unlike with CFCs, it is much harder to show people the problem—as opposed to many problems—and it is much harder to show the benefits, as opposed to the costs, of doing something about the reduction in biodiversity.

Where these problems are most obvious, however, is on the big issue of global warming. Again, we see a pattern of treaties and arguments about the scale of the problem, measures to deal with it, compliance with those measures, and the costs of their implementation. The 1992 UN Conference on Environment and Development (UNCED), also known as the Earth Summit at Rio, committed states under a program known as Agenda 21 to reducing their emissions of greenhouse gases to get temperatures back down to their 1990 levels. The 1997 Kyoto Protocol to the 1992 UN Framework Convention on Climate Change (UNFCCC) agreed at Rio, established a road map for reductions which gave developing states more time to reach targets. It also created a process of "trade and cap" by which firms were given quotas for their greenhouse gas emissions. If they reduced their emissions below their quota targets, they could trade the balance with other firms for money. Subsequent agreements steepened the target for emissions to five percent below the 1990 level and introduced penalties for non-compliance, but the tougher the agreements became, the more opposition from certain states they faced. The US pulled back from the process after Kyoto. Then, at follow-up conferences in Copenhagen (2009) and Cancun (2010) it joined with some newly industrializing states in a commitment to keep global warming only two percent above pre-industrial levels.

By the time the UN Conference on Sustainable Development (2012) was held on the twentieth anniversary of the Earth Summit, the US had still failed to ratify the Kyoto process and Canada had pulled back its commitment, its former government citing the size of the penalties it would face for non-compliance if it was still a party to the agreement. Several leaders of developed states failed to attend the Rio meeting, saying they were busy dealing with the global economic crisis. Those leaders who did attend were confronted by huge street protests made by environmentalists who had gathered from all over the world to demonstrate their anger at the lack of progress. Another multilateral conference known as COP (Conference of the Parties) 21 was held in Paris in 2015 to make a major effort to ease some of these disagreements and to move towards a much stronger global climate regime with firm targets for emissions and strong sanctions for those who ignore them. And in the same year, the US and China jointly committed themselves to pursuing targets regarding carbon emissions and to helping others to reduce their emissions too. There are no mechanisms for enforcing these pledges, however, other than the desire for governments to be seen to keep their word and preserve the reputations of their states. At the time of writing (2017) however, the significance of the Paris agreement has been undercut by the withdrawal of the US under the Trump administration.

Key terms

anthropocentric An understanding of something, for example the natural environment, which prioritizes the satisfaction of human needs and wants over other ways of understanding it.

carrying capacity The amount of pollution a body of water or piece of land can remove or absorb without being spoiled or destroyed.

environment The natural and produced surroundings in which living things live and act.

precautionary principle The idea that the consequences of a danger are so bad that action to avert it should not be left until there is complete certainty and agreement that the danger exists.

sustainability The ability to live in ways which do not consume, spoil, or destroy resources faster than they can be replaced.

Key takeaways

- Over the last forty years there has emerged a strong international consensus among scientists, governments, and citizens that the global environmental system is changing.

- Over the same period, there has emerged nearly as strong an international consensus among scientists, governments, and citizens that these changes are related to human activities, mainly those associated with industrialization.

- The main areas of change have been a rise in global temperatures, a decline in biodiversity, and a reduction of the ozone layer, all of which are harmful to life on the planet.

- There has emerged a strong international consensus that these changes should be stopped or slowed by reducing emissions of greenhouse gases, reducing pollution, and increasing sustainable economic practices.

- There exists a little disagreement about whether these changes are taking place, bigger disagreement about whether there is much people can do about them, and a great deal of international disagreement about who should adopt more environmentally friendly policies, how quickly, and who should pay for them.

- There are many environmental treaties. They are most effective where the problem is clear and fixable without too much expense—the Montreal Protocol on the ozone layer, for example. They are least effective where the problem is widespread, expensive to fix, and requires the cooperation of many people with other priorities they find more pressing—the Kyoto protocol, for example.

Exercises

1. In what ways does global warming matter and to whom?

2. How do the positions of developed states like the US and the members of the EU differ from the positions of developing states like China and India, on the question of restricting carbon emissions?

3. In what ways does the rise of environmental issues show how international relations have changed?

4. In what ways does the handling of environmental issues to date show how international relations have remained the same?

12.4   The future of natural resources, populations, and the environment in an era of uncertainty

As noted at the beginning of the chapter, the sources of the debate about the environment and global environmental policy are perhaps the most important examples of the uncertainty in international relations today. There has been great progress made in raising environmental awareness on the part of governments and peoples. Most people now claim to accept the principle of sustainable development as this applies to how natural resources are exploited. Trees should not be cut down at a rate faster than they can be replaced, for example, and water should not be taken from aquifers in greater quantities than it can be replaced over the same period of time. Most people claim to accept that the rate at which we pour waste into rivers should not exceed the carrying capacity of those rivers to absorb or remove the waste. Most people also accept that their activities can have a damaging impact on the environment of others, and that people in one state should accept responsibility for the environmental impact they have on people in other states. The sulfur emissions produced by power plants in Ohio and Britain fall as acid rain killing life in Canadian and Norwegian lakes respectively, for example. Not long ago, Americans and Britons would have said "tough luck; not our problem." That is no longer the case. Very few "climate skeptics" and virtually no scientists now reject the claim that the planet actually is warming up. Most people, but not as many, agree in general terms that something can and must be done.

It is on the specifics, however, where uncertainty is strongest, disagreement is at its most intense, and diplomacy faces its greatest challenges. The planet may be warming, the skeptics concede, but it has warmed and cooled in the past, and the present warming pattern is complex—witness the slowdown at the start of this century. In part, some of the skeptics acknowledge, this global warming may even be the result of human activities. However, they ask, are we sure that anything we can do will influence this trend? Before we set about imposing massive costs on our economies and transforming the way each of us lives so we can lower our carbon footprints, we had better be sure that it is worth the effort in terms of actually slowing global warming. Might it not be better to prepare for the consequences of global warming than to try to reverse it? Surely it is easier to move people away from areas where the sea is rising and storms destroy property, than it is to reverse a planetary climate trend whose causes are complex?[21] Besides, who is going to pay for all these changes to smokestack filters, car exhaust systems and ways of generating electrical power? What is to become of the workers in factories and mines which have to be closed because of the quest for clean energy?

Everyone agrees these costs should be fairly distributed with help provided to poorer states. Developed states like the US and the members of the EU, however, argue that they are doing their part in cutting emissions while newly industrializing states like India and China are hugely adding to the problem of greenhouse gas emissions. They are becoming rich while developed states are stagnating. The newly industrializing states should pay their fair share. The newly industrializing states reply, we are all in this mess because of two centuries of industrialization by the developed states. It now is our turn to grow, even if not to US levels of wealth, and fairness suggests that the developed world should pay more than us or anyone else in terms of cutting its emissions.

Arguments have been made worse by the fact that the parties to the arguments do not trust one another. Environmentalists often see the skeptics as selfish actors who simply do not care about the fate of the planet and most of its people so long as they are getting rich. How else do you explain agribusinesses taking huge risks experimenting with the unknown consequences of genetically modifying crops, oil companies' deep water drilling where they can do very little if something goes wrong, drug companies refusing to allow cheaper generic versions of their life-prolonging vaccines against HIV/AIDS to be produced until the patents run out, and electricity producers persisting with expensive and vulnerable nuclear power even though there is no satisfactory solution to the disposal of the dangerous waste it creates? More recently, how do you explain a US president who has suggested that the whole environmental issue is a Chinese trick intended to slow down China's economic rivals?

From the other side, similar doubts are expressed about the motives of environmentalists. The suspicion is that they are not driven by concerns for the environment, so much as hostility to the big corporations, the riches they generate, and the lifestyle of consumption they promote. Even if big sports utility vehicles were not wasteful of finite resources and producers of dangerous greenhouse gases, skeptics suspect that environmentalists would still be against them because of the bad values they think they reflect: conspicuous consumption, one-upmanship, and aggression. 'Why are the Europeans so opposed to genetically modified foods when there is no evidence that they are harmful?' the skeptics ask. Is it because the Europeans cannot compete economically in this area? And why, the skeptics ask, do environmentalists seem to willfully ignore the real progress made in deep sea drilling techniques, and lowering vehicle emissions, and why do they want to close the door to developing further improvements?

The trouble with these hostile mirror images is that there is something to both of them. Matters of fact and science are inextricably mixed up with matters of value and belief. What we might now call environmental disasters have happened before. Britain, for example, lost nearly all its forests over a thousand-year period. Place names like the Forest of Bowland reflect what used to be, although there is hardly a tree to be seen in these "forests" today. Ireland lost over a half of its population in the mid-19th century when the non-native potato crop—an import from the Americas on which most of the population had come to rely—failed. The population level has never fully recovered. The Mediterranean islands of Malta have no rivers, streams, woods, and little topsoil thanks to a sequence of what we now recognize as bad farming practices. The islanders' water comes from desalinization plants or bottled imports. The former is salty as it is drawn from the sea. The latter is expensive. It may be wrong that these things happened. They may have been avoidable, and people certainly suffered. Yet, the skeptics note that life goes on, and very good lives are lived in each of these places despite these "disasters."

We are certain that some natural resources, particularly sources of energy like oil, are being used at a rate greater than they are being replaced. It can take millions of years for oil to form naturally. We are certain that, absent some great scientific discoveries, the population of the world cannot aspire to the standards of living and rates of consumption presently enjoyed by the majority of people in the developed world. We are certain that climate change is taking place and nearly as certain that human activities, notably those from which carbon emissions result, are a major factor in climate change, although the consequences are complex and not well understood. We are even certain that the states of the world are taking these issues seriously and are trying to negotiate collective measures which will reduce the sources of the problems, are trying to develop new and sustainable ways of providing energy and food, and are trying to assist and encourage their populations as they make the transition to "post-carbon" economies and societies based on renewable resources and sustainable practices. What we are uncertain about is the rate at which non-renewable resources are being used, how fast and how extensively climate change is occurring, and how fast and how deep the transition to another way of living needs to be. Above all, we are uncertain whether the governments of states and the people they represent, no matter what they say about the need for sustainable development based on the careful stewardship of renewable resources, have the capacity to do what they say they want to do. The gains of environmentally sound policies often lie in the future and are collective gains. The costs of doing something often occur right now and are relative costs, paid more by some than others. The costs of doing something are presently to be carried mainly by the wealthy and powerful. The costs of not doing anything often lie with those least able to protect their interests. It might be a good time to raise taxes on fuels to promote more efficient use of them while the price of oil is low, for example, but how do you sell this to consumers (and voters) who are just getting by and enjoying the windfall of cheap gasoline/petrol?

As a practical matter, therefore, new arguments in environmental politics about how fast do we need to change our ways and how deep do the changes need to be often play out along the lines of older arguments. On the one hand in these arguments are those who do well from the way things presently are and say the possibilities exist for others to do well, too. On the other side are those who do less well and say the world is set up to keep things this way. To these arguments, often presented as between rich and powerful of the Global North and the poor and weak of the Global South, we turn in Chapter 13.

Recommended reading

Jeremy R. Youde, *AIDS, South Africa, and the Politics of Knowledge*, Aldershot, 2007.

David Joseph Wellman, *Sustainable Diplomacy: Ecology, Religion, and Ethics in Muslim-Christian Relations*, New York, 2004.

Ronald B. Mitchell, *International Politics and the Environment*, London, 2009.

Matthew Peterson, "Green Politics" in Scott Burchill, Andrew Linklater, Richard Devetak, Jack Donnelly, Terry Nardin, Matthew Paterson, Christian Reus-Smit, and Jacqui True, *Theories of International Relations* (4th edition), Basingstoke, 2009.

Sonja Boehmer-Christiansen and Aynsley J. Kellow, *International Environmental Policy: Interests and the Failure of the Kyoto Process*, Aldershot, 2003.

Notes

1 Michael T. Klare, *Resource Wars: The New Landscape of Global Conflict*, Holt Paperbacks, New York, 2002.

2 Nick Mead, "China versus US consumption," *DATABLOG, The Guardian*, August 3, 2010.

3 Luke Baker and Justyna Pawlak, "Insight: As Ukraine Looks West to Europe, Russia's Shadow Looms," *Reuters*, October 1, 2013 at http://www.reuters.com/article/2013/10/01/us-eu-ukraine-russia-insight-idUSBRE99008920131001

4 Donella H. Meadows, Dennis L. Meadows, Jergen Randers, William W. Behrens III, *The Limits to Growth*, Universe Books, 1972.

5 Michael R. Edelstein, Astrid Cerny, and Abror Gadaev (eds.), *Disaster by Design: The Aral Sea and Its Lessons for Sustainability*, Bingley, 2012.

6 Patrick Walters, "Aral Sea Recovery?" *National Geographic*, April 22, 2010, accessed at http://news.nationalgeographic.com/news/2010/04/100402-aral-sea-story/

7 Lester R. Brown, *Outgrowing the Earth: The Food Security Challenge in an Age of Falling Water Tables and Rising Temperatures*, Earth Policy Institute, International Publishers, Washington DC, 2004, accessed at http://www.earth-policy.org/books/out/ote6_2

8 UNICEF Press Center, "JMP Report 2008—Progress on drinking water and sanitation: special focus on sanitation" July 17, 2008 at http://www.unicef.org/media/media_44093.html

9 "As world passes 7 billion milestone, UN urges action to meet key challenges," *UN News Center*, October 31, 2011 at http://www.un.org/apps/news/story.asp?NewsID=40257#.Uk8k7BAtY24

10 Thomas R. Malthus, *An Essay on the Principle of Population*, London, 1798.

11 Warren S. Thompson, "Population," *American Journal of Sociology* 34 (6) 1929, pp. 959–75.

12 *China Daily (Europe)*, June 4, 2013, http://europe.chinadaily.com.cn/china/2011-04/29/content_12418282.htm

13 *Black Death*, http://www.history.com/topics/black-death

14 Jason Beaubien, "Botswana's Stunning Achievement Against AIDS," *Listen to the Story*, National Public Radio, http://www.npr.org/2012/07/09/156375781/botswanas-stunning-achievement-against-aids

15 See Stephanie Nebehay and Barbara Lewis, "WHO slashes budget, jobs in new era of austerity" in *Reuters*, May 19, 2011 at http://www.reuters.com/article/2011/05/19/us-who-idUSTRE74I5I320110519

16 Susan Greenhalgh, *Just One Child: Science and Policy in Deng's China*, University of California Press, Berkeley, 2008.

17 See Joseph Charlton, "Skip work, have sex: Russians celebrate 'day of conception' as sporting community continues to criticise Putin's anti-gay legislation" in *The Independent*, September 12, 2013 at http://www.independent.co.uk/news/world/europe/skip-work-have-sex-russians-celebrate-day-of-conception-as-sporting-community-continues-to-criticise-putins-antigay-legislation-8812840.html for the eighth anniversary of this holiday.

18 See Simone Bertoli and Herbert Brücker, "Selective Immigration Policies, Migrants' Education and Welfare at Origin," (abstract) *CEPR Discussion Paper No. DP8196*, Social Science Research Network, 2011 at http://papers.ssrn.com/sol3/papers.cfm?abstract_id=1749817

19 David R. Keller (ed.), *Environmental Ethics: The Big Questions*, Wiley Blackwell, Oxford, 2010.

20 Jacqueline Peel, *The Precautionary Principle in Practice: Environmental Decision-Making and Scientific Uncertainty*, Federation Press, Sydney 2005.

21 Henry Nau, *Perspectives on International Relations* (3rd edition), CQ Press, Washington, 2012.

13 North-South gaps and old-new gaps

Preamble

Listen to politicians, professors, preachers, experts, and diplomats talk about international relations, and soon you will hear them stressing the importance of cooperation. Whether to create economic prosperity or to achieve environmental sustainability, they suggest, we have to cooperate because, in the words of a former British prime minister, "We are all in this together."[1] Global problems, like the environment which was examined in the previous chapter, require global solutions. Everyone suffers without the cooperation necessary to increase economic growth and solve environmental problems.

Perhaps this is so, but a glance at the world suggests that very often people are not "all in this together" in the sense of all benefitting equally when something good happens or suffering equally when something bad happens. We see great inequalities among people in terms of just about everything human beings need and value. Even an environmental disaster, for example, will hurt some people far more than others, and some may even benefit from it. Consider how rising sea levels would affect the following: poor people who live close to the ocean in poor states; rich people who live next to the ocean in poor states; poor people who live next to the ocean in rich states; rich people who live next to the ocean in rich states; and people in the businesses of building sea walls and making pumps. They may be all in this together, but with greater versus lesser levels of vulnerability, greater versus lesser prospects of receiving help, and more versus fewer options in the face of a shared problem.

When we start thinking of inequalities and gaps in these terms, we start to move away from the realm of science and discussions between experts and towards the realm of politics and the sort of arguments noted in Chapter 2 between people about who gets what and why. You are more likely, for example, to have developed views about why there are rich and poor in the world and what, if anything, to do about the gap between them than you are likely to have developed views on why global warming is occurring or how we explain the apparent pause in the rise of global temperatures at the start of the 21st century. Inequality is a difficult issue to debate. At its worst, it becomes a shouting match between those who maintain that the rich and powerful run the world for their own benefit and will do anything to keep themselves on top, and those who say the poor and weak are so because they are lazy, stupid, and inferior. It may be that one or other of these positions is correct, or that they are both correct (they're probably both wrong). As we shall see, however, the arguments are not simply driven by political and economic interests. They often turn on how people define things, what they think is important and, especially, what they think is tolerable and intolerable.

An exploration of the dimensions of global inequality usually begins with a barrage of absolutely depressing statistics revealing the conditions in which many people live and the different life opportunities facing human beings in the lottery of where they happen to be born. This chapter will do that too, and then it will look at some of the arguments about why gaps and inequalities matter and in what ways. There are Realist, Liberal, and Radical Post-positivist approaches to understanding why gaps in terms of inequality exist in international relations. This chapter will devote more attention to Radical approaches, however, since these have become very influential if explaining how these gaps have developed. Chapter 14 will focus more on what, if anything, to do about these gaps, examining Liberal arguments for how to narrow them and more recent Radical proposals for how to rethink them.

13.1	Dimensions of global gaps and inequality

Learning objectives

1. Identify seven key quality of life indicators which can be used to demonstrate the existence of global gaps and inequalities.

2. Describe how using different measures can suggest different conclusions about whether the global income gap is narrowing or widening.

3. List the different dimensions along which human equality/inequality can be experienced.

We see inequalities in terms of what people have, how they are treated, and thus how they live, everywhere. You probably know from personal experience that life isn't always fair, although we all tend to remember the times things broke against us rather than the times they ran for us. You probably also know where to go in your hometown to see street people of all ages who have somehow fallen off, or never climbed onto, the ladder of life. You may have fallen off yourself at times or worry that you are going to do so. Most of us think that in these terms we are very lucky (although a little more luck wouldn't hurt). We use statistical data, however, to provide a more general and systematic, if not always more clear, picture of how life is not fair both within states and at the global level.

One way of representing this inequality is illustrated by the life expectancy figures in Table 13.1. A rough indicator of how long people are likely to live is provided by the state in which they happen to have been born, an event over which they have no control.

Another way to look at this fairness is by looking at household income and seeing what percentage of the population in a state has less than a particular

Table 13.1 Life expectancy at birth: selected states plus Hawaii and Mississippi (2012)

State	2008	2009	2010	2011
Afghanistan	48	48	48	49
Haiti	61	61	62	62
Cuba	79	79	79	79
Switzerland	82	82	82	83
United States	78	78	78	79
Hawaii	–	–	–	81
Mississippi	–	–	–	75

Note: these figures provide very rough guides. They vary within states by gender, race, social class, and region, for example, and different sources will provide different figures.

Source: for sovereign states, *World Bank* at http://data.worldbank.org/indicator/SP.DYN.LE00.IN and for US state figures, *World Life Expectancy* at http://www.worldlifeexpectancy.com/members.php

figure. For example, the World Bank used to use one US dollar a day, since revised to $1.25, as a benchmark figure (data from the Human Development Reports of the United Nations Development Agency can be found at this link: http://hdr.undp.org/en/content/human-development-index-hdi).

In 1995, the UN World Summit for Social Development noted the distinction between **absolute poverty** and relative poverty. It also put forward the Copenhagen declaration defining absolute poverty in the following terms. "Absolute poverty is a condition characterized by severe deprivation of **basic human needs**, including food, safe drinking water, sanitation facilities, health, shelter, education, and information. It depends not only on income but also on access to social services."[2] When people are deprived of basic human needs, death, suffering, social breakdown, violence, and war can result. **Relative poverty**, in contrast, may be seen as a condition in which people lack, or are deprived of, a level to which a community believes needs and wants ought to be satisfied; this level will be higher in developed states than in less developed states. It will also include less tangible notions of dignity and status, alongside more material concerns like food and shelter. Someone regarded as poor in Sweden or Canada, for example, might be regarded as well off by someone from South Sudan or Burma. It is much easier to identify absolute poverty, and to secure agreement that something should be done about it, than it is to identify relative poverty and agree that something should be done about it. The first concerns the basic requirements of human life and touches on what appear as basic and universal human values. Ideas about relative poverty, in contrast, are more dependent on contexts and have socially constructed elements to them.

Even with the elements of absolute poverty, it is still possible to argue over what precisely is meant by "severe" deprivation. How much education, access to information, or health care would be needed to move people from being severely deprived to merely being deprived to being satisfactorily provided for? Nevertheless, there is broad agreement on the following elements of the picture of global gaps and inequalities.

■ First, in a world with a total population closing in on 8 billion people, about a billion of them continue to live in conditions of absolute poverty. Many people have moved beyond absolute poverty largely thanks to economic growth in the newly industrializing states like China, Brazil, and India. However, this positive trend has been offset by population growth which has kept the figure at a billion.

■ Second, this absolute poverty is geographically concentrated in specific parts of the world, sub-Saharan Africa, for example, and to a declining extent, South Asia. People who live in absolute poverty in these areas are also the most vulnerable to natural disasters, diseases, and wars and other forms of organized violence.

■ Third, in any given part of the world on any of the indicators mentioned, those more likely to experience both absolute and relative forms of poverty include children, women, old people, regional, ethnic and racial minorities, people in lower socio-economic classes, and people who live in the countryside. They do so, not because of so-called "natural factors," like vulnerability to illness or physical weakness. The developed world shows that policy can compensate for such factors. They do so primarily as a result of the way dominant social values and priorities in vulnerable societies suggest how scarce resources should be allocated to their disadvantage.

■ Fourth, thanks to rapid economic growth, many people and several states are beginning to escape the conditions which produce absolute poverty. Thanks to fast industrialization and economic development, states like China and Brazil are moving beyond the low death rates which characterize the first phase of the demographic transition (see Chapter 12). However, there are arguments about both the sustainability of this route out of poverty in the future and about what it is doing in terms of relative poverty. Do the new middle class being created in states like South Africa and Mexico, for example, represent the future for nearly everyone in those states or are they destined to remain a minority? And what are the implications of the widening incomes gap which is developing between this new middle class and the established well off?

We can add two more observations which are not as clear cut. The first is the general sense that poverty is a bad thing about which something should be done, especially when it co-exists with great wealth. We may argue about how far equality should go—for example, the old socialist view, "to each according to his needs," regardless of his contribution does not secure universal agreement even among old socialists.[3] However, everybody says they agree that people should not be deprived of food, shelter, health-care, and education just because they start out life poor, and just about everybody agrees with the idea of equal opportunity or, at least, that everybody deserves a fair shot in life.

It offends our sense of fairness then when we see the sorts of images presented by the Global Post's *Great Divide* Project (see link at https://www.pri.org/collections/great-divide-global-income-inequality-and-its-cost). This uses a statistical compilation of measures known as the Gini coefficient which capture the range of inequality which exists in different states on things that people value like income and life expectancy. The project presents photos from around the world which illustrate the consequences of this inequality.[4] The data captured by the

Gini coefficient and other data-gathering exercises like the UN Development Agency's Human Development Index can be used to illustrate which states have more and less inequality in these terms. Images of famine victims like the one from a "Doctors Without Borders" hospital in Kenya are particularly disturbing, especially when we know that Kenya is a relatively wealthy, successful East African state with a high-end tourist industry attracting travelers from all over the developed world (follow link at http://www.spiegel.de/fotostrecke/photo-gallery-famine-in-east-africa-fotostrecke-70580.html).[5] Contrast this with the images in the film "Jambo!" put out by the Kenyan Tourist Board to promote tourism in Kenya by presenting images of high living standards and fun which is not available to the vast majority of the country's population (follow link at http://www.youtube.com/watch?v=_qHXEBH_aM8).

Most of us are familiar with the big scandals of recent years when it has been revealed that poor people all over the world have been paid very small sums of money for producing clothing and sport shoes which are then sold for hundreds of dollars in the developed world. In some cases, children have effectively been sold by their families into **indentured labor** in very poor conditions to produce, for example, soccer balls for export. Some children and women are also, in effect, treated like slaves and are trafficked and traded for sex. They are punished and sometimes killed when they object. The World Health Organization tells us millions of children under the age of five die every year (6.9 million in 2011), and that more than half these deaths could have been "prevented or treated with access to simple, affordable interventions."[6] We all agree that too much inequality is wrong and that everyone should have a fair shot in life. Many of the solutions to the worst consequences of inequality and the gaps between rich and poor can be put into practice fairly easily. Then why does absolute poverty persist, and why do many of these gaps between rich and poor appear to be growing?

Key terms

absolute poverty   A condition in which people lack, or are deprived, of basic human needs.

basic human needs   Sufficient food, safe water, safe sanitation, adequate shelter, and access to health care, education, and information.

indentured labor   An arrangement, usually in return for money up front, in which a person is bonded to work for another person for a number of years and/or until the money plus interest is paid off.

relative poverty   A condition in which people lack, or are deprived, of a level to which a community believes needs and wants ought to be satisfied; this level will be higher in developed states than less developed states.

Key takeaways

■ Most people agree that human beings have basic human needs which have to be satisfied if they are to live full, healthy lives.

- The extent to which people's basic human needs are satisfied is widely understood to depend greatly on the geographical location and level of economic development where they live.
- The extent to which people's basic human needs are satisfied can also depend on their race, ethnicity, nationality, gender, class, and age, together with the political and economic order in which they live.
- Nearly all people agree that the resulting inequalities in terms of, for example, life expectation and incomes, particularly between people living in the developed world and the developing world, should be reduced.
- Some of the gaps resulting from these inequalities are narrowing, others are persistent, and some are getting wider.
- There are political and economic arguments about what is happening to these gaps and why.

Exercises

1. Describe some of the possible consequences when people are deprived of their basic human needs.
2. How does relative poverty differ from absolute poverty, and why might there be less agreement about the need to solve problems of relative poverty?
3. Describe two factors which can make the persistence of poverty particularly upsetting and strengthen interest in putting an end to it.

13.2 | Realists, Liberals, and the significance of global inequality

Learning objectives

1. Describe how Realists understand the role of global inequality in the power politics of international relations.
2. Explain how Liberals see global inequality as a problem of knowledge, **reason**, **reasonableness**, and interests.

Recall that Realists think self-interested states are the most important actors in international relations (see Chapter 2). They say these states are chiefly concerned with maintaining and increasing their security by maintaining and increasing their power. Classical Realists stress how the character of states reflects and amplifies aspects of human nature. Neo-Realists stress how the logic of anarchy forces very different sorts of states to behave in basically the same ways if they are to survive and prosper.

As a consequence, and until recently, therefore, Realists have not been very interested in explaining global inequalities, divides, and gaps in terms of human needs, except perhaps **human security**. Even then, they have been more interested in state security on the assumption that if the state is secure, the human beings inside it will also be secure. More importantly, Realists have been far more interested in the consequences of inequality than in its causes. What happens in a world where some states have more power than others? How do the ways we answer this question shape our attitude to power?

Realists' answers are that states will try to get more power and that they are smart to do so. They add that since power today depends upon having a large, developed, growing, and competitive economy, then governments should be interested in economics. A strong economy producing healthy, educated citizens is a source of power. As far as international relations are concerned, however, the poor—as the old Christian teaching has it—are always with us. So make sure you do not become one of the poor states or, if you are poor, get rich as quickly as you can. To be poor is to be weak, and in an anarchical international system weakness is dangerous.

How then are we to explain the interest of governments in North-South divides, global gaps, and the resulting poverty and human misery? As human beings, Realists argue, statesmen will be neither more nor less interested in these issues than the rest of us. As statesmen, however, they have to put the interests of their own state first. Thus, they will engage with the issue of global poverty in the following circumstances.

- First, they will do so when appearing to care serves the interests and security of their state. There is no point annoying other governments and people by being truthful about not caring about others when being truthful offers no gains but may incur costs. According to Realists, whatever the political leaders of powerful, developed states attending a UN conference on international development actually think, they will join in the general humbug about how ending global poverty should be a priority for everybody and claim it is already a priority for their own state. They will then present a long list of the many things they are doing to contribute to its reduction.

- Second, statesmen will actually care about reducing poverty and closing gaps where they think the failure to do so may weaken the position of their allies and thus their own position. Thus, according to Realists, the US sends large amounts of money to Egypt partly to ease the problems of poverty because Egypt is an ally, and a stable and prosperous ally is more capable of being useful. By the same logic, the US does not send large amounts of money to Iran or Cuba because they are rivals of the US. The less stable and prosperous they are, therefore, the better.

- Third, statesmen will take arguments about reducing poverty and narrowing gaps seriously when their state will benefit, receiving money and other forms of assistance as a consequence. It is not surprising, Realists argue, that the UN General Assembly takes the lead on producing these initiatives. It is an institution which adopts resolutions supported by the majority of its member states. The majority of the states in it—being undeveloped or less developed—stand to benefit from measures undertaken in the name of reducing poverty and narrowing gaps between rich and poor. Nor should we be surprised, Realists note, when we see the diplomats of successfully developing states like Brazil and India pursuing interest-driven assistance policies in poorer states like Sudan and Sri Lanka, while at the same time asking to be treated as poor states still in need of help themselves from the developed world.

In addition, Realist theorists have attempted to address the criticism that they have little to say about inequality, poverty, and injustice by developing the arguments about hegemons and stability.[7] If the world wants any kind of developed international economic order, the Realists say, it has to take account of the realities of international politics. There is no overarching government to make the rules and to encourage and enforce compliance with them. There are multiple small, poor, weak, and self-interested states producing free-rider problems. As we saw in Chapter 2, a consequence of this, according to some Realists, is that the world needs a big power, or group of powers, to act as a hegemon or quasi-government. A hegemonic power is not only the strongest power in the international system. It is so strong relative to other states that it can create a system of rules to govern all states' interactions and uphold that system by providing incentives for others to comply with the rules, and punishments for those who do not.

Realist political economists applied this argument to the historical periods dominated by the Liberal hegemons, Britain, and the US. Both Realists and Radicals sometimes present the current world order as a system of rules maintained by US military and economic power. Both are interested in what is currently happening to what they see as US hegemony and its ability to maintain the current world order. However, other systems, for example, the Soviet Union's socialist system during the Cold War, Germany's various economic orders in Eastern and South Eastern Europe in the 1930s, and the Japanese Co-Prosperity Sphere in World War II can all be understood in hegemonic terms. The point, according to some Realists is that someone is needed to maintain order. Beyond that, the Realist political economists—or at least those in the Western, developed world—agree that the best hegemonic order for doing something about poverty, inequality, and a host of other economic concerns is one which safeguards Liberal political and economic principles. A hegemon which is Liberal in its own political and economic principles is the best guarantor of such an order.

Liberals agree about these principles but are less sure about the need for a single hegemon to impose and uphold them. Recall from Chapter 3, that Liberals think that interest-directed individuals are the most important and valuable actors in human affairs. They say these individuals are concerned with maximizing their good, usually but not exclusively defined in material terms. Individuals are reasoning and usually reasonable actors capable of cooperating and competing, as well as engaging in conflict to advance their interests. Most importantly, they are capable of learning about themselves and their circumstances and applying their acquired knowledge of both to improve their lives. As a consequence, therefore, Liberals have also not been very interested in explaining global inequalities, divides, and gaps which exist in terms of human needs, although for reasons which differ greatly from those of the Realists.

Liberals approach equality and inequality in two ways. The first is in terms of rights. Individuals have equal rights to things people value, for example, life, liberty, and property. No one person has a stronger claim to her life or holding property than another person, and in this sense they are all equal. In a second sense, however, people are clearly unequal. Some are more intelligent than others, for example, and know more and can figure things out more quickly. Some are stronger than others—physically or emotionally—and are capable of working harder than others, and willing to do so. Liberals generally agree that people can be differentially rewarded on the basis of their different capacities or, to put it another way, if they can get more than others without encroaching on other people's rights then so be it. Liberals do argue, however, about how much more and what individuals can do with it.

When they look at the global inequalities described earlier, therefore, Liberals note the following. Some of them are caused by ignorance or, better, absence of knowledge. People who know about bacteria and washing your hands in clean water after they have been to the bathroom, for example, get less sick and live longer than people who do not.[8] Education and the provision of clean water supplies solve that problem. Sometimes, however, education and water are not provided, because the people in a position to do so, usually the government, are just as ignorant as the people, or have no money to pay for these services, need or want to spend their money on other things, or simply do not care about the people who need these services. Sometimes also the people themselves do not like what education teaches them since it suggests they change the way they live. Sometimes, for example, they will not use clean water from new wells because it looks wrong or tastes funny. Sometimes they will refuse immunization for themselves and their children because they believe it will make them sick.

As we shall see in Chapter 14, Liberals have arguments among themselves about what to do when confronted by these sorts of problems. They usually revolve around how to allocate responsibility and obligation for doing something and how to balance the rights of those affected by these efforts. If people don't want to wash their hands and use the clean water, for example, that's their business, but what should be done if they fall sick, make others sick or do not let their children wash their hands and use clean water? Much more importantly, if governments say they have no money for the improvements, then who should pay for them, and if governments clearly have the money but choose not to make the improvements, what should be done to them to make them pay and by whom?

For Liberals, therefore, the causes of global inequality are very clear in a generalized sense. They arise from combinations of ignorance, selfishness, and ineffective systems of rules. The causes, however, are not nearly as important as the difficulties raised by trying to fix the problems. Never mind how people came to be so unequal, how we are going to deal with the fact that they are? For others, however, there is no possibility of alleviating the consequences of global inequality until one has a clear understanding of the reasons for why it exists, why it does not go away, and why it is possibly getting worse. These reasons, Radicals argue, are rooted in the very specific character of the way in which a capitalist world economy evolved after the great European political, social, and industrial revolutions of the late 18th and early 19th centuries.

Key terms

human security   An idea which suggests people's wish to live as free as they can from threats to their material and psychological wellbeing, with also the sense that states and state security do not always deliver human security.

reason   The idea that human beings use their intelligence to understand and solve the problems which face them.

reasonable   The idea that human beings will include the wishes and wants of other people in their reasoning and, possibly, the idea that they do so because they empathize with the wishes and wants of others.

Key takeaways

- Realists (see Chapter 2) are more interested in the consequences of global inequality and poverty for the relations of states than their causes and effects on human beings.
- Some Realists argue that a state exercising hegemonic power offers the best prospect for global order and that a Liberal hegemon offers the best prospect for a Liberal global order fostering economic development, if not necessarily economic equality.
- Liberals (see Chapter 3) accept some forms of inequality, and see some other forms of inequality as arising from ignorance, wickedness, and bad rules and institutions

Exercises

1. Under what circumstances do Realists say governments become interested in global inequality and poverty?
2. In what ways do Liberals say people are equal and in what ways do they say people may be unequal?

13.3   Radical and Southern perspectives on global inequality

Learning objectives

1. Describe the characteristics of **world systems**.
2. Describe the characteristics of **empires** and **imperialism**.
3. Explain the processes of **uneven and combined development**.
4. List the ways in which Radicals say the poor and weak are kept dependent.

"Radical" and "Southern" are not entirely satisfactory terms for the perspectives we are about to examine. Radical suggests the need for a fundamental change from the roots up. However, it also suggests views which are somehow wild, extreme, and outside the mainstream. In large parts of the world, the views we are about to examine are regarded as straightforward and mainstream. "Southern," of course, refers to the Global South, not the geographical one, and many people who subscribe to the views described here live in the Global North. As we saw in Chapter 4 on Post-positivist approaches, however, it is difficult to find a label which does not have problems. "Revolutionary" has the same problems as "radical." "Marxist" or "marxian" runs into the problem that not all the ideas we are about look at are consistent with Marx's own arguments. "Post-positivist" captures much of the intellectual side of these perspectives, but not their political or economic dimensions.

While they are hard to name, however, recall that all these approaches have the following in common. First, they focus on **production** and **reproduction**, meaning the ways human beings make and continue to make their lives out of their material surroundings. This involves working on nature, for example: planting crops, making iron, and cutting trees for lumber. It also involves what Marx called forces of production—the technical means available, for example, water mills, steam engines, nuclear power plants—and relations of production—the way people and their lives are organized around production such as masters and slaves, lords and serfs, and owners and workers. Finally, production also involves ideology—a system of ideas which help keep production going by makings sense of what is going on to the people involved when they ask questions like "why are things set up the way they are?" and "why do I have the position which I occupy in the scheme of things?"

The second thing these approaches have in common is their view that throughout history, relations of production have involved **exploitation**. Exploitation can refer simply to putting something to use or extracting a benefit from it. A state or a company can exploit oil reserves in its territory or offshore, for example, and a person can exploit a friend who works at a pizza place to get free pizza. Exploitation as it is being used here, however, conveys the sense that something is being unfairly taken. In this sense, according to Marx's collaborator, Friedrich Engels, exploitation began once human communities were able to produce more food than they consumed. The surplus food allowed the creation of two groups of people who did not have to produce the means of living, but got to consume more than their share—priests and warriors. Priests explained why they did not work yet got more than their share by telling stories of gods and magical beings who said this was right. Warriors hit anybody who didn't believe what the priests said and anybody who tried to make trouble. Together, in this view, and as we saw in Chapter 2, priests and warriors set up the Gangster state as a protection racket.

While economies have become far more sophisticated and productive today, Radicals maintain that exploitation remains at their core. Through work, the majority has always created the wealth available for consumption. This remains true even in an era where production appears to be increasingly automated. By ownership and control, the minority consumes more than its fair share of the wealth, thus creating and recreating inequalities. The vital point to grasp from Radical perspectives, therefore, is that inequality and poverty are not unfortunate byproducts of an economy or system of production and exchange. The system is set up the way it is to create and preserve inequality through exploitation.

Archaeologists and anthropologists delve deep into prehistory to show how extensive systems of production and exchange existed among simple societies long before there were states or anything much like them. As we saw in Chapter 9, people traveled great distances to exchange goods for economic and religious reasons. Goods themselves circulated through long chains of exchange between peoples who never met, and probably did not know of each other.[9] Using historical and sociological approaches, Immanuel Wallerstein invites us to think of these processes in terms of world systems analysis.[10] He does not use "world" in a global sense. He uses it to shift our thinking away from the idea of a series of national- or state-based economies linked by international economic relations and towards the idea of a single system on a bigger scale with a primary division of labor and regular economic exchanges. This world system overlays, transcends, and sometimes ignores the political units existing at the same time. Thus, we can think in terms of a Mediterranean "world," a Greek "world," and a Roman "world," each of these worlds exhibiting long-running flows of trade, investments, and cultural exchanges.[11]

Wallerstein and other world system analysts are particularly interested in the world system which they see emerging centered on 14th-century Western Europe, and which, they say, provides the basis for today's global economy. What they identify is the regular movement of bulk goods from different parts of the world on a regular basis. Silver from South America, tobacco and sugar from the Caribbean, and spices from the East Indies (now Malaysia, Indonesia, and the Philippines) were imported into Spain and Portugal. From there they circulated into the rest of Europe, in return for simple manufactures—farm tools, textiles, and clothing, for example, especially from the region of what is now northeast France, Belgium, the Netherlands, and southeast England. Later, the system expanded, initially to include the great grain producing estates in what is now eastern Germany and Poland. Eventually there emerged the famous trade triangle of manufactures from Europe exchanged for African slaves who were shipped to the Americas to produce cotton, tobacco, and sugar for export back in Europe (for an image of the slave trade triangle see, http://www.liverpoolmuseums.org.uk/ism/slavery/triangle.aspx).

As the slave trade triangle suggests, a key assumption of world systems analysis is that these exchanges are usually unequal and exploitative. One party benefits from them more than the other because it is more powerful, rich, clever, and confident than the other. It maintains its position by actual acts of violence and by what Johan Galtung calls **structural violence**. Slaves and workers would be punished if they objected to participating in unequal exchange. So long as the fear of punishment was in people's minds, however, then violence could be said to be structurally present. Without the presence of violence in this sense, people would simply refuse to participate or they would rise up in revolt.

A world system can be divided up in these terms into a center or core, on the one hand, and a periphery outside it, on the other. In **center/core-periphery** analysis, as Galtung describes it, the center is always occupied by a minority of people who possess more of everything that human beings consider valuable than people at the periphery who are always the majority (for representations of the world in terms of Center/Semi-Periphery/Periphery see the following links:

https://www.google.com/search?q=images+of+core-periphery

and

https://www.google.com/search?q=images+of+core-periphery&rlz=1C1G-GRV_en&tbm=isch&source=iu&pf=m&ictx=1&fir=pYGVYR6gUIJ_wM%253A%252CAs0nuOXxIvjjfM%252C_&usg=__4Q23r3cv4QRyTM-KhJpe4pRPnoNQ%3D&sa=X&ved=0ahUKEwi5y5Pmr-LWAhWJ3YMKHU_sDv4Q9QEILDAC#imgrc=lhFrjonwvuPLjM:).[12]

The world as a whole can be mapped in terms of centers, semi-peripheries, and peripheries depending on what is traded and the direction of the overall flow of wealth. So too can each region, state, or any other political unit in the world, and the interests of each center are aligned with each other, as are the interests of each periphery. Thus the governments and elites of the US, the EU, and developing states in Africa are on one side in arguments about who gets what, and the poor people living in the peripheries of the US, the EU, and developing states in Africa are on the other.

Liberal economists and Liberal political economists sometimes make human history sound like a set of smooth flowing processes and self-producing systems delivering human progress. However, Radicals want us to note that the world system which emerged between the 1400s and the 1600s did so as the result of massive human effort, conflict, and suffering. Had you looked at the contenders for building a world system in 1400, you would have probably bet on China rather than Western Europe. China had a long-running, stable political order, a sophisticated civilization, and an advanced technological base with which to work. The Europeans were still pining for the great days of the Roman Empire, arguing over whether the Emperor or the Pope should lead Christendom, and trying to carve out as much independence as possible for their relatively small kingdoms, dukedoms, and free cities. One of the fascinating aspects of history, however, is the surprises it produces. They generally result from the fortuitous combination of several causes occurring at the same time. In Western Europe's case, it was some improvements in marine engineering and navigation techniques which let ships cross oceans, improvements in metal casting which allowed for better cannon and muskets, and political rivalries which had kings and queens on the lookout for new sources of revenue and resources to support their wars with each other, that set an age of exploration and expansion in motion.

The Spanish and Portuguese took the lead. Spain sent explorers and soldiers into the Caribbean, Central America, the southern part of North America, eastern South America, and across the Pacific to the Philippines. Portugal did likewise southward down the coast of Africa, around the Cape of Good Hope, across the Indian Ocean to the Arabian Peninsula, India, the Malay Peninsula, the East Indies, and eventually China. In 1494, Pope Alexander VI facilitated the Treaty of Tordesillas by which Spain and Portugal divided the world to the west beyond

Europe—both known and unknown—between them. It was followed in 1529 by the Treaty of Zaragoza which did the same for the lands to the east of Europe. Needless to say, the vast majority of the world's population had no idea this carve up was taking place, and it was far beyond the power of Spain and Portugal to actually put it into effect.

Nevertheless, other Europeans were not far behind in expanding overseas. In the 17th century, England, France, and the Netherlands began by fishing the waters off North America and attacking the treasure fleets of the Spanish and Portuguese. Piracy was soon supplemented by the establishment of trading posts, naval stations, **colonies**, and plantations in the Americas, Africa, the Arabian Peninsula, India, the Pacific Islands, and Oceania. The Russians also began to expand, first southwards into the Crimea and the Caucasus, but eventually across Central Asia and Siberia towards India, China, and the Pacific. Over the next three hundred years, through a series of attacks against native peoples, wars against each other, and great projects for economic development, the major European powers essentially established a limited measure of control over the whole world, either directly through empires or through settlers who had subsequently declared their independence.

The term empire can mean several things. The source of the word is in the Latin term *imperium* suggesting rule, power, and authority. It can be used for any political system that has an emperor at its head. Thus Serbia and Brazil were both termed empires for a while for this reason, although neither was what is generally regarded as an empire. Usually, the term suggests the rule of one people over other peoples. A distinction is made between overseas empires of the sort once possessed by the Portuguese, the British, and the French, and contiguous or continental empires of the sort once possessed by the Austrians and Russians (the Spanish empire was a combination of both at its height). The Soviet Union was sometimes called an empire because it was claimed that Russians, in effect, ruled over the other nationalities. Many Russians would still object to this, maintaining that the Soviet Union was more of a commonwealth, albeit a repressive one, since Communist Party leaders from all the nationalities participated in the government. The United States is also sometimes called an empire by those who think that, in effect, it rules over other peoples. If so, however, it does so mainly indirectly, and an indirect empire seems very different from a direct empire.

The empire on which the sun never set

Are empires good or bad things? No one openly calls for the return of empires today because the historical ones were undemocratic, exploitative, and racist in the way they were organized. They were also inefficient in economic terms. However, they were not all bad and they did accomplish some good things. Consider the British Empire (Figure 13.1). It was the largest of the European overseas empires. At its fullest extent in 1922, it covered just under a quarter of the world's total land surface and had a population of over 450 million people. It began with the English conquests of Wales and Ireland and the union with Scotland between the 13th and

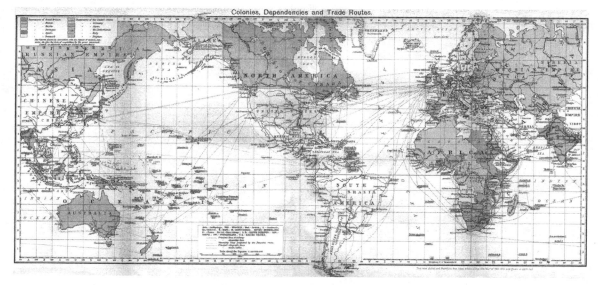

Figure 13.1 An old map of the European Empires in 1900, focusing on the British Empire
(Source: World History Archive/Alamy Stock Photo)

17th centuries. This resulted in the creation of a British union ruled largely from London. English fishing camps in the New World were followed by settlements on the eastern seaboard of North America and the pursuit of the fur trade into the northern interior. In the 18th century, Britain lost control of its American colonies, but held on to British North America (Canada) and its possessions in the Caribbean. It also expanded into India, Burma, the Malay Peninsula, southern Africa, and Oceania (Australia and New Zealand). In the 19th century, Britain gained control of Egypt, Cyprus, the western coast of the Persian Gulf, Hong Kong, and large areas of eastern and western central Africa.

By the 20th century, the tide had begun to turn against the British Empire. The so-called "white" or settler dominions of South Africa, Australia, New Zealand, and Canada saw themselves as increasingly more equal partners with Britain and, along with Ireland, had effectively won their independence by the early 1930s. Even so, the British Empire acquired new territories in the form of League of Nations mandates in Palestine and Iraq as late as 1919. After World War II, however, in the late 1940s, India, Pakistan, Burma, and Ceylon (Sri Lanka) became independent, followed by Malaysia in the 1950s and nearly every other colony in the 1960s. By 1980, all that remained were a few islands and territories. One important exception, the colony of Hong Kong with a booming economy and a population of over five million was handed back to China in 1997.

The remnants of the British Empire attract attention now only when there are arguments, for example, about handing back Gibraltar to Spain or handing over the Falkland Islands to Argentina. Unless they can be shown to be economically valuable, the British would probably be glad to see them go. However, the local inhabitants want to stay British and public opinion in Britain is easily aroused in their favor. Today, the empire lives on in a very loose association of its former members, the Commonwealth (formerly British Commonwealth) headed by Queen Elizabeth. Their heads of government meet every two years. Britain itself, however, faces the prospect that even Scotland may break away and become independent

The British today have mixed feelings about their empire. It was acquired and held with a great deal of violence, thieving, and deception. There were always arguments about whether it was a source of British power or a distraction and drain on its resources. As Britain itself became a parliamentary democracy with everybody voting in the 20th century, British rule over other people against their will was hard to square with what were now British principles. On the other hand, there is a great deal of pride in what their forebears, the relatively few inhabitants of some small islands off the coast of France managed to achieve abroad, a global civilization elements of which exist to this day, and at home, a multicultural society enriched, but also challenged, by its encounters with the peoples of its former colonies.

As we saw in Chapters 2 and 9, for Realists and mercantilists, empires are part of the story of the rise and fall of great powers. Great powers acquire empires to gain their resources, peoples, and strategic locations as sources of strength. They lose them through military defeat or when they become too weak to prevent other great powers from taking them or the local people rising up against them. For Liberals, empires are part of the story of what misguided states used to be tempted to do. Keeping control of other peoples is an inefficient way of gaining access to their resources and markets, and an illiberal way of maintaining political order because it does not involve the consent of the governed. The empires of Liberal states might have brought some good political, social, and economic reforms to their colonies—for example, establishing fair administration, starting schools, and managing the building infrastructure like railroads—but having one people bringing good things to another people or peoples is never the best way of doing it for either party.

For Radicals, however, empires are part of the story of unequal encounters between peoples. Over and over again, the peoples of Europe arrived in distant lands. They killed native peoples, either directly and intentionally through military operations or indirectly and carelessly through infecting them with disease or poisoning them with drugs like opium and alcohol. Those who were left were drawn into economic systems which exploited them or were displaced by European colonists who settled their former territories. The Europeans were able to do this because they were always richer, stronger, and better organized for war and control than the native peoples.

To be sure, the stronger had often preyed on the weaker in all parts of the world throughout human history. Radicals acknowledge that it was not only Europeans who built empires and exploited one another when they got the chance. What was different about the European empires, however, was the new driving force provided by the capitalist economic systems which developed in the European states in the 19ᵗʰ century. As Marx argued, capitalism's need for profit, and thus for constant growth, innovation, and access to cheap resources, gave it a competitive and exploitative dynamic which had never been seen before. Its guns and cheap goods made it impossible to resist.[13]

Indeed, radical communists like Vladimir Lenin argued that by the end of the 19ᵗʰ century an entirely new stage of capitalism called imperialism had emerged. According to Lenin, the search for profit and the pressures of competition had forced firms to merge first into ever bigger combines or cartels, and then with the banks into monopolies. These monopoly capitalist states increasingly had to look overseas for territories, resources, and weaker peoples to exploit. Once the world had been completely divided up between these monopoly capitalist states, there would be nothing left but to re-divide it through wars undertaken by imperialist states against each other.[14]

There had been arguments among 19ᵗʰ-century Radicals about whether capitalism was the precondition of world revolution or a developmental dead end which had to be destroyed. Marx himself went back and forth on the issue. He would point to what the British were doing in India, for example, developing roads, railways, and factories, and say they were bringing the revolution to India much sooner than it would otherwise come. In Ireland, however, he argued the British were stifling the revolution by forbidding industrial development which would rival the mainland's economy and insisting on developing only agriculture to feed Britain's growing working class.

Lenin shared Marx's equivocation. On the one hand, he worried that the workers of the developed capitalist states had become what he called a "labor aristocracy," still exploited but doing well enough to throw in their lot with the capitalists. On the other, he argued that the wars to re-divide the world would bring about the collapse of capitalism and that socialist revolutions would then occur in the leading capitalist states. These revolutions would spread to the rest of the world, eventually bringing about communism and the end of exploitation and inequality. To begin with, World War I and the Bolshevik Revolution in Russia seemed to confirm Lenin's more optimistic view. In the end, however, it was his more pessimistic view which proved more accurate from a Radical standpoint.

The problem, according to Leon Trotsky, was one of uneven and combined development. Trotsky had been one of the leaders of the 1917 Bolshevik revolution in Russia along with Lenin. The failure of the Bolshevik revolution to ignite successful revolutions elsewhere led to arguments among the Bolshevik leaders about the future of communism. Trotsky maintained that it was a mistake to see all states developing in the same way through the same stages towards capitalism and the emergence of a revolutionary working class which would overthrow it in each state. Different parts of the world had developed at different rates, and when global capitalism combined these unevenly developed states and regions together, interesting things happened.

The good news, from the Radicals' point of view, was that all states did not have to go through the same stages of development to reach the revolutions which would bring inequality to an end. Russia, for example, was able to have its revolution first even though it was not the most developed capitalist state. It had come to capitalism late, and therefore, some of its industrial organization was of the most modern and advanced type. Similarly, colonies might not have to go through centuries of development like the Europeans. Revolutions might emerge there suddenly, quickly, and unexpectedly.

Some people today, greatly influenced by Trotsky's thought, note the way capitalism is constantly creating new inequalities in its search for innovation and profits.[15] Consider, for example, how the Information Revolution has created a new "digital divide" between those with access to the Internet and those without. Consider also the ebb and flow of urban populations in the developed world. First, everyone who is able to do so moves from the countryside to the cities where profits can be made and wages are higher. Then, everyone who can moves from the cities to the suburbs where industry has re-located because the costs of doing business became lower there. Now, everyone who can is moving back into the cities because the cost argument has reversed itself. For Trotsky, these conditions of permanent turbulence brought with them the conditions of "permanent revolution," a constant struggle against inequality and the processes which created it.

More important, for our purposes, is the bad news about uneven and combined development from the Radicals' point of view. Capitalism's encounter with different societies brings about three types of development: **dependent development**; distorted development; and, some have argued, the "development of underdevelopment." These are consequences which, the Radicals argue, maintain old conditions of inequality, create new ones, and seem almost impossible to escape.

The idea of the underdevelopment of development is perhaps the hardest of the three to grasp.[16] It involves taking a broader view than usual of what is meant by development. Take, for example, the Africans who were brought to the Americas as slaves. We can imagine that they came from cultures with their own standards of living and sense of themselves as a collective identity. The passage to the Americas, separation from one another in the process of being sold and bought, and their subsequent plantation lives destroyed all that and replaced it with something from which very little good came, unless you believe that the experience of suffering can produce good things. The descendants of these Africans in the Americas today can be said to be living with that burden, although it clearly weighs more heavily on some than others. Similar claims can be made about the impact the Europeans had on the cultures and identities of Native Americans. Elsewhere, the native population of Australian island of Tasmania was exterminated by a combination of violence, infection, and neglect. And today many people in East Africa are more vulnerable to droughts and famines now their subsistence agriculture has been replaced by cash crops for export which cannot be eaten. In short, the argument is that development has, at least in some places, made life worse for some peoples. It is hard for people in the developed world to come to terms with these facts when they are used to seeing statistics about how, on the whole, when development arrives, death rates fall, life expectancies increase, and people live better lives.

The idea of distorted development is well illustrated by comparing a political map of western Africa with a map of the main ethnic groups in the same area.

The sovereign states reach in from the coast to the interior, one next to the other. The Gambia, for example, consists of a small strip of land on each side of the Gambia River. The basic infrastructure of roads and railways does the same thing. Until relatively recently, telecommunication between these states was often routed to Europe and back out again (although in the age of the Internet and the convoluted routing of e-mail traffic, this no longer seems so strange). While the political organization is roughly from the coast to the interior, however, the basic ethnic groupings in West Africa are roughly situated in layers stretching from east to west. This disconnection between the states and ethnic groupings in the region results from European colonialism. The Europeans landed on the coast in search of slaves. Then they moved into the interior to find and develop resources, establishing separate colonies with separate governments and different forms of political, economic, and legal organization. As a result people with a common identity, for example the mainly Moslem Hausa Fulani tribes of northern Nigeria and northern Ghana, northern Benin, northern Togo and northern Cote d'Ivoire were separated by colonial borders, merged with southerners who were similarly separated from one another, and encouraged to acquire a new common national identity chiefly through the languages of their respective colonizers. The local elites which replaced the European powers when these colonies became independent in the 1960s accepted these borders. They did so, on the assumption that more troubles would be created by trying to change them. The ethnic, cultural, and religious conflicts in the region which persist to this day, however, indicate how distorting and disruptive the European presence was and continues to be (look at the distribution north of the Bight of Benin on the ethno-linguistic map of Africa with political boundaries overlaid at https://tracingafricanroots. wordpress.com/maps/ethno-linguistic/).

Nigeria: the giant of Africa

Nigeria is one the largest states in Africa with a population of over 170 million people. After a gradual process of being taken over by the British through the 19th century, it became independent in 1960. The British were there for a relatively short time. There are stories of old people in West Africa watching the British flag hauled down for the last time at independence who had seen it hoisted for the first time at the end of the 19th century when the British formalized their control. Contacts with Europeans date back to the 16th century, however, when the Spanish and Portuguese exploited and expanded the practice of slave taking which the African kingdoms and empires of the region pursued in their wars with one another.

There are over 500 tribes in Nigeria, but the biggest three groupings, accounting for over 60 percent of the population are the Yoruba concentrated in the southwest, the Ibo (Igbo) in the southeast, and the Hausa-Fulani in the north. These groups have their own strong cultural identities, but one of the strongest—religion—reflects the influence of peoples from beyond the borders of the state. People in the south tend to be Christians, reflecting the presence of European missionaries and educators in the past. The people in the north tend to be Muslims, reflecting the influence of Arab traders who crossed the Sahara Desert from the Maghreb and further afield.

Nigeria is rich in resources, with a large agricultural sector producing cocoa, peanuts, cotton, palm oil, and rubber, among other crops and commodities. It has industries based on processing these. It has a young, fast growing population that is the product of rich and creative cultures. Above all, however, Nigeria is rich in oil, much of which it exports to the US. Oil is the principal source of income for the Nigerian economy. The state's size, wealth, and fast growth since independence have made it a leader in its region and a spokesperson for Africa. Neighbors, the African Union, the developed world, and the UN all look to Nigeria, for example, when peacekeeping forces need to be established and supplied with troops.

However, within six years of independence the state had experienced several military coups. These culminated in a civil war which began in 1967 when the mainly Ibo area broke away, declaring itself the independent republic of Biafra. The rebellion was crushed after a long and bloody war which lasted until 1970. Between one and three million people died. Nigeria experienced a series of military governments from 1966–79 and 1983–98. Since then it has had elected governments although the elections have been widely viewed as neither fair nor free.

Nearly everyone agrees that tribalism is a problem. Despite massive efforts to reform the politics of Nigeria along federal lines, parties and politics reflect tribal and ethnic interests, more than ideological differences about how to run the state. Corruption also plays a part. Generals and others have enriched themselves while incompetently managing the economy and running up huge debts despite the oil wealth. To be fair, however, Nigerian politics, like politics in many places in the world, reflect the belief that you get into politics to look after your family and people, and that to do this requires building up patronage networks of people who exchange favors. Outside intervention, primarily because of the oil, has complicated Nigerian politics. France, for example, backed Biafra in the civil war while Britain and the Soviet Union backed the government. International oil companies have engaged in environmentally damaging practices in the Niger delta where much of the oil is found and have been implicated in the harsh treatment of any local people who object to harmful policies too strongly.

Most recently, Nigeria has not escaped the rise in Islamic radicalism. A movement known as Boko Haram (loosely translated as Western Education is Harmful) has emerged in the north. Its members have attacked Christians who have retaliated against Muslims in the south, and most notoriously it has kidnapped young women from boarding schools, ostensibly on the grounds that they are receiving inappropriate education. The Nigerian army has been accused of overreacting by killing innocent people in the north to intimidate the rest of the population. There is widespread agreement that Nigeria has underperformed since independence to the point of dysfunction. In spite of great wealth generated by oil revenues, the economy has not diversified sufficiently, and most of the population has not benefitted from the uneven economic growth which has resulted. Nigerians are the first to blame themselves (or each other) for these failings, but they are also aware of how many of their problems result from the terms on which their state was set up in the first place, dividing peoples who used to live together and forcing peoples together who used to live apart.

The imperial states of Europe were interested in developing their colonies. They organized the local people into building ports, roads, and railways, and they brought their own experts in to create telegraph, telephone, and radio broadcasting networks. The imperial states also developed systems of administration, education, and healthcare. The British said they were preparing their colonies for eventual independence. The French maintained they were bringing their colonies up to a level of civilization from which they would be able to become part of France, the native inhabitants as French as anyone else. Whether their governments and people actually believed this, the Radicals maintained, it was not the case. Actual development took place only to the extent that it helped the imperial powers more efficiently and cheaply exploit the resources of their colonies. It was Raúl Prebisch, an Argentinian economist who directed the Economic Commission for Latin America in the 1950s, who called this dependent development, which he said resulted from **structural dependence**.

Prebisch's problem was one shared by many in the developing world. We have won our political independence and the right to manage our own affairs. We have our own government, our own armed forces, money, national bank, and our own flag and postage stamps just like states in the developed world. So how come we are not getting rich like the developed world? Why does the "modernization thesis" (which we shall examine in Chapter 14) not seem to work for us? The newly independent states of Asia and Africa were asking this by the 1960s. The problem was doubly tough for Prebisch, however. His state, Argentina, and the other states of South America had been independent for well over a century. Yet still they were stuck producing primary commodities for export which enriched only a minority of their population. Prebisch and other dependency theorists claimed that primary products like minerals, meat, and cereals were always faced with a **declining terms of trade** problem. That is to say, over time the price of primary product exports fell against the price of manufactured imports. As a result, a state like Argentina would have to export more and more wheat and beef to pay for the same quantity of imported machinery, vehicles, and aircraft. At the end of World War II, Argentina had been as wealthy as Canada and predicted to grow faster. By the 1960s, however, it had been left in the dust. What was to be done?

Prebisch's answer was that Argentina should move beyond producing things like cereals, timber, beef, and iron ore for export, and get into manufacturing its own locomotives, aircraft, military equipment, and vehicles both for the home market and for export. To accomplish this, however, three things were needed. First, there had to be people capable of making these more profitable goods. Second, there had to be the technical expertise which knew how to make them and how to organize the production of them. Third, there had to be capital to invest in the people, the experts, the factories, and the infrastructure which would make this kind of production possible.

States like Argentina had the people. They did not have enough people with the right skills, however, or the experts or the capital which would pay for these. The home-based commodity industries barely generated enough profit to pay the rising bill for imports. They could not provide the capital to invest in developing the new sectors. Therefore, states like Argentina were dependent on foreign expertise and foreign capital, and these were largely only available for investment in the commodities sector of the economy. We will help you raise beef and mine ore more efficiently, the developed world seemed to be saying, but we will not let you make cars and trucks because that is what we do.

Argentina, according to Prebisch and other theorists of *dependencia* as they called it, faced a world economy which was structured by the developed states to their advantage. Grow grain, and the capital flowed in from abroad. Try to develop heavy engineering and it was like running into a wall—no capital. The results, according to the Radicals, were dismal. More capital—not just money, but human capital too, the best minds and the best athletes, for example—flowed out of a dependent state than flowed in. Political instability was generated by tensions between the relatively few commodity producers and finished goods importers (known as the comprador class) who benefitted from the status quo and the workers and business people (known as the national bourgeoisie) who wanted to develop and benefit from a modern economy at home.

A state like Canada might do relatively well with a commodities-based economy delivering a high standard of living. It might even be allowed a measure of industrial development so long as this was primarily geared for export. However, it would always be a dependent, second-class citizen in the international order. Argentina, for example, was allowed to make Ford Falcons long after they disappeared from the US market but not allowed to make the latest Ford car models. Brazil could produce weapons, but not the very latest weapons. Canadians might get rich, but only at the price of watching their oil and gas flow south to help create better jobs in the US, and when the price of commodities fell or resources were used up, they had to accept the spectacle of whole towns essentially closing down. If they didn't like it, they could reflect on the blockades, embargoes, and interventions to which states like Cuba, Chile, and Iran were subjected when they protested too much.

Key terms

center/core-periphery The idea that any social system, including the international system, can be divided into a minority at the center or core which possesses most of the things that people value and a majority on the periphery or edge which does not.

colonies Territories which are not part of a state, but controlled by it and usually overseas; properly speaking with people from the state settled there permanently.

declining terms of trade   A situation in which the price of some goods tends to fall over time against the price of the goods for which they are being traded requiring more of them to be sold to obtain the same amount of the other goods.

dependent development   The idea that the form which development takes in poorer parts of the world is shaped, distorted, and limited by the needs of development in richer parts of the world.

empires   A political system where the rulers of one people also rule over other peoples with the objectives of exploiting them, helping them and building up the economic and political power of the system.

exploitation   Putting a resource or good to use (exploiting a deposit of iron ore, for example), often, but not necessarily, with an element of unfairness or taking advantage when the term is applied to people exploiting one another.

imperialism   A stage in the development of a state's economy, according to Lenin, where its businesses cannot make sufficient profit at home and so they invest in less developed areas abroad, but also used to describe policies of rule and exploitation pursued by empires.

production   Usually the creation of material goods from raw materials, but also the creation of all the material and non-material elements of human life can be viewed as forms of production.

reproduction   The ongoing and repeating process by which the elements of human life are created.

structural dependence   The idea that poor parts of the world are prevented from developing by the rich world's control of expertise, capital, and force.

structural violence   The idea that a social system which depends on the use or the threat of force to hold together has violence as part of its structure.

uneven and combined development   The idea that the process of development does not take place at the same rate in all parts of the world, but that each part of the world is connected by it.

world system   A connected system of production which transcends the boundaries of states.

Key takeaways

- Radicals maintain that inequality and poverty result from the exploitative way in which production is organized.

- Radicals see a world system linked by uneven and combined development.

- The present world system is more exploitative than past ones, according to Radicals, because it is a capitalist one which exploits weaker actors to compete effectively, grow, and create profits.

- In world systems theory, systems are divided into centers or cores—each with a minority which has the most of everything people value—and peripheries—each with a majority which has less of everything people value.

- Cores keep peripheries dependent on them, limiting and distorting the ways in which they can develop.

Exercises

1. Why do Radicals regard the relationship between owners and workers as one of exploitation?
2. Why, according to Radicals, did becoming independent from the European empires not solve the problems of the former colonies?
3. Why, according to Radicals, should Canada worry even though it is rich?

13.4 The future of North-South and new-old gaps in an era of uncertainty

Dependency theorists rank among some of the most pessimistic Radicals when it comes to doing something about global inequality together with the material poverty and social indignities which they see resulting from it. Developing states were no longer colonies of empires but, dependency theorists argued, they might as well be. Through policies of neo-colonialism, rich states continued to control them even though they were independent. Prebisch, himself, was not so pessimistic. As we shall see in Chapter 14, he had a strategy by which he believed developing states could find their own way forward along the dimensions of economic, political, and human development. Developing states should make things themselves rather than importing them from the developed states, and when they had to trade, they should trade with each other rather than the developing states, using the UN to organize their cooperation and to lobby for concessions from the developed states. However, the question of both North-South and old-new gaps has become far more complicated since Prebisch's time in the 1960s. As was suggested in Chapter 12, it is unlikely that North-South gaps are going to be closed by the rest of the world achieving levels of development and consumption presently enjoyed in the rich states of the North because of the environmental damage in which such an effort would result. While some of the BRICS, for example, have been enjoying impressive rates of growth, they are not looking to become like North America and Western Europe in terms of the scale and character of the individual consumption patterns of their citizens. If they are beginning to close gaps, it is in terms of things like military power, diplomatic influence, and overall market share.

In addition, and as we shall see in Chapter 14, a new sort of gap is increasingly attracting attention—not that between different parts of the world or between different states, but between the rich and the poor, the educated and the uneducated, the skilled and the unskilled, the employed and the unemployed, plus the old and the young, within states. The result, or so it seems at times, is not uncertainty about how to achieve human development. What we see, instead, are fierce arguments between several competing viewpoints whose advocates are all equally certain that they know the best way to achieve human development and, more importantly, what human development should truly mean.

Recommended reading and viewing

Karl Marx, *The Communist Manifesto*, Moscow, 1969, http://www.marxists.org/archive/marx/works/1848/communist-manifesto/

Robert W. Tucker, *The Inequality of Nations*, New York, 1977.

Deepak Lal, *Poverty and Progress, Realities and Myths about Global Poverty*, Washington DC, 2013.

Michael Parenti, *The Myth of UnderDevelopment*, 2007, http://www.youtube.com/watch?v=5eKMspN-7Co

Madsen Pirie, *Economics is Fun: Globalization*, Adam Smith Institute, 2012, http://www.youtube.com/watch?v=shepp7De_4o&list=PL06A6035D1EAF3D0E

Global Poverty Project UK Launch, http://www.youtube.com/watch?v=gdIe2qSZJuQ

Notes

1 The former British Prime Minister, David Cameron, often made this claim, in this case speaking after riots in British cities in 2011. Cameron's Conservative Party argues that pro-business, free market policies eventually benefit everyone who works hard and does their best. Its opponents think this is wrong, that Cameron does not believe it, and that he was simply being cynical; see http://www.conservatives.com/News/Speeches/2011/08/David_Cameron_We_are_all_in_this_together.aspx

2 Copenhagen Declaration at http://www.unesco.org/education/pdf/COPENHAG.PDF

3 Karl, Marx, "Critique of the Gotha Program," *Marx/Engels Selected Works* Vol. 3, Moscow, 1973.

4 For the Gini coefficient, see the following link: http://web.worldbank.org/WBSITE/EXTERNAL/TOPICS/EXTPOVERTY/EXTPA/0,,contentMDK:20238991~menuPK:492138~pagePK:148956~piPK:216618~theSitePK:430367,00.html. For the Human Development Index see the following link: http://hdr.undp.org/en/statistics/hdi

5 Clemens Höges and Horand Knaup, "Famine in East Africa: a Catastrophe in the Making," *Spiegel Online International*, July 21, 2011, http://www.spiegel.de/international/world/famine-in-east-africa-a-catastrophe-in-the-making-a-775338.html

6 "Children: Reducing Mortality," *World Health Organization Media Center Fact Sheet No. 178*, September, 2012, http://www.who.int/mediacentre/factsheets/fs178/en/

7 For example, Robert Gilpin, *The Political Economy of International Relations*, Princeton, 1987, and Stephen D. Krasner, *The Third World Against Global Liberalism*, Berkeley, 1985.

8 See, World Health Organization, *WHO Guidelines on Hand Hygiene in Health Care: A Summary*, WHO/IER/PSP/2009.07, World Health Organization Press, Geneva, 2009.

9 Barry Buzan and Richard Little, *International Systems in World History*, Oxford, 2000, and Jared Diamond, *Germs, Guns and Steel: The Fates of Human Societies*, New York, 1997.

10 Immanuel Wallerstein, *World Systems Analysis: An Introduction*, Durham, 2004.

11 Ferdinand Braudel, *The Mediterranean and the Mediterranean World in the Age of Philip* II (Vols I and II), Berkeley, 1996.

12 Johan Galtung, *A Structural Theory of Imperialism*, Oslo, 1971.

13 Karl Marx, *The Communist Manifesto* (Marxist Internet Archive, Marx and Engels Library) accessed at http://www.marxists.org/archive/marx/works/1848/communist-manifesto/ch01.htm

14 V.I. Lenin, "Imperialism: The Highest Stage of Capitalism," in *Lenin: Selected Works* (Vol. I), Moscow, 1963.

15 Justin Rosenberg, "The philosophical premises of uneven and combined development," *Review of International Studies*, 39, 3, July 2013, pp. 569–597.

16 Andre Gunder Frank, *The Development of Underdevelopment*, New York, 1966.

14 Economic, human, and political development

Preamble

Everyone is interested in economic, human, and political development, although they argue over what these terms mean. There is a global consensus around the claim that economic development is the foundation on which the other two are built. The Taliban and ISIS might be exceptions to this claim, since they emphasize observing what they regard as the teachings of Islam above all else. However, our usual outliers, Iran and North Korea, are not. The Iranian leader, Ayatollah Khamenei, and North Korea's First Secretary, Kim Jong-un, would broadly agree with Americans and Europeans that the road to a powerful, secure state and a prosperous, happy people begins with figuring out how to create wealth efficiently, fairly, competitively, and profitably. What they would disagree on is how to do this.

Indeed, the international relations of the 20th century can be seen as an extended argument between people with different views on how to accomplish economic growth and development. Capitalists said maximize wealth through free markets, then secure states and prosperous, free peoples will emerge almost as byproducts. Socialists said put wealth creation under the control of states which will allocate resources where they are most needed according to complex plans. These socialist states will make decisions based on rational considerations and avoid the wasteful and unfair anarchy of private competition and profit-seeking. Social democrats looked for a middle way in which states moderated, regulated, and facilitated the operations of free markets in favor of ordinary people without killing off the vitality, risk-taking, and competition which those markets encouraged. Fascists also looked for a middle way in which states moderated, regulated, and facilitated the operations of free markets in favor of building up the power of the state and the group which controlled it without killing off the vitality, risk-taking and competition which free markets encouraged.

Until recently, this extended argument was considered effectively settled. World War II had exposed the great moral and practical shortcomings of Fascism. Nazi Germany, Fascist Italy, and militarist Japan simply could not compete with the productivity and capacity for innovation of either the capitalist United States or the socialist Soviet Union. The Cold War had exposed the weaknesses of socialism, when the Soviet Union buckled under the strain of delivering rising living standards while competing in an arms race with the United States. And, although this might have been less clear at the time, the Cold War could also be said to have gravely weakened social democracy. Without the threat of socialism on the other side of the Iron Curtain, social democratic governments were far less able to leverage concessions like higher taxes and fairer income distribution from private wealth-holders when Western economies ran into difficulties.

Thus by the end of the 20th century, as we noted in Chapter 4, Francis Fukuyama could wonder whether we had reached "the end of history" in terms of arguments about how to organize human affairs, and he could worry about the effects of this on people's willingness to strive for greater things.[1] For once, if only briefly, certainty replaced uncertainty as a global consensus (the so-called Washington consensus considered in Chapters 9 and 10) seemed to emerge about establishing free market economies with political democracies. Given what people seemed to want—freedom coupled with rising standards of living—this combination looked like being the only game in town from now on. As we know already, however, neither history nor arguments about how to organize economies and for what purposes have come to an end. This is because the popular version of Fukuyama's argument suffered from three over-simplifications.

The first of these is that socialist states were never as socialist, and the capitalist states were never as capitalist as they liked to present themselves. Indeed, the big story, whether in capitalist America, communist China, or social democratic Germany, has not been about states versus markets, but rather about the resilience of the state as a director of, and participant in, modern economies.

The second oversimplification is the idea that everyone wants development and that other forms of development depend on economic development. Most people would like to be better off in material terms. However, they give different answers as to how much better off they would like to be, and how they rank being better off in relation to other things which are important to them. Both the rise of religion and the emergence of concerns about sustainability and limits to growth (see Chapter 13) have affected people's attitudes to development.

The third oversimplification is to see arguments about the best way to organize politics and economics as separate from the struggle for power and influence in the world. They are not. Americans, for example, may regard democracies and free markets as the best combination for delivering development. There may even be some objective sense in which this is actually true. However, as the US declines (relatively), and as China rises, we should not be surprised to see Chinese understandings of development and Chinese arguments about the best politics and economics for delivering it attracting more attention. If India continues to grow quickly, we shall also see more attention to Indian views on development. As states and peoples consider how best to define, pursue and deliver economic, human, and political development, uncertainty is edging out certainty once again. Or, as was noted at the end of Chapter 13, competing certainties—the Chinese, Anglo-Saxon, and European models, for example—are emerging with the arguments going on within states, as much as between them.

| 14.1 | Undeveloped, underdeveloped, and developing peoples and states |

Learning objectives

1. Explain the shift in terminology from undeveloped through underdeveloped to developing when discussing changes in peoples and states.
2. List the ways in which the US can be described as more developed than China.
3. Discuss the assumptions behind the idea that human development and political development depend on economic development

Development is an idea more easily used in the natural sciences than in the social sciences.[2] We can think of the processes by which an organism grows bigger, becomes more complex, and perhaps even matures and reproduces itself. However, we also think of how an organism decays, declines, and dies as part of its process of development. Development may also simply refer to things happening or finding out more about what is happening. For example, news reports often use development in the sense that there have been developments in a news story about a court case, the birth of a royal baby, or negotiations between the United States and Russia.

The problems begin when we try to apply the idea of development to human societies. The problems are well illustrated by the difficulties academics, governments, and international organizations have experienced with the terminology used to describe rich and poor states and societies. In the 19th century, when European empires dominated much of the world, a simple distinction was made between those states and peoples who were "developed" and those who were "undeveloped." To be developed was to be rich, powerful (or aligned with the powerful), and civilized. Thus, for example, the US, France, and Denmark could be seen as developed. India, Ethiopia, and the Pacific Islands could be seen as undeveloped.

There were at least two problems with this distinction between developed and undeveloped. The first was that very few places and people were completely undeveloped. Accordingly, people looked for other terms. "Underdeveloped" allowed that some development existed, but it also implied that there had been a failure or a problem in the sense that we talk about, for example, a baby born with underdeveloped lungs. "Underdeveloped" peoples, especially once they ceased to be colonies and became independent states, were very sensitive to this implied judgment. Therefore, terms like "less developed" or, better still, "developing" were adopted. The latter, in particular became much more popular since it suggested that, wherever a state or people were right now in terms of development, they were on the road to somewhere better. Today, we often see this problem finessed by referring to types of states with acronyms, for example AISs (Advanced Industrial States) and LDCs (Less Developed States).

The second problem concerned the idea of being "civilized." This was, and remains, much harder to get around. The European empires and other developed states at the time spoke in terms of "a **standard of civilization**."[3] A state which met this standard would have a responsible government committed to upholding the rule of law and the rights of its people. The people too would be "civilized" in that they would respect one another's rights and accept the lawful rule of their government. From inside the developed European states, this standard appeared obvious and universally applicable. Governments which ruled arbitrarily and peoples who were governed by their passions and ignorance in their relations with one another failed to meet the standard of civilization and needed encouragement, help and control from outside to improve. With luck and wisdom, all the states and peoples of the world would meet the standards of civilization eventually.

However, from outside these developed states, this standard of civilization looked particular (Western, Liberal and Christian) rather than universal, self-serving rather than benign, and hypocritical rather than genuine. It allowed rich white people not only to set the rules for all the rest, but to break those rules in their dealings with people of other races (and poor white people) when they wanted to do so, like parents sometimes break their own rules when raising their children. In his early years as a British-trained and educated lawyer in India and South Africa, the Indian nationalist and pacifist, Mahatma Gandhi, experienced the racism of the British Empire first-hand, most famously when he was not allowed to travel in a railway coach reserved for whites even though he had the appropriate ticket. Thus, when asked on one occasion what he thought of Western Civilization, he famously replied that he thought "it would be a good idea," the implication being of course that the West was not civilized yet.

It helps to think in terms of two ideas. The first is "Civilization," singular and upper case. This suggests a universal code of moral, legal, political, and economic standards towards which all peoples and all states are developing. The second is "civilizations," plural and lower case. This suggests different and multiple sets of moral, legal, political, and economic standards. Thus we can speak of Western civilization, Chinese civilization, and Roman civilization, for example. The plural approach allows us to think about a number of interesting questions. Are civilizations in a process of **convergence** on a single set of standards—a global civilization?[4] If so, we might think of economic development in terms of economies becoming organized more around free market principles and priorities. We might think of human development in terms of individuals being richer and freer. And we might think of political development in terms of governments becoming more willing to hold elections in which more parties can compete and win.

If civilizations are not converging, or we do not want them to converge, then can we still identify key areas in which their expectations overlap, for example, over the basic needs of shelter, food, water, and security (see Chapter 13)? Or, as Samuel Huntington suggested, are civilizations likely to clash over their differences regarding what is important in human life?[5] And, most difficultly, can we speak in terms of some civilizations being more developed, higher, or better than others? If so, we are back to our old problem with "grounding" from Chapter 4. Where do we stand to make such judgments?

Think of Western civilization as we find it in the United States and "Confucian" civilization, as Huntington identifies it, in the People's Republic of China. Which state has the most developed civilization? Along some dimensions, this question seems easy to answer. For now at least, the US economy is bigger, more sophisticated and generates more wealth than China's. The gap between them is shrinking in terms of absolute size, but remains very large in per capita terms. Thus the US distributes more of that wealth to more of its people who live longer, healthier lives in which they consume more than their Chinese counterparts. The US political system also seems more developed, allowing people to think and say what they like about leaders whom they can try to replace through free elections. And Americans seem to have more fun, benefitting from a popular culture which is geared to entertaining them on their own terms. What does China have to offer? It has a very long history, which has given rise to a strong culture with its own distinctive philosophical, literary, and artistic traditions. The Chinese know where they have come from and who they are, even if they are less sure about where they are going. Their own culture is a source of identity and security. Children look after their parents, for example. They don't put them in care homes—at least they didn't until Westernization and modernization began to break down traditional family relationships. Most Chinese also know how to have fun without needing much stuff.

There would seem to be no contest between the US and China as to which has the most developed civilization. Which way do people move, for example, when given the chance—from China to the US or from the US to China? Applying the "veil of ignorance" test suggested by John Rawls, knowing nothing at all about your wealth, social status, and health, into which of the two would you sooner be parachuted to make your way in life?[6] The answer may seem obvious to you, and this might seem like evidence that there are certain things which everybody wants which some societies are better than others at providing. The vast majority of Chinese, however, would not make the same choice as you, providing circumstantial evidence, at least, that Chinese and American conceptions of the good life universally desired by all people are much more shaped by our respective cultures than we realize.

Western Civilization and the good life: the case of the Irish Travelers

The Travelers (*an lucht siúil* in Irish) are an Irish minority people which research suggests became a distinct ethnic group about 1,000 years ago. There are some 25,000 Travelers in Ireland, over 15,000 in Britain, and at least 10,000 in the US. Their numbers are hard to estimate since most of them maintain an itinerant lifestyle. They live in caravans (trailers and motor homes) and remain in one place for a relatively limited amount of time. They have a distinct language (Shelta) which combines elements of Gaelic Irish and Irish-English, and their own culture. In the past they made their living through horse-trading, dog-breeding, and selling and repairing kitchen pots and pans. In addition to these activities, today many Travelers are involved in the scrap metal industry and door-to-door companies which specialize in black-topping driveways, laying floor tiles, and house painting.

Like the Roma, Irish Travelers have often been called gypsies by the rest of the world in the mistaken belief that they originally came from Egypt. However, other than their life style and the suspicion with which mainstream society often regards them, the Travelers have no relationship to the Roma. Today, they come to the attention of settled communities when they suddenly appear on a piece of common land, unused private property, or in the layby at the side of a road, and set up camp for weeks and sometimes months. People then complain about Travelers engaging in anti-social behaviors like making a mess, making a noise, drinking to excess and fighting. In addition, concerns are expressed about their marriage practices (girls are married around 16–17), about their not paying taxes like everyone else and, above all, about their engaging in theft. In addition, the local authorities worry about how their life style affects the access of young Travelers in particular to good health care and good education.

The resulting arguments are familiar and have played out many times in many places before, for example, between American Indians, Australian Aborigines, and the Roma of southern Europe and the governments claiming authority over the territory on which they happen to be. On the one hand, many people say that the Irish Travelers are simply at odds with the demands of the modern, civilized life which most people want. That life requires people to live more or less in one place most of the time, respect property, obey the law, pay their taxes, and send their children to school so they can become productive citizens. In this view, Travelers are tragic holdovers from simpler times, cynical free riders benefitting from the contributions of the rest of us, or a combination of both. Either way, the argument is often made that they need to be eased towards their cultural or (according to extremist racists) physical extinction.

The Travelers' response is the same as that of threatened minorities and indigenous groups everywhere. We like who we are; and we like the way we live. Who is to say that one way of life is more developed or civilized than another, particularly to the extent that one way of life should give way so that another can prosper? We do no harm. Indeed, because of other people's belief that their societies are more developed and civilized than ours, we have been far more sinned against than sinning. When relations with the Travelers are badly handled, the result can be traumatic and polarizing like the 2013 eviction of hundreds of Travelers by police and private security firms at Dale Farm near London shown in Figure 14.1. The Travelers said they had permission to be on unused land. The authorities said their settlement had spread onto land where there was no permission for it to be, and that it was a becoming a public nuisance. When relations are better handled, organizations like the London Gypsy and Traveller Unit are formed to mediate between interested parties (http://www.lgtu.org.uk/).

Evaluating states and societies in terms of a single checklist of properties and values is dangerous. A single checklist always risks reflecting the priorities of a particular view. Instead, it is better to look at how different states and societies deal with conflicting perspectives on what human life is about and how it should be lived. However, for people with power and responsibility facing the problems of how to keep their followers secure and happy, all forms of development have

Figure 14.1 Evictions underway at the Dale Farm Travelers camp outside London in Essex, England, 2013

(Source: Graham M. Lawrence/Alamy Stock Photo)

come to be seen as dependent on the acquisition and production of wealth. Whether one wants a society of artists and poets, proletarians and peasants, or middle-class people and entrepreneurs, goes the argument, they have to be organized to feed, house, and supply themselves, or there will be no wealth for them to consume and no art or poetry for them to enjoy.

The idea that the economy comes first (President Clinton had a sign above his desk saying "The economy, stupid" during his 1992 election campaign so he didn't get distracted by other issues) seems obvious to us now. For much of human history, this was not the case. Of course wealth had to be generated in ancient Egypt, the Mesoamerican empires of the Maya and the Aztecs, and among the Bedouin peoples of the Arabian Peninsula, for example, to sustain their societies. However, they did not think about wealth creation in these terms, and still less in terms of economic development, growth, innovation, and change. Economic life was simply part of life. It was static for long periods, mainly took care of itself, and was subordinated to other priorities, except in times of great danger or great opportunity.

It was with the birth of modernity in Western Europe that ideas emerged about growth, development, and the priority of economic growth and economic development over other human interests. As we saw in Chapters 9 and 10, the idea of **capital** emerged then along with concerns about how it is best allocated to foster economic growth and development. Capital is a word with several uses. Sometimes it is used as a synonym for money. Think of it here, however, in terms of things of value to the processes of creating wealth. Thus we can speak of financial capital (for example, money), physical capital (for example, factories and their equipment), and human capital (you, me and other people when we are employed to create wealth).

Political economists closely studied the experiences of the British, other Europeans, the Americans, and the Russians in industrializing and triggering fast economic growth and development in the 19th century. They argued that attention needed to be paid to the accumulation of capital—how to build up wealth rather than just consume it; the concentration of capital—how to bring it from many places and purposes and use it in a few places on a few purposes; and the allocation of capital—what to use it on. Successful societies in terms of economic development found ways of capturing part of the wealth their economies created. As capital, this wealth could be concentrated and invested in more production, in expanding production to new products, and in improving the productive capacities all around by researching, developing, and employing new techniques of production. How best was that wealth to be captured as capital? How best was it to be allocated? And who best might do the capturing and allocating? These were the questions that confronted the developed states and peoples before they became developed, and still confront developing states and societies today.

Key terms

capital   Various forms of wealth available to be invested in further wealth creation. The accumulation, concentration, and allocation of capital are of great importance to economic development.

convergence   The idea that human societies are becoming more similar to one another in response to the universal interests and values of people and the technical, economic, legal, and political arrangements required to secure those interests and values.

standard of civilization   The idea that there is a single set of properties and values which identify being civilized and against which states and societies can be compared.

Key takeaways

■ Development usually refers to processes by which a system grows, becomes more complex, matures, declines, and ceases to be.

■ Development can mean the same thing when applied to human societies but invariably involves value judgments about what is desirable and what is better which have political consequences.

■ States and societies can experience economic, human, and political development, but it is widely, if questionably, assumed that economic development is a precondition for human and political development.

■ Economic development requires the accumulation of capital which can be concentrated and then allocated in the form of investment.

Exercises

1. In what ways might human development in the US be said to be less advanced than in Europe?

2. In what ways might economic development in Europe be said to be less advanced than in the US?

3. How can the children of Irish Travelers be raised according to the standards of civilization of authorities like the Irish government in regard to health care and education?

| 14.2 | Roads to development 1: primitive accumulation and state capitalism |

Learning objectives

1. Describe how processes of primitive accumulation work.

2. Explain how socialist states like the Soviet Union practiced a form of capitalism.

3. List the advantages and disadvantages of state capitalism.

There are several roads to the development of richer, stronger, more productive and complex economies. However, the governments and peoples of developing states and societies wondering how to accumulate capital must feel a bit like the reader of Hannah Glasse's recipe for baking a rabbit pie, "First catch your rabbit." The really hard part comes before they even get started. In his view of primitive accumulation, "previous to the division of labor," Adam Smith imagined a simple world before money, capital, loans, and investments, in which people began to accumulate the things (he called them stock) they needed to survive and work. Some people worked hard and piled up wealth and some did not. Then the ones with wealth started to put the ones without it to work, thereby accumulating more wealth.[7] The primitive accumulation practiced by the kings and emperors of the ancient world involved rounding up people—usually slaves and captives—for a project and forcing them to work in return for support only sufficient to keep them alive and allow them to reproduce. The Egyptian pyramids (Figure 14.2) were created by this system of **slavery** but so too, indirectly, were some of the finest buildings in England's seaports and the former plantations in the southern state of the US.

Today, slavery offends most people's moral sensibilities, although forms of it are still practiced. As we saw in Chapter 13, for example, some sex workers are effectively, if unofficially, owned by those who control them, and some indentured laborers are bound by forced agreements with their employers which mean, in effect, they will not be free until a long time has passed. Perhaps more importantly from a practical point of view, slavery is widely judged to be an inefficient way of concentrating capital for most forms of economic activity given

Figure 14.2 Results of primitive accumulation: the Pyramids of Giza, begun in 2584 BCE
(Source: Michael Snell/Alamy Stock Photo)

the available alternatives. Owners have to absorb all the costs of maintaining their slaves, and people motivated by fear alone generally do not work well.

Nevertheless, where labor is cheap or controlled, the tasks in hand require limited skills, and governments are ruthless, slavery in something like its historic form can resurface. The Soviet Union under Joseph Stalin in the 1930s mobilized large numbers of people—often political prisoners—and forced them to work in effect as slaves on big infrastructure projects like digging canals and building highways. Nazi Germany did likewise employing slave labor under even more terrifying conditions in its armaments industries during World War II. As recently as the 1970s, the Khmer Rouge revolutionaries in Kampuchea (now Cambodia once again) forced people out of the cities at gunpoint to work in the fields. And arguably, whenever local authorities put prisoners to work in return for nominal compensation, this could be regarded as a form of slave labor, although the punitive, restitutive, and rehabilitative purposes of this practice outweigh its economic significance.

The Soviet Union from 1917, its allies in Eastern Europe and Asia after World War II, and its allies in South East Asia and Africa from the 1970s, did not restrict themselves to economic development by primitive accumulation. Their leaderships were all inspired by a form of socialist ideology (see Chapter 13). Socialism maintains that big decisions about wealth creation and economic development should not be left in the hands of a minority made up of wealthy private citizens. This capitalist minority will exploit the majority, engage in wasteful competition with each other, and allocate resources according to profitability rather than real human need. Ideally the people, as the real wealth creators, should make these decisions, socialists argue. However, as a practical matter in a modern complex society this responsibility should be handled by the state on the people's behalf.

The Soviet model launched by Vladimir Lenin and the Bolsheviks (Soviet communists) involved putting most of the economy under public ownership administered by government departments and agencies.

In the 1930s, under Stalin, the Soviets developed a complex process of **economic planning** for five-year cycles by which resources were allocated and production targets were set for workers, peasants, farms, and factories. The Soviet system was regarded as a socialist one rather than a communist one because of its reliance on the state rather than the people themselves. However, as Leon Trotsky (see Chapter 13), one of the original Bolsheviks who had fallen out with Stalin and had been exiled and eventually murdered on his orders, pointed out, the Soviet model was a degenerate one at best. A bureaucracy had emerged which ruled for itself.[8] Other critics suggested that it operated as a state capitalist system. Soviet workers still worked for wages rather than the full value of the wealth they created, the profit, or difference between the two, being taken by the state instead of private companies.

The Soviet model delivered fast growth in its early stages, but it is generally seen as a blind alley today. Even at its most productive, planned economic development under the supervision of state agencies was often hugely wasteful in the allocation of resources. Its commitment to economic equality forced it to rely on coercion and ideological enthusiasm, rather than positive economic incentives to get people to work. Its claim to having a scientific understanding of what was best for people and how to achieve it contributed to the brutal treatment of any opposition with which the system had to deal. Once Stalin was dead, the leadership spent much of its time trying to see how much it could relax its political and economic control to stimulate economic growth without the Communist party losing power completely. All these problems were amplified whenever the Soviet model was established in other parts of the world where it was often seen as a foreign import. And as noted above, the Soviet model failed in its competition with the West, both in arms racing and in delivering rising living standards to ordinary people. When Mikhail Gorbachev attempted the major political reforms of *glasnost* (opening up the political process) and *perestroika* (restructuring the political and economic system) to end stagnation after 1985, the Soviet state collapsed and most of the non-Russian nationalities declared their independence leaving a rump Russian state behind.

Yet the Soviet experience still matters to states and peoples interested in economic, human, and political development today. It does so in several ways. First, the oppression, suffering, and killings which took place under Stalin have delegitimized **totalitarian** approaches to development where a powerful leadership exerts strong control over nearly all aspects of economic, social, and political life. Politicians who believe in a strong role for the state in economic development face an uphill battle in getting people to support them freely. Second, as we shall see below, many former communist states are still wrestling with the problems posed by shifting from socialist, centrally planned economies to ones in which more free market principles are employed.

Thirdly, however, and for all its eventual shortcomings, the Soviet experience provided a model of fast and relatively independent industrialization. In a period of less than twenty years, Russia was transformed from a backward, broken state into a great military power capable of taking on and defeating Nazi Germany, the most advanced military power in Europe at the time. Equally quickly, state capitalist approaches to development based on egalitarian principles delivered a level of education and health care to large numbers of people which they had never before experienced. Which bits of the Soviet experience might we salvage, we see the governments of some developing states asking, while avoiding the Stalinist horrors and eventual stagnation which accompanied state capitalist, centrally planned economies in the past.

Key terms

economic planning   In a state capitalist system, a process by which the central government allocates resources and sets production targets for the economy as a whole and sectors within it, both of which are controlled or owned by the state.

slavery   An economic system in which the producers have no control over their own lives and are treated as property to be owned and traded by their masters.

totalitarian   An adjective used to describe political systems in which governments seek to control and shape every aspect of the economic, political, social, and personal lives of their citizens.

Key takeaways

- Primitive accumulation is a term to describe how early economic activity resulted in the accumulation and concentration of wealth either through the hard work of some individuals or the coercion of many into working by the few.

- We associate primitive accumulation with the distant past and the beginnings of economic activity, but it may still reappear where ruthless people with power can coerce others, typically into large scale projects requiring low skills.

- State capitalism is a form of socialism in which the state controls or owns all or most of the sectors of the economy. It is associated with communist states like the former Soviet Union and the People's Republic of China.

- State capitalism can initially deliver very fast rates of growth and economic development through a system of central planning, coercion, and mobilizing ideological enthusiasm, but it seems able to deliver development only to a certain level after which it stagnates.

Exercises

1. In what parts of the world might we find coercive primitive accumulation occurring today?

2. What sorts of reasons might the government of a developing state give for still being interested in aspects of the Soviet model of development?

14.3   Roads to development 2: *laissez faire* capitalism

Learning objectives

1. Describe the assumptions about human beings on which *laissez faire* capitalism depends.
2. List the economic, legal, and political preconditions for economic development along *laissez faire* capitalist lines.
3. Explain the reasons given for *laissez faire* capitalism's triumph in the late 20th century.

The road to development suggested by *laissez faire* (literally French for "let do" or, more loosely, "leave it be") capitalism rests on the assumptions of Liberalism outlined in Chapter 3.[9] However, it is worth re-visiting them since they are of great importance to the operations of the contemporary global economy and to debates about how developing states should attempt to grow their economies, thereby enriching their people and making them feel more secure. For moral and practical reasons, the Liberal ideas from which *laissez faire* capitalism is derived claim that any economic or political system should prioritize the interests and talents of human beings seen as individuals. Individuals are rational beings who work and create wealth to satisfy their needs. They generate more wealth through working harder, getting others to work for them, trading, and investing in the wealth creation of others. The wealth they create, or which they are responsible for creating, should belong to them in the form of private property with which, Liberals argue, they have the right to do as they wish so long as this does not impact on the rights of others.

However, some people are smarter than others when it comes to figuring out how to create wealth. Some people are prepared to work harder than others. Some are prepared to take more risks in investing in enabling others to work. Any system of economics, the *laissez faire* argument runs, should operate in such a way as to reward with more wealth those who do more. In addition, however, their reward should also reflect the demand from other people for what they do. People should not be rewarded simply for working hard if no one wants what they produce. Most importantly, people should be able to earn more money from the sale of the goods they produce than it cost them to produce it, and those who own production processes involving the work of others should similarly be able to make more. This profit can be used to reinvest in, improve, and expand production, and it can be used to support and improve the producer's living standards—an incentive for people to work hard.

In determining what ought to be done or what needs to be done, Liberals argue, each individual is the best judge of his or her interests, and each individual is generally an unreliable judge of other people's interests. This is why *laissez faire* approaches trust neither governments nor private companies to make economic decisions on the big scale of national economies and markets. Both are just composed of self-interested individuals. Therefore, let individuals be free to make their own decisions about how hard they want to work, what they want to invest their efforts and wealth in, and the terms on which they will buy and sell their wealth and labor with other individuals. They can do this in an open market in which the only restrictions are to respect the lives and property of others, to keep promises and honor contracts, and to compete fairly.

In these **open markets**, capital is accumulated and concentrated not by decisions of the state or any powerful individual. It is accumulated and concentrated by the decisions of multiple individuals trying to act in their own best interests. The possibility of profits provides the incentive to work hard, invest, and take risks. The possibility of these efforts being unrewarded or resulting in a loss of wealth justifies the profits on the occasions that these efforts are successful. Therefore, the Liberal advice to developing states and societies is that they approximate the following principles as closely as they can as soon as they can. The transition is often referred to as a process of liberalizing or **liberalization**. It has the following steps.

- First, developing states need to establish the principle of the **rule of law**. Many societies have systems of law, but these often serve as a way of rationalizing and justifying the way in which the powerful, especially the governments of states, go about getting what they want. The rule of law suggests a system of rules which seeks to be just and fair and honest, which has its own independent ways of reasoning, and to which everyone—rich, poor, powerful, and weak—are equally subject.

- Second, developing states need to ensure that this rule of law protects the rights of all individuals and especially their **private property rights**—the rights to acquire and hold private property and to use it as they wish providing this does not encroach on the rights of others. In particular, property rights should be protected from efforts by governments or others to restrict or override them except in exceptional circumstances such as in time of war or in the course of a natural disaster.

- Third, developing states need to establish open markets where individuals can freely trade their property, labor and capital (investments in stocks and shares, for example). These markets should be subject to the same sort of protections as property rights from attempts by governments to restrict, rig or override them.

- Fourth, developing states should establish governments whose authority is limited to protecting individuals from law breakers by upholding and enforcing the law, and protecting them from foreign invasions by maintaining armed forces or raising these forces as necessary. Governments might provide public goods like roads from which everybody benefits, but which no individual has an interest in providing. They might try to develop human capital by investing in education and health care. However, the claim that what a government proposes to do is a public good or public interest should always be treated with caution, and private methods of providing goods should to be preferred and sought after.

- Fifth, the governments of developing states should withdraw from economic activity such as directly owning, controlling, or investing in production, and refrain from policies which are intended to redistribute wealth from some individuals to others (by taxation, for example). They should borrow modestly and tax as little as possible, focusing their taxation mainly on consumption (sales taxes) rather than production (income taxes), thereby encouraging savings and work.

■ Sixth, developing states should make their governments representative of, and accountable to, the individuals on behalf of whom they act. This does not necessarily mean a fully fledged democracy with universal suffrage. Initially at least, it could mean a government which subjects what it wants to do to the rule of law, or it could mean a government which is chosen by significant stakeholders—primarily property owners, for example.

Supporters of *laissez faire* capitalism acknowledge that these conditions can be difficult to fulfill. Ignorance, fear, and the vested interests of those who do well out of the old ways of doing things can stand in their way. However, the argument runs, they are clear, just, and accord with the universal aspirations of human beings to be as free as possible to improve upon their lots in life. Establish these principles in a developing state, and you will see capital concentrated and allocated in the most efficient way possible. Economic growth will accelerate to the point where it is self-sustaining. Some individuals will become very wealthy and everyone will, sooner or later, be better off. If you need further convincing, supporters of *laissez faire* capitalism argue, just look at some of the wealthiest and most secure states and societies in the world today. The United States, Canada, Britain, Germany, France, Italy, and Japan are all among those which came closest to following these principles in the course of their own development. Until the end of the Cold War, Russia, China, and the rest of the communist world were among those who did not.

Key terms

liberalization A process by which states and societies abandon old economic practices in which the government is heavily involved and put Liberal principles regarding government, property rights, and individual rights into practice.

open markets A concrete or virtual space—such as a town square, stock exchange, or social media exchange site—where individuals are equally free in legal terms to exchange publically goods, services, and capital for investment.

private property rights Principles, often expressed in law, acknowledging that individuals can lawfully create, possess, and trade goods which belong exclusively to them and which cannot lawfully be taken from them against their will by other individuals, and only taken from them against their will by governments in exceptional circumstances.

rule of law A principle suggesting that political, economic, and other forms of human activity, particularly the conduct of government and the resolution of disputes, should conform to the law, and that all citizens and the government should be equally subject to the law, rather than the law being subordinated to the wishes of particular people, be they politicians, the wealthy, or the mob.

Key takeaways

- *Laissez faire* capitalism is based on Liberal assumptions about human nature, the importance of private property, the conditions in which wealth is most efficiently created, the arrangements regarding how its producers are most justly rewarded, and the sort of government which best guarantees these conditions and arrangements.

- *Laissez faire* capitalism suggests a set of principles based on the assumptions above which developing states and societies should adopt if they wish to accumulate, concentrate, and allocate capital as efficiently as possible.

- A developing state which applies these principles will have the best chance of achieving self-sustaining growth and development which is not dependent on loans and other forms of external support.

- These principles are difficult to put into practice for many reasons, but the most prosperous, secure, and highly developed states and societies in the world today are those which have come closest to putting these principles into practice.

Exercises

1. In what ways are developed states like the US *laissez faire* and in what ways are they not?

2. In what circumstances might an individual's right to hold property and do what they want with it be legitimately limited, and how?

14.4   Roads to development 3: practical experience

Learning objectives

1. List the basic types of developing states we can identify today.

2. Explain the assumptions of the **import substitution** and the export led positions in development debates.

3. Discuss the possible significance of the rise of China, India, and other quickly industrializing states for debates about development.

Theories often sound like claims about what the world is like, why it is like that and, as a result, a list of things people should do if they're smart. As we learned in the Introduction and Chapter 4, however, the relationship between theories and the world is complicated and often messy. Certainly theories affect what people do. So do many other things, however, and what people do, in turn affects the theories.

This is particularly true in the case of theories about economic development and what people, states, and societies actually do. We cannot, for example, find any state which completely followed the Soviet model in the past—not even the Soviet Union. A small private sector of economic activity survived there through most of its history. Nor can we find any developing state which completely follows the model of development suggested by *laissez faire* capitalism above, although many governments today claim that they strongly subscribe to its principles. Nevertheless, we can identify some broad, real world types by employing the following dimensions: size; current level of economic development, extent and type of government/state ownership in the economy; and elite attitudes towards the import and export of goods, services, and investments.

First, we can identify states which are making a transition away from the Soviet model of extensive ownership by the state, to one in which an independent private sector emerges. Cuba and the former Soviet republic of Belarus provide examples of states which are making this transition slowly and reluctantly, as their governments seek to stay in power. Poland provides an example of a state in which many of the effects of nearly fifty years of communist rule are fast diminishing.

Second, we can identify states which have attempted to achieve economic development by government-led policies which encourage the domestic private sector to produce goods at home to substitute for imports from abroad. In the past, Argentina, Chile, and Ireland all provided examples of this strategy. Most developing states still offer some encouragement to home producers for the home market, but as an overall development strategy this approach is discredited and made difficult by international trade agreements.

Third, we can identify states which have attempted to achieve economic development by government-led policies which encourage the private sector to produce goods for export abroad. There are at least two types of such states. The first type are those which possess large quantities of a particular resource—oil or gas, for example, and very little else. Initially, at least, for states like Saudi Arabia and Iraq, the export option is the only one available to them. The second type possesses more diversified economies capable of producing certain kinds of goods and services which they export to offer at competitive rates abroad. As we shall see below, Taiwan, South Korea, Hong Kong, and Singapore are all examples, formerly known as "Asian Tigers" because of the fast rates of growth this strategy delivered.

Most developing states pursue a complex, and sometimes contradictory combination of these approaches. Smaller states are more likely to be focused on a single strategy and a few sectors of their economy. Larger states like China, India, and Brazil are more likely to be engaged in pursuing development through a combination of import and export strategies, strongly supporting state owned or directed enterprises in some sectors, while stepping back and letting both domestic and foreign private actors operate freely in others. In addition, larger states—China especially—are significant because of their potential for changing the rules of the economic system in which development takes place and for providing new models of development for others to follow.

The challenge for developing states, nearly everyone agreed after World War II, was to accumulate a sufficient concentration of capital to be allocated to domestic economic activity. Once this was accomplished, it was expected that the developing states would reach a "take off point" of self-sustaining growth and start to catch up with the developed states.[10] This did not happen in any straightforward sense. Developing states kept importing finished goods and struggled to pay for them with exports of primary products. As we saw in Chapter 13, dependency theorists from developing states argued there were structural reasons like the declining terms of trade which weighted economic relations in favor of the developed states. These economic arguments were backed by a simple political one. Why are we Argentines, Brazilians, and Irish buying goods from rich foreigners when we could be earning money and employing our own people making the same goods right here at home?

Economists like Prebisch and Singer said an Import Substitution Industrialization (ISI) was needed. Developing states should try to satisfy their own needs by their own efforts as much as possible. If they had to import though, then better they did so from other developing states than from the developed world. Similar conclusions had been reached by the government of newly independent Ireland some thirty years earlier. Even though it had won its political independence in the 1920s, by the 1950s nearly 90 percent of its imports still came from Britain and 90 percent on its exports went to Britain. The Irish government had put up protective tariffs against imports and used a combination of public and private investment to foster their own "infant industries." However, the results were disappointing. By the 1960s, Irish living standards were falling behind those of the rest of Western Europe. Emigration was on the rise to Britain and the US. Many companies depended on government funds to keep them in business and people in jobs. And to cap it all, the level of economic dependence on Britain had not shifted much. What was the point of being independent, the Irish started to ask, if most of the problems which independence was supposed to solve were still there?

Other developing states attempted the same approach as Ireland with similar results. Today, ISI is associated with uneconomic steel mills and national airlines costing developing states huge sums to support until they finally go bankrupt. Larger developing states, like India and Brazil, did better than small ones because they had larger domestic markets to sell to and productive sectors of the economy which could be taxed by the government to help the unproductive sectors and keep the jobs they supported with subsidies. As we shall see below, however, even most of them ran into difficulties in the 1970s and 1980s when they borrowed from abroad to finance this approach.

Liberal economists identified two problems with ISI. First, it ignores the law of comparative advantage outlined in Chapter 3. According to Liberal economists, people and states ought only to produce goods and services when they have a good chance of doing so competitively—that is at a better price or with better quality than the products of their rivals. Producers in small developing states could not do this by concentrating on their home market and protecting their industry from the industries of bigger, more developed states. The home market was rarely big enough to enjoy the necessary economies of scale which allow goods to be produced at the lowest price. Protection would remove the pressure to be efficient, innovative, and thus competitive with bigger, more experienced rivals. The end result would be shoddy goods produced at a loss. At least it would be so long as the ISI state could protect its home market.

The second problem was that throughout the second half of the 20th century, it was becoming harder to pursue traditional policies of protection. States negotiated, first through the GATT process and then through the World Trade Organization, agreements by which they steadily reduced tariffs called duties on each other's manufactured goods (see Chapter 9). These agreements were monitored for violations by states themselves, regional trading organizations, the World Bank and, eventually, the World Trade Organization, all of which would impose penalties like fines or retaliatory duties on violators. This regime of **trade liberalization** was steadily extended from banning most duties to preventing states from giving their own firms an advantage through using public funding to help them run or government purchasing policies which favored home-produced goods.

How then were developing states to grow if ISI did not work—either because it was wrong in principle or because it was facing an increasingly hostile environment? There was an alternative to the disappointing performances of states like Brazil, Argentina, India, and Ireland after World War II. Over roughly the same period, South Korea and Taiwan managed to transform themselves from agricultural backwaters into industrial powerhouses, while Hong Kong and Singapore achieved similar rates of growth by developing their financial service sectors. How did so-called "Asian Tigers" do it?

There are two main parts to the answer. The first is that these states pursued a strategy of **export-led development** in sectors of the economy where they enjoyed or could create a comparative advantage over producers in the developed world. They specifically targeted goods required by the developed world. Thus, South Korea had plenty of iron ore and plenty of cheap labor at the end of World War II, but was mainly an agricultural economy. It moved steadily from exporting ore to processing some of it into iron and steel. On this heavy industrial base, it moved into sectors like ship building and car manufacturing. And as its stock of concentrated capital grew, South Korea diversified into other labor-intensive industries like electronics, exploiting the skills and competitive labor costs of its workforce to increase its exports. Today, you probably take for granted the presence of reliable, relatively inexpensive, Korean cars. However, the Korean car industry only made its first cars in the 1950s, first exported them in the 1970s, and achieved its current reputation (except among older people) for producing cars which compete with Japanese, German, American models across the full range only in the early 21st century.

The second part of the answer to how the export-led model of development succeeded lies in the way in which capital was concentrated and allocated. In each case, governments played big and often controversial parts. They engaged in decisions about where capital should be allocated. In South Korea, for example, the government made sure that a few big family-owned companies which were committed to the export strategy received the lion's share of investment. One of the consequences of the export-led strategy was that domestic consumption was kept low. In each of the "Tigers," authoritarian governments made sure that political opposition to maintaining low living standards was kept weak by using repressive measures. During the 1970s in Chile, when a leftist party was elected to form a minority government committed to ISI and socialist policies, a coup was launched against it by the armed forces with encouragement from the US. The resulting military government then intimidated and crushed the remaining opposition while instituting export-led reforms under the advice of economists from the University of Chicago.

During the Cold War, it was easy to rationalize these strong and sometimes violent measures taken by governments as part of the struggle against communism. No government in the capitalist world wanted to judge the South Korean and Taiwanese governments too harshly if they "cheated" by unfairly aiding their own big companies when both of them were in the front line against Soviet Russia and communist China. Even violent repression of opposition was justified and sometimes supported—as in Chile, Argentina, and much of Central America—on the grounds that were the communists to win, the repression would be much worse and economic development would give way to economic stagnation. After the Cold War, however, Liberal economists expected, and nearly all governments said they agreed, that *laissez faire* capitalist principles would be much more strongly applied worldwide. With communism defeated and import substitution discredited, there would no longer be any good reasons for governments to interfere in the operations of their own economies to provide their producers with unfair advantages. Developing states would privatize those parts of the economy their governments had owned and support only those measures which allowed for free and fair competition to achieve export-led growth in open markets.

This has not happened. The governments of developing states have remained closely involved in economic activity for a number of different reasons. However, they can all be summed up by paraphrasing Bill Clinton—"it's the politics stupid."

- First, people in much of the developing world expect states and governments in general to be the best leaders of economic development, even if they do not trust their own particular government and politicians. The populations of former colonies remember (and are taught) that it was politics which won their freedom and independence from empires, while economic exploitation kept them captive. Even if, as we shall see below, the politicians are often regarded as corrupt or incompetent, the people of developing states seem to think, at least, they are "our" politicians from our country. The financiers, executives, and experts, no matter how rich, efficient, or clever they may be, are often regarded as working for someone else abroad.

- Secondly, the economic and political elites of developing states, particularly smaller ones, see the state itself as the only organization capable of taking on and competing with the big corporations from abroad. It may not be able any longer to own completely industries which trade internationally, but the state can enter into partnerships with both domestic and foreign owners. It can make strategic decisions in an attempt to pick winners and develop them through financing and other forms of support into national champions which will compete effectively in the world economy.

- Thirdly, the governments of developing states are not just interested in efficiencies which deliver international economic competitiveness. They are also interested in acquiring, keeping, and exercising political power. When a government makes decisions about the allocation of economic resources, it does so believing this will develop the state in the direction it wants it to go. It also does it knowing that it gains leverage over clients in the private sector who hope to benefit from its patronage, and support from those citizens who have jobs as a result. When the government of a developing state surrenders that power to foreigners and international markets, it may get more efficiency. However, this may come at the price of lost jobs and opportunities for patronage which weaken its political position.

Egyptian bread and economic reform

The governments of developing states often have little room to maneuver between economic and political disaster. The case of Egypt is instructive. Since the 1960s Egyptian economic growth has been unable to keep pace with the growth of its population. It is a classic example of the demographic trap examined earlier where improvements in health conditions quickly improve the survival rate of newborns. One result is persistent and growing unemployment. On several occasions Egypt has struggled with its balance of trade. As a result, its government has also struggled with its balance of payments, and it has had to apply to international institutions like the World Bank and the International Monetary Fund (IMF) for loans. The IMF has said it will lend Egypt money on condition that it reforms its economic policies to reduce the likelihood of similar problems in the future.

One of the things the IMF generally asks is that governments reduce their own spending so they can reduce the tax burden on their citizens and make their economies more attractive to investors. Specifically, in Egypt's case, they have asked it to remove the subsidies it pays to keep the price of bread, a staple in the Egyptian diet, low. This and other subsidies, the IMF says, cost money the government can ill-afford. It also distorts the market for bread, allowing the population—including many people who do not need help—to become over-reliant on artificially cheap bread for which domestic producers cannot grow sufficient wheat at controlled prices. However, every time the government tried to reduce the subsidy in the past dating back to the 1970s, the result was widespread political demonstrations. Indeed, the protests that helped remove President Mubarak in 2011 took place against a backdrop of rising prices for wheat, rice, and food in general. The Egyptian poor could afford no rise in their cost of living, and the Egyptian middle class were angered by the loss of this subsidy.

In addition, the governments and supporters of developing states point out, there is an element of hypocrisy in demands from the developed world that they should reform their economies in accordance with the principles of *laissez faire* capitalism. All the arguments above should apply to the developed states just as much as to developing states. The developed world has been very interested in liberalizing trade in manufactures and services where it enjoys an advantage, but much less interested in liberalizing trade in agricultural products where the developing states have a chance of competing (see Chapter 9). Some developed states, like France, continue to play a leading role in their national economies trying to give general direction to the way in which they should develop. Others continue to protect and help national champions like aviation companies or petro-chemical companies break into and establish a position in global markets. And all developed states will protect some uncompetitive sectors, at least for a time, citing national security reasons or socio-cultural reasons to avoid job losses in parts of the state with a weak economy, strong political representation or both.

Today, therefore, developing states face a challenge in which theory and practice appear sharply divided. The Soviet Union fell in 1990–91, and the centrally planned socialist economies held together by its political power and military strength collapsed along with it. These events gave a great boost to the argument for *laissez faire* capitalism. Yet the emerging success stories in terms of development had followed different roads during the Cold War. South Korea and Taiwan had seen strong and repressive governments heavily involved in decisions about how capital should be concentrated and allocated in support of an export-led strategy. Like the states of the European Union, they had also been quite protective of their home markets. Chile's government had taken a more hands-off approach to economic development, but a hands-on approach to political control and oppressing opposition to change by using murder and intimidation. There might have been a case for these illiberal practices when containing the Soviet Union was the number one priority, but it would be much harder to justify any of these departures from Liberal economic and political norms today. The other examples of spectacular success, Singapore and Hong Kong, had taken different routes to becoming major players in services industries like banking, finance, and insurance. However, they were both small islands in exceptional circumstances—Hong Kong was neither a state nor a democracy—which had found niches in the world economy. They did not look like promising models for anyone else.

The result, therefore, was a mix. On the one hand, the governments of developing states attempted to institute *laissez faire* capitalist principles where they could see an obvious advantage to doing so, or where they had to as a condition of securing investments from international financial organizations or trading agreements with more liberal developed states. On the other, they tried to maintain their control of sectors of the economy when this helped them with their power and patronage, when they tried to build up national champions to compete on the world stage, and when they were scared of reforms which would lose jobs, raise prices and strengthen political opposition. Like the developed states, they would all maintain they subscribed to *laissez faire* principles as far as this was practically possible. As we have seen in the discussion of trade rounds (see Chapter 9), they would accuse each other of falling short of these principles. Meanwhile, liberal economists would praise them when they adopted the right reforms, and point out the opportunity costs, inefficiencies and lack of economic sustainability of approaches in which the state stayed involved through high

Figure 14.3 A picture of Xi Jinping, president of China since 2012, and a bust of Mao Zedong (1893–1976), leader of China's communist revolution on sale in a Beijing market in 2014

(Source: Lou Linwei/Alamy Stock Photo)

taxation, high spending, and giving orders about where to invest and what to produce. Nearly everyone agreed with the orthodoxy that liberalization was best in principle and bemoaned the difficulties of achieving it in practice.

At least that was the case until recently. Now, that orthodoxy has been challenged from an unlikely source, the communist People's Republic of China. And the challenge has gained weight because of major difficulties in an unlikely place in the world economy, the capitalist states of the developed world, the United States and the European Union in particular.

China has had a long and for the most part, glorious history as one of the great centers of world civilization for over two thousand years. However, modernity has been very hard on it. As we noted above, the Chinese Empire surrendered its lead in technological and economic development to the Europeans between 1400 and 1800. By the start of the 20th century it was being economically exploited by most of the European great powers plus the United States and Japan. While Japan borrowed ideas from the West, adapted them to its own preferences, and became a modern great power, China's efforts at reform left it weaker and more divided than before. The Japanese invaded China before World War II but were unable to conquer it completely. They left in 1945 and a civil war resumed which the communists under Mao Zedong won in 1949.

With its large territory, huge population, and considerable natural resources, China always had great potential. However, the Chinese communists never seemed to be able to realize it. Mao claimed to be a Marxist-Leninist. Like Lenin in the Soviet Union, however, he faced the problem that he headed up a revolution which was supposed to be based on the urban industrial working class in a state with a mainly agricultural economy and peasants. Mao studied the Soviet experience closely, and he based his revolution on changes in the countryside first. Like other communist regimes, the People's Republic quickly achieved some basic improvements in the health and education of China's vast population, but then it stalled.

Mao had two great fears: that the Soviet Union's leaders would try to pull rank in the international communist movement and tell China what to do; and that China's Communist Party members, like their Soviet counterparts, would lose their revolutionary zeal and become flabby bureaucrats concerned only with protecting their own privileges. To deal with the first fear, Mao broke with the Soviet Union in 1960 when it refused continued support for China's nuclear program. He also attempted to devise a program of fast industrialization suited for mainly agricultural states. It was called "The Great Leap Forward" and was based on the small scale, widespread production of iron by peasants in their own compounds. To address his second fear, Mao instituted a series of programs known as "The Great Cultural Revolution," by which senior Communist Party officials and others would be publicly criticized, sent into the countryside for re-education, and sometimes imprisoned and killed. Both programs were disasters. The Great Leap Forward produced very little iron and, by distracting peasants from their farm work, resulted in reduced crops and great famine in the countryside. The Great Cultural Revolution left all but a few of Mao's closest advisors under his wife's leadership terrified that they were going to be denounced. When Mao died, these advisors were soon arrested and steps taken to make sure that no individual could wield such power in the Chinese Communist Party ever again.

Deng Xiaoping became the most influential Chinese leader. It soon became clear that he was interested in ending China's economic stagnation and building it into a prosperous world power. Even in a political system like China's, which makes much use of slogans and aphorisms, Deng was noted for his sayings. His pragmatism about economic systems was reflected in his view that "the color of the cat—black or white—did not matter so long as it caught mice," and that China was like a person fording a river by "feeling the stones" with your feet. Most importantly, he is supposed to have declared "Poverty is not socialism; to be rich is glorious," which would have been sacrilege in Mao's more egalitarian, anti-consumerist times. What Deng meant initially was that China would experiment with some market reforms the way other communist states had, and Cuba continues to do so today. In the 1980s, under **"socialism with Chinese characteristics"** or "market socialism," he increased the amount of private property it was possible to own, allowed some market-based trading and competition between producers, and invited foreign investment and technological expertise into China.

To begin with, the consequences were small. In the late 1980s, even after Deng's reforms had attracted considerable international attention, Chinese GNP was estimated to be about the same as that of Belgium or the Netherlands. Nevertheless, under successive Chinese governments a clear strategy emerged.

Special economic zones were created, initially along the coast. In these, privately owned industries taking advantage of cheap labor with very few rights produced exports for the developed world. These zones grew, people at all levels within them became richer, and production began to move up the ladder from cheap plastics to higher technology goods requiring more developed labor skills. Today, China is a major exporter of a full range of goods to both the developed and developing world. It was reported as overtaking Japan's economy in 2011 in terms of net worth. If it maintains its present rate of growth, it was estimated in 2012 that China could overtake the US economy in the same terms as early as 2014 (it did not).

China's spectacular growth has been export-led so far. However, it is not simply following the path blazed by the former Asian Tigers on a larger scale. Despite growing urbanization, much of the population continues to live in the countryside. Despite the fast growth of the private sector, large sections of the economy remain in state ownership. The Chinese government, and thus the Chinese Communist Party, exercises tight control over strategic decisions about capital concentration and allocation at the national level, as well as tight control over the amount of money in circulation, the cost of borrowing it, and the quantity and value of the money which can be converted into foreign currency. The Chinese Communist Party continues to govern and represses all but the gentlest opposition expressed *sotto voce*. Clearly, the lesson its leaders have learned from what it sees as the disasters of *glasnost* and *perestroika* under Gorbachev in the Soviet Union is that economic liberalization comes first and political democratization comes a very distant second.

Figure 14.4 Modern Beijing subway station
(Source: Asia Photopress/Alamy Stock Photo)

The Beijing subway

The Beijing subway (Figure 14.4), intended as a showcase for modern China, also provides a useful snapshot of the contrasts and contradictions which exist there. The trains are built in China, very advanced, covered in adverts for consumer products, and on some lines have commercials and news projected onto the tunnel walls. They become very crowded in the rush hour but are clean, the atmosphere is relaxed, and young people with guitars sometimes come into the carriages singing popular songs—not what you usually associate with subways in communist states. The system underwent a big expansion in the early 21st century with equipment being updated, old lines being extended, and new lines being built in time for the 2008 Beijing Olympics. At each station, however, passengers funnel through a security check like at an airport. In the central area, lots of uniformed security personnel surround each scanning machine. They are accompanied by policemen who look like soldiers and who sometimes move around in pairs at a quick march. On the platform, more uniformed staff monitor where passengers are waiting for the train and let them know if they think they are standing in the wrong place by shouting at them. As the train comes into the station another uniformed man can be seen standing at ease behind the driver. Sometimes he can be seen hurriedly standing up and getting into his place as the train comes out of the tunnel. There is a genuine security risk of course, just as there is on subway systems in other parts of the world. However, the approach to security on the Beijing subway system reflects two other things: the desire of the communist state to exert a presence and have a high profile in public places; and the large number of people for whom jobs have to be found.

Does China provide a viable model of development for other states? Liberal economists and supporters of *laissez faire* capitalism are doubtful. China's impressive growth rates, they argue, come from the bits of economic policy it does right and the special economic zones where market principles are allowed to operate. China's performance has been good, but it could have been so much better if China had undertaken liberalization across the whole state. In addition, China has grown so fast because the communist policies of the past ensured it started from a very low level of development in the first place. Now the easy gains have been made, China will face tougher challenges maintaining its growth rates, and it will have to manage the **rising expectations** of a huge and growing population which has seen a relatively few people growing very rich. Meanwhile, the majority is losing the social safety net of full employment and very cheap health care which the old socialist system claimed it provided.

The more optimistic critics see China gradually moving in the right direction. Under China's current president, Xi Jinping, the public sector, although huge, is shrinking. Democracy—or political participation—although very limited, is beginning to develop at the local level, and corruption is increasingly punished at all levels. The more China wants to participate in the world economy, the more interested its government is becoming in getting its producers to conform to international regulations about intellectual copyright, currency manipulation, safety, and protections for workers. Given what the Chinese government wants, an influential state and a prosperous society, and given what all governments have to do to achieve this in a globalized, networked, highly competitive economy, there is only one direction for China to move, the optimists argue. The only question is how fast and how painfully the state will make the transition.

The more pessimistic critics are not sure that China wants to make this transition. They argue that the Chinese communists are mainly interested in strengthening themselves and weakening their rivals both at home and abroad. Xi Jinping is tightening his personal grip on the Communist Party and the government at the center, and big restrictions are placed on the access which Chinese people have to the Internet and social media. China, they argue, is ruthlessly pursuing raw materials and sources of energy around the world without care for human rights, to fuel an export strategy which creates massive trade and finance imbalances with the developed world. The only good news, the pessimists say, is that the strategy is unlikely to work. Even China no longer wants to lend Americans money to buy Chinese goods. It is losing its labor costs advantage to other developing states where people will work for less. Some companies are moving jobs back to the more skilled work force of the developed world as China's labor cost advantage shrinks. If China is to maintain the growth which keeps its leaders rich and pays for its expanding armed forces, it will have to start selling goods and services to its own people and reward them enough so they can afford to buy Chinese goods and services. Once it starts doing this, China's people will begin to demand change and the communist order will be swept away as it was in the Soviet Union and Eastern Europe.

To the governments and many of the people of some developing states, however, China's "peaceful rise" presents a different picture. They see a state which maintained a rate of growth between seven and nine percent even during the great economic downturn after 2008. Over the same period, the economies of the developed world were either stagnant or shrinking. They also see a state which has accumulated a great amount of foreign capital from the success of its exports which makes the governments of other developing states want to increase their own **sovereign wealth funds**. More importantly, the Chinese government can access this capital, which is often held by companies of which the Chinese state owns at least half, and use it to make loans and investments both at home and abroad. The "One Belt, One Road" initiative noted in Chapter 9 is one of the results of this strong position. The Chinese communists may not be democratic, and they may not have a great respect for human rights and political opposition. The Chinese people do not seem too disturbed by this, however, so long as the economy keeps growing and China keeps gaining more respect around the world. Further, the governments of many developing states are grateful that the Chinese do not follow the practice the developed states have of asking about them about their human rights records before investing in their economies. What the developed states see as a cynical disregard on the part of the Chinese for human rights, the governments of some developing states present as respect for sovereignty, cultural differences, and local conditions. Food, health care, and jobs for all are what are needed now, they argue. Individual rights to speak one's mind, to criticize the government, and to oppose its policies can come later. As China's television and press services are fond of pointing out, however, an open political opposition and a free press, as these operate in the West, seem to be a mixed blessing, especially if you are trying to get anything done.

China's future and the issues to which it gives rise are key sources of the uncertainty in international relations today. At present, the government of a state like India, with a growing population which may overtake China's in the future, needs very fast economic growth to cope with this demographic challenge. Since independence, India has been a democracy. For many years its government closely regulated the Indian economy to protect its markets from international influence. More recently, the Indian government has listened to the call from the developed states to liberalize its economy, and it has enjoyed some successes. India is developing a leading presence in the global market for information technologies, and its success in developing low-cost, English-speaking call centers is well known in the developed world. However, India has not enjoyed growth on China's scale. Today it sees a struggling United States and Europe whose advice to deregulate seems to be a major source of their own big problems in the banking sector. Worse, deregulation seems to prevent their governments tackling these problems, and allows the finance they are creating to flow abroad.

No one of importance in the developing world is advocating a return to communism. One only has to compare the darkness of communist North Korea with the brightness of South Korea in satellite images to realize that road has proved a failure (Figure 14.5). The Marxist part of the Chinese experience looks more and more like an aberration of history. The strong government part of the Chinese experience, however, fits in with China's historic needs and looks attractive to others faced by similar problems. If growth recovers in the developed states, China may remain an outlier arguing with itself about what to do next, as its population ages, its labor costs begin to rise, and it loses its competitive edge. If growth does not recover strongly in developed states, however, the debate about the role of the state in economic development will intensify. And if China continues to prosper, this will be reflected in the principles on which the global economy operates. Specifically, the state's role in the economy will no longer be seen as a matter for regret incurring huge opportunity costs which needs to be reduced wherever possible. Instead, it may come to be seen as an essential tool for making possible fast, targeted, independent economic development.

Key terms

export-led development   A process by which a state develops industries for the export of goods so that it can pay for its imports from abroad.

import substitution   A process by which a state cuts down imports, and thus dependence on abroad, by developing industries which concentrate initially on supplying the domestic market.

Figure 14.5 North Korea (in shadow) and South Korea (light) by night from space provide an indicator of different levels of economic development and different priorities
(Source: Universal Images Group North America LLC/Alamy Stock Photo)

rising expectations   A situation where people believe that better lives for themselves and their children will be achieved. It is often linked to the claim that people are more likely to demand change and more likely to revolt, not when things are absolutely desperate, but when they experience some improvement which encourages them to believe that things actually could be a lot better.

socialism with Chinese characteristics   The idea that socialism in China would be different from other places (for example, its initial base being in the countryside). The term has been extended to capitalism with Chinese characteristics to suggest differences between capitalism in China and elsewhere (for example, its retaining a strong and guiding role for the state).

sovereign wealth funds   Capital accumulated by governments through taxation or, more often, through direct income from the activities of companies which states wholly or partially own, they can use for investment in other economic projects. This is viewed as unfair, inefficient, and market-distorting by Liberal economists.

trade liberalization   The process by which restrictions on international trade such as duties, quotas, and domestic preferences in government purchasing have been reduced through international negotiations.

Key takeaways

■ Three basic roads to development have been attempted by developing states and their societies: through government-controlled, centrally planned economies; through creating import substitution industries (ISI); and through creating industries for export-led development.

■ The stagnation and eventual collapse of the Soviet Union fatally delegitimized central planning, and the success of the US and other developed states boosted the principles of *laissez faire* capitalism as the ideal to which all states interested in growth and freedom should be aspiring in the late 20th century.

■ With some reluctance and great difficulty, developed states moved towards adopting these principles. They also focused on export-led development rather than ISI, but a combination of state and private involvement remained the norm.

■ The great success (so far) of China's blend of Marxist-Leninist political principles with capitalist economic principles, especially at a time when the developed world is experiencing great economic problems, has re-opened the questions of which is the best road to economic development and what is the best role for the state in it.

Exercises

1. What sort of development was the Soviet model good at delivering and why did it eventually stagnate?

2. Why did states like Ireland want to develop their own industries geared to the domestic market, and what difficulties did they face?

3. To what extent do you think that political repression in places like Chile and China is justified if it helps make possible sustained economic growth and rising living standards?

14.5	Other factors influencing the road to development: aid and corruption

Learning objectives

1. List the forms of aid or **development assistance** available to developing states.
2. Describe the arguments for and against aid.
3. Explain why corruption in developing states is regarded as a major problem.

The governments and societies of developing states do not simply choose which development road to take and launch themselves on it. Lots of other factors are in play (see Chapters 9 and 10). The availability of loans—whether direct or indirect investment—is even more important to developing states than developed ones. So too is the supply of expert technical knowledge needed to develop and efficiently produce innovative, competitive products. Developing states struggle to accumulate their own capital, and they often feel weak and dependent in their negotiations with developed states and multinational corporations. That is why poor states with poor human rights records like Sudan and Zimbabwe are pleased to see China achieve a position where it is capable of investing in them. Unlike the developed states, their governments think, China is "one of us." It has gone through what we are going through, and knows it should stick to business concerns rather than asking awkward questions about how we treat our people.

Some developing states have had to confront the difficult circumstances of their own creation by the former colonial powers (see Chapter 13). Peoples have often been divided and then thrown together with fragments of other peoples in forms of political organization which are not indigenous to any of them. Finally, and most recently, concerns about environmental sustainability and possible limits to growth pose huge question marks over where development should be heading once developing states escape "the demographic trap." Can the planet support 193 states consuming and polluting at the same rate as China and India, never mind Europe and North America, today (see Chapter 12)? In this final section of the chapter, however, we will restrict ourselves to two more immediate issues: the role of foreign aid in development and the problems posed by corruption.

Foreign aid involves the transfer of a benefit from one state (the donor) or society to another (the recipient) without an equivalent exchange. It is nearly always a sensitive issue, and this is reflected in the different terms which are used to describe it. "Foreign aid" suggests charity and a patronizing attitude to some. Terms like "development assistance" and "Overseas Development Assistance" (ODA) are more often used today. A distinction is usually made between **human-**

itarian assistance, usually provided in an emergency like a natural disaster, and development assistance, provided to help a state develop its economy and society and politics. A distinction is also usually made between **bilateral assistance**, provided state-to-state, and **multilateral assistance**, usually provided by states and civil society actors to an international or regional agency which then distributes the pooled assistance.[11] Private actors such as the Bill and Melinda Gates Foundation are also becoming more important in development assistance. We have already examined foreign aid from the point of view of those who give it (see Chapter 5). Here we examine it primarily from the point of view of the recipient states and societies. For them, there is one big question. Does foreign aid work?

Humanitarian assistance is clearly beneficial in the short term. Donor states and civil society actors usually provide humanitarian assistance after disasters like floods, earthquakes, and famines out of a straightforward moral compulsion to rescue people and keep them alive. Governments may think of the "newspaper headline benefits" of helping and the "headline costs" of not doing so when others are stepping in. They may enjoy the opportunity of offering help, as when Cuba offered doctors to the US after Hurricane Katrina in 2005. It knew the US would find the offer embarrassing and would likely have to decline it. And prestige is a consideration. The French are proud of their specialist teams who can find and rescue people from badly damaged buildings, and others admire them. Similarly the world is aware that only the US can deploy large numbers of transport aircraft almost anywhere in the world. These are minor considerations, nevertheless, when compared to dealing with the humanitarian challenges posed by natural disasters. The recipients of emergency humanitarian aid are usually just grateful for any help they can get, at least in the short term.

In other than the short term, however, humanitarian aid can become problematic. Donor states often do not deliver all they promise, and they may lose interest once a disaster is no longer headline news. Even the help that is received can become controversial. Food aid, for example, can lower the price of food in the recipient's markets, discouraging local farmers, and it can provide a source of patronage and power to local Big Men and their armed gangs who gain control over its distribution. Refugee camps, although intended as temporary arrangements, can allow more permanent solutions to be postponed. Many of the victims of Haiti's 2010 earthquake are still living in tents and other temporary accommodations. As noted in Chapter 8, some Haitians have caught diseases like cholera, possibly from soldiers of the UN peacekeeping force sent to protect them. Many Palestinians still live in what are, in effect, permanent refugee camps established some seventy years ago in the Lebanon, Jordan, Syria, the West Bank, and Gaza. There is also little evidence that humanitarian aid on its own improves relations between hostile states. For example, Greece offered its old rival Turkey help, and the US offered Iran help after their earthquakes in 1999 and 2003 respectively. However, this "disaster diplomacy" had few lasting positive political effects.[12]

The benefits of ODA to recipient developing states depend on two things: what, if anything, the donor expects in return, and the form of the assistance. In the past, states provided help to one another for three reasons: to make other states into allies; to make these allies stronger; and to influence these allies into doing what the donor state wanted done. Historically, therefore, this help was often of a military nature. Britain, for example, bankrolled the European alliances which fought France's Napoleon at the turn of the 18th and 19th centuries. Germany and Italy armed the Spanish nationalists in the Spanish civil war in the 1930s. Even today, if the destination of US ODA, for example, is plotted and military assistance is included, the map corresponds quite well with a similar one of the major US security interests. Israel gets the most as a close ally and even closer friend. Egypt gets the second most as a state which the US regards as critical to the balance of power in the Middle East.

States also provided aid in the hope of obtaining political support. Today, the search for supporting votes on resolutions in international organizations like the UN General Assembly has replaced the search for support for favored candidates to place on the thrones of European states that took place in the past. And aid is sometimes provided in an attempt simply to neutralize the effects of similar assistance to recipients from rival states. In the Cold War, the Soviet Union provided assistance to communist Yugoslavia to try to draw it back into the Soviet alliance system, while the US provided it with assistance to try and keep it a friendly neutral. China and the US find themselves in a similar competition over Pakistan today.

If the aid comes in the form of gifts of goods and cash, and if the political price involves voting in support of the donor state's position at the UN, or even joining some form of alliance, this might seem a reasonable bargain to the government of the recipient developing state. Paraguay, for example, continues to recognize the Nationalist government in Taiwan as the legitimate government of all China in return for economic assistance. Playing great power rivals off against each other in the quest for benefits might seem to be the ideal position. This is rarely how it seems to the governments in question, however. For them, it seems much more like a dangerous tightrope act in which they try not to alienate one or both of their suitors. Further, even gifts have a way of creating dependent relations. This can happen at the political level. Egypt's army, for example, has been built up into the largest and most modern Arab army in the Middle East thanks, in part, to the massive transfers of assistance from the US noted above. As a result, it is a powerful player in Egyptian politics. The political upheavals in Egypt associated with the Arab Spring or Awakening show, however, that Egypt's people are not sure they regard this powerful army as a benefit. The army, itself, is constrained in what it does by its dependence on US support. Without it, the payroll for the troops would dry up, training programs would decline and equipment could not be properly serviced.

Dependencies are also created by the economic benefits to themselves which donor states often expect to have. As anyone who has a cell phone or cable television service contract will know, the provision of a phone or cable equipment for free or at a favorable rate is usually just the beginning of a long-term relationship in which the money subsequently flows in one direction with service, repair, and upgrade fees. The same can be true of goods like military equipment, civilian aircraft, and data management systems.

Donor states sometimes issue export credits, which the recipient state has to use buying things from the donor's economy. As a consequence, stories about the purchase of inappropriate goods at uncompetitive prices sometimes hit the headlines. In the past, for example, Canadian companies have exported pumps designed for operating in the Arctic and portable buildings with roofs designed to bear heavy snow loads to Africa. US aid packages have contained large quantities of personal deodorant. Despite questions about the distorting effects of US and Canadian shipments of rice, wheat, and grain to markets in parts of the world that have experienced food shortages, these shipments persist long after the crises have passed. American and Canadian farmers and agribusiness who benefit from their governments' food purchases strongly object to any attempt to stop them.

Great efforts have been made to avoid these kinds of mistakes and distortions. Many donor states have shifted the weight of their foreign aid programs from bilateral to multilateral efforts. This consolidates individual states' contributions into a greater pooled effort administered usually by an international or regional organization. Multilateral aid is also much less likely than bilateral aid to have the appearance of "strings attached," which donors' conditions and expectations generate. The organization of aid programs has become much more sophisticated as well, with efforts to target the right sort of aid where it is needed and to provide clear measures of its performance in particular situations to demonstrate value-added. The UN Millennium Development Goals program established at the start of the century has provided a set of ambitious targets in this regard and a framework for achieving them.[13] The governments of donor states say they give aid to generate economic development in other states as a good in itself. They also accept the Liberal view that economic development creates trading partners. The more a state's economy develops, the bigger a market it becomes for exports and the safer a location it becomes for investments. In addition, developed states argue that development is likely to help other states become democracies which respect human rights and are committed to peaceful ways of settling disputes.

In these macro terms, we can see foreign aid playing a part, but only a part, in the sort of economic development which integrates developing states into the global economy. However, this kind of development has critics in terms of its fairness and sustainability (see Chapters 12 and 13). The self-interests of donor states still get in the way. It is still by no means clear, for example, that economic development always leads to political democracy or that donor states always place a priority on its doing so when they have other interests at stake. Self-interest also influences the debate about whether aid should be focused on those developing states which are well-placed to use it and possibly become trading partners, or those states and people who most need help, but from whom there is little prospect of economic return.

As a result, aid remains controversial at the micro-level. Why, for example, did Ireland help Saudi Arabia develop its dairy industry in the 1980s just because Ireland had great experience in the field? Saudi Arabia is rich and Ireland is not. These sorts of questions become pointed in times of austerity like the present. Why, for example, is Britain providing aid to Pakistan and India when they are both nuclear powers, India has a space program, Pakistan is buying F16 combat aircraft from the US, and the British government is instituting deep domestic spending cuts? Surely charity begins at home, opponents argue, instead of spending a fortune on foreigners. And why, until recently, have US soldiers, diplomats, engineers, medical workers, and teachers in Provincial Reconstruction Teams been building schools and hospitals in Afghanistan for people who do not seem to like them or cannot take care of themselves?

The sums spent are also argued over. In 1970, the UN set 0.7 percent of Gross National Product (GNP) as a target for aid spending by developed states.[14] This is a tiny amount according to the supporters of development assistance programs, especially compared to the 2–5 percent developed states typically spend on their own social welfare and defense, and only a handful of states reach that target today. The US, for example, while the biggest donor in absolute terms, looks quite ungenerous by the UN measure. In contrast, opponents note the absolute figures are still large and, they claim, could be put to better use, for example, spent at home or used to reduce taxes. Besides, opponents argue, aid makes both its recipients abroad and those who benefit from their purchases at home lazy and dependent on government-subsidized benefits. In short, the day-to-day debate about foreign aid becomes a subset of the big debate in developed states between Liberal economists, *laissez faire* capitalists, and social conservatives, on the one hand, and social liberals, big corporations, and supporters of interventionist governments on the other, about the best way of achieving economic growth and development at home.

There is one problem with foreign aid on which they are all likely to agree, however. That is the issue of corruption. Corruption refers to the process by which the moral purity and integrity of an individual or society breaks down. It also refers to the actions or processes which result from that breakdown, specifically rule breaking and taking illegal or unfair advantage of being in a position to make, apply, and enforce rules. Corruption is generally regarded as bad because it rewards those who break the rules, penalizes those who keep to them and, perhaps worst of all, puts pressure on the good to become bad if they are to prosper.

It is possible to identify political, economic, and legal corruption operating on different scales in a society. Petty corruption is small scale, for example, if your professor accepted a cash payment to give you a good grade. Grand corruption occurs when a more powerful or influential person is engaged in a similar practice, for example, a university president making sure that the children of major donors always got good degrees. And systemic corruption occurs when an entire organization routinely operates along these lines, the whole university routinely falsifying grade reports, for example, to make the school look good.

It is widely assumed in the developed world that developing states have large amounts of political, economic, and legal corruption at all three of these levels. It is also assumed that foreign aid provides a point of focus for corrupt individuals and can cause increasing amounts of corruption. This assumption is based on some of the experiences which people from the developed world have when they travel to underdeveloped states. Officials at all levels from customs and immigration officers at the airport, through officials processing permits, to senior government ministers making their minds up over letting a major contract go ahead may all expect an unofficial payment for their services. The assumption is also based on a sense that even after large sums of money have been provided, development often seems uneven, slow or non-existent. Where has all the money gone? Finally, assumptions about corruption in the developing world can sometimes rest on views which are at best hypocritical and at worst racist.

There is sufficient agreement in principle about the unwanted consequences of corruption that a series of international agreements have been reached and measures adopted to counter it. Most UN members, for example, have ratified the UN Convention on Corruption adopted by the General Assembly in 2003. This commits states to combatting corruption through a series of measures: adopting the principle of **transparency** in their political and economic relations to prevent corruption; criminalizing corrupt practices to signal that they are unacceptable; and punishing those found guilty of corruption to enforce the laws against it. The convention also commits states to cooperating with each other in trying to reduce cooperation and in compensating or recovering the assets of those who have been victims of corruption.[15] In addition, a number of non-governmental agencies such as Transparency International have developed a number of indices of corruption. With these, they monitor the actions of states, their officials, and their citizens to establish league tables which rank states in terms of their levels of corruption (examples of the way they present levels of corruption may be seen at https://www.transparency.org/news/feature/corruption_perceptions_index_2016).[16]

Despite the global consensus that corruption is a problem, however, the issue remains controversial. Developing states resent the charge that they, in particular, are the problem and find it embarrassing. Too much attention, they argue is paid to petty corruption. What harm is there in the pittance that minor officials might extract in the form of bribes when their pay is so low? Indeed, some Liberal economists have argued that under certain conditions, where economic activity is slowed by inefficient bureaucratic processes, for example, a little "greasing of the wheels" may actually be helpful. Further, the blame for corruption associated with development assistance and foreign trade and investments generally, cannot just be laid at the door of developing states. For them to be accepting bribes and favors means that the political officials and business executives of developed states must be offering bribes and favors. People only complain about bribery, the argument goes, when "sore losers" have been "out-bribed" as well as outbid on a contract by someone else. Besides, look at how developed states behave when the corruption and sharp practices of their own people are revealed by sources like WikiLeaks. They seem to devote more resources to catching the whistle-blowers than to punishing the offenders.

Finally, one of the biggest charges against developing states is that they are riddled with systemic corruption from top to bottom. Entire political systems, it is claimed, are run for the benefit of the particular leader, family, clan, tribe, or religious grouping which happens to be in charge, using nepotism to promote and appoint the right people rather than the best people, and oppression to deal with objections. The leadership of Iraq under Saddam Hussein, for example, was dominated by people from his home town of Tikrit. Worse, if the opposition actually does find a way into power, it does precisely the same thing, kicking out the old guard and looking after its own. What these states need is political development, the critics say, to provide a system of equal opportunity in which talent and hard work, rather than birth and identity, shape people's destinies, where there is a place for constructive opposition near the center of power, and where leaders will step down when they are defeated in free and fair elections.

Until these conditions are established, corruption, and violence will be endemic, while revolution and civil war will be ever-present possibilities.

Key terms

bilateral assistance   Development assistance provided from one state to another.

development assistance   Transfers of goods, money, and services, usually from developed states, international organizations, or private actors to developing states and societies. Its primary purpose is to assist in the economic, political, and social development of the recipient state.

humanitarian assistance   Help provided to rescue people and keep them alive, usually during and after a natural disaster or a war.

multilateral assistance   Development assistance provided by a group of states and others through an international organization. It is assumed that multilateral assistance will be less guided by selfish motivations of the donors.

transparency   The principle that political and economic decisions, plus the criteria on which they are based, should be open to public scrutiny.

Key takeaways

- All developing states use foreign aid and face the issue of corruption.
- Humanitarian assistance helps people after disasters; development assistance is designed to help economic, political, and social development.
- Aid can be bilateral, state-to-state, or multilateral, provided by many states usually through an international organization or agency.
- There are often arguments about the extent to which the self-interest of donor states affects the amount and suitability of the aid they provide to recipient developing states.
- There are often arguments about the way corruption in developing states wastes and misdirects development assistance.
- Development assistance often gets caught up in broader arguments about the role of states in helping people versus the need for people to help themselves.

Exercises

1. What sort of development aid would you expect the governments of developing states to prefer?
2. In what ways can military aid be regarded as development assistance?
3. What mistake does public opinion in developing states often make about levels of development assistance?
4. How does the principle "Charity Begins at Home" often play out in developed and developing states?

| 14.6 | Uncertainties about economic, human, and political development |

The arguments against corruption and for flying straight with free markets and democratic governments under the rule of law instead are powerful ones. Nevertheless, people from developing states argue, they are based on a major collective memory loss, ungenerous judgments, and assumptions about politics and government which can be culture-bound and hypocritical. What is forgotten is that the political cards which the governments of many developing states have to play were dealt to them by the colonial powers when they carved up the territories they occupied into colonies that suited them and not the local people and conditions. What is ungenerous is to fault developing states for their performance over less than seventy years of independence in tackling challenges which took the developed world three centuries to work out. And states like Britain, France, and even the US did not have more developed states breathing down their neck the way developing states do today. What is culture-bound and hypocritical is to see the political systems of the developing world purely in terms of corruption and dishonesty. In most societies of the world, the individual is supposed to come second to the groups of which they are a part. Looking after your family members when you are in a position to do so is not nepotism in their view. It is a moral obligation. Politics is not the competition of parties representing individuals. It is the wheeling and dealing of different groups within a society for their shares of the spoils.

There may be not one road to modernity but many. Modernity itself may mean different things to different people. And currently there is a great deal of uncertainty about the Western model of development even in developed states themselves, where anger at rising levels of inequality, fear of terrorism and, by extension, migrants, plus concerns about what people will do in an increasingly jobless economy, abound. China's success with state-led growth, Iran's experiments with Islamic banking which keeps interest to a minimum, and India's experiments with micro-financing focusing on small projects often owned and managed by women, suggest there may be many roads forward, yet each of these examples generates its own uncertainties. China's economic success is undercut by expansionist military policies which have alienated all but one of its immediate neighboring states. Iran's Islamic experiments take place against a backdrop of increasing impatience on the part of the younger and more urban elements of its population who often sound like they wish to rejoin the modern, developed world. India's micro-financing projects can seem like a drop in the ocean when set against the scale on which its economy operates and the scale of the challenges it faces. And all three face a problem which they share with the developed world. Development takes place unevenly, widening the gap between the relative haves and the relative have-nots, even when everyone is benefitting in absolute terms.

In the midst of these uncertainties, only one thing seems certain. People and peoples need time and space to explore their respective ways forward. To paraphrase former president Bill Clinton one last time, it's neither the economy nor the politics, stupid! It's the cultures.

Recommended reading

Stephen Brown, *Struggling for Effectiveness: CIDA and Canadian Foreign Aid*, Montreal, 2012.

Richard Mallet, *The Future of Foreign Aid: Development Cooperation and the New Geography of Global Poverty*, Basingstoke, 2012.

US Department of State, *Foreign Assistance: Various Challenges Impede the Efficiency and Effectiveness of US Food Aid*, Washington, 2012.

Interview with Dambisa Moyo, author of *Dead Aid: Why Aid is Not Working and How There is a Better Way Forward for Africa* (New York, 2009) on You Tube, http://www.youtube.com/watch?v=BFABdPOpr2A&list=PLE327717CA0322879

UN Development Program, *Empowered lives. Resilient Nations* at http://www.undp.org/content/undp/en/home.html

Notes

1 Francis Fukuyama, "By Way of an Introduction," *The End of History and the Last Man*, New York, 1992, p. xi.
2 Stephen Chilton, *Defining Political Development*, Denver, 1987.
3 Gerrit W. Gong, *The Standard of Civilization in International Society*, Oxford, 1984.
4 Thomas Friedman, *The World is Flat: A Brief History of the 21st Century*, New York, 2005.
5 Samuel Huntington, *The Clash of Civilizations and the Remaking of World Order*, New York, 1998.
6 John Rawls, *A Theory of Justice*, Cambridge, 1971.
7 Adam Smith, *Wealth of Nations* (Book Two), "Introduction," New York, 1909, accessible online at http://www.bartleby.com/10/200.html
8 Leon Trotsky, *The Revolution Betrayed* (available online at http://www.marxists.org/archive/trotsky/1936/revbet/ first published 1937).
9 The ideas and assumptions of *laissez faire* capitalism are sometimes called "neo-liberalism," especially by those critical of them. The term is confusing since used in this sense, neo-liberalism is not neo-anything but actually Liberalism. Neo-liberalism was also used in the 1930s to indicate a form of Liberalism which gave a stronger role to the state than that envisaged in classical Liberalism.
10 W.W. Rostow, *The Stages of Economic Growth: A Non-Communist Manifesto*, Cambridge, 1960.
11 For a typical breakdown of how a state and its civil society actors organizes its ODA see *Statistics for International Development 2012* provided by the British Government's Department for International Development at https://www.gov.uk/government/publications/statistics-on-international-development
12 For more information see *Disaster Diplomacy*, the website of the Disaster Diplomacy organization at http://www.disasterdiplomacy.org/
13 See *UN Development Goals 2015* at http://www.un.org/millenniumgoals/
14 See "The 0.7% target: An in-depth look" in *Millennium Project* at http://www.unmillenniumproject.org/press/07.htm#01
15 "United Nations Convention Against Corruption," *United Nations Office on Drugs and Crime* at http://www.unodc.org/unodc/en/treaties/CAC/
16 See the website of Transparency International at http://www.transparency.org/

15 Conclusions

The main theme of this text has been uncertainty. We live in a time when it is not clear what is happening to international relations. We also live in a time in which the subject of International Relations seems to add to the uncertainty. When people are asked what the key elements of this uncertainty are, their answers will very much depend on who they are, where they live, and their position in society. As we noted in Chapter 4, a Yanomami mother in the Brazilian jungle worries about the outsiders who may destroy the forests on which the way of life of her people depends, yet provide medicines and health care which make birthing a less dangerous process. A Chinese steel worker will be proud of his country's new power and wealth, but worry whether his government can reform itself and the economy without both falling apart, so that he can keep on getting a little bit richer and hope for a bit more freedom. Most American workers will worry about whether the US will remain the richest, strongest state in the world, and whether military engagements across the globe, even when they are to help other people, will keep the US strong or sap its strength. They will be glad that the US remains a technological leader with all the benefits that this can provide in, for example, health care, yet worry about whether they can afford that care. Like many people elsewhere, they will also worry about how globalization seems to be increasing inequality between the very rich and the rest, and whether they will still have jobs in an era of manufacturing increasingly undertaken by robots and 3D printers.

When people who study international relations are asked the same question about uncertainty, they try to be more objective. Even so, the concerns of their own state will shape what they think are the big issues. American academics, for example, are very interested in how global order is maintained, the role of the US in maintaining order, and the role of different forms of power—hard, soft, smart—in maintaining the US role. European academics are often fascinated by the European Union and wonder whether it represents a new way to conduct international relations—possibly even the future of international relations in general. Armenian, Bangladeshi, and Ethiopian academics are probably much less interested in these questions. They are much more interested in the problem of how weak states and poor regions get what they want from the international system without losing control over their own destinies.

However, most International Relations academics will agree that there are three sources of uncertainty which matter to everybody, even if everybody is not equally interested in them.

■ The first source of uncertainty is the shifting balance, or shifting distribution, of power between states in the world. The most obvious examples of this shift are the rise of China and Asia generally, plus the relative decline of the US and Europe, but other states and regions are rising and falling too.

■ The second source of uncertainty is the revolution in communication and information technologies, which has made possible the rise of the networked knowledge economy and a global civil society caring about human rights and environmental sustainability more than about states and national interests.

■ The third source of uncertainty is the stresses posed by the way we live on the environment and the possibility that the resulting environmental changes call into question the sustainability of our present ways of life.

Just about everyone among the academics agrees that power and wealth are flowing away from the Western developed states of North America and Europe and towards the fast rising states of East and South Asia, particularly China, India, and Indonesia, and, albeit to a lesser extent for now, the rising states of South America and Africa, particularly Brazil, Nigeria, and South Africa. What there is less agreement about is how fast this change is taking place, whether it is irreversible, what consequences may flow from it, and to what extent this shift matters when compared to other things that are going on. Have we years of American leadership ahead of us still? Are we heading towards an era of collective leadership, or is there going to be a struggle for power from which a new global leader may eventually emerge? If so, how are we to keep that power transition and the struggles which may accompany it as peaceful as possible?

Just about everyone among the academics agrees that the Internet, big data, and powerful computers which are often themselves cheap and small have produced cheap, widely accessible information which it is increasingly difficult to conceal. People know more about what their governments get up to, but governments and other powerful actors know more about what their people get up to as well. What there is less agreement about is how important these changes might actually be. Does it matter that states and other powerful actors cannot seem to keep secrets, are increasingly vulnerable to cyber-attacks, and may be invaded as a result of their human rights abuses, or are we simply seeing novel developments which will be easily accommodated as states and others adjust their behaviors?

Finally, just about everyone among the academics agrees that environmental change is taking place and is so as a result, in part at least, of human activities. States and others have committed themselves by international treaties to setting targets for their carbon emissions and shifting to environmentally sustainable economic practices. What they cannot agree on, however, is how big the changes are, how hard and in what ways we should work to address them, and whether states or people in general actually have the will and the ability to live up to the commitments they are busy making.

So how are we to respond to this uncertainty? What would it take to remove some of this uncertainty from international relations? Each of the main theoretical approaches we have examined has its own response. Realists look to history and find the answer lies in power and the ability to establish and maintain a specific international political order. When one great power state has been stronger than the rest, its ideas have dominated—for example, France in the 17th century, Britain in the late 18th and 19th centuries, the US in the late 20th century and possibly still today. If people want a settled, peaceful life at home, they'd best support their local sheriff. If they want a settled, peaceful life internationally, then they'd best support the global hegemon. Of course, history also suggests that great powers rise and fall. In between hegemons, we have periods in which a balance of power or, if they can cooperate, a concert of the powerful states performs the job of the hegemon, not always successfully. Balances of power and concerts between several states are harder to operate than a system relying on one state.

As a practical problem, therefore, the questions from a Realist point of view become, can the US hang on to its hegemonic position and, if not, can someone else, presumably China, replace it? If one great power state cannot dominate, then is a small group of great power states who see eye-to-eye and can act in concert the next best option? This is very much the working assumption to which today's governments say they are committed. Can the US and its Western allies manage the world together? Can they socialize the emerging great power states like China and India and other members of the G20 into playing their part? From the emerging powers' points of view, however, the question has a different spin. Can the US and its Western allies make the sorts of concessions necessary for China, India, and Brazil to cooperate with them? Like the rest of us, Realists struggle to answer these questions and as a consequence, they often default to advising that their own particular state remain as strong as it can. After all, that is what all the other great powers will be doing if they are smart. In the US case, staying strong may allow it to remain the hegemon for some time to come. And if it fails to remain the hegemon, or as President Trump seemed to be suggesting early on, no longer wants to be a hegemon, then it is still better to be strong than to be weak. The great problem in the Realist way of seeing things is that of convincing other states that they should not try to be the hegemon, or it is if you are the hegemon. If you are one of the other states, the great problem is how to convince the declining hegemon that it should retire and let someone else have a go. Either way, Realists say, only once you have the order problem solved can you give serious attention to the other sources of uncertainty.

How do Liberals respond to this uncertainty? Given that human beings remain organized in sovereign, territorial states, Liberals share much of the Realist view of history. However, their enthusiasm for a hidden hand guiding the wellbeing of free markets is not extended to the operations of the balance of power which arises in a system of sovereign states. They prefer the hegemon—a powerful, developed state, or group of states which, in addition to safeguarding security, maintains the rules which make efficient trade and development possible, and upholds human rights on a global scale. In addition, however,

Liberals have a sense that human reason, economic necessity, and technological developments are pushing everybody—states, international and regional organizations, transnational private companies, civil society actors like human rights groups and environmental groups, and individual human beings—towards a single, integrated, networked, rule-governed, global future in which borders matter less, collective identities are less distinct, and people will live richer, more secure, but less diverse and, in terms of jobs and careers at least, less settled, lives.

As a practical problem, therefore, the questions from a Liberal point of view become: can the gains of the postwar Liberal economic order be protected and extended through globalization and, if so, by whom? This is not so much a question of whether a state or states will be powerful enough to undertake this task, in the way the Realists understand it. It is much more about how to get people at all levels of society in all states to hang on to their reason, exercise their reasonableness, and keep their nerve as globalization goes through a rough patch. It involves convincing people of the following: first, that the widening gap between the wealthy few and the rest will either be self-correcting or correctible by policy; second, that a certain amount of risk and change in life is not only inevitable, it is desirable; and third, that for delivering what most people in the world seem to want, in the medium to long term, nothing beats a liberal world order in which property is respected, promises are kept, trade is free, and finance lightly regulated. In short, Liberals tell us to be happy because the world is moving in the right direction and, as a consequence, the other sources of uncertainty will be, indeed are being, reduced. Nevertheless, Liberals worry about how people, particularly politicians and governments and, to a lesser extent, criminals and terrorists, preying on ordinary people's insecurity, greed, and stupidity, are perfectly capable of messing things up.

How do Post-positivists respond to uncertainty? For most of them, it is not a problem to be solved or even eased. It is a condition which much of the world already accepts and which the rest of us should start getting used to. Indeed, from a Post-positivist perspective, the costs of trying to get rid of uncertainty are often higher than those of living with it. Hegemons, for example, be they Liberal, communist, Fascist or today, corporatist, do not resolve uncertainty. Rather, they impose one way of seeing the world over others and, sooner or later, they fail with often terrible consequences. A Liberal hegemony may be preferable to the others insofar as it stresses human rights, gender equality, individual freedom, and economic wellbeing, for example, but it does so at a price which is usually paid by those on whom these values and other ideas about progress are being imposed.

Post-positivists have their own uncertainties. For example, have the information and communication revolutions strengthened the powerless many or the powerful few? As a series of protests against globalization, old-fashioned dictatorships, and mass abuses of human rights around the world have made clear, people, as individuals and as groups, are engaged in international relations as never before. People with independent sources of information and the independent capacity to generate information greatly complicate the problem of control and maintaining order. However the same information and communication technologies which have enhanced people power have also greatly strengthened the ability of states and other powerful actors to out-produce other producers of information, to frame debates, and to know more and more about what is going on, at least at home. In Syria, the Internet and cell phones may have helped people tired of President Assad and his human rights abuses rise up against him. In the Philippines, the same technologies help President Duterte wage a violent war against drug dealers and other street criminals with considerable public support, and in Turkey, they allow President Erdoğan to tighten his grip on power and present nearly all his opponents as traitors and terrorists.

What Post-positivists are reasonably certain about, however, is that for now, the world is becoming more plural with no one in a position to impose a single vision on it, but lots of actors, not just states, increasingly able to promote their visions of the world, loudly, instantly, and above all, intrusively. President Trump's declaratory Tweets about what must and must not happen, and what the US will and will not do, may be extreme examples of how this noisy world is being produced. Just as Prussians, Russians, and Austrians responded in kind to the *levée en masse* of big armies made possible for the French by their revolution in the 18th century, however, so too today everyone is responding to the new technologies of communication and information through the social media they make possible. Very small terrorist groups can produce Internet images of them-selves and their objectives which make them look as powerful, professional, and attractive as big states and multinational corporations, at least to some audiences. Government officials step out of secret negotiations and tweet their take on what is going on—some do it in the meetings as they are happening. Intelligence agency hackers expose embarrassing e-mail traffic during the election campaigns in states for which they wish to make trouble. Everyone, it seems at times, is now in a position to shout at one another, to provoke one another's emotions, and score points off one another in front of audiences in much the way the European monarchs used do this in the 18th century when they became angry with one another.

If this is the case, then we are coming full circle. As we noted in the Introduction, international relations used to be mainly about diplomacy. The relations of states were managed by an international set of professional diplomats. These diplomats shared an outlook and special skills designed to preserve the peace among their egotistical sovereigns who found cooperation with each other very hard, but mutual misunderstanding very easy. Certainty for these diplomats was rarely a virtue, and the diplomat who claimed to be certain about what was happening and what ought to happen would often be regarded as a menace. What these dip-lomats valued among themselves were civility and mutual respect, a preference for co-existence without all arguments having to be resolved, and an acceptance of the ambiguities of living in a complex and plural world. Their challenge was not to fix the world's problems, but to hold it together while others tried to solve those problems or, more often than not, in the absence of problems being either solved or solvable.

International relations today in an era of uncertainty confront problems to which there are many solutions but few which are agreed upon and, thus, deliverable. This applies both to "new" issues like climate change and population growth, and to "old" ones like North Korea's nuclear weapons and Syria's civil war. What they require is diplomacy of the sort outlined above, only not just the diplomacy of the state-serving professionals. Now, as each of us is drawn by our lives, jobs, and interests into international relations, we all need to acquire something of this diplomatic outlook and its skills if we are to prosper, while trying to make the world a better place and avoiding making it any worse.

Index

Note: Page number in **bold** type refer to **tables**
Page numbers in *italic* type refer to *figures*
Page numbers followed by 'n' refer to notes